The Great Siou
Campaign of 18
Day-by-Day

The Great Sioux Campaign of 1876, Day-by-Day

FREDERIC C. WAGNER III

McFarland & Company, Inc., Publishers

Jefferson, North Carolina

ISBN (print) 978-1-4766-8214-3
ISBN (ebook) 978-1-4766-4527-8

LIBRARY OF CONGRESS AND BRITISH LIBRARY
CATALOGUING DATA ARE AVAILABLE

On the cover: Sioux Indians attacking a company of the Seventh Cavalry,
June 24, 1867, sketched by T.R. Davis (Library of Congress);
Wind Cave National Park, South Dakota © 2022 Zack Frank/Shutterstock

Printed in the United States of America

*McFarland & Company, Inc., Publishers
Box 611, Jefferson, North Carolina 28640
www.mcfarlandpub.com*

To my wife, Lisa,
with whom all things are possible,
and whose love has stood off the cold,
the bleak, and the heartache…

and to her mother, Josephine,
whose unequivocal support was always there.
May she rest in everlasting peace.

… and to my friends
who have ridden these trails with me, day-by-day,
Max Reeve, Michael Olson, Scott Nelson, and Frank Bodden

Table of Contents

Preface and Author's Notes

This book is an example of a series of notes evolving and coalescing over time; time in this case being defined as more than twenty-two years. The data contained herein are from myriad sources and the work can be considered a "synthesis" of works by myself, other writers, historians, campaign participants, and historical documents from U.S. archives. With the exception of the timing work involving the actual battle of the Little Big Horn and its lead-up along the Rosebud Creek, as well as a number of my newer discoveries and logical conclusions over the last fifteen years, not everything in this book is a recitation of my own direct research: rather, it is a compilation of the research and writings of many others—that synthesis I mentioned—all of whom I list here in alphabetical order, not by contribution. So, in acknowledgment and thanks, I list Marc Abrams; Steve Andrews; MaryLou Backus; Michael Badhand; Sandy Barnard; Captain Albert T.S. Barnitz; William W. Boyes, Jr.; Lieutenant James H. Bradley; Kingsley M. Bray; E.A. Brininstool; Jeff Broome; James S. Brust; Walter Mason Camp; John M. Carroll; Laudie J. Chorne; George M. Clark; Evan Connell; Melissa A. Connor; Kurt Hamilton Cox; Walt Cross; Roger Darling; Ephriam D. Dickson III; Michael Donahue; James Donovan; Charles G. du Bois; Fred Dustin; James R. Foley; Katherine Gibson Fougera; Prof. Richard Allan Fox, Jr.; Katherine Gibson; Colonel William. A. Graham; Dr. John S. Gray; Jerome A. Greene; Kenneth Hammer; Richard G. Hardorff; Gordon C. Harper; Dale O. Harris; John P. Hart; Grace Raymond Hebard; Paul Hedren; Jason E. Heitland; Heitman Register; Raymond C. Hillyer; Frazier Hunt; Robert Hunt; James S. Hutchins; John Keegan; Joe Kelly; Robert J. Kershaw; Elisabeth Kimber; James B. Klokner; Dr. Charles A. Kuhlman; Orin Grant Libby; Bruce R. Liddic; Major Edward S. Luce; Colonel French L. MacLean; Neil Mangum; Billy Markland; Dr. Thomas B. Marquis; Douglas C. McChristian; Chuck Merkel; Diane Merkel; Gregory F. Michno; Ron Nichols; Michael L. Nunnally; Loyd J. Overfield II; Jack Pennington; Brian C. Pohanka; Bob Reece; Bill Rini; James S. Robbins; Peter G. Russell; Sam Russell; Douglas D. Scott; Antony Shaw; Larry Sklenar; Vern Smalley; Paul Stekler; Edgar I. Stewart; Glenwood J. Swanson; Private William O. Taylor; Linda Terrell; Private Peter Thompson; U.S. Army Command and General Staff College; U.S. National Archives; Second Lieutenant Charles A. Varnum; Herman J. Viola; Dr. L.G. Walker, Jr.; Russell F. Weigley; James Welch; James Willert; P. Willey; Roger L. Williams; and Private Charles A. Windolph.

This book, while not in a traditional narrative or formal outline, is formatted differently in what I call a "bullet-narrative." Were I to flesh-in every item and every entry, it would probably take a thousand pages or multiple volumes, not to mention ophthalmic problems with crossing eyes. Much of the commentary is my own, but some is paraphrased and some quoted directly from the sources listed above to save length, and as is my usual wont, I try not to interject opinion—my own—but will sometimes leave in the opinions of those I quote even if they may differ from my own. Quotes from original sources, be they men who fought at the battle, or those who served on the campaign, or from original letters and telegrams, have all been highlighted in italics. In many cases, standard, modern-day military rank abbreviations have been used, i.e., SGT for sergeant, LTC for lieutenant colonel, CPT for captain, and so forth, primarily for brevity's sake, but more because after almost sixty years from first entering the Army, I simply cannot get those abbreviations out of my head. A glossary immediately following this preface will explain all the cryptic abbreviations used throughout, but it should be noted there is *no* consistency in the presentation of ranks and titles throughout the book. The reader, once accustomed to the continuing archival reports, should understand why, but will also see the interspersed three-letter abbreviations, as noted. At other times, the full rank may be spelled out, or old-usage abbreviations such as "Lt. Col." and such will be noticed.

I am a copious footnote-endnoter, and this book has more than seven hundred endnotes for only eight chapters, and while that is not up to my usual prolix standards, it is considerable for this type of endeavor. The timing work I allude to was developed for and presented in my book *The Strategy of Defeat at the Little Big Horn* and expanded briefly in my later work *Marcus Reno in the Valley of the Little Big Horn*. A comparison of all three works will show the necessary consistency of an analysis that has stood the test of time. The major difference between the three is in this book's presentation: it is easier to follow events presented in this format ... hopefully.

Unless otherwise noted, all times from June 22 through June 25 were developed, researched, vetted by data from the United States Naval Observatory, tested, and compared to primary sources, by me, again, having used all the sources and resources available in their determination (those of June 25—Chapter 7—are especially highlighted). The reader will also get prompts from time to time alerting him or her to the various changes in the formatting of the text. Once again, this has been done for ease of following each specific unit/command/event.

I have chosen to end the book with an entry from September 23, 1876, from First Lieutenant Edward Settle Godfrey's field diary. The campaign itself struggled on, other Army units and commanders separating and dogging the various Sioux and Cheyenne clans as they broke up, some returning to the agencies, fighting and dying along the way, or simply wandering off, Sitting Bull eventually winding up in Canada before finally surrendering in the United States. This campaign and the battle along the Little Big Horn River formed the tribes' last great hurrah, proud peoples, victims of their own ways, their own habits, their own customs. Their immense power, brought together for a summer "jamboree" and earmarked by everything we know about how Indians acted, rode, behaved, scouted, and fought, was in final, full array, the stuff of legends and lore. As the campaign withered down the following year and finally ended, the 7th Cavalry went on to fight farther west, different peoples, but never again on the scale of that summer in 1876. Territorial wars officially ended in 1890, and the frontier declared closed, but it was this great campaign of 1876 that was the death knell of the Plains Indians.

Glossary of Terms
and Abbreviations

This book uses many abbreviations, and in a number of cases, abbreviations that are not standardized until we arrive at modern-day militaria. The following attempts to provide a modicum of interpretation for most of these terms. Abbreviations from the original documents found in the text have been left alone, and the reader may note there are variations of the terms seen below, but those variations are easily decipherable. It should also be noted, as a general rule I use only the singular when describing Indian tribes, i.e., "Cheyenne," not "Cheyennes," regardless of the number of people referred to. There is no correct-incorrect way of doing this, just a personal preference. The reader will notice exceptions, but those exceptions are only in quoted documents or books. The modern-day military lingo is from the U.S. Army style guide.

1LT—first lieutenant

1SG—first sergeant

2LT—second lieutenant

7th Cavalry, 2nd Infantry—not "Seventh Cavalry" or "Second Infantry"

AAAG—acting assistant adjutant general

AAG, Ass't Adjt Gen.—assistant adjutant general

ACS—assistant commissary of subsistence (the quartermaster officer)

ADC—(in any format) aide-de-camp

ADJ—adjutant

BG—brigadier general

Co.—company (the military unit)

CO or C.O.—commanding officer

COL—colonel

Company A, etc.—not "A Company" (modern)

CPL—corporal

CTMP—chief trumpeter

D. T.—Dakota Territory

EM—enlisted men

FAL—Fort Abraham Lincoln

Head Qts. or HQ—headquarters

I/7I—Company I, 7th Infantry

Inst.—"instant," meaning the referenced month

L/2C—Company L, 2nd Cavalry

LBH—Little Big Horn (generally referring to the river)

LG—lieutenant general

LT—lieutenant

LTC—lieutenant colonel

MAJ—major

M.T.—Montana Territory

MTC—Medicine Tail Coulee

OD—officer of the day

PRD—Powder River Depot

PVT—private

QM—quartermaster

RCOI—The Reno Court of Inquiry

SGM—sergeant major

SGT—sergeant

SSR—Sharpshooters' Ridge

TMP—trumpeter

Troop vs. Company—regimental cavalry units were known as "companies" in 1876; changed to "troops" in the 1880s

Ult.—"ultimo," meaning the previous month being referenced: latest, last

USMA—United States Military Academy

W.T.—Wyoming Territory

Prologue:
Historical Vignettes

On August 19, 1854, twenty-nine infantrymen from Fort Laramie were killed over an incident involving a "dead" cow. This became known as the Grattan Massacre. More than a year later—September 3, 1855—in what was called Harney's Battle, troops wiped out a Sioux village on Blue Water Creek (off the North Platte) in Nebraska, in retaliation for the Grattan massacre.

- In 1859 the first Yellowstone Expedition took place. It was a scientific (topographical) expedition led by Captain William F. Raynolds. Jim Bridger was the chief guide and on October 19, 1859, a half-breed scout named Mitch Boyer was hired on to guide a side expedition led by a civilian named J. Hudson Snowden to explore the Pumpkin Butte area.
- On, November 29, 1864, Colorado militia at Sand Creek mostly wiped out a peaceful Cheyenne village under Black Kettle.
- After the Civil War it was estimated there were 125 tribal groups totaling some 270,000 Indians in the American West.[1]
- The Powder River Expedition from Fort Laramie was conducted from July to October 1865 and commanded by Brigadier General Patrick E. Connor.
- In mid–July 1866, Red Cloud's War began. The army invasion of the Powder River country was the primary cause. This "invasion" consisted of the building of two forts (a new Fort Phil Kearny and Fort C.F. Smith) and the use of the Bozeman Trail. A third outpost, Fort Reno, was already standing, though the name had been changed from Fort Connor to Fort Reno. On December 21, 1866, Captain William J. Fetterman and eighty soldiers were led into a trap by Sioux marauders and wiped out not far from Fort Phil Kearny.
- Fort Fetterman was established July 19, 1867, at the junction of La Prele Creek and the North Platte River, seventy-five miles from Fort Laramie.
- Hayfield Fight, August 1, 1867 (the hayfields at Fort C.F. Smith).
- Wagon Box Fight, August 2, 1867 (near Fort Phil Kearny).
- Fort Ellis, three miles from Bozeman, was established August 27, 1867. It was located on the eastern end of the Gallatin Valley, on the left bank of the East Gallatin River.
- On June 1, 1867, Lieutenant Colonel George Armstrong Custer's summer campaign began with six companies of the 7th Cavalry—A, D, E, H, K,

and M—totaling 338 enlisted men, fourteen officers, and one surgeon. The command departed Fort Hays, Kansas, and moved to Fort McPherson, Nebraska. From there Custer proceeded to camp near present-day Benkelman, Nebraska, on the Republican River (June 22–28). There were a number of skirmishes until the expedition ended at Fort Wallace, Kansas, on July 13, 1867. On the morning of June 24, the Indians attacked the 7th Cavalry's camp. This was Custer's first fight with Plains Indians. On June 26, Captain Albert T.S. Barnitz (Company G)—not part of Custer's immediate expedition—suffered eleven casualties including five killed, one and a half miles northwest of Fort Wallace. On the same day, 600–700 Indians attacked lieutenants Sam Robbins (Company D) and William Cooke (HQ, in charge of sixteen wagons) ten miles south of present-day Edson, Kansas. A fifteen-mile running fight ensued, lasting more than three hours. Two soldiers were wounded and five Indians killed. On the night of July 5–6 Custer camped at Riverside [stage] Station on the South Platte River, Colorado Territory, and on July 12 the command discovered the remains of Lieutenant Lyman S. Kidder (2nd Cavalry) and eleven soldiers near the north bank of Beaver Creek, Kansas.

- Desertion was a huge problem for the frontier army. While troops laughingly called it "The Grand Bounce" or "Taking French Leave," the army found it less hysterical. Between 1867 and 1891, some 88,475 out of 255,712 soldiers—34.6 percent of enlistees—went AWOL.[2]

- Red Cloud's War culminated with the farcical Laramie Treaty of 1868. The assemblage of Indians at this treaty was reputed to have been larger than the village gathered at the Little Big Horn in 1876. Red Cloud finally signed this treaty on November 6, 1868, at Fort Laramie.

- From the time of the 1868 treaty ending Red Cloud's War there were a number of Indians outside the reservations. These were termed "hostile." By 1875, "outlaws"—Indians who had left the reservations—had brought the number to about 3,000, all under the leadership of Sitting Bull. By the time of the 1876 expedition, these numbers had been greatly inflated, but the military still believed only 500 to 800 warriors would be encountered and these could be handled easily by any of the three columns designated for that campaign. Military authorities were unaware so many Indians had slipped off the reservations, for the reservation agents had failed to report these desertions. These Indians were known as the "winter roamers."

- November 27, 1868—Battle of the Washita, Indian Territory [Oklahoma], against the Southern Cheyenne: Black Kettle's village. General Field Orders Number 8, issued by General Sully, established Camp Supply. It was located near the junction of Wolf Creek and the North Canadian River. While supposed to be temporary, it lasted until 1895. General Field Orders Number 10, Headquarters, District of the Upper Arkansas, outlined the plan of attack that led to the Washita battle. Prior to the battle, Custer had organized an ad hoc group of close to forty sharpshooters under the command of First Lieutenant W.W. Cooke. Custer asked for and received adequate ammunition for training as he put together a very efficient program of drill and target practice.[3] Before the attack, Captain William Thompson (Company B) said to Custer, "'General, suppose we find more Indians than we can handle, etc.' Custer said gruffly, 'Hell, all I am afraid of we won't find half enough. There are not Indians enough in the country to whip the 7th Cavalry.'"[4] The scout, Ben Clark, rode alongside of Custer who would allow no one to get ahead of him.[5] Clark said the village consisted of about sixty lodges (Sheridan's report said fifty-one).[6]

- The Yellowstone or Stanley Expedition, July–September 1873, was commanded by Major General David Stanley. It was to support the Northern Pacific Railway surveying parties. It consisted of ten companies of the 7th Cavalry commanded by Custer. Companies D and I, under Major Marcus Reno were not with this expedition; they had been ordered to Pembina, Dakota Territory, and were escorting a party surveying the U.S.-Canadian border. Stanley gave Custer fairly free rein and Custer would move ahead with a small detail scouting for suitable routes. There were two sharp clashes with the Sioux: August 4, 1873, near the confluence of the Tongue River and the Yellowstone, and August 11, 1873, near the mouth of the Big Horn River. First Sergeant John Ryan (M/7C) estimated the Indian strength at 1,500 in the fight near Pompey's Pillar (August 11). During these engagements, Custer had one of the command's best shots—Private John H. Tuttle (Company E)—set up as a sharpshooter. He set up and killed three warriors before being shot in the brain and killed. In the fight of August 4, Custer's advance command consisted of companies A and B. Captain Myles Moylan (A) was ordered to stay within reach of support and Custer moved ahead to pursue the Indians.

- Yellowstone Wagon Road and Prospecting Expedition, February–May 1874: from Bozeman, down the Yellowstone past the Bighorn, up the Rosebud, then westward to the ruins of Fort C.F. Smith (this is the *eastern* Rosebud, not the *western* Rosebud that flows into the Stillwater west of the Bighorn River). The expedition was strictly looking for gold and had several encounters with angry Sioux.

- The Black Hills Expedition, commanded by George Custer, took place between July 2 and August 30, 1874. "On one occasion on the return trip Custer was warned by a group [four] of Cheyenne warriors that Sitting Bull at the head of a war party of 5,000 Sioux was preparing to ambush the column in the Short Pine Hills. The command was alerted, but no Indians were seen, although they did find the abandoned camp of a very large body of Sioux. The size of the camp caused Luther North to remark that it was probably just as well that the Indians had departed before the soldiers got there, to which Custer replied that with the 7th Cavalry he could whip all of the Indians in the Northwest."[7] The expedition consisted of six companies of the 7th Cavalry stationed at Fort Abraham Lincoln; four companies of the 7th stationed at Fort Rice; Company I, 20th Infantry; Company G, 17th Infantry; and sixty-one Indian scouts from forts Lincoln and Rice.

- In 1876 there were only eleven generalcies in the entire army and the country was divided into four military divisions:
  - o The Atlantic
  - o The South
  - o The Pacific
  - o The Missouri: Lieutenant General Philip H. Sheridan, headquartered in Chicago. The division extended from Illinois to Utah and from the Canadian border to the Mexican border. Sheridan commanded it from 1869 to 1883. It was disbanded in 1891–1892. The Missouri consisted of five departments:
    - ‹ Dakota: MG Winfield Scott Hancock, 1869–1872; BG Alfred Terry, 1872–1886; HQ in St. Paul, Minnesota. The department included Minnesota, Montana, and the Dakota territories, north and south.
    - ‹ Platte: BG Christopher Auger, 1869–1872; BG Edward Ord, 1872–1875; BG George Crook, 1875–1882; HQ in Omaha, Nebraska. Its area of responsibility was Nebraska, Iowa, and Wyoming and Utah.
    - ‹ Missouri: BG John Pope, 1870–1882; HQ at Fort Leavenworth, Kansas. Department was responsible for Illinois, Missouri, Kansas, the northern end of the Texas panhandle, New Mexico, Colorado, and the northern half of Oklahoma.
    - ‹ Texas: Joseph Reynolds, 1870–1872; BG Christopher Auger, 1872–1875; BG E.O.C. Ord, 1875–1880; HQ in San Antonio. Responsible for most of Texas and the southern part of Oklahoma.
    - ‹ The Gulf: BG Christopher C. Augur, HQ in New Orleans.
- Weather extremes for the 1876 campaign were brutal. Lieutenant Woodruff, who was with Colonel John Gibbon on this campaign, claimed temperatures reached as low as -40° in March and as high as 111° in August. There were no roads, no re-supplies, and no changes of clothing; only buffalo and Indians.[8]

PART I

Day-by-Day

Carpe diem
—Odes 1.11 of Q. Horatius Flaccus ("Horace"),
65 BC–8 BC

1

Genesis

October 15, 1875–March 31, 1876

OCTOBER 15, 1875—FRIDAY—*Military Correspondence & Intelligence Reports*—From the Dakota Department of the Acting Assistant Adjutant General: "Reports interview with Crow Breast by C. O., Fort Buford, and the intention of the hostile Indians under Sitting Bull to make war on the whites."[1]

OCTOBER 19, 1875—TUESDAY—*Military Correspondence & Intelligence Reports*—From the Dakota Department of the Acting Assistant Adjutant General, "Reports anticipated Indian depredations at the Berthold Agency."[2]

OCTOBER 21, 1875—THURSDAY—*Military Correspondence & Intelligence Reports*—The commanding officer of Fort Stevenson, "Relative to anticipated trouble at Ft. Berthold and troops sent there."[3]

OCTOBER 27, 1875—WEDNESDAY—*Military Correspondence & Intelligence Reports*—The commanding officer of Fort Stevenson, "Reports return of troops to their posts. No further trouble looked for."[4]

NOVEMBER 3, 1875—WEDNESDAY—At a secret White House meeting, President Ulysses S. Grant and a few selected cabinet members—Secretary of the Interior Zachariah Chandler, Assistant Secretary Benjamin Cowen, and Secretary of War William W. Belknap—and Lieutenant General Philip Henry Sheridan, commanding general of the Military Division of the Missouri headquartered in Chicago, as well as Brigadier General George Crook, commanding general of the Department of the Platte, attended. A decision was made to launch a war against the so-called Northern Sioux, those Indians not considered agency Indians. Sheridan was assigned to command the military operation. The army commander, William T. Sherman, was not at this meeting.

FALL—WINTER, 1875–1876—Lieutenant Colonel George Armstrong Custer and his wife Elizabeth "Libbie" Bacon Custer, are in New York, on leave.

NOVEMBER 4, 1875—THURSDAY—An announcement appears in the press saying the army would no longer make any effort to keep settlers out of the Black Hills.[5] From the time of the 1868 treaty ending the so-called Red Cloud War there were a number of Indians living outside the reservations. These were termed "hostile," and by 1875, others termed "outlaws"—Indians who had left the reservations—had brought the number to about 3,000, all under the leadership of Sitting Bull. (These Indians were also known as "winter roamers.") A government-sponsored expedition in 1875 prospected the same area as George Custer's 1874 Black Hills expedition, all of this, of course, patently illegal based on the 1868 treaty. Another inept government commission was dispatched to attempt to get the Sioux to sign away the gold-bearing areas of their reservation as well as the entire non-ceded territory. In September 1875, the Sioux forced the commission to flee. By the time of the 1876 spring-summer expedition, Indian numbers had been greatly inflated, but the military still believed only 500 to 800 warriors would be encountered in any campaign and these could be handled easily by any of three assigned columns. Military authorities were unaware many Indians had slipped off the reservations, for the reservation agents had failed to report these desertions.

NOVEMBER 9, 1875—TUESDAY—Erwin C. Watkins, a newly-appointed Indian inspector—and Republican Party hack from Michigan—releases a report containing comments about Indians refusing to cede the Black Hills and claiming they were murderers, plunderers, and disrespectful of government authority. Watkins wrote,

> The true policy in my judgment, is to send troops against them in the winter, the sooner the better, and *whip* them into subjection…. The Government owes it … to the frontier settlers who have, with their families, braved the dangers and hardships incident to frontier life. It owes it to civilization and the common cause of humanity.[6]

General P.H. Sheridan—At this same time, General Sheridan writes to Brigadier General Alfred Howe Terry, Commanding General, Department of Dakota, telling him while orders forbidding miners to enter the Black Hills would not be rescinded, the army was no longer to stop them from entering the Indians' sacred land.[7]

NOVEMBER 12, 1875—FRIDAY—*Military Correspondence & Intelligence Reports*—General Terry's Annual Report lists the nine companies of the 7th Cavalry stationed in his district as follows: at Fort Lincoln, companies A, C, D, F, and I, and regimental headquarters; at Fort Rice, companies H and M; and at Fort Totten, companies E and L. The three remaining companies—B, G, and K—were stationed in the Department of the Gulf commanded by Brigadier General C.C. Augur, headquartered in New Orleans.

NOVEMBER 21, 1875—SUNDAY—*Military Correspondence & Intelligence Reports*—The commanding officer of Fort Stevenson, "Reports information relative to Unkpapas and Sitting Bull."[8]

DECEMBER 1, 1875—WEDNESDAY—From Zachariah Chandler, Secretary of the Interior, to William W. Belknap, Secretary of War: "I have the honor to inform you that I have this day directed the Commissioner of Indian Affairs to notify said Indian, Sitting Bull, and the others outside their reservations, that they must return to their reservations before January 31, 1876; and that if they neglect or refuse so to move, they will be reported to the War Department as hostile Indians, and that a military Force will be sent to compel them to obey the order of the Indian Department." (The Commissioner of Indian Affairs was Edward P. Smith, but Chandler's actual order to Smith was dated December 3, 1875.)

At the time, the Indian agents in the various areas and agencies were: James S. Hastings, Red Cloud Agency at Camp Robinson, Nebraska; E.A. Howard, Spotted

Tail Agency in northwestern Nebraska (today, this is known as the Rosebud Indian Reservation and is the home, primarily, of the Brulé Sioux. Disaffected tribesmen from Spotted Tail were the ones occupying a small camp on the east side of the Little Big Horn River on the flats below Weir Point at the time of the Little Big Horn battle); John Burke, Standing Rock Agency; William W. Alderson, Fort Peck (1LT-Dr. Holmes Paulding, an army officer and military surgeon with Colonel John Gibbon's Montana column, did not care for him, calling him a liar)[9]; Dexter E. Clapp, New Crow Agency; and Dr. Valentine McGillycuddy, Red Cloud Sioux Reservation. Other agents in the territory were: Bingham, Dr. H.F. Livingstone, Beckwith, and Reily.

DECEMBER 2, 1875—THURSDAY—*Military Correspondence & Intelligence Reports*— The commanding officer of Fort Stevenson, "Encloses letter for Indian Agent, Ft. Berthold relative to hostile intentions of Sioux, at mouth of Little Missouri."[10]

DECEMBER 3, 1875—FRIDAY—*Military Correspondence & Intelligence Reports*— From the Department of the Interior, "Correspondence concerning status of certain wild bands of Sioux. Covering report of Indian Inspector Watkins."[11]

Side Notes—As we are beginning to see—and will continue to see—intelligence reports were flowing constantly between posts.

DECEMBER 6, 1875—MONDAY—Edward P. Smith, the Commissioner of Indian Affairs, directed the Indian agents at the major Lakota agencies to advise the Sioux leaders their bands must surrender to the agencies no later than January 31. Runners were to be sent out to inform the various tribes.

SOME TIME IN DECEMBER 1875—Generals Terry and Sheridan meet in Chicago to devise plans for the upcoming campaign. Early intelligence estimates given to Sheridan indicated the Sitting Bull–Crazy Horse bands numbered no more than about 160 lodges with some 270 warriors, wintering somewhere in southeastern Montana.

DECEMBER 22, 1875—WEDNESDAY—*Military Correspondence & Intelligence Reports*—From the Commanding General, Department of the Platte, "Referring to endorsement of Commissioner of 20th inst. from Interior Dept. relative to hostile Sioux. States that military operations may be commenced against when such action becomes necessary."[12]

Crook/Wyoming Column—On this same day, Brigadier General George Crook, the commanding general of the soon-to-be Wyoming column, notified headquarters his troops could take the field whenever necessary. Crook's initial order-of-battle for the campaign—the Big Horn Expedition—would consist of twelve companies as follows—

- Companies A, D, E, F, and M, 3rd Cavalry, the entire mounted complement from Fort D.A. Russell (outside of Cheyenne);
- Companies B and E, 2nd Cavalry, from Fort Sanders near Laramie, Wyoming Territory;
- Company A, 2nd Cavalry, from Fort Fetterman;
- Companies I and K, 2nd Cavalry, from Fort Laramie; and,
- Companies C and I, 4th Infantry, from Fort Fetterman.[13]

General P.H. Sheridan—General Sheridan wanted a quick winter strike at the hostiles, the majority of whom were reported to be wintering near the mouth of the Little Missouri River, some one hundred miles from Fort Abraham Lincoln near Bismarck in the Dakota Territory.

DECEMBER 28, 1875—TUESDAY—*Military Correspondence & Intelligence Reports*—From the Commanding General, Department of Dakota, "Gives opinion as to the feasibility of operations against Sitting Bull's Indians should they refuse to obey the orders of the Commissioner of Indian Affairs to remove to their reservations."[14]

JANUARY 1, 1876—SATURDAY—*Military Correspondence & Intelligence Reports*—At the beginning of the year, Fort Laramie was garrisoned by companies C, E, F, G, and H, 9th U.S. Infantry, along with the regimental band and field staff; and companies I and K, 2nd U.S. Cavalry.

JANUARY 4, 1876—TUESDAY—*General P.H. Sheridan*—Sheridan writes to Sherman stating, "General Terry is of the opinion that Sitting Bull's band ... is encamped at or near the mouth of the Little Missouri...."[15] General Terry also indicated he could move on short notice and seven companies of the 7th Cavalry should suffice in bringing the hostiles to bay. He indicated the troops should take only a few days rations and the campaign would have to be a complete surprise because the soldiers would not be able to follow the Indians were they to scatter.

JANUARY 10, 1876—MONDAY—*Military Correspondence & Intelligence Reports*—Report from Dexter E. Clapp, Crow Agency, Montana Territory—"Reports parties of Sioux in the vicinity of the Big Horn. Two men killed and one wounded, and that they are moving toward agency."[16]

Generals Phil Sheridan and George Crook leave Camp Supply in the Indian Territory for a five-day turkey shoot along the Canadian River. Prior to departing from Chicago, Sheridan wrote General Sherman that both Crook and Terry were ready to launch a winter campaign against the Sioux Indians. According to the guide and interpreter Ben Clark, who accompanied the party on this trip, Sheridan and Crook discussed war plans and Sheridan asked him to come serve as chief of scouts. The group returned to Camp Supply and then headed to Fort Dodge where they boarded their train on January 18, having reportedly bagged 140 turkeys. Two weeks later, the deadline passed for the winter roamers to come in to the agencies. As the deadline passed, the Secretary of the Interior officially turned over responsibility to the War Department. On February 8, 1876, Sheridan ordered generals Terry and Crook to launch their winter campaigns.[17]

SOME TIME IN JANUARY 1876—*Military Correspondence & Intelligence Reports*—Colonel Daniel Huston, commander of Fort Stevenson (located north of Fort Lincoln) advised Terry the hostiles had moved southwest along the Little Missouri toward the badlands.[18] Shortly thereafter, it was reported the Indians were "on the Yellowstone, probably as high up as Powder River."[19] Estimates remained at five hundred lodges. In Captain Charles King's article, "Custer's Last Battle," contained in the August 1890, edition of *Harper's Magazine*, King sets the locales for a number of tribes as the Sioux first made their appearance in areas west of Minnesota:

the Yellowstone and its tributaries were the territories of the Crow; the prairies of Nebraska, the Pawnee; the Black Hills region, Cheyenne and Arapaho; the western areas of the Big Horn range and the valleys between them and the Rockies, Shoshone (Snake); and the north shore of the Missouri River, Cree.[20]

JANUARY 22, 1876—SATURDAY—*Military Correspondence & Intelligence Reports*— From the Department of the Interior, "Encloses copy of communication from the Commissioner of Indian Affairs recommending that forcible restraint be laid on Sitting Bull's and other bands of hostile Indians should they fail to meet the requirements of the Government before January 31, 1876."[21]

FEBRUARY 1, 1876—TUESDAY—*Military Correspondence & Intelligence Reports*— Headquarters of General W.T. Sherman—"Time allowed for Sitting Bull's band to come in having expired, the Interior Department recommends the adoption of forcible measures by the War Dep't."[22]

FEBRUARY 2, 1876—WEDNESDAY—*Military Correspondence & Intelligence Reports*— From the Adjutant General—"Furnishes copy of letter relative to the probable movements of Sitting Bull and his band."[23]

Montana Column Trains—Captain Edward Ball, with a detachment from Company H, 2nd Cavalry, leaves Fort Ellis—located at the eastern end of the Gallatin Valley on the left bank of the east Gallatin River near the town of Bozeman, Montana Territory, some three miles distant—escorting a wagon train with supplies for the Crow Agency along the Stillwater, one hundred miles away.

FEBRUARY 7, 1876—MONDAY—Authority was received to commence operations against the hostile Indians. It was around this time Terry was informed Sitting Bull had moved to the Dry Fork of the Missouri River, some 200 miles farther to the west, while Bloody Knife—George Custer's favorite Arikara (Ree) scout—reported no Sioux camps on the Little Missouri. In addition, Terry received information the Sitting Bull/Hunkpapa camp was no more than thirty to forty lodges and no more than seventy warriors.[24] Indian agents however, reported more than ten times that number of lodges. Captain Robert Hughes, Terry's aide-de-camp and brother-in-law, declared Terry believed Sitting Bull's personal following consisted of some five hundred lodges.[25] In all likelihood, Terry got that impression from the Indian Office that estimated there would be no more than 3,000 men, women, and children off the reservations.[26] Confusing matters, however, military authorities were told there would not be more than a "few hundred" warriors and not united. Estimates ranged from 500 to 800 warriors, with 500 being the most commonly assumed. Again, agents put the figures much higher. Furthermore, the military was told Sitting Bull only had seventy-five warriors in the Dry Fork camp and Crazy Horse's village contained no more than 120 lodges with 150 warriors at the extreme.[27] Despite the fact both generals Terry and Crook realized and calculated Indians would slip off the reservations during the spring, historian Edgar I. Stewart wrote, "military leaders ... assumed that any one of the three columns could defeat any force of the enemy that it might encounter. The main difficulty ... would be to catch the Indians and force them to fight or surrender."[28]

FEBRUARY 8, 1876—TUESDAY—*Military Correspondence & Intelligence Reports—* From the Commanding General, Department of Dakota—

> Says letters received from Fort Stevenson show that Sitting Bull has left the Little Mo. River and is now on the Yellowstone as high up as Powder River. Suggests that Col. Custer be directed to report to him on his return to Lincoln. Forwards letter relative to Sitting Bull's band having left camp on Little Mo. & being now on the Yellowstone in vicinity of Calf's Ear Butte.[29]

*General P.H. Sheridan—*Sheridan wired Terry and Crook that operations against the hostile Sioux had been ordered.[30] A telegram was sent by General Philip Sheridan on this date to General Terry (there was no corresponding message to Crook). The telegram read as follows: "Headquarters, Military Division of the Missouri, Chicago, February 8, 1876. Confidential. The Secretary of the Interior and the Commissioner of Indian Affairs have requested, and War Department has ordered, operations against hostile Indians. Papers will be forwarded tomorrow. (Signed) L.C. Drum, Asst. Adj. Gen."

> Sheridan to Terry—"You are therefore ordered to take such steps with the forces under your command as will carry out the wishes and orders above alluded to. General Crook will operate from the south in the direction of the headwaters of Powder River, Pumpkin Buttes and Big Horn River; and all Departmental lines will be disregarded by the troops until the object requested by the Secretary of the Interior is attained. I am of the belief that the operations under your direction and those under General Crook should be made without concert, but if you and he can come to any understanding about concerted movements, there will be no objection from me."

FEBRUARY 9, 1876—WEDNESDAY—Civilian traders Paul McCormick and Newman Borchardt leave Fort Pease, located on the north bank of the Yellowstone River, for Fort Ellis, seeking military help against marauding Sioux.

Side Notes—Fort Pease was built by three Bozeman traders, former Crow Agency agent, "Major" Fellows D. Pease, Paul W. McCormick, and Zadok H. Daniels. It opened on June 24, 1875, and was established as a trading and "wolfing" post. The fort consisted of small log huts connected by a stockade line. "Fort Pease is situated directly on the bank of the river, at the edge of a wide open prairie. Directly opposite, on the other side of the river, a steep rocky bluff rises up almost perpendicularly from the edge of the water...."[31] It was never a military post and was inhabited by hunters and trappers only. Daniels and Pease "soon drifted into other pursuits and the enterprise eventually became known as McCormick & Company."[32]

A follow-up telegram to Terry, dated February 9, 1876, read as follows:

> Your telegram of Eighth (8) received. I have no specific instructions to give you about Indian hostilities. If Sitting Bull is on the Little Missouri as heretofore supposed to be, and cannot be reached by a quick march, as you formerly contemplated, I am afraid but little can be done by you at the present time. I am not well enough acquainted with the character of the winters and early springs in your latitude to give any directions, and you will have to use your best judgment as to what you may be able to accomplish at the present time or early spring.
>   (Signed) P.H. Sheridan, Lieut. General.

FEBRUARY 10, 1876—THURSDAY—General Terry receives his official orders to commence operations against the hostile Sioux. At the time, the 7th Cavalry was scattered in various locations: at Fort Abraham Lincoln were the regimental headquarters and companies A, C, D, F, and I. Companies E and L were located at Fort Totten;

companies H and M at Fort Rice; and companies B, G, and K were on detached service with the Department of the Gulf.

Colonel John Gibbon was ordered,

> ...to move eastward with all the troops that could be spared from the various garrisons in Montana.... Gibbon was not to seek to destroy the power of the Sioux Nation unless an unusually favorable opportunity should present itself, but was to attempt to hold the Indians south of the Yellowstone and prevent them from crossing over to the north bank....[33]
>
> These instructions to Gibbon constitute a further illustration of a policy which was to be in evidence again and again throughout the subsequent months, to surround the Indians and keep them from running away. But, despite the fact that the white man did not seem to be able to comprehend it, the Sioux and the Cheyennes ... had not the slightest intention of running away.[34]

According to Gibbon, the original plan called for his column to move,

> ...directly on Fort C.F. Smith by what was called the Bozeman wagon-road, then to cross the Big Horn River and move eastward, with the expectation of striding [*sic*?; striking?] any hostile camps which might be located in that vast region watered by the Little Big Horn, Tongue, and Rosebud....[35]

These orders were later changed after it was learned of the Crook/Reynolds fight on the Powder River on March 17. It was thought best for Gibbon to remain on the left bank of the Yellowstone in an attempt to prevent Indians from crossing northward.

Side Notes—Communications between the Terry-Dakota column and the Crook-Wyoming column were virtually impossible. For Crook to communicate with Terry he would have had to send a dispatch from wherever he was located to Fort Fetterman in the Wyoming Territory. A telegram would then be sent to department headquarters in Omaha. That message would be relayed to division headquarters in Chicago and in turn to Terry's department headquarters in St. Paul, Minnesota. From that point the telegram would go to Bismarck, the western terminus for the telegraph in 1876. Then the telegram would have to go aboard one of the steamboats to either Glendive or the Powder River Depot, a little later in the campaign. Then it would be sent by courier to Terry, wherever he was in the field. This entire process would have taken at least two weeks.[36]

FEBRUARY 15, 1876—TUESDAY—George and Libbie Custer arrive in St. Paul, Minnesota, George's leave now over. Custer spends the next two weeks at Department of Dakota headquarters conferring with General Terry.

Montana Column Trains—Captain Ball and his H/2C detachment return to Fort Ellis from the new Crow Agency. (See February 2.)

FEBRUARY 16, 1876—WEDNESDAY—*Military Correspondence & Intelligence Reports*—From Lieutenant Colonel Huston, Fort Stevenson, Dakota Territory—"Encloses copy of extract of Commissioner from the Indian Agent at Fort Berthold saying Sitting Bull states: 'he has no hostile intentions towards his agency, and as soon as he trades his robes and dried meats, he is going to the Black Hills to drive out the gold hunters.'"[37]

FEBRUARY 17, 1876—THURSDAY—*Military Correspondence & Intelligence Reports*—From the Interior Department—"Encloses correspondence reporting Crazy Horse and Black Twin leaders of hostile Sioux on their way to Red Cloud Agency."[38]

A press dispatch from Omaha, Nebraska:

It is stated on the most competent and reliable official authority that the Sioux, Cheyenne, and Arapahoe Indians have been and are yet making the most extensive preparations possible for an outbreak in a very few weeks. They have been purchasing large quantities of ammunition and arms wherever they could get them, going as far south as the Indian Territory for this purpose. It has been known for some time past that the best fighting men had deserted the agencies, and are moving in the Big Horn, Powder River, and Tongue River countries, concentrating and arranging forces for this war. There are at the agencies and on the reservations only those who are too infirm or disabled to be of use, and the families of those Indians who have left. So far as known, the Indians will likely strike the frontier settlements, and unless something is promptly done they will do terrible work before they can be overpowered.[39]

Crook/Wyoming Column—General Crook and his staff leave Omaha for the field. They traveled on the Union Pacific Railroad to Cheyenne.

FEBRUARY 18, 1876—FRIDAY—*Military Correspondence & Intelligence Reports*— From the Adjutant General—"Furnishes copy of letter from Interior Dep't transmitting reports in relation to Sitting Bull and his band."[40]

Major Brisbin's Mission—The civilian traders, McCormick and Borchardt, reach Fort Ellis and file their plea for assistance against the Sioux. Major James Sanks Brisbin wires General Terry for permission to assist the traders. (See February 9.)

Crook/Wyoming Column—Crook and his staff arrive in Cheyenne.

FEBRUARY 19, 1876—SATURDAY—*Major Brisbin's Mission*—Terry receives a dispatch from Brisbin informing him of the traders at Fort Pease (located about fifteen miles north of Junction City, on the north bank of the Yellowstone, six miles below the Big Horn–Yellowstone confluence) holding off a party of Sioux. Terry grants permission.

Custer requests from the Adjutant General's office seventy new recruits to replace those soldiers due for discharge prior to May 1.

FEBRUARY 20, 1876—SUNDAY—*Military Correspondence & Intelligence Reports*— From the Commanding General, Department of Dakota—"Furnishes official copy of telegrams relative to attack on Fort Pease and relief sent from Fort Ellis."[41]

FEBRUARY 21, 1876—MONDAY—*Military Correspondence & Intelligence Reports*— From the Interior Department—"Transmits copies of letters from Commissioner of Indian Affairs and Agent Bingham reporting Sitting Bull and his band to be peaceably inclined."[42]

Terry informs Sheridan of the plans he worked out with Custer. It called for the initial jump-off on April 15.

Crook/Wyoming Column—Companies A, D, E, F, and M, 3rd Cavalry, the entire mounted complement from Fort D.A. Russell, depart the fort heading north to the Hunton ranch (near Bordeaux, Wyoming). From there they would head directly to Fort Fetterman, bypassing Fort Laramie. Companies B and E, 2nd Cavalry, from Fort Sanders near Laramie, depart for Fort Fetterman.

FEBRUARY 22, 1876—TUESDAY—*Military Correspondence & Intelligence Reports*— From the Commanding General, Department of Dakota—"Forwards extract of telegram stating that Sitting Bull is moving on Fort Peck."[43]

Major Brisbin's Mission—Major Brisbin leaves Fort Ellis in an attempt to rescue the traders at Fort Pease. The military complement at Fort Ellis in 1875–1876 consisted of Company C, 7th Infantry (Captain D.W. Benham); and four companies of the 2nd Cavalry under the command of Major James Sanks Brisbin: Company F (Captain George L. Tyler and Lieutenant Charles Francis Roe), Company G (Captain James Nichols Wheelan), Company H (Captain Edward Ball), and Company L (Captain Lewis Thompson and Lieutenant Samuel Todd Hamilton). Brisbin takes the four 2nd Cavalry companies, twelve infantrymen from C/7I under Lieutenant William Quinton to handle a cannon; forty or fifty civilians under Lieutenant Lovell H. Jerome (H/2C); and a small wagon train with rations. First Lieutenant-Dr. Holmes Paulding went with them.

11:30 AM—Brisbin's cavalry halts to wait for the wagons.

4:30 PM—Brisbin goes into camp about 1½ miles below "Quinn's Ranch," eighteen miles from Ellis.

General Terry tells Sheridan of his Sioux campaign strategy: "I think my only plan will be to give Custer a secure base well up on the Yellowstone from which he can operate, at which he can find supplies, and to which he can retire at any time the Indians gather in too great numbers for the small force he will have."[44]

Crook/Wyoming Column—Companies B and E, 2nd Cavalry from Fort Sanders, crossing through the Laramie Mountains following the Collins Cut-off, pass the Hunton Ranch and continue directly toward Fort Fetterman. Crook and his staff leave Cheyenne and spend the night at the John Phillips' ranch.

FEBRUARY 23, 1876—WEDNESDAY—*Major Brisbin's Mission*—5:30 AM—Brisbin breaks camp.

NOON—Brisbin halts at Benson's Landing (not far from present-day Livingston, Montana) to await wagons.

1 PM—March resumes, but wagons cannot keep up and Brisbin halts again at Shields River, three miles from Benson's.

6 PM—After brutal weather came up, Brisbin ordered camp at Countryman's Ranch on the Yellowstone.

8:30 PM—Main body arrives at camp, pitch dark, and according to Dr. Paulding, "wind blowing like blue blazes."[45]

Crook/Wyoming Column—AFTERNOON—Crook and his staff arrive at Fort Laramie.

FEBRUARY 24, 1876—THURSDAY—In a *New York Tribune* dispatch from Cheyenne, Wyoming Territory:

> It would be extremely difficult to give an accurate estimate of the number of Indians now off their reservations and roaming over the region which is to be traversed by the present expedition. Probably there are from 12,000 to 15,000 men, women, and children, and of this number not more than 3,000 warriors could probably be mustered.[46]

Major Brisbin's Mission—In the early morning Brisbin resumes his march. The wind had not abated, and he halted briefly at Hunter's Hot Springs and then proceeded 4½ miles to the Yellowstone where he attempted to cross. The river was covered with ice and despite being only one hundred yards wide, Brisbin decided to continue and find a flowing ford. Finally, the column crosses, and a little below the crossing goes into camp on the south banks of the Yellowstone.

Crook/Wyoming Column—Crook spends the entire day at Fort Laramie working on the expedition.

FEBRUARY 25, 1876—FRIDAY—*Military Correspondence & Intelligence Reports*—From the Commanding General, Department of Dakota—"Forwards official copies of telegrams relative to concentration of troops at Fort Ellis to operate with the cavalry on the Yellowstone against hostile Indians in that Section."[47]

General Terry instructs Gibbon to move as soon as he is able. A letter was sent from Headquarters, Fort Rice, to the Assistant Adjutant General, Department of Dakota, stating some 35,350 rounds of Springfield carbine ammunition, as well as 12,589 rounds of .45 pistol ammunition were on hand.[48]

Major Brisbin's Mission—The winds finally abated and Brisbin's column moves on. The road was firm so the wagons kept pace.

4 PM—Brisbin goes into camp along the river.

Crook/Wyoming Column—Crook and his staff, as well as Colonel John Jones Reynolds—who was to command the expedition, Crook expecting to be more of an on-looker—depart Fort Laramie heading for Fort Fetterman.

FEBRUARY 27, 1876—SUNDAY—General Terry orders Gibbon to prepare all the troops that can be spared and prepare to move eastward against the hostiles. At various spring dates, troop strength of the three columns were as follows: Crook (June 30, 1876, muster rolls): 1,059 (as of May 29); Gibbon: 431; and Terry: 1,059, consisting of 321 infantry, and the 7th Cavalry (eventually leaving from Fort Abraham Lincoln): 738. Total uniformed personnel for the campaign: 2,549 (also, see March 17). "While the 'Organization of the Army under the Act of March 3, 1889,' [*sic*; 1869] allowed a maximum strength of 100 and a minimum of 50 privates per infantry company, Congressional efforts to economize military expenditures in subsequent years put a cap of 25,000 men on the enlisted strength of the Army by 1877. 'As a result, a ceiling of 37 soldiers per company was imposed on the infantry, which usually meant less than 25 men for duty.'"[49]

Major Brisbin's Mission—Near the mouth of the Stillwater, Brisbin meets Lieutenant Charles Schofield (L/2C and battalion adjutant) with thirty-one Crow scouts from the Crow Agency. Two more miles and the column went into camp.

Crook/Wyoming Column—Crook, Reynolds and their staffs arrive at Fort Fetterman.

FEBRUARY 29, 1876—TUESDAY—*Military Correspondence & Intelligence Reports*—From the Commanding General, Department of Dakota—"Furnishes copy of telegram to Col. Gibbon relative to movement against Indians and authorizing him to enlist 25 Indian Scouts and hire two interpreters."[50]

General P.H. Sheridan—General Sheridan dispatches Lieutenant Colonel Wesley Merritt (9th Cavalry) to investigate reported food shortages at the Red Cloud Agency.

MARCH 1, 1876—WEDNESDAY—*Military Correspondence & Intelligence Reports*—From the Commanding General, Department of the Platte—"Gen.

Reynolds command takes the field tomorrow. I don't want cartridges. All right about 'Mike.'"[51]

Crook/Wyoming Column—Brigadier General George Crook departs Fort Fetterman, Wyoming Territory, with two companies of infantry and ten companies of cavalry under Colonel Joseph J. Reynolds, almost 900 men including auxiliaries, heading for the Powder River country. *This movement kicked off the Great Sioux War.*

> The column followed the old Phil. Kearney road to the Powder River at Fort Reno, thence moved direct to the headwaters of Tongue River, thence down the valley of the Tongue River to Red Clay, and thence by the valley of Otter Creek across to the Powder River, a short distance west of the forks....[52]

Crook departed with approximately 700 men of ten cavalry companies and two infantry companies: 3rd Cavalry: A, D, E, F, and M companies; 2nd Cavalry: A, B, E, I, and K companies; and the 4th Infantry: C and D companies. In addition, he counted thirty-five scouts, guides, and herders; 156 civilians for five pack trains; a wagon train of eighty-five wagons; and ambulances; and 892 mules.

Side Notes—Some of the best pack masters in the West were Hank Hewitt, John "Yank" Bartlett, Tom Horn, and Tom Moore.[53] George Crook, while in Arizona fighting the Apache—before he was transferred north for the 1876 campaign—took a fierce interest in pack trains and the mules hauling the equipment. He,

> ...initiated a system that got rid of ill-fitting military pack cushions and replaced them with Mexican-inspired cushions stuffed with straw that evenly distributed the heavy packs on the mules. Several saddle blankets were layered on the mules to prevent sores, with the *aparejo* (pack saddle) placed over them before the load was added.

Mules could carry close to 300 pounds.[54] Properly conditioned animals could carry 275 pounds, but without grass as feed, they required twenty pounds of grain a day.[55]

Major Brisbin's Mission—Brisbin reaches Baker's Battlefield (of 1872). The scout George Herendeen and another trader from Pease are met and join the column. Shortly, trying to cross the Yellowstone, the ice broke and three horses from G/2C and seven mules were lost.

Dakota Column and ***Gibbon/Montana Column***—Both columns were stymied by bad weather, neither being able to move.

Military Correspondence & Intelligence Reports—At some time in March, the Interior Department ordered all hunting south of the Red Cloud and Spotted Tail agencies halted, despite post permission. This was in contravention of Article 11 of the 1868 Laramie Treaty. This forced ever more Indians off the reservations.

MARCH 2, 1876—THURSDAY—Secretary of War William W. Belknap—a Grant Republican—resigns under a cloud of suspicion over the sale of post traderships (six days later President Grant replaced him with Alonso Taft). Democrats under Heister Clymer, Chairman of the House Committee on Expenditures, continue to press forward with their investigation.

MARCH 3, 1876—FRIDAY—*Military Correspondence & Intelligence Reports*—From the Commanding General, Department of Dakota—"Forwards extract of telegram from C.O. Fort Lincoln stating that Sitting Bull is encamped on Tongue River.

A party of Gros Ventres who went to his camp left there [with] all their ammuni‑ tion."[56]

Major Brisbin's Mission—Brisbin manages to cross the river near Pompey's Pillar.

MARCH 4, 1876—SATURDAY—*Major Brisbin's Mission*—4 PM—Brisbin arrives at Fort Pease to relieve its occupants (see February 22). The original party consisted of forty-six men; however, six had been killed, eight wounded, thirteen escaped, and the remaining nineteen were found alive and unhurt. No Indians were seen, but war lodges for about sixty Sioux were found. Brisbin was furious, for the Sioux had not been in the area for six weeks. The trappers, hunters, and traders—nineteen of them—were "as worthless subjects as one would wish to see."[57]

General P.H. Sheridan—LTC Wesley Merritt reaches the Red Cloud Agency to investigate food shortages.

MARCH 5, 1876—SUNDAY—*Gibbon/Montana Column*—Dr. Holmes Paulding wrote, "In camp outside the stockade. The ass outs [*sic*] are all drunk and disorderly; one of them had a row with [Lieutenant] Schofield last night and got jugged."[58]

MARCH 6, 1876—MONDAY—*Major Brisbin's Mission*—NOON—Brisbin begins his march back to Fort Ellis. Many of the trappers protested, but Brisbin's orders were to take all the personnel and provisions back to Fort Ellis. The column moved ten miles, crossed the Yellowstone, and went into camp.

MARCH 7, 1876—TUESDAY—Train service on the Northern Pacific had been sus‑ pended until April because of the heavy snows, but knowing George Custer had to get to Fort Lincoln, a special train was laid on to transport him, Libbie, several oth‑ ers, some artillerymen to man the Gatling guns for the upcoming campaign, plus some merchandise for the Bismarck retailers. At Crystal Springs, sixty-five miles east of Bismarck, huge snowdrifts blocked the train and the Custers were forced to make other arrangements to get to Fort Lincoln.

MARCH 8, 1876—WEDNESDAY—*Major Brisbin's Mission*—Snow began, but Bris‑ bin's column moved on.

Colonel Gibbon wrote the following letter to General Terry.

Fort Shaw, M. T.
March 8th, 1876

My dear General,

Yours of the 21st February reached me yesterday and I was very glad to learn the particulars of the programme. Since the receipt of your telegrams I have been using every effort in prepar‑ ing to get off. The contractor promises to have wagons here the last of this week (10th) to move the companies from here and I hope to start the command for Ellis on Monday (13th). It will take ten days to get to Ellis if we have *no storms*. For the last two days a heavy snow storm has been raging, which may delay the arrival of our wagons, but the command will leave here at the earliest possible day. To save time I have ordered the company from Baker to move at once to Ellis with post-wagons and if snow is not too heavy on the range from this storm that company will get there ahead of us. I have directed the Commanding Officer of Ellis, if the contractor has [*sic*] not at Ellis on the 18th, the transportation called for, to proceed at once to hire wag‑ ons and start a part of our rations and forage for the new agency (my proposed depot) under escort of the Baker Company. Should that company not get to Ellis in time I will then send one

of the cavalry companies as they will probably be back by that time. Then when this (Fort Shaw) command gets to Ellis it need not be delayed probably more than a day. The great object is to get across the range from Ellis before the roads soften, and you will perceive we will be pretty close on to the 1st of April even if not interrupted by storms. Hence the necessity for some special agreement in regard to transportation after the expiration of the present contract of which I telegraphed you. The decision of the freight matter on the Baker expedition ought to be on record in the Chief Quartermaster's Office. During April I do not think we shall have any trouble in crossing streams, but after they rise our operations are liable to be a good deal hampered both in regard to our movements, and in getting additional supplies from Ellis; for the Yellowstone when it gets up is "booming" and the ferry opposite Ellis is a poor and slow one. Hence the importance of supplies by steamer up the Yellowstone. (My first objective point will be C.F. Smith or the mouth of the Big Horn dependent upon whether we can cross that stream at the mouth.) After crossing the Big Horn my next objective will be any camps or Indians I can hear of in that vicinity. There must be some, tho' I hear most of them are about Tongue river. To get there I may have to go down the Big Horn from C.F. Smith and then down the Yellowstone; and this I understand will conform to what you expect in the programme from my command. The route to be finally adopted will depend upon the information to be derived from guides, which I expect to employ at the agency, and there too I expect to enlist my Indian scouts (Crows) and can possibly induce a good many more to join us with the hope of sharing in the plunder. I would like to know, beforehand, if possible, General Crook's probable course. Should our scouts encounter each other it would be important they should know it and I propose to mark mine with a strip of red rag or flannel on the left arm, so that we will know them ourselves. I shall make arrangements at Ellis for the forwarding of mail matter by expresses so that if necessary we can communicate in a few days by telegraph. Benham telegraphs me that Brisbin, it was reported, would be at the new Agency on the 6th. I think it best not to leave him out there till I join him, as in addition to the fact that his command will probably need some refitting [*illegible*] their hurried departure and trip, his coming back may induce the hostiles to think that all danger from this direction is over and give us a better chance to strike them unawares.
It ought not to take long to finish up this matter satisfactorily, and all I ask is if we do it and there is no longer any necessity for my services in the field you will send me a leave or orders to go east as I am very desirous of going but this is to depend *entirely* on the developments of the future and the circumstances at the time.

Very truly yours,
(Signed) John Gibbon

True copy respectfully forwarded for the information of the Lieutenant General,

Alfred H. Terry
Brigadier General
Headquarters of Dakota
March 21, 1876

MARCH 11, 1876—SUNDAY—*General P.H. Sheridan*—LTC Wesley Merritt returns through Fort Laramie. Six days later—March 17—he files his report outlining the food shortages at the Red Cloud Agency.

MARCH 12, 1876—SUNDAY—The Custers arrive at Fort Abraham Lincoln, brought there by a special sleigh driven by Tom Custer and a stagecoach driver. Custer immediately orders Major Marcus Reno at Fort Lincoln and Captain Frederick William Benteen at Fort Rice to get their commands ready for a prolonged stay in the field. Reno orders four to six weeks training, concentrating on company and battalion drill, but not on horsemanship or individual close-quarters combat training. Hour-long target practice—reduced to thirty minutes—was also ordered.[59]

MARCH 14, 1876—TUESDAY—*Military Correspondence & Intelligence Reports*—From the Commanding Officer, Fort Russell—"Reports no news from Gen. Crook since 7th. Col. Sheridan is at Cheyenne and notes arrival of Gen. Merritt at Red Cloud."[60]

Gibbon/Montana Column—Captain Walter Clifford and his E/7th Infantry leave Camp Baker (later, Fort Logan)—along Smith's/Deep Creek—digging their way through snowdrifts toward Fort Ellis. Clifford was to meet J.H. Conrad's supply train from Fort Shaw, then escort the wagons to the new Crow Agency and await Gibbon's arrival with five companies of the 7th Infantry. First Lieutenant William Isaac Reed would remain at Baker; Captain Richard Comba (D/7I) would guard the post. Clifford's route is nicely summarized by historian James Willert:

> …south through the broad valley of Smith River. Snowlaced cottonwood and aspen trees bordered the riverbank, and the mountains to either flank were generously crowded with snow-shrouded Ponderosa pine and Douglas fir. The foothills, grass-carpeted in spring, interlaced with fingers of evergreen and deciduous tree growth, were also under the deep snow blanket.[61]

Major Brisbin's Mission—Brisbin and Captain Tyler decide to return to Fort Ellis by "carriage." While attempting to cross Boulder Creek, the carriage tipped over and both officers were caught in the icy stream. Tyler was hurt so bad Lieutenant Roe had to assume command of F Company. Brisbin recovered, but needed crutches.

MARCH 15, 1876—WEDNESDAY—*Military Correspondence & Intelligence Reports*—From the Commanding General, Department of Dakota—"Repeats telegram from Major Brisbin, 2nd Cavalry relative to his arrival at Fort Pease and the condition of affairs there."[62]

Custer receives a telegram summoning him to Washington for the Clymer hearings. Custer orders Major Reno and Captain Benteen to ready the regiment for an extended stay in the field.

Gibbon/Montana Column—Clifford proceeded "up the valley to the head of Smith River's south fork (near present-day Ringling, Montana). Here the company probably crossed the low divide known as North Pass, between that drainage and Shields River."[63]

MARCH 16, 1876—THURSDAY—*Gibbon/Montana Column*—Clifford, after passing over the summit of the range, turned west, and went up Flathead Creek to cross the Bridger Mountains at Flathead Pass. "The ascent … to the summit snaked through a narrow, timbered canyon…."[64]

Crook/Wyoming Column—Frank Grouard and other scouts tail two Indians trailing game tracks. They determine there is an Indian camp on the Powder River. Crook instructs Colonel Joseph J. Reynolds to take four companies of the 3rd Cavalry and two companies of the 2nd Cavalry—fifteen officers and 359 EM—to strike the village the following day.[65] Crook instructed Reynolds to capture the pony herd and take away as many supplies as possible, while Crook would take the remaining four companies of cavalry and the pack train and re-join Reynolds on Clear (Lodgepole) Creek the following evening. At dusk Reynolds breaks camp and heads for the

Powder moving up the north fork of Otter Creek. The night had heavy clouds, obscuring whatever moonlight there may have been. The ground was frozen and snow-covered.

MARCH 17, 1876—FRIDAY—*Military Correspondence & Intelligence Reports*—
From the Commanding Officer, Fort Russell—"Relative to intelligence from expedition under General Crook."[66]

From Lt. Col. M.V. Sheridan, A-d-C—"Reports arrival at Fort Laramie, and states that Gen. Crook had established Supply Camp at [Fort] Reno, and left that point on the seventh, nothing heard from him since."[67]

From the Commanding General, Department of Dakota—"Forwards copy of telegram from C.O. Fort Shaw stating that the command marched this morning, 12 officers and 194 men."[68]

Gibbon/Montana Column—10 AM—(*Gibbon's watch was set on Fort Ellis time, which was supposed to be San Francisco time. The times used here are not known to be either San Francisco or St. Paul, but are consistent.*) Captain Charles Cotesworth Rawn (Commanding Officer, I/7I, and as senior officer, commander of this battalion of the 7th Infantry) leaves Fort Shaw (about twenty miles west of the future site of Great Falls, Montana) with five companies—A, under Captain William Logan and First Lieutenant Charles Austin Coolidge; B, under Captain Thaddeus Sanford Kirtland and Second Lieutenant Charles Austin Booth; H, under Captain Henry Blanchard Freeman and Second Lieutenant Frederick Monroe Hill Kendrick; Rawn's own Company I, with First Lieutenant William Lewis English and Second Lieutenant Alfred Bainbridge Johnson; and K, (under Captain James Madison Johnson Sanno) and ten mule-drawn contract wagons with rations for ten days; twelve officers, 195 enlisted personnel. Also with them were Second Lieutenant Charles Albert Woodruff (Company K), commander of the Gatling battery (two guns), and First Lieutenant James Bradley (Company B) and twelve mounted infantrymen as scouts. The column runs into severe snow and the roads were a mass of mud and slush.

The Annual Report of Major Gillespie carries the strength of the Gibbon column as twenty-seven officers, 409 EM.[69] Lieutenant James Bradley claimed Captain Rawn commanded the column when it left Fort Shaw.[70] Freeman took over later when Rawn suffered severe snow blindness. Gibbon forbids all trumpet, bugle, and drum calls for fear of the hostiles using them for anything. Gibbon wrote:

> The original intention was to move the Montana column directly on Fort C.F. Smith, by what was called the Bozeman wagon-road, then to cross the Big Horn River and move eastward, with the expectation of striking any hostile camps which might be located in that vast region watered by the Little Big Horn, Tongue, and Rosebud.[71]

Clifford's journey became easier after crossing the summit. He entered the rolling terrain known as the "Springhill Country."

3:30 PM—Rawn's column camps at Eagle Rock near Birdtail Divide. Because of the bad weather they were able to make only eleven miles. At night, the temperature plummets to -40°.

Major Brisbin's Mission—10 AM—Brisbin's column returns to Fort Ellis, bringing with it the "rescued" citizens.

Crook/Wyoming Column—Some time before dawn, Colonel Reynolds had reached the bluffs west of the Powder. He could see the Indian camp on the river's west bank. The Indians had posted no guards. Reynolds' plan called for the cavalry to converge on the camp from the north, west, and south.

7:30 AM—The attack was scheduled for this time, but was delayed because of the difficulty of the terrain and the routes.

9 AM—Led by the guide, Frank Grouard, Reynolds' cavalry attacks the Cheyenne village of Old Bear and Little Wolf located on the Powder River. The village consisted of about 105 to 110 lodges—some say only sixty-five, including about ten to fifteen Sioux (the warrior He Dog being among them)—and 500–700 Indians, 250 of whom were warriors (author Neil Mangum says 200 warriors and 700 inhabitants).[72] The attack was successful, but Reynolds eventually withdrew, leaving three dead and one wounded soldier behind and destroying huge amounts of supplies the military could have used. Writer Dr. Thomas B. Marquis claimed there were only about forty Northern Cheyenne lodges under Old Bear, located on the west bank of the Powder River. A number of the inhabitants were still alive in 1933.[73]

The attack began with a charge by Captain James "Teddy" Egan's Company K, 2nd Cavalry, supported by Captain Anson Mills' battalion. Captain Alexander Moore's (F/3C) battalion was to position itself north of the camp to preclude the Indians' escape, but he failed to accomplish his mission and most of the Indians escaped in that direction. The village contained "tons of dried buffalo meat and robes … and vast quantities of ammunition."[74] The Northern Cheyenne warrior, Wooden Leg—who was also there—said only one warrior was killed. He also claimed there were only three or four Sioux lodges in the village. The Sioux youngster, Black Elk erroneously claimed this was Crazy Horse's village,[75] and the same impression was given to the Spotted Tail Indian agent, E.A. Howard, by General Crook who informed him of Reynolds' attack.[76] Apparently an old woman, wounded in the fighting, told Reynolds Crazy Horse had been there.[77] Both Minneconjou and Oglala Sioux were in the camp. Crook misidentified this camp as being that of Crazy Horse with some Northern Cheyenne and Minneconjou.

11 AM—Reynolds begins to torch the village and everything in it. As Reynolds destroyed the village, Indians gathered on the bluffs. Other Indians began infiltrating through the brush along the river. The troops' led horses were also becoming a concern.[78] As the village burned, Mills' troops held the center position with Moore on his left and Egan protecting the right flank. As warriors on the bluffs and along the river fired on Moore's and Egan's troops, they were forced to pull back, leaving Mills without flank protection. Reynolds ordered Mills to pull back and ordered Captain Henry Erastus Noyes (I/2C)—who Reynolds had allowed to unsaddle, rest, and boil coffee—to support him. It took Noyes an hour to comply.

1 PM—Noyes arrives to support Mills' pullback. Mills and Egan begin withdrawing.

1:30 PM—Reynolds begins to withdraw upstream to meet Crook and the supply train. Several wounded and dead were left behind. Four soldiers were killed, six were wounded.[79] Seven hundred Indian ponies were captured. By the following morning—because of a token guard posted to watch the herd—the Indians had recovered virtually all their horses.

Indian Village—On this date it appears Crazy Horse's small village of about thirty tepees was located on East Fork of the Little Powder River. At about the same time, Sitting Bull was on Spring Creek, a tributary of the Powder.[80]

General P.H. Sheridan—LTC Wesley Merritt files a report to General Sheridan indicating the food shortages at the Red Cloud Agency were real, but caused more by issuing rations to visiting Indians than by any chicanery. He also warned in his report that these shortages should be made up promptly because Indians were leaving the reservations to join the northern bands.

MARCH 18, 1876—SATURDAY—*Military Correspondence & Intelligence Reports*—From Assistant Adjutant General, Department of the Platte—"Reports latest information regarding movements of Gen. Crook."[81] From Commanding Officer, Fort Russell—"Telegram sent in obedience to dispatch calling for information in regard to Gen. Crook and condition of affairs."[82]

Gibbon/Montana Column—7 AM—Lieutenant James Bradley departs William John's ranch (near the head of Little Prickly Pear Canyon).

8 AM—The column breaks camp.

1 PM—Lieutenant Bradley captures two deserters from Company K, privates Charles Keating and James McFarland, some four miles beyond Helena. After depositing the deserters in the Helena jail, Bradley stays at the St. Louis Hotel—his men at the Overland Hotel—determined to join the column the next day.

4 PM—The column camps on the Dearborn River: seventeen miles for the day.

Montana Column Trains—5 PM—Wagons arrive in camp. At night the temperatures were estimated to be -40°.

Crook/Wyoming Column—Concerned about finding Crook, Reynolds decided to travel 100 miles south, back to the supply base at Fort Reno. Around noon, as Reynolds prepared to break camp, Crook's column was spotted.

MARCH 19, 1876—SUNDAY—*Military Correspondence & Intelligence Reports*—From Lt. Col. Sheridan, Fort Fetterman—"Reports his arrival at that post and intelligence from Gen. Crook."[83]

From Assistant Adjutant General, Department of the Platte—"Relative to latest information of the movements of Gen. Crook's command."[84]

Gibbon/Montana Column—8 AM—March began again. It was bitterly cold with heavy winds, below freezing temperatures, and heavy snowdrifts.

1 PM—Camped at Kreuger's ranch, a march of thirteen miles through heavy snow drifts. Captain Rawn, now snow-blind, became incapacitated and was forced to pass command to Freeman. The contract surgeon, Dr. Charles Hart, suffered frostbite and would leave the column at Helena.

Montana Column Trains—3 PM—Wagons began arriving after much difficulty, including a number having tipped over. In the meantime, the J.H. Conrad wagon train from Fort Shaw reaches Fort Ellis.

MARCH 20, 1876—MONDAY—*Military Correspondence & Intelligence Reports*—From Lt. Col. Sheridan, Fort Fetterman—"Nothing heard from Crook today; weather moderating."[85]

Gibbon/Montana Column—7:15 AM—Weather moderates and Freeman's men march eighteen miles through mud and slush. Captain Rawn leaves column to return to Fort Shaw.

2:15 PM—After an eighteen-mile march, Captain Freeman camps in a cove of the Little Prickly Pear Canyon. The weather had moderated and snow turned to slush and mud. Clifford reaches Fort Ellis.

Indian Village—Remnants of Old Bear's Powder River camp reach Crazy Horse's Oglala village near Charcoal Butte [*a butte, by definition, is taller than it is wide*]. These two groups set out in search of Sitting Bull's Hunkpapa camp, thought to be at Chalk Butte, some fifty miles east of the Powder River. There, they find not only Sitting Bull—whose camp was larger than the Cheyenne and Oglala, combined—but they find Lame Deer's Minneconjou Sioux there as well. As they all decided to band together for better protection against the whites, it was arranged that the Cheyenne should always be first in line of march while the others followed because it was felt the soldiers were waging a war of extermination against the Cheyenne. Because the Oglala were their "first friends," they would be second in the line of march and since the Hunkpapa only wanted to be left alone and not fight, they were to be last.[86] This was also the way the camp at the Little Big Horn was arranged. When they traveled, the Oglala followed the Cheyenne, the Minneconjou following next, and the Hunkpapa last.[87]

MARCH 21, 1876—TUESDAY—*Military Correspondence & Intelligence Reports*— From the Commanding General, Department of Dakota—"Forward copy of letter from Col. John Gibbon relative to programme of the expedition under his command."[88]

Gibbon/Montana Column—7 AM—Troops begin their march but make only five miles and after 2½ hours on the road, go into camp to give the men some rest. The day was bright, clear, and warm. Two more troopers were discovered missing. A party from the mounted detachment was sent after them. One was apprehended, but the other, Private John McCarty (H/7I) escaped.

9:30 AM—They go into camp after only five miles. Camp was made at William John's Ranch at the head of Little Prickly Pear Canyon on the old Helena and Fort Benton stage road. That night, privates Henry E. Sturgeon and Charles Symes (both, H/7I) deserted.

Indian Village—More of Old Bear's people reach Crazy Horse at Charcoal Butte.

MARCH 22, 1876—WEDNESDAY—*Military Correspondence & Intelligence Reports*— From Lt. Col. Sheridan, Fort Fetterman—"Nothing heard from Gen. Crook today. Will start back tomorrow via Laramie."[89]

From Gen. George Crook, Fort Reno—"Reports the destruction of Crazy Horse's village by Gen. Reynolds and part of the command on the 17th inst. and recommends immediate transfer of Red Cloud and Spotted Tail Agencies to the Mo. River."[90]

Gibbon/Montana Column—7 AM—Freeman's command is on the march. Weather was warm and clear.

1:30 PM—After a march of seventeen miles, Freeman goes into camp at four miles from Helena near the widow Durgin's ranch. Gibbon and his quartermaster officer, Lieutenant Joshua West Jacobs (regimental quartermaster), passed by and headed into Helena. The deserters Keating and McFarland were returned to duty and went unpunished.

MARCH 23, 1876—THURSDAY—*Gibbon/Montana Column*—6:45 AM—March resumes.

2 PM—Freeman goes into camp having covered eighteen miles through heavy mud. His camp was located near the Spokane House, a wayside inn.

Montana Column Trains—Clifford leaves Fort Ellis with his E/7I (from Camp Baker) and a twenty-eight-wagon contract supply train carrying 100,000 pounds of supplies to establish a field supply depot at the new Crow Agency (Agent Dexter E. Clapp) on the Stillwater (see April 1, 1876).

MARCH 24, 1876—FRIDAY—*Military Correspondence & Intelligence Reports*— From the Assistant Adjutant General, Department of the Platte—"Notes dispatch from Gen'l Crook dated Fort Reno Mar. 22nd. Will be at Fetterman on 22nd (?). Send no more mail there, all well."[91]

General Terry sends a telegram to General Sheridan: "The most trustworthy scout on the Missouri recently in hostile camp reports not less than 2,000 lodges and that the Indians are loaded down with ammunition."[92]

> General Terry, not unaware of the growing strength of the Sioux, apparently planned to establish a secure base of supplies well up the Yellowstone River.... Terry realized that if the hostiles who regularly passed the winter in the valleys of the Yellowstone and Powder rivers should be able to concentrate their warriors in one camp or in contiguous camps, they could not be attacked by a small force without great risk of defeat ... the ordinary estimate was three fighting men to a lodge....[93]

Gibbon/Montana Column—6:30 AM—7th Infantry breaks camp.

1:30 PM—Freeman makes camp at Indian Creek Ferry. Column made eighteen miles. Lieutenant Bradley returns and assumes command of the mounted detachment (Lieutenant Woodruff had commanded it in Bradley's absence).

MARCH 25, 1876—SATURDAY—*Gibbon/Montana Column*—6:30 AM—March continues over decent terrain. While Bradley claimed the day was cold and windy, Lieutenant Coolidge—now the acting surgeon, still refusing a horse, preferring instead to walk with the men—called the day warm.

2:45 PM—The column goes into camp near "Galen's residence" having made twenty-one miles.

MARCH 26, 1876—SUNDAY—*Military Correspondence & Intelligence Reports*— From Gen. George Crook, Fort Fetterman—"Sends congratulations. Desires authority to visit Chicago for the purpose of consultation."[94]

Gibbon/Montana Column—6:15 AM—Column breaks camp. Because the bridge over the Madison River was down, the command had to detour, turning left and crossing the river on a ferry, one mile below the junction of the Jefferson and Madison rivers and some 200 yards above the mouth of the Gallatin River.

12:45 PM—After traveling fourteen miles, the command went into camp ½ mile beyond "Gallatin City," a mere collection of wooden buildings including a gristmill.

4 PM—Gibbon and Jacobs visit the camp.

NIGHT—Two more troopers desert; nine total, only three caught.

Crook/Wyoming Column—Crook returns to Fort Fetterman where he immediately prefers charges against Colonel Reynolds. In turn, Reynolds preferred charges against captains Moore and Noyes. Both Reynolds and Moore were found guilty and were suspended, though President Grant remitted their sentences. Reynolds resigned in 1877; Moore in 1879. While found guilty, Noyes received only a letter of reprimand.[95]

Crook used three staging areas to prepare for the upcoming summer campaign: Fort D.A. Russell (near Cheyenne), Fort Laramie, and Fort Fetterman. Additional troops were even brought in from other departments. At Fort Fetterman, Crook stockpiled 300,000 pounds of grain; thousands of pounds of pork, coffee, sugar, and beans; ammunition; a herd of beef in excess of 1,200 head; and several hundred wagons.[96] Crook, rather than return to Fort Laramie, went directly back to his headquarters in Omaha.

MARCH 27, 1876—MONDAY—*Gibbon/Montana Column*—6:10 AM—The column resumes its march.

12:45 PM—After marching eighteen miles, Captain Freeman goes into camp near Cockerill's Bridge over the West Gallatin. The troops are now well broken-in, with virtually no more blisters or marching problems (Fort Ellis was now sixteen miles away). Having spent the night in Helena, Gibbon and Jacobs pass by the 7th Infantry's camp and reach Fort Ellis. While at Ellis, Gibbon learns of the March seventeenth Reynolds fight Crook's command had with the Sioux-Cheyenne village and the fact they were farther east on the Powder River.

MARCH 28, 1876—TUESDAY—George Custer arrives in Washington, D.C., by train.

Gibbon/Montana Column—6:15 AM—Freeman breaks camp.

NOON—Passing through Bozeman, Freeman's battalion arrives at Fort Ellis. This completed the 183-mile march from Fort Shaw. Lieutenant Jacobs had brought with him scout Henry Bostwick and hired one of the Fort Pease trappers, John W. Williamson. He also hired six teamsters—Wes Thomas, Charles Willis, Phil Huskey, George Bickle, Sam Lutz, and George Black.

MARCH 29, 1876—WEDNESDAY—*Military Correspondence & Intelligence Reports*— From the Commanding Officer, District of Montana—"Reports the hiring of 22 wagons each to haul 5,500 lbs, and that he is exercising all possible economy."[97]

Custer testifies before the Clymer committee.

MARCH 30, 1876—THURSDAY—*Gibbon/Montana Column*—7:30 AM—Captain Freeman and his five companies—along with Lieutenant Bradley, his mounted scouts, and a fifty-team train—depart muddy Fort Ellis, heading east toward the Yellowstone, while Gibbon remains, planning to leave with the cavalry column. At Fort Ellis, Gibbon queries Terry by telegram; he requests to be allowed to seek Sitting Bull north of the Yellowstone instead of south. Suggests to Terry the Sioux are on Dry Creek (far to the north; Brisbin thinks this) and that he should be allowed to hit them in that area. The telegram dated March 30, 1876, Colonel Gibbon to General Terry:

In view of the information from Genl. Crook, am I not operating in a wrong line by going south of the Yellowstone instead of north of it? Brisbin reports a large fresh lodge pole trail leading north from mouth of Rosebud. He thinks Sitting Bull is on Big Dry Fork toward which his trail leads. Must I limit my offensive operations to Indian reservation lines or may I strike Sitting Bull wherever I can find him? (sgd) Gibbon

NOON—After a difficult march across the Bozeman/Yellowstone pass, Freeman puts his command into camp along Fleischman's Creek. They had traveled 10½ miles. Regulations for the campaign were put in place, e.g., guard duty: it was to be the function of one infantry company per day, with the company's senior officer as Officer of the Day.

2:30 PM—The slower moving wagon train arrives in camp.

AFTERNOON INTO NIGHT—Snow began and cold, blustery winds arose.

MARCH 31, 1876—FRIDAY—*Military Correspondence & Intelligence Reports*— From the Commanding General, Department of Dakota—"Furnishes copy of telegram from Col. Gibbon asking for instructions, and copy of reply thereto."[98]

Terry wires Gibbon, telling him not to go south of the Yellowstone and also telling him Sitting Bull was not on Dry Creek, but in all likelihood, on the Powder. Terry wants Gibbon to move to the mouth of the Big Horn. Also tells him he can strike any Indian force he finds: "...be careful not to neglect the great object of keeping between the Indians and the Missouri."[99]

The original plan had been for Gibbon to march east and destroy any Sioux camps to be found in the valleys of the Little Big Horn, the Rosebud, or the Tongue rivers. The news of Reynolds' fight on the Powder River, however, changed things. It was now thought the hostiles were *not* out in large numbers and it was felt they would flee northward as Crook pressed them. Gibbon was to press forward, as rapidly as possible, on the north side of the Yellowstone. The Indians' two principal crossing places of the high-rising river, "were just above and just below the mouth of the Rosebud...."[100]

Telegram dated March 31, 1876, Terry to Gibbon:

Dispatch received. Until I learn what General Crook's further movements will be, and until Custer starts I think you ought not to go south of the Yellowstone but should direct your efforts to preventing the Indians from getting away to the north. I doubt that Sitting Bull is on Big Dry Fork. All information here points to the Powder river as his present location and General Crook is positive that such is the fact. I think that if you move to the mouth of the Big Horn, by the time you reach it I shall be able to send you information of the movements of Crook and Custer upon which you will be able to determine your course. If, however, you find that you can strike a hostile band anywhere, do it without regard to reservations; but, in doing it be careful not to neglect the great object of keeping between the Indians and the Missouri. Custer has been delayed by the blockade of the North Prairie road. We have not yet been able to [*illegible*] his train or his supplies. I hope that the road will be open next week. Make ample arrangements for communications with Ellis. (sgd) Terry.

Gibbon/Montana Column and the *Montana Column Trains*—Because of the weather Freeman remains in camp. He receives a message from Gibbon instructing him to move two days further on and await the contract wagons.

2

Exodus

April

APRIL 1, 1876—SATURDAY—Custer sends a telegram—probably to Terry—informing him scout Charlie Reynolds reports, "from 300 to 600 lodges under Sitting Bull are now en route to (Fort) Berthold."[1]

Gibbon/Montana Column—7:15 AM—Freeman breaks camp. His route takes him past Quinn's Ranch (half-way between Fort Ellis and the old Crow agency) to the Yellowstone where he skirted the river at Benson's Landing, then marched east to Shields River (earlier known as "Twenty-five Yard Creek").

Montana Column Trains—Captain Clifford (E/7I) reaches and establishes a field supply depot at the new Crow Agency (Agent Dexter E. Clapp) on the Stillwater. Clifford brought twenty-eight wagons with supplies, but did not know of Gibbon's change of plans and would wait there for the arrival of the Montana column.

9 AM—Captain Lewis Thompson (Commanding Officer, L/2nd Cavalry) in command of four companies of the 2nd Cavalry (F, G, H, and L) and a civilian wagon train leaves Fort Ellis. First Lieutenant–Dr. Holmes Paulding, Assistant Surgeon, is with them, along with Second Lieutenant Edward J. McClernand (G/2C), who was detailed to Gibbon's staff as the Acting Engineer Officer. The roads were so bad they could make only seven miles, encountering severe difficulty in crossing Bozeman Pass. The cavalry's commander, Major James Brisbin, begged Gibbon to go along. Not only was Brisbin very heavy, but he was suffering from bad arthritis and had to ride in an ambulance and walk on crutches.

1:45 PM—After traveling some nineteen miles, Captain Freeman goes into camp on Shields River. Freeman receives a message from First Lieutenant Levi Burnett, the adjutant, not to wait for the contract wagons, but to move to the new Crow agency as quickly as possible. After sunset Thompson moves into camp, only some seven miles from Fort Ellis.

APRIL 2, 1876—SUNDAY—6:30 AM—*Gibbon/Montana Column* and the *Montana Column Trains*—Freeman is on the march. The day was warm, bright, and clear. Dr. Paulding, accompanied by the cavalry battalion adjutant, Lieutenant Charles Brewster Schofield (L/2C), leaves Fort Ellis with whiskey and his medical supplies, all turned over to him by Lieutenant Coolidge. They reached the cavalry column that day. By early morning Thompson and the cavalry leave camp and cross Middle

33

Creek, but because of difficulties negotiating the roads, they were able to make only three miles before going into camp again. Because of the steep grades they had severe difficulties moving the wagons. The snow is all gone now and the roads much better.

11:15 AM—After traveling some seventeen miles east, Freeman goes into bivouac near Dr. Andrew J. Hunter's hot springs resort, known officially as "Yellowstone White Sulphur Springs." As the column camped for the evening, sentinels were posted. The system adopted was for one company, each day, to provide all the guards. The men would be grouped in combinations of three, lying down, only one man required to remain awake. Instead of a verbal challenge and password, a whistling system was adopted. Bradley disliked this, thinking it was more dangerous to the troops than it would be successful in keeping Indians confused. This system was used for the duration of the campaign.[2]

1:30 PM—The wagon train—escorted by Bradley's mounted detachment—arrives in camp.

Indian Village—The combined Cheyenne–Powder River village and Crazy Horse's small village of about thirty tepees arrived at Sitting Bull's camp on Spring Creek, a tributary of the Powder.[3]

APRIL 3, 1876—MONDAY—*Gibbon/Montana Column*—Colonel John Gibbon, Major James Brisbin (Commanding Officer, 2nd Cavalry battalion and of Fort Ellis), First Lieutenant Levi Burnett (Adjutant, 7th Infantry), First Lieutenant Joshua Jacobs (Regimental Quartermaster, 7th Infantry), and Lieutenant Samuel Todd Hamilton (L/2C) leave Fort Ellis in a furious snowstorm. Gibbon wires Terry before leaving that he and the rest of the expedition are off. His command consists of twenty-seven officers, 409 enlisted men.

10 AM—Rain, then sleet and snow begin falling. Thompson's cavalry column moved along Billman Creek. From there they continued about eleven miles to Fleischman's Creek, crossed, eventually reaching Benson's Landing. After a brief pause, they moved to Shields River and went into bivouac. Snow now became a fierce storm and the wagon train fell several miles behind.

5:30 PM—Gibbon's column overtakes Thompson's bivouacked cavalry (at Shields River), thirty miles out of Fort Ellis by this time. Gibbon sends a courier to Freeman. Hot words were exchanged between Gibbon and Brisbin, and Thompson, probably because Thompson had allowed the train to fall behind.

Montana Column Trains—6:15 AM—Freeman and the wagon train break camp and ford the Yellowstone.

10:30 AM—Weather got worse during the march, heavy snow falling. After traveling sixteen miles Freeman ordered camp when they arrived at Big Boulder Creek. The wagons were corralled because of the threat of Indians. Captain Logan's Company A took guard duty. The snow continued all night.

APRIL 4, 1876—TUESDAY—*Military Correspondence & Intelligence Reports*—From the Commanding General, Department of Dakota—"Reports the expedition fairly off today (April 3rd); total 409 men and 27 officers, Signed Gibbon, Com'dg Dist."[4]

Telegram dated April 4, 1876, from St. Paul, Minnesota, to Adjutant General, Division of Missouri, Chicago—"The following just received from Fort Ellis April 3rd expedition fairly all off today total four hundred and nine men and twenty-seven officers signed Gibbon Com'd'g District."

Custer testifies before the Clymer committee for a second time.

Montana Column Trains—6:45 AM—Freeman and his infantry, despite the snow, break bivouac and begin their march again while Bradley takes the point. It is still bitterly cold and the snow affected travel. The column moved only nine miles.

10:15 AM—Freeman reaches Big Deer Creek on the south bank of the Yellowstone and one mile from the river, seventy miles out of Fort Ellis. He orders the column into camp. A courier from Gibbon orders him back to the north side, to wait, opposite the mouth of Stillwater Creek. Soon, a courier arrives with a message from Gibbon that the cavalry would be delayed until the wagons caught up. Also, Gibbon had received news of the March seventeenth attack on the Cheyenne village by Colonel Reynolds, and he was concerned the escaping Indians would flee north, crossing the Yellowstone. Freeman's column was to head down the Yellowstone and try to intercept the Indians, rather than heading toward old Fort C.F. Smith.

Gibbon/Montana Column—Gibbon/Brisbin and Thompson's cavalry remain in camp along Shields River. Finally, around midnight, the last of the wagons arrive at the cavalry's Shields River camp.

APRIL 5, 1876—WEDNESDAY—*Military Correspondence & Intelligence Reports*— From the Commanding General, Department of Dakota—"Forwards copy of letter from the C.O. Fort Stevenson, D. T., enclosing letter from Indian Ag't at Fort Berthold advising him of the location of Sitting Bull's camp and of his intention to come to that agency and trade."[5]

Montana Column Trains—6:15 AM—Freeman and his infantry, along with his wagon train, break camp. Lieutenant Bradley, riding point, encounters a group of one hundred white prospectors under William Langston at Bridger's Creek (earlier known as Emmill's Creek). They were heading for the gold fields of the Black Hills. Then, in the early morning, the cavalry and wagon train leave Shields River. After fording the Yellowstone and traveling 19.6 miles, Gibbon and the cavalry go into camp, still well behind the infantry.

11:10 AM—Having traveled fourteen miles, Freeman orders his troops into camp.

APRIL 6, 1876—THURSDAY—*Montana Column Trains*—6:10 AM—Freeman breaks camp and moves along the Yellowstone's south bank until bluffs blocked his passage. The cavalry also breaks camp.

10:55 AM—After a rocky fording of the river to its north bank and traveling twelve miles, Freeman goes into camp opposite Stillwater Creek. The weather had improved immensely and many men went fishing.

Gibbon/Montana Column—NOON—Cavalry crosses Big Boulder Creek. Moving very quickly they travel twenty-one miles and camp along Big Deer Creek. Lieutenant Charles Roe wrote to his wife: "The expedition is still involved in mystery, our big chief keeping his knowledge, if he has any, sealed in his bosum [*sic*]...."[6] From here, Gibbon sent a message to agent Dexter Clapp at the New Crow Agency seeking the services of scout Mitch Boyer and some Crow scouts.

APRIL 7, 1876—FRIDAY—*Gibbon/Montana Column* and the *Montana Column Trains*—Infantry remains in bivouac awaiting Gibbon's arrival. After crossing Bridger Creek, the cavalry—having marched about twenty miles—go into camp along the south bank of the Yellowstone, two miles west of where the cliffs closed in the valley. Gibbon, Brisbin, and their staffs continued on.

3 PM—Gibbon and the 2nd Cavalry overtake and join Freeman's infantry in camp opposite the New Crow Agency.

APRIL 8, 1876—SATURDAY—*Gibbon/Montana Column*—10 AM—In the pouring rain, Captain Thompson and the 2nd Cavalry reach Freeman's camp. Mitch Boyer and Muggins Taylor arrive and are enlisted as scouts. Gibbon wrote of Mitch Boyer:

> Whilst seated in my tent … a man, with the face of an Indian and the dress of a white man, approached the door, and, almost without saying anything, seated himself on the ground; and it was some moments before I understood that my visitor was the expected guide. He was a diffident, low spoken man, who uttered his words in a hesitating way, as if uncertain what he was going to say. He brought the news that the Crows were waiting to see me....[7]

~10 AM—As the cavalry rode into camp, Gibbon, Brisbin, Freeman, Burnett, and Bradley—guided by Boyer—left for the Crow agency. The party traveled some eighteen miles through rain and sleet, then snow, past Countryman's Ranch, then they forded the Yellowstone, eventually arriving at the agency, where they were greeted cordially by Agent Clapp. They found Clifford and E/7I there (having left Camp Baker on March fourteenth). Snow continued to fall throughout the afternoon and evening.

APRIL 9, 1876—SUNDAY—*Gibbon/Montana Column*—MORNING—The re-united column begins moving down the north bank of the Yellowstone. At Countryman's Ranch, the cavalry and wagons forded the river to its south bank, while the infantry continued to march along the north bank. About twelve miles on, the cavalry and wagons were forced to re-ford the river to its north side. After a total of fifteen miles, the cavalry and wagons went into camp.

10 AM—Gibbon holds council with the Crow. Pierre Shane (*aka*, Chane, Chene, Chienne), a French-Canadian and the agency interpreter, stood by to translate. Lieutenant Bradley wrote, the Crow chiefs in attendance were Blackfoot, Tin Belly, Iron Bull, Bull That Goes Hunting, Show His Face, Medicine Wolf, Old Onion, Mountain Pocket, Crane In The Sky, Sees All Over The Land, One Feather, Spotted Horse, Long Snake, Frog, Small Beard, Curly, Shot In The Jaw, White Forehead, Old Crow, Old Dog, White Mouth, and Crazy Head. There was another named Adada-A-Hush. Bull That Goes Hunting had the largest following, but Blackfoot seemed to have the most influence. Initially, the meeting did not go well.

AFTERNOON—Gibbon sends Clifford's company (E/7I) down the valley to join the rest of the expedition. Lieutenant Jacobs was told to bring up the wagons and load the supplies, some 100,000-lbs worth. By late afternoon, Clifford (E/7I) joins the rest of the infantry column. In the evening, Gibbon, with suspicions the Sioux are somewhere in the Big Horn valley, meets with a group of about two hundred miners from Bozeman who were heading off to the Black Hills via the old Fort C.F. Smith route and the Big Horn. They agree to try to flush any hostiles they meet up to the Yellowstone so Gibbon can deal with them. Some Crow agree to accompany the miners.

APRIL 10, 1876—MONDAY—*Gibbon/Montana Column***—Gibbon enlists twenty-three Crow as scouts, and two interpreters, Tom LeForgé and Barney "Bravo" Prevot, join as well. Lieutenant Bradley issued the scouts a piece of red "squaw-cloth" about 6"-wide to be worn on the left arm, above the elbow.[8]

Montana Column Trains—By afternoon Lieutenant Jacobs had arrived with the train of empty wagons, escorted by Lieutenant Edward J. McClernand (G/2C) and a cavalry detachment, probably from his own company. Heavy, wet snow began falling again.

APRIL 11, 1876—TUESDAY—*Gibbon/Montana Column***—9 AM—Gibbon's party leaves the Crow agency early so as to avoid being snowed in, but there was eighteen inches to two feet of snow on the ground already. By the time they reached the Yellowstone, the mountain snow had abated, with only about two inches on the ground and clear weather. The column fords the Yellowstone, but two mules in harness are lost. They continued east along the river's north bank, for about fifteen miles. *Montana Column Trains*—Camp Supply was established on the Yellowstone, west of Clark Fork (111.5 miles from Fort Ellis), primarily because they had more supplies than wagons to carry them.

Lieutenant Bradley outlined the command's strength: Gibbon and staff—three officers; 7th Infantry battalion (Freeman) of six companies—thirteen officers, 220 enlisted personnel; 2nd Cavalry battalion (Brisbin) of four companies—ten officers, 186 enlisted men; non-combatants: one officer, twenty men. Totals—twenty-seven officers, 426 men; one 12-pound Napoleon gun; two .50-caliber Gatling guns (all under the command of Lieutenant Woodruff); twenty-four government and twelve contract wagons.

APRIL 12, 1876—WEDNESDAY—*Gibbon/Montana Column* and the *Montana Column Trains***—Gibbon's command remained at Camp Supply. Captain William Logan's A/7th Infantry is left in charge; supplies under the command of Lieutenant Joshua W. Jacobs (7th Infantry), the expedition quartermaster. They were to remain until wagons could be sent back to load the supplies. Lieutenant Coolidge would remain at Supply as "medical officer."

APRIL 13, 1876—THURSDAY—*Gibbon/Montana Column***—7:15 AM—Gibbon's column leaves Camp Supply, as the campaign now began in earnest. More Crow scouts arrived to fill out the complement. Bradley scouted forward, but because he had no interpreter and no means of communicating with the Crow scouts, a number of them slipped back and rode with the column, afraid of meeting the Sioux. The progress was slow because of very soft ground. The column made only 11½ miles because of the muddy roads (probably a little west of Park City, Montana). Tom LeForgé arrives and was able to help Bradley with the Crow.

3 PM—Gibbon goes into camp.

9 PM—Campfires extinguished. Pickets posted. Ball's H/2C given guard duty.

APRIL 14, 1876—FRIDAY—*Gibbon/Montana Column***—6 AM—Lieutenant Bradley and his mounted scouts depart camp. Bradley, having worked closely with LeForgé, gained control of the Crow and scouted effectively for a breadth of ten to twelve miles. This would become virtually a constant, daily routine.

7 AM—Main column departs camp, but because of the melting snow and mud, progress was very slow, especially for the wagon train that must always be kept in sight.

2 PM—Cavalry arrived in camp. The column made 14.2 miles and established camp near Clark Fork, a southern tributary of the Yellowstone.

Montana Column Trains—3:30 PM—Wagon train arrives in camp. Particular vigilance was paid this night because of the increasing possibility of meeting hostile Sioux.

APRIL 15, 1876—SATURDAY—*Gibbon/Montana Column*—6:45 AM—Bradley and his scouts depart camp.

7 AM ±—Main column departs camp.

6 PM—Column travels 17.35 miles. Camps just below Baker's Battleground, forty-three miles from Camp Supply (west of, but near Huntley).

Side Notes—On August 14, 1872, Clifford's E/7I, English's I/7I, and all four of the cavalry companies took part in the Baker fight against the Sioux. Officers involved were Jacobs, English, Lieutenant Alfred B. Johnson, Clifford, Lieutenant George Shaeffer Young, Roe, Wheelan, Doane, Logan, Rawn, McClernand, Ball, Lieutenant James G. Macadams, Thompson, Hamilton, Lieutenant William I. Reed, Captain George L. Browning, Lieutenant William Quinton, and Schofield.[9] The battle resulted from the troops' protection of a Northern Pacific Railroad surveying party. Gibbon sent out companies C, E, G, and I, 7th Infantry, and companies F, G, H, and L, 2nd Cavalry, all under the command of Major Eugene M. Baker, 2nd Cavalry. A Sioux raiding party estimated at 800–1,000 warriors discovered the party. Baker was drunk, so Captain Rawn—disgusted at his commander—essentially took command. Because of quick thinking action by the likes of Rawn and Logan, the Sioux were routed, losing some forty warriors, with possibly as many as one hundred wounded. One soldier—Sergeant McClaren (C/7I)—and one civilian—a man named Francis—were killed, and three troops were severely wounded. According to Lieutenant Edward Settle Godfrey in his revised 1908, *Century Magazine* article, the Hunkpapa Sioux warrior, Gall, led the Sioux raiding party.[10]

Indian Village—By mid–April the Indian camp had grown to somewhere around 400–500 lodges, with 1,200 to 1,500 warriors.[11] They traveled north, heading down the eastern tributaries of the Powder River, eventually reaching the Powder itself. As they moved, they picked up the Sans Arcs Sioux. According to Wooden Leg, the camps were still separate, though close. When the Sans Arcs joined, they brought about as many as the Oglala and Minneconjou, though more Indians kept joining in small groups. At this point—and the date is problematic—Wooden Leg thought the comparative size of the various tribes to be as follows: Cheyenne: fifty lodges; Oglala: sixty to seventy lodges; Minneconjou: sixty to seventy; Sans Arcs: sixty to seventy; and the Hunkpapa: 150 lodges. This would total between 380 and 410 lodges.[12] While still early in the campaign, Wooden Leg's estimates above, fit very nicely with the estimates of Bradley and Boyer with what they eventually saw on the Tongue

River and Rosebud Creek. The tribal herds were kept separate. Farther down, the Blackfeet Sioux—the smallest of the groups—joined, probably as the tribes reached the Powder River itself. A few Waist and Skirts (Santee) joined. They had no horses and used large dogs to carry their meager possessions. This was probably the Ink-paduta band returning from Canada. Some Brulé joined, as well as Assiniboine. The Cheyenne war chief, Lame White Man and some more Cheyenne joined here. When they reached the Powder, they turned west toward the Tongue River, camping several times before reaching that stream. A large group of Cheyenne, led by Dirty Moc-casins, joined at the Tongue River, doubling the size of the Cheyenne village.[13] Other Indians were also joining along the way, increasing the size of each group. At each camp, the direction of march for the next move was determined by the amount of game reported by their scouts.[14]

APRIL 16, 1876—SUNDAY—*Gibbon/Montana Column*—6 AM—Gibbon sends Lieu-tenant McClernand with a working party to find a ford to the south side of the river. Lieutenant Bradley went with them, forded the river, and took a position on the heights below Pryor Creek.

9:35 AM—Column breaks camp and after traveling four miles, fords the Yellow-stone to its south bank. They crossed the river near the present-day town of Huntley. The weather was fine, but ford was deep and swift. Lieutenant Schofield's horse fell in a hole and the two were almost drowned.

MID-AFTERNOON—The column makes only seven miles. After crossing Pryor Creek (also known as "Shooting at the Bank Creek," by the Cheyenne), then moving back toward the Yellowstone, Gibbon orders camp on the creek. He described it as, "a deep, rushing torrent of muddy snow water, with high banks," while Clifford called it, "the dirtiest stream I have ever seen ... as black as ink, and thicker than milk—a stream of liquid mush, in fact."[15]

EARLY EVENING—Bradley leaves his "perch in the hills," and heads into camp, having seen no sign of hostiles. Apparently, however, some of the scouts saw some "strange horsemen."

APRIL 17, 1876—MONDAY—*Gibbon/Montana Column*—4:30 AM—Reveille. Humid and overcast; threatening rain.

8 AM—The column departs camp, led by Bradley and his mounted troop-ers. They went about three miles, then halted to allow the trains to catch up. When the wagons joined, the column moved on to Cachewood (Arrow) Creek, five miles; crossed it (dry), and continued down the valley. Near sunset they had made about sixteen miles, camping just below Pompey's Pillar, sixty-six miles out. Gibbon, anx-ious to find the whereabouts of the Sioux, discussed it with Bradley and the latter sent Muggins Taylor out toward the Big Horn River, thirty miles distant. Fourteen extra Crow scouts, who had been nothing but tag-alongs, were also sent forward to recon-noiter. Gibbon decided to remain in camp the following day.

Side Notes—The explorer, William Clark carved the following in its soft sandstone: "W. Clark July 25th, 1806." Pompey's Pillar was named by Lieutenant William Clark in 1806. He named it in honor of Sacajawea's baby son (the child's father was Tous-sant Charboneau and the boy's real name was Jean Baptiste Charboneau), who

Clark nicknamed, "Pomp," Shoshone for "chief." Clark affectionately called the boy, "Pompy." When the Lewis and Clark expedition came upon the rock, Clark called it, "Pompy's Tower." Some time later, when editors were preparing Clark's journals for publication, his sloppily written notes were changed inadvertently and the rock was mislabeled, "Pompey's Pillar," the editors believing Clark had named it for the ancient landmark in Alexandria, Egypt.

APRIL 18, 1876—TUESDAY—*Gibbon/Montana Column*—Gibbon's command stayed in camp, sending out scouts. Large buffalo herds were seen grazing quietly in the Big Horn valley. This told the troopers the Indians were not too close, for if they were, the herds would be moving.[16]

APRIL 19, 1876—WEDNESDAY—*Military Correspondence & Intelligence Reports*—From the Department of the Platte—"Repeat telegram relative to the condition of affairs at the Red Cloud and Spotted Tail Agencies."[17]

Telegram dated April 19, 1876, from Omaha, Nebraska, Assistant Adjutant General, to Headquarters, Mil. Div. of the Missouri, Chicago, Ill—

> The following telegram received from the commanding officer District of the Black Hills, Fort Laramie, Wyo., April 18, 1876, Adjutant General, Department of the Platte, Omaha, Neb. Commanding officers at Robinson and Sheridan report by courier that no Indians have left either agency with their families since the fight on Powder River. A few men only went out to bring in their own people and some have returned accompanied by Northern Sioux. Cheyenne at Red Cloud are alarmed and talk of going South. Indications are that the punishment of Crazy Horse [*sic*] affects the Ogallallas favorably. Major Jordan thinks three hundred of this band would go with expedition against Northern Indians if they could retain what they captured. Northern Sioux have stolen their stock lately. No bad feeling shown at either agency. A few miners have been killed near Black Hills. Will telegraph any change. Signed Bradley Lieut. Colonel.

In the same telegram—"I have instructed the Commanding officer District of Black Hills to keep me fully posted on condition of affairs at Red Cloud and Spotted Tail agencies. George Crook, Brigadier General."

A letter from Headquarters, Cheyenne Agency, D. T., April 19, 1876, To the Assistant Adjutant General, Department of Dakota, St. Paul, Minn.—

> Sir:
>
> The Interpreter at this Post reports that he has information from the Indians to the effect that a party of half-breed whites coming from the Red River Country in the vicinity of Fort Terry [?], are, and have been for over a month, encamped near the Black Hills, north of Bear Butte, and that they are carrying on an extensive trade in ammunition with the Indians. He says that Indians tell him these half-breeds held a council with the principal hostile chiefs in the course of which they (the half-breeds) stated that it was their intention to assist the Indians against the whites by trading for their ammunition which under present circumstances they could not obtain anywhere else. They also say that the half-breeds have one cannon with them.
>
> The Interpreter also reports that a brother of Bull Eagle, who left the hostile camp on the 9th inst. arrived here yesterday. This Indian says that the main camp of the hostile Indians was, when he left it, headed for a distance of about twenty-five miles along the mouth of the Powder River and along the Yellowstone, and consisted of about three thousand bodies. This Indian also brings us the first reports that we have had through Indians, of the recent fight that General Crook's Command had with the Indians. He says that the Indians of the camp routed by Gen'l Crook's forces arrived at the main hostile camp a few days before he left it, and that he has conversed with Indians of the routed camp, and learned from them that the attack of the cavalry

on their village was a complete surprise, the Indians not being aware that there were any soldiers within hundreds of miles of them, and that their first intimation of their presence was seeing the "white horse soldiers" charge through the village; he further stated that the Indian women and children at once ran to "the rocks," that the men fired one volley at the soldiers and also ran to the rocks or cliffs and from there continued the fire on the troops while the fight lasted and that when this was over, they returned to the camp and found four dead soldiers and five dead Indian men and one woman. They positively assent that this was the only loss in killed they sustained, and also positively deny that any living (wounded) soldiers fell into their hands. They saved sufficient provisions from the burned camp to support them for the march to the main camp, a distance of about eighty miles, and recovered nearly all the ponies, which had been captured by the cavalry within a day or two after the fight. The Indian says that the village attacked was not Crazy Horse's band; that Crazy Horse was at the time of the fight with the main camp on Powder River, and that the Indians routed were fifty-five lodges of Cheyennes and ten of Ogallalla Sioux.

This Indian who claims to be sent by the hostile chiefs as a messenger to this Agency to ascertain the chances of them obtaining ammunition and stores here, and that the hostile Indians are thoroughly roused and threaten to make an attack on the whites which shall be as complete a surprise to them as was the attack of the cavalry on their village. He furthermore says that the head chiefs are organizing small predatory war parties and raiding them out in all directions; that the chiefs who were heretofore opposed to war with the whites, now harangue their young men and council them to make an organized attack on some unprotected trading post, with a view to obtaining by force the ammunition they cannot procure by other means.

> I am, Sir, Very respectfully, Your obedient Servant,
> (Sgd) George Ruhlen, 2nd Lieut., 17th Inf., Comd'r Post.

Gibbon/Montana Column—7:30 AM—With Bradley again in the lead, the column breaks camp. Blustery winds, swirling sand.

9 AM—Column reached Fly Creek: water standing in holes; the creek not running. The valley began to narrow here and while Captain Freeman decided to keep the infantry on the river's south bank, the cavalry and wagons prepared to ford to the north side. At this point, the river was 580 feet wide, but only forty inches deep. The column—less the infantry—crossed. After only 2½ miles, however, they were forced to re-cross to the south side, the river now some 632 feet wide and three feet deep. After making 18.6 miles they went into camp at 4:45 PM amidst a large copse of cottonwoods. Still no sign of the Sioux.

APRIL 20, 1876—THURSDAY—Custer released by the Clymer committee and the Adjutant General and leaves Washington, D.C.

Gibbon/Montana Column—7:40 AM—The march resumed; day dawned clear. Bradley and his scouts were several miles ahead. As they moved farther downstream, they noticed the river rising higher and Gibbon knew he had to cross to the north side before it became impassable. Mitch Boyer was constantly in the water searching for a suitable crossing point, ripples indicating a shallower area. Captain Ball led the final crossing to the north side of the Yellowstone. After crossing, they traveled another mile and a half through a sagebrush-covered bottom, then ascended to a high plateau, passing the mouth of the Big Horn River. From the heights, they could see Fort Pease, six miles below the Big Horn. Four miles across the plateau they reached the head of Fort Pease valley.

5 PM—Having traveled 17.2 miles, the column went into camp at Pease Bottom, two miles west of the abandoned fort (between Bighorn and Myers). Despite seeing the tracks of two horses—they turned out to be wild—there was still no sign of the Sioux, though they were deep into Sioux country.

APRIL 21, 1876—FRIDAY—*Gibbon/Montana Column***—4 AM—Reveille.**

10 AM—As Gibbon prepared to move, two riders were seen approaching. One was Will Logan, the young son of Captain Logan; the other, Sergeant William Thompson (A/7I), both from Logan's camp along the Stillwater—they had ridden about one hundred miles. They brought an urgent dispatch from General Terry dated April 15, 1876, from St. Paul, ordering Gibbon to go no farther than the Big Horn. The dispatch tells of Crook's column not moving until mid–May (actually, it would be May 29) and of the Dakota column not yet moving.

Crook's column had at least three reporters with it: Thomas B. MacMillan (Chicago *Inter-Ocean*); John F. Finerty (*Chicago Times*); and Reuben B. Davenport (*New York Herald*). There was probably someone from the *Army and Navy Journal* along as well. The dispatch also tells Gibbon the Sioux appeared to be in much greater numbers than Gibbon was originally led to believe; Crook's Powder River victory was hollow, at best; and Gibbon was to cease his advance until further orders.[18] At 10:40 AM, Gibbon penned a dispatch to Terry informing him of the extent of his advance; he wrote, he now felt the Sioux are "…in the direction of the Black Hills mines first, whatever they do afterwards."[19] He also decides to order Captain Logan to move the supply depot to Pease, and he informs Terry of same. He decides as well, to send a cavalry scouting party toward old C.F. Smith to communicate with William Langston's prospectors. Gibbon now moves the column alongside the old abandoned Fort F.D. Pease (104 miles out and 215.32 miles from Fort Ellis). The fact Fort Pease was in the same condition as it was when Brisbin's command left it a few weeks earlier indicated to Gibbon the Sioux had not been in the area.

APRIL 22, 1876—SATURDAY—*Military Correspondence & Intelligence Reports***—** From the Department of Dakota—"Furnishes copy of telegram directing Major Moore and Co.'s C, D, and I, 6th Infantry, to proceed up the Yellowstone to meet expedition under Lt. Col. Custer."[20]

Gibbon/Montana Column—1 AM—Gibbon detailed four cavalrymen to carry mail back to Ellis. The command remained bivouacked and at four PM it began raining.

APRIL 23, 1876—SUNDAY—*Gibbon/Montana Column* **and the** *Montana Column Trains***—**6:30 AM—Captain Freeman's company (H/7I) is sent back to Camp Supply with an empty wagon train—twenty-seven wagons[21]—to bring up the supplies; eighteen-day round trip. Five of the wagons—under the escort of Lieutenant Frederick M.H. Kendrick and a small detachment—were to return to Fort Ellis: discharged contract teams of John W. Power's wagon train. There, Kendrick would wait for the E.G. Maclay & Co. Diamond-R supply wagons.

APRIL 24, 1876—MONDAY—*Gibbon/Montana Column***—**NOON—a rather hot day—Gibbon orders Captain Ball, with two companies of the 2nd Cavalry (his own H and Roe's F, around eighty men; Dr. Paulding later wrote it was ninety-seven white men and one Indian, total), on a scout up the Big Horn River to old Fort C.F. Smith, some seventy-five miles from the Big Horn's confluence with the Yellowstone. Ball was also to try to contact the Black Hills mining party if it was still in that vicinity. The command was to return via Tullock's Creek. Lieutenant McClernand, the acting engineer officer, accompanied the column, as did LeForgé and Jack Rabbit Bull. One source claimed other Crow scouts went along as well, though neither Bradley nor McClernand make mention of it. Some pack mules were taken. Apparently, George Herendeen and Muggins Taylor also went along.

Montana Column Trains—2 PM—CPT Freeman's wagon train traveled twenty-two miles and camped on the north bank of the Yellowstone, opposite Pompey's Pillar.

2:15 PM—*Captain Ball's Scout*—Ball's column crosses the Yellowstone just above the mouth of the Big Horn, 5½ miles from Fort Pease. Around 2:30 PM, Ball halts to make coffee and rest the animals, resuming his march at 6 PM.

11:30 PM—Ball moved into camp near Wood Creek, sixteen miles from the Yellowstone, 21½ miles from Fort Pease. Pickets were posted and the horses hobbled.

Gibbon/Montana Column—Back at Fort Pease, Bradley's scouts continued to roam the territory.

APRIL 25, 1876—TUESDAY—*Captain Ball's Scout*—9:15 AM—Ball's column resumes its march, covering sixteen miles and halting at 1:20 PM on the left bank of the Big Horn River. The troops rested while the animals grazed.

6:40 PM—Ball resumes his trek up the Big Horn. At around 7:10 PM they reached the Little Big Horn confluence, and continued heading up-river. Ball entered the valley from the southeast, into a green and attractive meadowland area, then briefly halted a short distance from the present town of Hardin, Montana.[22]

11:30 PM—Having covered thirty-two miles for the day, Ball halts, making camp in a small cove of the Big Horn. During the day, smoke had been observed in the Big Horn Mountains, making the troops wonder if that was where the Sioux were … accounting for the lack of any signs of their presence in the Big Horn Valley.

Montana Column Trains—Having covered twenty-five miles, Captain Freeman makes camp three miles below the mouth of Pryor's Creek.

Indian Village—Sitting Bull's village, now with Crazy Horse's, has moved to the confluence of the Mizpah and Powder and will remain there until about April 28.[23]

APRIL 26, 1876—WEDNESDAY—*Captain Ball's Scout*—6 AM—Ball's command leaves camp and fords the Big Horn—2½ feet deep—spending most of the day riding through enormous herds of buffalo. After crossing the river, Ball moved another 1½ miles, then stopped to make breakfast, resuming the march at 1:30 PM. They moved about six miles to a place opposite Beauvais Creek, and continued on.

2 PM—Ball fords Rotten Grass Creek, about ten feet wide and very shallow (1½ feet deep), clear and cold water.

6:05 PM—Ball's command crosses Soap Creek: high banks, firm, pebbly bottom, clear and cold. Around sunset Ball makes camp. They covered only about twenty miles because of frequent stops to allow the horses to graze. McClernand described the area as the finest tillable soil he had seen in Montana: no stones, cactus, or sagebrush, and plenty of water. Smoke was seen in vicinity of Fort Smith, three miles away.

Montana Column Trains—Captain Freeman's column makes another twenty-five miles, camping near the mouth of "Cannon Creek."[24] Freeman meets the mail carriers there.

APRIL 27, 1876—THURSDAY—*Military Correspondence & Intelligence Reports*—Letter from Major Marcus Reno, Commanding at Fort Lincoln to the Assistant Adjutant General, St. Paul, dated April 27, 1876—"Sioux scout from Standing Rock reports all young men are leaving reservation with best ponies. They report going to fight Crow Indians, but he says they are going to join Sitting Bull. (Sgd) Reno, Commd'g."

George Custer having once more been ordered back to Washington arrives in the city, ostensibly to testify again in the Belknap hearings. It seems Belknap may have orchestrated the ploy to keep Custer from the campaign.

Gibbon/Montana Column—Lieutenant Bradley sends six Crow scouts down the Yellowstone as far as the Rosebud (nearly sixty miles) to look for Sioux.

Captain Ball's Scout—Captain Ball remains in camp most of the day. He said later it was the finest land he had seen in all of Montana.

5:15 PM—Ball's column begins its move through the "hayfields" of Fort C.F. Smith and after three miles reached the abandoned fort, seventy-five miles from the mouth of the Big Horn. They stop for a while to look around, leaving the old fort site at 7:05 PM. The weather became cool and rain threatened. Finally, at midnight Ball halts and makes camp on Rotten Grass Creek, having traveled eighteen miles for the day.

Montana Column Trains—Meanwhile, Freeman makes twenty-two miles and is now within a day's march of Captain Logan's supply camp. Mitch Boyer and the young Will Logan continue on ahead.

APRIL 28, 1876—FRIDAY—*Military Correspondence & Intelligence Reports*—From the Commanding General, Department of Dakota—"Furnishes copy of letter relative to the traffic in ammunition between half breed whites and hostile Indians and to the recent fight between Gen. Crook's command and Indians. Forwards copy of telegram from C.O. Fort A. Lincoln stating that Sioux Scout from Standing Rock Agency reports all young men leaving reservation with best ponies."[25]

A man named Boucher, living near the Spotted Tail Agency, was known to be an arms trafficker.

Captain Ball's Scout—9:25 AM—Captain Ball is on the move, heading mostly east, and at 10:10 AM the command reaches a small tributary of Rotten Grass, moving up the creek, then over high, rolling hills, reaching the top of a high divide at eleven AM. After marching 7½ miles, Ball halts at noon.

2 PM—Ball is on the move again. At 3:25 PM the column reaches a small creek running northeast. They follow it for three miles where it joined another creek. They crossed the latter, moving another four miles until reaching Lodge Grass Creek (Indians called it Long Creek).

6 PM—The column reaches the Little Big Horn River. They turn left down the

river's west bank for about a mile, then camp on the west bank in a grove of cotton-woods. They had traveled 21½ miles for the day.

Montana Column Trains—Freeman's wagon train reaches Camp Supply. Lieutenant Frederick Kendrick, Sergeant George Stein, Corporal Patrick Ruddin, and eight privates (all H/2C) would escort the John W. Power wagons to Fort Ellis.

APRIL 29, 1876—SATURDAY—*Fort Abraham Lincoln*—Lieutenants Smith (E/7C) and Calhoun (L/7C) arrive at Fort Abraham Lincoln.

Captain Ball's Scout—8:45 AM—Captain Ball's advance continues down the Little Big Horn valley, noticing the ravine-cut bluffs on the east side of the river. Soon, the column passes through an area where a large Indian camp had been the preceding summer. The camp was located just below the mouth of Lodge Tail Creek and had been a Cheyenne camp, though McClernand and Paulding incorrectly identified it as Sioux.

12:45 PM—The command passes by the hills the 7th Cavalry was eventually to fight on. Ball makes a short camp on the site later occupied by the Indian village.

2:30 PM—Moving a total of some six miles down the Little Big Horn, Ball fords the river toward the east, crosses the Wolf Mountains and reaches a dry tributary of Tullock's Creek.

8:45 PM—Camp is made on another tributary of Tullock's, fifteen miles traveled since noon; twenty-seven miles for the day; and 140½ miles since leaving Pease.

Gibbon/Montana Column—NOON—Lieutenant Kendrick with his escort and four wagons, head out for Fort Ellis.

Montana Column Trains—1 PM—Freeman and Logan load the train and make ready to evacuate Camp Supply, heading back to Fort Pease. They move six miles.

APRIL 30, 1876—SUNDAY—*Military Correspondence & Intelligence Reports*—From the Commanding Officer, Fort Stevenson—"Forwards letter from Indian Agent Fort Berthold reporting the Sioux camp of 1,500 lodges a few days ride from the agency. They have plenty of meat and robes and their greatest desire is ammunition."[26]

In a letter dated April 30, 1876, from Fort Berthold, D. T., to Lieut. Col. Dan'l Huston, 6th U.S. Inf'y, Commanding, Fort Stevenson, D. T.

Dear Sir,

Your communication of 29th inst. at hand and noted. The latest and most reliable reports from the Sioux camp is that there is about 1,500 lodges a few days ride from this agency and small parties are going to different points to trade. They claim that they are going to fight the Crow Indians. I think they intend to make trouble somewhere. There is but 12 lodges here now on the other side of the river from the village. They say that these [*sic*; there are] two other parties coming in here if they have no trouble with the whites. They have plenty of meat and robes and their greatest desire is ammunition. None to be obtained here from either trader or Indians. They are to leave here tomorrow. Mr. Chas Reynolds will give you all the particulars; anything new will post you.

Yours truly,
C. W. Darling

As a result of the letter, above, a letter dated April 30, 1876, from Headquarters, Fort Stevenson, to Assistant Adjutant General, Dept of Dakota, St. Paul, Minn.

Sir,

In compliance with General Orders No. 19, Headqrs. Dept of Dakota series 1875, I have the honor to enclose herewith a letter received this day from the Indian Agent at Fort Berthold, D. T.

The Mr. Reynolds therein referred to gives no further information but merely confirms the report of the Agent.

Yours Respectfully, Your obedt Servt,

Dan'l Huston, Lieut. Colonel, 6th Inft'y, Brvt Colonel, U.S. Army, Commanding.

Captain Ball's Scout—3:20 AM—Reveille.

5:15 AM—With rain threatening, Ball begins his move down Tullock's Creek. At eight AM, having traveled nine miles, he halts to graze his tired animals.

12:30 PM—Ball's column is on the march again.

4 PM—Marching another eleven miles, Ball goes into camp having made only twenty miles for the day because of the stops to allow the animals to graze, and the creek being very crooked, with steep banks. Had not seen a single hostile Indian on the entire trip. Author and historian Edgar I. Stewart noted here: "The great majority of the warriors who were to overwhelm the Custer command several weeks later were still at the agencies on the Dakota reservation and were just beginning to leave there to join the hostile bands."[27]

Gibbon/Montana Column—Gibbon noted in his *American Catholic Quarterly* article, thinking at the time, that the hostiles "had all fled to the agencies."[28] Bradley's six Crow scouts return; no Sioux seen.

Montana Column Trains—Freeman and Logan continue down the Yellowstone. A light rain began falling in the afternoon.

Indian Village—Sitting Bull's village—with Crazy Horse's—has moved to the Tongue River, near where it is joined by Pumpkin Creek. They will remain here until about May fifth. From there they will move up the Tongue.[29]

3

Numbers

May

May 1, 1876—Monday—President Grant turns down Custer's request for an interview, making him wait more than five hours. Finally, he goes to the War Department and receives permission to leave the city. That night, Custer boards a train and heads for Monroe, Michigan, to visit his parents and a friend, John Bulkley.

Montana Column Trains—6 AM—Freeman and Logan resume their march with the wagon train. They would make camp two miles from Baker's Battleground. The weather was very warm; bright and clear.

Captain Ball's Scout—7:15 AM—Captain Ball resumes his march down Tullock's Creek. The stream was so crooked it required frequent crossings. After marching twelve miles Ball's troops reach the mouth of Tullock's, about one mile above where the Big Horn flows into the Yellowstone. By three PM Ball and Roe return from their scout along the Little Big Horn and Tullock's Fork. No sign of Indians. The trip was 178 to 180 miles. Their arrival was preceded by the wild shrieking of scouts on the bluffs opposite Fort Pease, howling that the far-off troopers were Sioux warriors. Gibbon writes a telegram for Terry:

> Captain Ball just in with two companies from Fort C.F. Smith. Went on Phil Kearny road as far as Rotten Grass Creek, thence over on Little Big Horn to Tullock's Fork and down that. He saw no sign of Indians. My [Crow] scouts report none on Rosebud. As soon as my supplies reach here, say in ten days, I propose, if no news comes from you, to move downriver.[1]

Gibbon/Montana Column—By now, six of the Crow scouts had deserted: boredom, too many rules imposed by Lieutenant Bradley.

Late night—John Williamson leaves Fort Pease for Bozeman with Gibbon's telegram.

**May 2, 1876—Tuesday—*Military Correspondence & Intelligence Reports*—Telegram dated May 2, 1876, from Reno, Commanding, Fort A. Lincoln, D. T., to General Ruggles, St. Paul—"Twelve (12) lodges of Hunkpapa at Berthold trading report several hundred lodges between here and Yellowstone waiting for expedition. Indians from camp attacked by Crook have joined Sitting Bull. Fuller details in letter from Col. Huston by this mail. (Signed) Reno, Commanding."

Gibbon/Montana Column—By now, Lieutenant Bradley wrote they were very perplexed at not having seen any signs of the Sioux. He opined about them having returned to their various agencies, awaiting another turn to take off, and believed this might be the case because of Crook's fight on the Powder. Nonetheless, Bradley still believed the Sioux were in the area. A heavy windstorm sets in, but the weather was warm.

Despite the warmth, because of the bad roads, Freeman was able to make only twelve miles and camped a little below Pryor Creek.

LATE NIGHT INTO THE FOLLOWING MORNING—A band of Northern Cheyenne warriors under Two Moon(s) steal Crow ponies during a storm. They took thirty-two Crow horses, plus Henry Bostwick's horse and mule. The Crow—upon discovering their horses had been swiped—stood around and cried. Gibbon wrote, "The Crows assembled at their camp, and cried, like children whose toys had been broken."[2] The Indians had seen the troops and were aware of the Fort Pease camp. They had even followed Ball's command to the Yellowstone. One Cheyenne warrior had sneaked into Pease and watched several officers playing cards in one of the buildings, Lieutenant Samuel Todd Hamilton being recognized later by this warrior and informed of it at Fort Yates.[3]

MAY 3, 1876—WEDNESDAY—*Military Correspondence & Intelligence Reports*— From Commanding General, Department of Dakota—"Forwards copy of telegram from C.O. Fort Lincoln with information that there are several hundred lodges of hostile Indians between Berthold and the Yellowstone waiting for expedition; that Indians attacked by Crook have joined Sitting Bull."[4]

***Gibbon/Montana Column*—**Crow ponies stolen by hostiles; signs of a fifty-man war party spotted. It began to drizzle in the morning, then the temperatures dropped and the rain changed to snow. By afternoon the valley was shrouded in fog. Twenty Sioux stole the horses while the rest remained in reserve. (Edgar Stewart claimed they were Cheyenne under Two Moon[s].[5]) There were seventeen Crow scouts remaining and none of them had horses. Bradley was upset and wrote that he believed Gibbon was wrong in granting the Crow the latitude to keep their horses wherever they wanted, rather than corral them as the cavalry did.

***Montana Column Trains*—**Because of the windstorm, Freeman was unable to move his wagons during the morning and early afternoon, but finally, at three PM, he was able to hitch his animals to their wagons and move.

***Indian Village*—**On this day, the Sioux village stood a little up from the mouth of the Tongue River. Close to 400 lodges and 800 warriors under Sitting Bull and Crazy Horse. The so-called winter roamers had moved leisurely down the Powder, almost to its mouth, then turned west.

MAY 4, 1876—THURSDAY—*Dakota Column*—Major Orlando Moore, Commanding Officer, Fort Buford, Dakota Territory, was ordered by General Terry to establish a supply depot at Glendive Creek/Stanley's Stockade, established during Stanley's 1873 Yellowstone expedition (near present-day Glendive, Montana). This consisted of Company C, 6th Infantry (Captain James W. Powell; Second Lieutenant Bernard A. Byrne, Acting Commissary and Acting Quartermaster); Company D, 6th Infantry (Captain Daniel H. Murdock; First Lieutenant Frederick W. Thibaut, Acting

Battalion Adjutant); and Company I, 6th Infantry (Second Lieutenant George B. Walker). Stanley's Stockade was built during the June 1873 Colonel David Sloan Stanley expedition for the Northern Pacific Rail Road survey.

In the morning of this day George Custer arrived by train in Chicago. He had his nephew, Autie Reed, with him, as well as his niece. While waiting for the train to St. Paul, Colonel Tony Forsyth handed Custer a telegram from Sherman instructing him to remain in Chicago to await further orders. He had been forbidden to go on the campaign. Custer had breached protocol by not seeing President Grant—a ploy—and by not getting permission from Sherman to leave Washington. Custer requested permission to at least serve his "detention" at Fort Lincoln instead of Chicago.

Gibbon/Montana Column—1 AM—Two couriers from Fort Ellis arrived. They had encountered four Indians—ten or twelve miles back—and one shot an arrow at them.

7 AM—Bradley dispatched Sergeant Joseph L. Farrell, five men, Tom LeForgé, and a Crow scout to look for a missing man, Private John Madden. Weather was chilly and cloudy.

3 PM—Having found Madden, Farrell and his detachment return to camp.

Montana Column Trains—9 AM—The Freeman/Logan supply train resumed its march, traveling seventeen miles, and then going into camp. Signs of Indians were observed: Dr. Paulding, Muggins Taylor, and a trooper—out on a hunting expedition—were followed closely by a band of Sioux.

MAY 5, 1876—FRIDAY—*Military Correspondence & Intelligence Reports*—From Commanding General, Department of Dakota—"Forwards copy of instructions to C.O. Fort Berthold relative to movement of troops to join the expedition against hostile Indians."[6]

Montana Column Trains—5 AM—The day dawns clear, and Freeman and Logan with the supply train depart camp. They have breakfast at Pompey's Pillar.

1 PM—Freeman and Logan resume march.

6:12 PM—Trains go into camp along a dry creek. They had traveled ten miles and this camp was awful: no grass, no water, and full of wood ticks.

Gibbon/Montana Column—Lieutenant Bradley sends out Crow scouts, on foot, in an attempt to find out where these Indians came from. Nothing. Lieutenant Kendrick's (H/7I) detachment arrives at Fort Ellis.

MAY 6, 1876—SATURDAY—Custer arrives in St. Paul, and finds General Terry is sympathetic to Custer's plight.

Montana Column Trains—5 AM—Freeman and Logan leave camp, but still have difficulty moving along Yellowstone's northern bank. The wagon train makes eighteen miles for the day.

Gibbon/Montana Column—Some time in the morning, Bradley sends out Crow scouts Half Yellow Face and Jack Rabbit Bull—mounted—who surprise three Sioux, and steal their horses. Bradley then seeks permission from Gibbon for another scout downriver and at night. At first, Gibbon refused, then relented, but told Bradley it would have to be the night of the seventh. Scout George Herendeen joins Gibbon at Fort Pease, and the mackinaw boat trader, Linas McCormick, also arrived at the fort.

NOON—There is a hailstorm for an hour.

MAY 7, 1876—SUNDAY—6:30 AM—*Montana Column Trains*—Freeman, Logan, and the wagons depart camp. They go twelve miles through badlands and camp on the Yellowstone, eight miles from Fort Pease.

Gibbon/Montana Column—In the evening Bradley heads out on a strong scout: seventeen mounted soldiers, Bostwick, LeForgé, and four Crow scouts. The consensus among the officers was Bradley's mission was foolhardy and dangerous.[7]

Crook/Wyoming Column—Lieutenant Egan of Crook's command meets a war party of one hundred lodges and some 700–800 warriors on the Powder River trail, all heading north. Each party ignored the other.[8]

Military Correspondence & Intelligence Reports—The Red Cloud Agency (Agent James S. Hastings) was reported to be virtually deserted.

MAY 8, 1876—MONDAY—General Terry's headquarters receives word from General Sherman that President Grant will allow Custer to go at the head of his regiment. Custer is instructed to be prudent, not to take along any newspapermen, and to abstain from "personalities."

Gibbon/Montana Column—3 AM—Fifteen miles downriver, Bradley discovers three abandoned Sioux war lodges that probably sheltered as many as thirty warriors. The three Sioux warriors the Crow had surprised on May sixth were, in all likelihood, from this party. Bradley rides on, fording They-Froze-to-Death Creek, and riding farther downstream until the party found where the Sioux had forded the Yellowstone to its south bank.

10:30 AM—Bradley, having continued down the north bank of the Yellowstone, goes into camp.

5 PM—Having rested a while, Bradley and his scouts break camp and continue their downriver scout, seeing more and more signs of Sioux. They moved about two miles and reached Great Porcupine Creek where they spotted a large herd of buffalo. Before he could stop them, the Crow charged into the herd, firing, and killing several. Bradley was upset because of the threat of Sioux about. Bradley decided to turn back here.

Montana Column Trains—6 AM—Freeman breaks camp at and at eleven AM, he and Logan arrive at Fort Pease along with Boyer and the wagon train. Gibbon decides to move his camp farther downstream, realizing there were only war parties and not the main camp(s) in this area.

MAY 9, 1876—TUESDAY—*Military Correspondence & Intelligence Reports*—From the Assistant Adjutant General, Department of Dakota—"Gen. Terry left for Fort Lincoln this morning."[9]

Terry and Custer leave for Fort Abraham Lincoln in the early morning hours.

Gibbon/Montana Column—2 AM—Bradley and his detachment camp on Froze-to-Death-Creek and at noon returns to Fort Pease convinced the Sioux are down the

Yellowstone and not in the interior, north or south. He had traveled some eighty-five miles. This established Bradley as a very fine scout, though Gibbon would never give him the credit he was due. Gibbon sends a telegram or note to Terry informing him of his intended move downriver. Gibbon's fear now is Sioux escaping north, into the wilderness.

The mackinaw trader, McCormick, left with the mail, hoping to return in sixteen days with fresh vegetables. At the same time, the troops refurbished several small mackinaw boats found at Pease, and Gibbon decided to take them, Captain Clifford's E/7I given the job of navigating. Scout George Herendeen claimed the boats were his, since he built them. Gibbon had offered him $50 a month to scout, but Herendeen had refused the pay, not wishing to be obligated to the army. He insisted on accompanying the troops with the boats. (*Once accepting the military's employment, the civilian scouts were subject to the commander's orders, similar to the troopers.*)

Crook/Wyoming Column—In the meantime, Brigadier General George Crook and his aide, Lieutenant John G. Bourke, leave Omaha for Cheyenne, then Camp Robinson and the Red Cloud Agency to try to recruit scouts. The agent—James S. Hastings—was extremely uncooperative.[10] After leaving Camp Robinson, Crook and Bourke headed for Fort Laramie.

MAY 10, 1976—WEDNESDAY—General Terry, his staff, and George Custer arrive at Fort Abraham Lincoln.

Gibbon/Montana Column—8:30 AM—Gibbon's entire column leaves Fort Pease for downriver. The march begins in rain and mud and follows General Stanley's 1873 trail. Clifford—in the boats—wrote that small parties of Sioux are seen, but no indication of any camps. The main column came across a number of deep ravines, difficult to cross. The valley gave way to difficult bluffs. Crow scouts capture two abandoned Sioux ponies. Sioux are now seen frequently, even single warriors. At noon heavy rains begin to fall. Gibbon called it a "furious rainstorm" and at three PM, John Williamson, the white scout from Pease, joined the column with mail from Fort Ellis.

4 PM–7:30 PM—The rain becomes heavier, drenching the column.

6 PM—The command turns right and descends a ravine leading to the Yellowstone.

7:30 PM—Gibbon goes into camp, having traveled 16¾ miles. Captain Clifford arrives with his company in the three small boats found at Fort Pease. These camps were usually "laid out in rectangular shape with one side along the river; and we had from 600 to 800 animals, mostly mules." Lieutenant Charles Roe said every night Indians were around or in the camp.[11]

MAY 11, 1876—THURSDAY—*Gibbon/Montana Column*—This turned out to be a layover day. The rain had stopped, leaving the day warmer. More signs of the Sioux found.

MAY 12, 1876—FRIDAY—*Gibbon/Montana Column*—7:20 AM—Gibbon starts out again, still following Stanley's trail of 1873. A short march brought them to Froze-to-Death-Creek with badlands on each side.

5:30 PM—After traveling some 18.9 miles, Gibbon camps in the Yellowstone

Valley. Fresh signs of Sioux were discovered along the banks of the river, though Lieutenant McClernand does not mention it in his journal. Scouts Barney Bravo and Little Face overtake the column, bringing back the six deserters, providing Lieutenant Bradley with several much-needed mounts for his scouts. By evening Lieutenant Jacobs (the Quartermaster Officer), Muggins Taylor, Henry Bostwick, Sergeant William Wilson (K/7I) are ferried across the Yellowstone to scout down to the Rosebud.

Indian Village—Sitting Bull's village—with Crazy Horse's—has moved up the Tongue River, mid-way between Pumpkin and Lay creeks. They will remain here until about May sixteenth.[12]

MAY 13, 1876—**SATURDAY**—*Military Correspondence & Intelligence Reports*—In a dispatch from Omaha, it was reported eighty lodges left the Red Cloud Agency in one day that past week.[13]

Gibbon/Montana Column—4 AM—Reveille sounded; remains in a layover. The day was hot and sunny. Bradley allows four unmounted Crow to cross the river in hopes of stealing some Sioux horses.

4 PM—The Jacobs party returns: unsure they had gone as far as the Rosebud and having seen no Sioux.

MAY 14, 1876—**SUNDAY**—*Military Correspondence & Intelligence Reports*—Telegram dated May 14, 1876, from Fort Pease, Montana, to General Terry, Commanding, St. Paul, Minn.—

> Captain Ball, just in with two companies from C.F. Smith, went out on Phil Kearny road as far as Rotten Grass; thence over on to Little Big Horn at Tullock's fork and down that. He saw no signs of Indians. My scouts report now on Rosebud. As soon as my supplies reach here, say in ten days, I propose, if no news comes from you, to move down the river. (Sgd.) Gibbon, Commanding.

Dakota Column—3:30 PM—Major Moore leaves Fort Buford (established on June 15, 1866. Latitude, 48 degrees, longitude, 103 degrees 57' 30"; located on the left bank of the Missouri River, near the mouth of the Yellowstone) for Stanley's Stockade (Glendive Creek) on the steamer "Josephine." (Mart Coulson was the captain of the steamer.) Three companies of the 6th Infantry were aboard (C, D, and I).

Terry telegrams Sheridan: "It is represented that they have 1,500 lodges, are confident and intend making a stand."[14] Terry received information from a number of independent sources and concluded the Indians were concentrated either on the Little Missouri or between that river and the Yellowstone. He then sends a telegram to Fort Ellis, to be forwarded to Gibbon, "directing him to move down the Yellowstone to 'Stanley's stockade,' to cross the river, and move out on 'Stanley's trail' to meet the column from Lincoln."[15] Major Marcus Reno, commanding Fort Abraham Lincoln in Custer's absence, had previously reported large numbers of Indians leaving the agencies.

Gibbon/Montana Column—7:45 AM—Gibbon breaks camp with rain threatening. In 3.7 miles the column reaches and crosses the Great Porcupine. While the wagons are crossing, Bradley continues on to "Castle Rock."

> Near Porcupine Creek while waiting for Gibbon's wagon train to cross, Bradley climbed a high butte, Castle Butte [*Castle Rock*]. I found the butte and wanted to climb it, but the bluff which

is sandstone had weathered inward. I would have needed a forty-foot ladder just to get to the top. I could see where Bradley climbed up and carved his name, but no cigar for this guy. The owner, whose license plate read "bitch," was helpful and showed me where Indian tipi rings were. I also saw the ruts of Stanley and Gibbon's wagon trains.[16]

4:45 PM—Having traveled 16.97 miles for the day, Gibbon goes into camp about one mile above the Little Porcupine Creek. He halts for six days, six miles above Rosebud Creek and one mile above the Little Porcupine (called Table Creek by Lewis and Clark), fifty-two miles downriver from Fort Pease. Right after pitching camp, a thunderous hailstorm erupted, accompanied by high winds, then heavy rain. While fierce, the worst of the storm lasted only ten to twenty minutes, blowing down tents, flooding the camp and soaking everyone. Rain continued throughout an extremely dark night. In camp, Gibbon decides to send out Lieutenant Bradley on another scout.

Montana Column Trains—Lieutenant Kendrick (H/7I) leaves Fort Ellis with a detachment of fifteen men and the Diamond-R train carrying 100,000 pounds of freight.[17]

MAY 15, 1876—MONDAY—*Military Correspondence & Intelligence Reports*—From the Assistant Adjutant General, Department of Dakota—"Gen. Terry's column left Fort Lincoln this morning."[18]

From the Assistant Adjutant General, Department of Dakota—"Departure of troops from Fort Lincoln delayed on account of rain."[19]

From the Commanding General, Department of Dakota—"States that reports place the Sioux camp on the Little Mo. river, that he has ordered Col. Gibbon to move Eastwards, and suggests that the Co-operation of Gen. Crook's Column would be desirable."[20]

Telegram dated May 15, 1876, from Fort Lincoln, D. T., to Ass't Adj't Gen'l, Military Division, Chicago, Ill—

Information from several Independent sources seems to establish the fact that the Sioux are collected in camps on the Little Missouri and between that and the Powder river I have already ordered Col. Gibbon to move eastward and I suggest that it would be very desirable for Gen'l Crook's column to move up as soon as possible. It is represented that they have fifteen hundred lodges are confident and intend to make a stand. Should they do so and should the three columns be able to act simultaneously I should expect great success. We start tomorrow morning. Alfred H. Terry, Brig. Gen.

Dakota Column—Terry originally wanted to start out this morning, but the rainstorm delayed departure until the seventeenth. Reports indicated Sitting Bull had assembled the Sioux and Cheyenne on the Little Missouri, ready for a fight.

Gibbon/Montana Column—Gibbon remained in camp on the Little Porcupine a short distance above the mouth of the Rosebud and on the opposite, north side, of the Yellowstone. The day saw plenty of rain and snow.

10 AM—Bradley's four unmounted Crow return reporting a Sioux trail of about thirty mounted warriors leading up the Yellowstone from the Tongue. Bradley, now believing the village would be found on the Tongue, seeks permission to go on another scout. Gibbon reluctantly agrees. Several officers again felt the mission was doomed to failure and there was a great deal of apprehension as the men began to depart. Bradley started out with his twelve mounted infantry. He also took eight

volunteer soldiers, including privates Elijah Hall and Henry Rice (both from Free-man's H/7I); none of the cavalry volunteered. In addition, he took the scout Bar-ney "Bravo" Prevo, five Crow scouts, including Curley, none of whom volunteered. Mitch Boyer was not on this scout. Toward evening, one by one, the men left camp and gathered in a copse of timber. They were ferried across the Yellowstone in Cap-tain Clifford's boats and gathered on the south bank in the dark. They headed south-east, crossing the Rosebud five miles out and resting for the night, fourteen miles out, total. The terrain was extremely difficult to negotiate and Bradley felt the Crow were deliberately leading the column into rough terrain. He paused to chastise them. They soon emerged into better country, confirming Bradley's suspicions, and crossed the Rosebud.

Montana Column Trains—E. G. Maclay & Company's Diamond-R train leaves Fort Ellis. Lieutenant Kendrick and his eight men formed the escort. Matthew Carroll accompanied the train; he would become wagon master for the Montana column.[21] According to Carroll, the train consisted of fourteen teams and twenty-eight wag-ons: the Diamond-"E" twelve teams; twenty-four wagons, ninety-seven mules and five horses; and a sub-train of two teams, four wagons and twenty mules, with freight, as per the bill of lading. Number of men employed, eighteen. Rain and snow, and the train had a rough time, making little headway.

MAY 16, 1876—TUESDAY—*Military Correspondence & Intelligence Reports*—Tele-gram dated May 16, 1876, from Headquarters, Military Division of the Missouri, Chicago, Illinois, to Brig. Gen A.H. Terry, Fort A. Lincoln, D. T.—

> Your telegram received. I will hurry up Crook, but you must rely on the ability of your own col-umn for your best success. I believe it to be fully equal to all the Sioux which can be brought against it, and only hope they will hold fast to meet it. Keep me as well posted as you can, and depend upon my full assistance in every respect. You know the impossibility of any large num-ber of Indians keeping together as a hostile body for even one week. (Signed) P.H. Sheridan, Lieut. General.

Gibbon/Montana Column—Shortly after midnight it became too dangerous to go on without first seeing what was ahead, so Bradley stopped to camp, rest his men, and allow the horses to graze.

4 AM—Bradley, furious at the Crow because they had deceived him again—they were still some five miles from the Wolf Mountains—advances another five miles, using ravines and avoiding ridges. The day started off foggy, but by the time they reached the hills it had cleared and the day became bright and sunny.

6 AM—Bradley, from a sheltered ravine, climbs to a high peak in the Wolf Moun-tains. They could now see the Rosebud valley for thirty miles above its mouth, but see no sign of Sioux. A high ridge ran between them and the Tongue River. Then, at around nine AM Bradley decides to move closer to the Tongue. The detachment pro-ceeds east and they find the trail of the thirty Sioux his unmounted Crow had seen earlier. Bradley feels this trail led from the Tongue, probably some fifteen to eighteen miles above its mouth. Almost certain of finding a village now, they proceed very cautiously. Ascending through a pine-covered ridge Bradley halts on the ridge sum-mit and glimpses the Tongue, five to six miles ahead.

4 PM—From some five miles downstream, Bradley spots a haze of smoke—no

tepees could be seen because of the terrain—which turned out to be a 300–400-lodge Sioux camp on the Tongue River (near Garland, today), thirty miles south of the river's mouth (Edgar I. Stewart writes it was about eighteen miles from the confluence with the Yellowstone[22]; Stewart was probably incorrect), and probably containing 800–1,000 warriors. While Bradley wanted to get closer—they could see only smoke plumes, no tepees—the Crow were adamant about not going any nearer. The Crow estimated 200–300 lodges. This village represented "nearly all the winter roamers gathered in one camp—the very target of the campaign."[23]

6 PM—Reluctantly, Bradley starts back, talked into returning by his Crow scouts. At some time near seven PM, Bradley halts to water the horses, allowing the men to eat. At some point here, the Sioux discovered Bradley's tracks and followed them all the way back to the Yellowstone and Gibbon's camp. At 9:30 PM, having moved very rapidly, Bradley halts for two hours to rest his men and horses. At 10:15 PM, at the Montana column's bivouac, pickets fired at what they believed were Indians, then at 11:30 PM, Bradley is on the move again. The night is very dark, but by now the Crow scouts seemed to know all the shortcuts and the easiest traveling route! Bradley still worried, however, about the thirty Sioux to his front.

MAY 17, 1876—WEDNESDAY—*Military Correspondence & Intelligence Reports*—From the Commanding General, Department of Dakota—"Gen. Terry's column left Fort Lincoln at five o'clock this morning."[24]

From the Commanding General, Department of the Platte—"Relative to Indian Scouts, who would accompany the expedition for what plunder they could capture. Leaves for Fort Fetterman in the morning."[25]

Dakota Column—4 AM—Reveille sounds for the Dakota column at Fort Abraham Lincoln. Too wet to start fires, so breakfast consisted of hard tack and water. Morning was raw and cold with heavy mist and fog. At five AM, the trumpeter at headquarters, signaling the taking down of the tents and preparations to move, sounded the "General." Units were bivouacked on a plateau about one-half mile below (south of) the cavalry barracks at Fort Abraham Lincoln (Missouri River on the east, the prairie to the west). "Boots and Saddles" now sounded: horses saddled and troops ready to mount.

The 7th Cavalry was divided into two wings, each with two battalions of three companies. The right wing under Major Reno, consisted of battalions commanded by Captain Myles Keogh (Company I) with companies B, C and I; and Captain George Yates (Company F), companies E, F, and L. The left wing was commanded by Captain Frederick William Benteen (Company H) with battalions commanded by Captain Thomas Weir (Company D) and companies A, D, and H; and Captain Thomas French (Company M) with companies G, K, and M.[26]

The Indian Office in Washington, D.C., had told Custer they estimated the winter roamers at 3,000 persons, i.e., 850 warriors. (That further tallied with Boyer's later estimates of villagers on the Tongue and Rosebud Rivers, i.e., 400 lodges, 800 warriors.) Writer and historian John S. Gray stated the winter roamers—those not living on the reservations set aside in the Treaty of 1868—represented less than twenty percent of the Sioux nation.[27] The majority, living on reservations could not support themselves. They had, so far, failed in becoming dry farmers. It was the winter-roamers who so resented the white man's incursion into the so-called "unceded" territory. Custer figured 1,000 warriors, plus another 500 coming out of the agencies, the so-called "summer roamers." What Custer did not know was Sheridan's attempts to control the agencies with larger garrisons drove exceptionally large numbers of Indians out of the agencies. These summer roamers joined the winter roamers. It was found that agency estimates were hollow indeed: the Spotted Tail Agency (Agent Howard): instead of 9,610, there were 2,315. The Red Cloud Agency (Camp/Fort Robinson was established on March 8, 1874, along the left bank of the White River in northwest Nebraska near present-day Crawford, Nebraska): instead of 12,873, there were 4,760. Eighty known warrior lodges had departed the Red Cloud Agency in the ten days prior to May sixteenth.[28] Cheyenne River Agency: instead of 7,586, there were 2,280. At the Standing Rock Agency: instead of 7,322, there were 2,305. (This agency was at Fort Yates, Dakota Territory [named Yates, December 30, 1878]. The post was established at the already existing agency on the Missouri River on December 23, 1874, to help control the Indians.) This showed that instead of 37,391, there were actually 11,660 present. These numbers were from a new census ordered under Army supervision, *after* the battle.[29] (Modern scholarship, however, appears to show the totals at each agency greatly inflated, at best. The late-John Gray's work, as well as that of scholars such as Ephriam D. Dickson III and Kingsley M. Bray indicate a Sioux population at about 16,000–17,000 souls, total, at that time.[30]) Sheridan reported that once he was allowed to take charge of the Indian agencies—July 22, 1876—he instructed his commanders to make a head-count. By September 1, 1876,

> "…it was found that those at Red Cloud numbered 4,760, nearly one-half less than had been reported by the agent. The count at Spotted Tail's agency was less than 5,000, whereas nearly double that number was alleged to be present at their agency, and were issued to." He went on: "Troops were also sent to occupy the Missouri River agencies to accomplish the same purposes, and the number of Indians found present was less than one-half to one-third than was reported present and issued to by the agents."[31]

Side Notes—What is so interesting here is the discrepancy between the numbers from the Indian Agency, what Custer believed, and the numbers in the telegram sent by Terry to Sheridan three days earlier, reporting 1,500 lodges (2,000 in a March 24, 1876, telegram). Scouts estimated there were some 3,000 fighting men in the village. Even Mark Kellogg, the civilian reporter for the Bismarck *Tribune* wrote:

> The latest information brought in by scouts from the hostile camps report Sitting Bull as having concentrated his entire camp near the Little Missouri River…. His force is given at 1,500 lodges. This estimate would enable him to put at least 3,000 warriors into the field.[32]

Some of this intelligence came from the scout, "Lonesome" Charlie Reynolds. When Reynolds made his report, the hostiles were camped along the Little Missouri. By the time the expedition set out—on this day—the Indians had moved to the Tongue River. Obviously, Terry's command knew nothing of this. Reynolds was convinced,

> …the Sioux intended to fight and that they would prove to be very troublesome customers. He reported that the hostile tribes had been preparing for war for a long time, supplying themselves with the best of Winchester repeating rifles and with plenty of ammunition, and that "*every move they were making meant fight.*"[33]

The *Chicago Times*—in a May 24, 1876, article—would report, "In all there are Cheyennes, Sioux, and others, some 3,000 ready to fight out this campaign against Gen. Crook. They have numerous allies and people well-informed place the actual hostile Indian camp at from 7,000 to 8,000 first class fighting men...."[34]

The correspondent for the *New York Herald*, Reuben B. Davenport, wrote, "3,000 bucks have left the Cheyenne Agency on the Missouri to join Crazy Horse. Louis [Richaud] reports that of forty-two lodges that went on the warpath from Red Cloud Agency, 17 returned... [May seventeenth] ...."[35] There is an interesting comment in Willert, *Little Big Horn Diary*, 90, regarding George Crook's Wyoming column.

> During the day's advance [June 4, 1876], Indian *sign* began to reveal a *significant* and unusual characteristic: pony tracks were everywhere in evidence, but the tracks of *dragging lodge poles* were not! [Lieutenant] Bourke observed: '...men were slipping out from Red Cloud and Spotted Tail agencies and uniting with the hostiles, but *leaving their families at home,* under the protection of the reservations.' ... If the women, children and other non-combatants were being left behind, and the *warriors only* were gathering, there could remain no doubt but that the Indians fully intended to fight the white man's armies.

Military Correspondence & Intelligence Reports—On June 6, 1876, Colonel Michael V. Sheridan—Lieutenant General Philip Sheridan's brother—dispatched a message to Terry: "Courier from Red Cloud Agency reported... [June 5, 1876] that Yellow Robe ... says that 1,800 lodges were on the Rosebud and about to leave for Powder River ... and says they will fight and have about 3,000 warriors." This now clearly indicated the military expected a large number of Indians, willing to fight. Terry received this message *after* the Little Big Horn fight.[36]

Lieutenant Edward Godfrey later wrote,

> ...about one-third of the whole Sioux nation, including the northern Cheyennes and Arapahoes, were present at the battle; he estimates the number present as between twelve and fifteen thousand; that one out of four is a low estimate in determining the number of warriors present; every male over fourteen years of age may be considered a warrior in a general fight ... considering the extra hazards of the hunt and expected battle, fewer squaws would accompany the recruits from the agencies. The minimum strength of their fighting men may then be put down as between 2,500 and 3,000. Information was dispatched from General Sheridan that from one agency alone about 1,800 lodges had set out to join the hostile camp; but that information did not reach General Terry until several days after the battle.[37]

Another factor neither Terry nor Custer were aware of—because it came much too late—was a report on June 20, 1876, from a Captain Pollock who telegraphed the Department Commander from Fort Laramie that....

> Jordon [?] under date of June 19 says Little Wolf, chief of Northern Cheyennes, left the agency Thursday (June 15) with 1,000 of his people, including 200 warriors for the north. All other Indians have gone to Ash Creek [Reno Creek] to attend the grand sundance commencing today.[38]

Side Notes—The area of operations for the three columns took in some 100,000 square miles. Crook's expedition in March 1876 had located Indians along Powder River, yet Terry's best information in mid–May 1876 had them along the Little Missouri River. Crook's mid–May 1876 intelligence reports placed them "on the *Blue Stone River,* MT, 300 miles from Fort Fetterman ... a stream which empties into the Yellowstone"[39] [See May sixteenth]. Willert also makes the point, "The task of each of the three principal … commands … had been explicitly stated: located [sic] the camps of the recalcitrants and destroy them."[40]

Many soldiers anticipated a short, sharp campaign, maybe no longer than two weeks. The following men were assigned Special Duty for all or part of the campaign:

Brainard, PVT George—Orderly for General Terry.
Murphy, SGT Robert L.—Orderly for General Terry.
O'Toole, PVT Francis—Orderly for General Terry.
Lynch, PVT Patrick—Orderly for General Terry.
Hughes, SGT Robert H.—Orderly-trumpeter for George Custer.
Dose, TMP Henry C.—Orderly-trumpeter for George Custer.
Martini, TMP PVT Giovanni—Orderly-trumpeter for George Custer.
Burkman, PVT John W.—George Custer's orderly/striker.
Goldin, PVT Theodore W.—HQ messenger. [Unsubstantiated.]
Callahan, CPL John J.—Hospital orderly and Dr. Lord's assistant.
Abbotts, PVT Harry—Dr. DeWolf's attendant.
Ryder, PVT Hobart—Hospital orderly for Dr. Porter.
Davern, PVT Edward—Major Reno's orderly.
McIlhargey, PVT Archibald—Major Reno's striker.
Korn, PVT Gustave—Captain Keogh's orderly. [*Unsubstantiated.*]
Kelly, PVT Patrick—Captain Keogh's striker.
Pickard, PVT Edwin H.—Captain Yates' orderly, then assigned to packs.
Deihle, PVT Jacob—Captain Moylan's orderly.
Lorentz, PVT George—Captain French's orderly.
Klotzbucher, PVT Henry—Captain French's striker.
Sanders, PVT Charles—Captain Weir's orderly.
Dorn, PVT Richard B.—Captain McDougall's orderly.
Penwell, TMP George B.—Lieutenant Godfrey's orderly, then Reno's trumpeter.
Rapp, PVT John—Lieutenant McIntosh's orderly/striker.
Hackett, PVT John—Lieutenant Wallace's orderly.
Harrison, SGT Thomas Wilford—Lieutenant Edgerly's orderly.
McVeigh, TMP David—Lieutenant De Rudio's orderly.
Strode, PVT Elijah T.—Lieutenant Varnum's orderly.
Trumble, PVT William—Lieutenant Hodgson's orderly.
Kramer, TMP William—Possibly Lieutenant Harrington's orderly.
Clear, PVT Elihu F.—Lieutenant Hare's orderly.
Klawitter, PVT Ferdinand—Libbie Custer's orderly at Fort Lincoln.

Dakota Column—The sun rose at 5:05 AM, local time and by six AM the wagon train was on the road, escorted by the infantry. Major George Gillespie, Chief Engineer of the Military Division of the Missouri, in his 1876 annual report, reported the column's strength as: thirty Indian scouts; forty-five officers; and 905 enlisted men.[41]

Lieutenant Edward Maguire, in his annual report, listed fifty officers; 968 enlisted personnel; 190 civilian employees; and 1,694 animals. He also included forty-five Indian scouts, guides, and interpreters.[42] Maguire was given a four-mule ambulance for his instruments and men. The odometers were attached to its wheels.

The *Army and Navy Journal* of July 15, 1876—after the battle—listed again the strength of the units leaving Fort Lincoln: 7th Cavalry: twenty-eight officers, 747 enlisted men; 6th and 17th Infantry: eight officers, 135 enlisted men; a Gatling gun battery of two officers, thirty-two enlisted personnel and three Gatling guns (making a total of five on the campaign); and forty-five Indian scouts, making a total of 952 uniformed personnel, plus Terry's staff.[43]

Mark Kellogg, the correspondent for the Bismarck *Tribune,* claimed 1,207 men left Fort Lincoln.[44]

The column was accompanied by a herd of cattle to supply fresh meat. Private Walter Sterland (Company M, 7th Cavalry)—detailed to serve as quartermaster butcher at regimental headquarters—told Walter Mason Camp, there were seventy-seven head of cattle at the campaign's start.[45]

According to retired army colonel and author, French MacLean, the column consisted of the following: 752 mules; thirty-two quartermaster horses; 695 government horses; twenty-six battery horses for the Gatling guns (these would be the so-called condemned horses); ninety-five private horses; seventy-four hired horses to haul supplies; and 114 six-mule wagons, used mostly to haul grain forage for the horses: 3,000–5,000 pounds per wagon.[46] (First Sergeant John Ryan of Company M claimed these wagons could haul up to 6,800 pounds.) The two lead mules were called "leaders" and were generally smaller in size. The middle pair was usually slightly larger and called "swings." The two mules closest to the wagon were "wheelers" and were larger and much stronger than the others.[47] MacLean also claimed Captain Tom French, the Company M commander, may have had his own wagon—smaller—and if this is so other officers probably had one as well.[48] This wagon would carry the officer's tent, extra clothes, cot, chair, writing table, Sibley stove, cooking stove, Dutch oven, camp kettle, and mess ware for four people. His orderly would also probably ride in it.

In all, there were approximately 166 wagons, though the *Army and Navy Journal,* in a later edition, listed 151.[49] These were broken down as follows: 114 six-mule government-owned teams would be primarily used to haul forage for the animals. Obviously, they would become lighter as the animals ate the forage. Each would carry 3,000 to 5,000 pounds of cargo. Then there were thirty-seven two-horse teams. These were smaller; civilian-owned and under contract to the government. They contained mainly camp equipment, ammo, and sundry supplies, and were generally carrying 1,500 to 2,000 pounds of cargo. In addition, there was variously reported, thirty-five, forty-five, or eighty-five pack mules, along with some seventy other vehicles: ambulances, etc., and 179 civilian drivers. According to historian John Gray, quartermaster trains were mule-drawn and could only make about twenty miles a day.

With all this, there was a shortage of horses: seventy-eight 7th Cavalry recruits had to walk because their horses had not yet arrived from St. Paul, Minnesota.

As the column moved out from Fort Lincoln, it headed northwest for the bench-land above the fort and west of Fort McKeen, the old, abandoned infantry post named for Colonel Henry Boyd McKeen (or McKean) who died at Cold Harbor. Construction began in June 1872 and the post housed the 6th Infantry. On November 19, 1872, the fort's name was changed to Fort Abraham Lincoln.

When Custer arrived in late summer of 1873 after the Yellowstone Expedition another post had been built on the adjacent plain ... inherited the name Fort Abraham Lincoln when the infantry fort on the bluff was abandoned. West of the parade ground stood Custer's home, flanked by those of subordinate officers. In February of 1874 ... Custer's home was luxuriously rebuilt: a thirty-two-foot living room with a bay window, billiard room on the second floor, library, plenty of space to exhibit his gun collection and stuffed trophies. Behind the house were gardens, enclosed by a fence to keep out the dogs. At some later date a ballroom was added....[50]

6:45 AM–7 AM—The 7th Cavalry was passing in review at the barracks.[51] The scouts led the parade, first passing by the log huts of the Ree, located south of the garrison and intoning a dirge-like chant Libbie Custer hated. The command was formed in a column of fours (Lieutenant Godfrey referred to it as a "column of platoon"[52]). The column then passed "laundress row," the cabins occupied by the troopers' families. Tear-streaked wives, some wailing children: a lot of sorrowful women. The column entered the parade ground where it halted one last time so the officers could embrace their wives. The band then switched over from *Garryowen* to *The Girl I Left Behind Me*. It then passed Officers' Row and began its "long ascent to the plain above."[53]

The ground was damp, so there was little dust on this first day and by seven AM the infantry and wagons were assembled on the hill. After the parade the cavalry joined the infantry and wagons and the column formed up. The general order of march was as follows: one battalion as advance guard; one battalion as rear guard, behind everything; one battalion on each flank. The rear guard would assist any wagon that had broken down. The flank battalions were to remain within 500 yards of the column and never go beyond or get behind the train by more than a half-mile. On the flanks, one company was allowed to get one half mile ahead of the train, then it would halt and dismount, resting the horses. When the other two companies caught, the routine would continue. That way there were always two companies along each side of the train. In rough country, flankers were sent out farther to insure against surprise attacks. Custer and his aides led, followed by one cavalry company selected each day from the advance guard. Then the lead two companies in the forward battalion (which changed each day) were under Lieutenant Edward Maguire's charge and served in "pioneer" duty, e.g., bridging, road building, etc. Then came the Gatling guns. The government wagons, followed by the civilian wagons—all closely supported by the infantry—were in the middle. The wagon train was assembled in a column of fours. To the sides on the wagons were the beef herd and spare horses (the horse *remuda*) and mules. The scouts fanned out to the front.

Each cavalry company was assigned one wagon: five days rations and forage; troops' mess kit; officers' mess kit, tents, and baggage; ten days' supplies for the officers' mess; and each troop horse carried between eighty and ninety pounds of ammunition, plus the rider.

Between 1:30 and 2:30 PM the column moves some 13½ miles—almost due west over rolling prairie with numerous hillocks—and camped on the Heart River (here, about three feet deep and thirty yards wide; empties into the Missouri, right near Bismarck)—**Heart River, Camp 1**.[54] In 1997, this locale was approximately one mile south of the Northern Pacific Railroad siding at Lyons, North Dakota, and 1½ miles above the confluence of Sweetbriar Creek.

The camp was established in the bottom, which is about 500 feet square, and was fenced in on three sides by high bluffs, the fourth side being bounded by the gentle slope leading to the prairie…. The grass was good and plentiful, and there was no lack of wood. A slight rain fell during the night.[55]

This was the first water since leaving Fort Lincoln, not uncommon on this or any other campaign. There were no additional trails. "In 1876 there was not a ranch west of Bismarck, Dakota, nor east of Bozeman, Montana."[56] The site chosen was "beautifully located on level grassy plateau nearly surrounded by the Heart River. A fringe of trees borders the river's edge—many of which … are dead and dry so [there] can [be] roaring fires tonight."[57] The camp was located on the same ground where Custer's command had stopped for an afternoon lunch when returning from the 1874 Black Hills Expedition. General David S. Stanley's expedition had also camped there in 1873, en route to Fort Rice. Unfortunately, however, the site was overrun by rattlesnakes the soldiers promptly disposed of.

The main guard generally consisted of four or five non-commissioned officers (NCOs) and twelve to fifteen privates. One NCO and three privates would be posted at prominent points. Reveille was generally to be at 4:20 AM; stable call, supervised by an officer, followed reveille. "Two hours after reveille, the command would be on the march."[58]

Gibbon/Montana Column—In the meantime, around daylight on the Yellowstone River, Lieutenant Bradley has reached the base camp and reports to Colonel Gibbon, crossing the river to reach him. (The camp had been preparing to move.) Gibbon now decides to remain in camp, preparatory to an attack on the Indian village. His orders had been to move his camp farther downriver on the seventeenth, but in his after-action dispatch to Terry, he tells of his scouts finding a Sioux camp on the Rosebud [*sic*, the Tongue River; Gibbon's error] and he decided to attack it, setting out on this day. He would leave only Captain Sanno's K/7I to guard the camp and supply train, leaving an attack force of about 392 men: five companies of infantry: A, B, E, H, and I, 7th Infantry; and four companies of cavalry: F, G, H, and L, 2nd Cavalry; a total of thirty-four officers, 350 enlisted men, plus Crow scouts and eight civilian "camp followers." He would also take some thirty pack mules. Within an hour of Bradley's arrival back at camp, Indians were seen on the prairie across the river.

9 AM—The move to cross the Yellowstone began. The cavalry was to cross first, establish a defensive perimeter on the south bank, then ferry the infantry across by the mackinaw boats. The river, however, had become a raging torrent of muddied water and there was great difficulty getting the horses into the water. By noon Gibbon is attempting to ford the Yellowstone, but it remained a torrent and after having four horses drown, he abandoned the effort. To make matters even more embarrassing, some seventy-five to a hundred Sioux were watching the fiasco from across river—and beyond carbine range—thereby negating surprise. Some of the Indians even got within 200 yards of Bradley's men, still on the south side of the Yellowstone.

5 PM—Very few cavalry mounts had made it across and the effort was abandoned. There is some confusion here, however. Historian James Willert claimed Sergeant John McCabe (H/2C) helped try to get the horses across the river,[59] but historian Loyd Overfield claimed McCabe was sick at Fort Pease.[60] John Gray claimed Gibbon's failure to cross the Yellowstone dispirited him for the rest of the campaign,

a claim of some dubiousness. He also blew his opportunity to reap further important intelligence by not following up on Bradley's coup.

Montana Column Trains—EVENING—According to Matthew Carroll, Second Lieutenant Lovell Hall Jerome (H/2C) joined the wagon train,[61] but this also seems suspect. Jerome was at Fort Ellis, in arrest since March 17, 1876. (Jerome had been on a mission in February, so he may have been released by this time.)

10 PM—A false alarm arouses the nervous camp.

Indian Village—Sitting Bull's village—with Crazy Horse's—has moved to a point between the Tongue River and Rosebud Creek. They will remain here until about May 20.[62]

MAY 18, 1876—THURSDAY—*Military Correspondence & Intelligence Reports*—From the Assistant Adjutant General, Department of Dakota—"Forwards tabular statement showing the composition of Gen. Terry's Command and its approximate strength."[63]

Dakota Column—2:40 AM—Reveille sounded (Terry's diary records reveille at three AM).

5 AM—The column was ready to go (sunrise was at 5:04 AM, local sun time), but has problems crossing the Heart. A corduroy road had to be laid: planks, cottonwood logs, branches, and earth.

8 AM—Finally the Terry-Custer column begins crossing after Lieutenant Maguire's engineers and infantry prepared the road and riverbeds. By 8:30 AM the train is across the river.

9 AM—The column is moving, but it is slow: they are trail-less and entering unknown terrain laced with many narrow streams.

10:30 AM—Terry halts the command for a brief rest.

1:45 PM—A campsite is located on a plateau approximately fifty feet above a tributary of Sweet Briar Creek and consisting of about seventy acres. They had gone 10¾ miles (24¼ miles, total from Fort Lincoln)—*Sweet Briar Creek, Camp 2*.

2 PM—Terry arrives in camp (his diary records the distance at 10.8 miles). The countryside was glacial moraine, with many immense boulders and small round hillocks. It is approximately two miles west of the present-day Sweetbriar Station of the Northern Pacific Railroad.[64] Off to the southwest could be seen the Dakota badlands.

3 PM—Heavy rains with fierce lightning struck and lasted for about twenty minutes, then a steady rain fell at intervals.

6:10 PM—The last of the wagons arrived.

Terry's dinner consisted of roast beef, mashed potato, warm biscuits, and raw onions in vinegar for salad.

Steamer "Josephine"—11 AM—While all this was going on, the steamer "Josephine," with Major Moore, arrived at Stanley's Stockade (Glendive) and unloaded troops and supplies. Once unloaded, Moore heads back to Buford to retrieve more supplies.

Gibbon/Montana Column—The rain affected more than the Dakota column, however, for Gibbon and Brisbin got sick as the rain hit farther west as well. Wagon

Master Matthew Carroll says he joined the train this day "while breaking camp on Hunter's bottom on Yellowstone River (Hunter's Hot Springs)."[65]

Some time shortly before noon, Mitch Boyer, two Crow, and captains Wheelan (G/2C) and Thompson (L/2C) head out on a three-day scout down the north side of the Yellowstone toward the Tongue River (about forty miles distant). The objective was to make sure the Sioux had not slipped down the Tongue and crossed the Yellowstone to the north. Then, in the afternoon, four unmounted Crow were sent out by Bradley to steal Sioux ponies. By five PM the wagons had pulled up to camp for the night. The train had "no guide, and no one in [the] train who knows the country below Baker's battle-ground."[66]

By evening it was still rainy and cloudy, though shortly thereafter the rain turned to snow. At dark, Bradley and twelve of his mounted infantrymen—along with scout LeForgé—and five Crow begin a move upriver to meet expected couriers from Fort Ellis. They moved twelve miles before establishing a bivouac: no fires.

Crook/Wyoming Column—After leaving Camp Robinson, Crook and Bourke headed for Fort Laramie. At Laramie Crook received a telegram informing him Terry had departed Fort Lincoln, though it gave the date as the sixteenth rather than the seventeenth. After a short time, Crook and Bourke leave Laramie on this date bound for Fort Fetterman.

MAY 19, 1876—FRIDAY—*Military Correspondence & Intelligence Reports*—From the Assistant Adjutant General, Department of Dakota—"Forwards copy of telegram from Col. Gibbon saying that Capt. Ball just in reports no sign of Indians—proposes to move down as soon as supplies reach him."[67]

Dakota Column—4:20 AM—Wake-up call for the Dakota column. Not yet raining, but heavy clouds and cool weather. Terry's diary has the column beginning its move at five AM, though other sources claim the column began its march closer to 6:30. They encountered rough and broken country, with more huge boulders, deep ravines, bogs, and even prairie dog villages. Only a mile from the encampment, the column was faced with the problem of Sweet Briar Creek, swollen by the rains to a fast-running creek, almost fifty feet wide and ten feet deep. They detoured to the south. Again, rain threatened; the ground was very soft and once more the wagons became mired. The good news was scout Charlie Reynolds brought back a pronghorn antelope!

7:20 AM—The command halts to close up and at ten AM scouts from Fort Lincoln reach the column with mail. By 10:35 AM the march is resumed, halting again at 11:30 AM for camp. At noon, an advanced party, consisting of Custer and Terry, pitched camp after traveling about 13½ miles (37¾ total): ***Crow's Nest Butte, Camp 3***, also called Buzzard's Roost Butte or, by the troops, Turkey Buzzard Camp. It was a flat stretch along the southwest edge of present-day New Salem, North Dakota. It was a miserable site, with no water, no wood, little grass, and wet buffalo chips. And once more a furious thunderstorm with large hailstones, pelted the troops, until suddenly around 1:15 PM the violent storm subsided and a bright sun and heavy winds began drying things out. At some time after six PM the last of the wagons arrived and were corralled in the center of the bivouac with the horse and mule remuda picketed just beyond. The tents came next, the pickets just beyond those, then on the highest ground, the mounted pickets (vedettes). The night was cool and very windy with more heavy rains. At sunset mail was sent back with One Horn and Red Foolish Bear, two of the Ree scouts.

Gibbon/Montana Column—Farther west, Gibbon and Brisbin were still sick and the falling snow made traveling miserable for Lieutenant Kendrick and the Diamond-R wagon train. Little progress being made previously, they remain in camp. Wind blew in ferociously from the west and heavy snow remained on the hills.

9 AM—Bradley meets the messengers; it was still raining. After eating breakfast, Bradley's detachment and the couriers head back to camp around ten AM.

The Thompson/Wheelan scouting party—preparing to move—stops suddenly when Boyer and the Crow scouts report forty to fifty Sioux warriors ascending the Yellowstone on its south riverbank, twenty miles downriver from Gibbon's main camp. As the Indians moved westward up the river seeking a suitable ford, they left their led-horses under the care of two or three young warriors. Boyer and Hairy Moccasin (James Willert said it was Goes Ahead; Freeman wrote it was Hairy Moccasin and one other Crow[68]) swim the river in an attempt to steal the ponies left behind with the Sioux youngsters. The Sioux youngsters run off the horses and Boyer and Hairy Moccasin swim back. The scouting party continues to the Tongue River but finds nothing except the trail where Bradley had turned back after spotting the winter-roamers' village.

At noon the four unmounted Crow sent out in the afternoon of the day before, are on the high summit of the Wolf Mountains where Bradley had spotted the Sioux village. They run across a Sioux war party of several hundred warriors and are barely able to escape, leaving behind their horse-stealing ambitions. The warriors disappear into the Rosebud valley, heading downstream toward the confluence.

Indian Village—This is very likely the day the Indians reached the Rosebud. Wooden Leg said their first camp was about seven or eight miles up from the stream's confluence with the Yellowstone River.[69] While the distance is a little short, it fits with later descriptions. All the camps were on the east side of the creek. Charcoal Bear—the chief medicine man of the Cheyenne—joined the camp here. He brought more Cheyenne with him.[70] The camp remained in this area for six or seven days, then moved about twelve miles up the stream.[71] The warriors had spotted Gibbon's command trying to ford the Yellowstone, and reported this to the village. They were warned to leave the white men alone; the village was set up for defense, not aggression.[72] This is the same as their camp on the Little Big Horn on June 25, 1876. Wooden Leg said the Indians were unaware they had been spotted at this camp.

Gibbon/Montana Column—3:30 PM—Bradley reaches camp with the two mail couriers. Finally, at six PM, the rain and snow finally stop. Wagon Master Carroll journals that they can finally move in the morning, though the going would probably not be easy.

MAY 20, 1876—SATURDAY—*Military Correspondence & Intelligence Reports*—
From Assistant Adjutant General, Department of the Platte—"Statement of strength and designating the Companies of Gen. Crook's Command."[73]

From General George Crook—"Reports interview with Miner from Fort Phil Kearny who states that he saw no sign of Indians on his trip and intimates that they are following the Buffalo."[74]

Dakota Column—5 AM—Reveille. The day was greeted by more heavy rains in the early morning. Terry orders out Reynolds, Lieutenant Maguire, and ten Ree scouts to find a suitable crossing over the Muddy, some nine miles ahead. At between 7:30 and eight AM the troops began to move (Terry's diary has the advance guard leaving at 7:45 AM), finding Maguire and company. It was now raining intermittently, and many coulees cut the terrain making it very slow going for wagons.

9 AM—The first creek was crossed, 4¼ miles from the start. A rest was ordered, then at 11:15 AM the march began again. Terry's diary says the Little Muddy was reached at noon, but the main command reached the Little Muddy River at 1:30 PM, making only 9½ miles for the day (47¼ miles from Fort Lincoln). This camp was the ***Hail Stone Creek, Camp 4***. Despite being in camp, preparations were made for the following day's move and at 2:45 PM bridge building began.

9:15 PM—George Custer sits down and writes his first letter to Libbie, and at 9:30 PM scouts were sent back with messages and mail, after dark so as to avoid hostiles: Bull Stands In Water, Red Star, and Strikes The Lodge were the couriers[75] (James Willert claimed the scouts were One Horn and Red Foolish Bear[76]). That night there was more heavy rain.

Gibbon/Montana Column—The day also starts out with a steady rainfall and Gibbon orders the column to remain in camp.

8 AM—The four unmounted Crow sent out earlier, return, reporting the large body of Sioux—several hundred warriors; one report claiming 700!—moving toward the mouth of the Rosebud from the direction of the Tongue.[77] At between nine and 9:30 AM, after hearing the Crow's report of the large body of Sioux, Gibbon orders his column out in search of Boyer and Captain Thompson's detachment downriver. Gibbon's command, less Captain Kirtland's B/7I, leaves camp looking for signs of the Sioux. They cross the Little Porcupine and travel 8.66 miles, camping one to two miles below the Rosebud and staying there for two weeks. A drenching rain continued falling. Across the river are the Big Wolf Mountains and farther east, a line of broken ridges on the west side of the Tongue River. No Indian crossings were found and Lieutenant Bradley continues his scout for another thirteen miles, passing the confluence of the Rosebud and Yellowstone, but turns back when he discovers Thompson's trail. He cannot, however, find Thompson, and heads back upstream. Unknown to Bradley, a Sioux war party had crossed the Yellowstone farther downriver and had come upon his trail, following it. Returning by eleven PM, Bradley reaches Gibbon's camp, having gone about twenty-two miles down and back. Then, at 11:45 PM, Sergeant Bernard Belicke (C/7I) was accidentally killed by a sentry in the Little Timber camp.

Montana Column Trains—The Diamond-R wagon train started out, an east wind drying the roads to make travel easier: roads were "heavy," but drying. That noon the Diamond-R wagon train halted for two hours, finally camping along Little Timber Creek.

May 21, 1876—Sunday—*Military Correspondence & Intelligence Reports*—From General George Crook—"Acknowledges receipt of dispatch but no letter. Is informed that Buffalo are moving west, and that the Indians must keep near them."[78]

***Steamer "Josephine"*—**Major Moore again heads to the Stanley's Stockade (Glendive) depot on the "Josephine," with more supplies.

***Dakota Column*—**2 AM—Scout Charlie Reynolds saddles up and heads out to seek a good route of advance for the day.

3 AM—dawn—reveille was sounded, and the advance was ordered for five AM, but then postponed when Terry ordered a route change. There was still occasional rain; a very gloomy, misty start to the day.

6:30 AM—The column moved across the Little Muddy after Maguire's engineers built a bridge. The ground was marshy and initially uphill, straining the mules pulling the wagons. The route was now about two miles north of that taken in the 1873 and 1874 expeditions, with the weather continually threatening. The column continually halted and began again: seven AM, the column halts; nine AM, command moves again; ten AM, command halts; eleven AM, the command moves. At noon the sun finally came out and the day became much warmer; also, the column entered grassy valleys, with long, flat and gently sloping hillsides. Wagons now made much better time, but a toll was already being taken on the men and animals. One mule had to be shot, another left behind. Three men had to be carried in an ambulance: two were sick, one accidentally shot himself in the heel while mounting.

The command halted again at 12:10 PM, and resumed its march at 2:45 PM. During the afternoon they passed by "Maiden's Breasts" or "Twin" Buttes. Other butte names in the area were: "Rattlesnake Den," "Wolf's Den," "Dog Teeth Butte," "Rainy Butte," "Cherry Ridge." The reporter, Mark Kellogg, filed a dispatch for the *New York Herald,* published in the June 19, 1876, edition: "...the term hill is never heard on the Plains; every prominent elevation is spoken of as a butte; instead of ridges one hears only of divides, while valleys are seldom heard of, but in their stead one constantly hears of ravines...."[79]

After the "pioneer" battalion bridged another crossing and after traveling 13½ miles (60¾ miles from Fort Lincoln), camp was made at 3:30 PM—***Head of Hay Creek, Camp 5.*** Camp location was approximately 8½ miles north and one-half mile west of present-day Glen Ullin, North Dakota. The terrain was rocky, but with plenty of water and fair grassland. Nearest wood was a small stand of cottonwoods two miles away.

***Gibbon/Montana Column*—**Weather cool and cloudy with an east wind, and Gibbon orders Lieutenant Jacobs to take their empty wagons and some men from each company and go back up-river to retrieve their tents and equipage. Bradley and Captain Clifford and his men would go along to retrieve the boats left there. Jacobs and Bradley arrive at Kirtland's camp during the morning, load everything and proceed back downstream. Bradley and Clifford move back down the river to an old abandoned and burnt-down trading post, old Fort Van Buren.

4:30 PM—The Thompson-Wheelan-Boyer scout returns to the new Gibbon camp with its news.

5 PM—The bivouac is complete.

Montana Column Trains—6 AM—Diamond-R wagon train departs camp.

NOON—The Diamond-R train halts for lunch. Wagon Master Carroll and Lieutenant Jerome rode ahead of the train all day.[80]

4 PM—Kirtland's wagons arrived carrying the supplies from the previous bivouac.

6 PM—Having covered twenty-one miles on good roads, the Diamond-R train camps for the night around on Sweet Grass Creek; good grazing. They arrived too late to attempt a crossing of the creek.

MAY 22, 1876—MONDAY—*Dakota Column*—3 AM—Reveille. It was a brisk morning, bright and clear. Good night's feed for animals. Hot breakfast and coffee for troops, and at 4:25 AM–4:40 AM the column moves out, Captain Benteen's wing on the left, Major Reno's on the right, Charlie Reynolds and Bloody Knife in the lead, followed by Terry, Custer, and Kellogg; 44° and clear skies. During the march Reno spends a lot of time leading the regiment because Custer rides farther ahead with Terry. The ground was wet, but firm; no dust (the wagon tracks can still be seen today!). They expected to have to cross the Big Muddy, but instead, traversed a muddy plain that proved to be the creek's headwaters.

10 AM—The column hits Custer's return trail from his 1874 Black Hills expedition, about 6½ miles southeast of present-day Hebron, North Dakota. Column stops for lunch.

NOON—The advance party had made 15½ miles (seventy-five miles from Fort Lincoln) and Terry decides to go into camp near the headwaters of the Knife River, seven miles east of Young Man's Butte, because of the proximity of wood and water. Temperatures were now in the mid-sixties, with much drier territory, rock-strewn with sage and prickly-pear cactus (and rattlesnakes). Reynolds bags three more antelope. In the early afternoon the column moves on, catching up with the advance. They have to cross a tributary—Thin-Faced Woman's Creek—of Knife River: a dry riverbed, but with twelve-foot-high embankments that had to be cut down. Finally, at one PM, after a teamster accident with an overturned wagon, the column goes into camp: *West of Hebron, Camp 6.* This camp was about 3½ miles west of present-day Hebron, North Dakota. There was new grass (after an old prairie fire) for the horses, plus plenty of wood, game birds, etc. That evening the band entertains the troops.

> On [today's] photo the campsite would be between and encompassing the two rectangular fields with stripes on them. Due to the fact there were so many wagons the campsite took up at least two sections and may have spilled into more. North of the campsite is a high bluff dubbed "George's Butte."[81]

Gibbon/Montana Column—Three troopers from Gibbon's column go out hunting for antelope and buffalo and stumble into the Sioux war party—eight to ten strong—that had followed Bradley's trail. The soldiers managed to escape and head back to camp to warn Gibbon. The colonel now sends Captain Wheelan's G/2C downriver two or three miles with orders to then cut north; Bradley heads upriver to do the same thing; and the Crow scouts are sent directly north. The Sioux, however, avoid the trap by moving north.

5:30 PM—Wheelan's company, Bradley, and the Crow return to camp without seeing any appreciable Indian signs. Gibbon, however, is now fully aware the Sioux are watching him.

11 PM—As a precautionary move, the train mules are put in a corral.

Montana Column Trains—9 AM—The train, having difficulty crossing Sweet Grass Creek—having to repair roads—is finally on the move, on an up-grade, but traveled only ten miles for the day. At noon, after moving only about four miles, the train halts "at mouth of canyon below the forks, where we found a good spring, being the only water in the creek."[82] The train finally got through the canyon after some rough going—only two miles—and went into camp; no water for the mules.

Indian Village—As noted, some time after May 16, the hostile camp moved west to the Rosebud valley and was increasing in size as Indians from the agencies were joining. The first Rosebud camp was about seven or eight miles up from the Yellowstone.[83]

MAY 23, 1876—TUESDAY—*Dakota Column*—3 AM—Reveille.

5 AM—The command breaks camp and is on the march at 5:20 AM. Weather was cool—48°—clear, breezy; southerly winds, indicating a warming trend: a comfortable day, with no clouds; traveling over prairie grasslands. "To the north were 'badlands'—deep ravines and 'boggy' watersheds of the Knife River region—and, to the south, more 'badlands' and many buttes.... Buttes dotted the region as well, and *depressed* wooded ravines presented deep, impassable barriers...."[84] Temperatures moved into the upper fifties. For the first time, they spot elk and Custer pursues. He discovers a fresh campfire and indications of hostile Indians, "a short distance beyond the high, round hillock—known as Young Man's Butte (two miles east of present-day Richardson, North Dakota)."[85] Author James Willert makes reference here to Terry's decision to camp west of the butte and scout the region for Indians. Furthermore, he writes, "If the Indians proved [to be] recalcitrants, and could be induced to proceed peacefully back to the reservation, as they had been ordered, he would permit no violence against them...."[86] This is another indication of the mission: return the hostiles, peacefully, to the reservations.

6:30 AM—The command halts and at 7:05 AM begins to march again.

8 AM—Terry arrives with the advance at the place where he chooses to bivouac.

8:20 AM—To rest troops for harder day's march, Terry decides to go into camp early: *Young Man's Butte, Camp 7.* Made only eight miles (now eighty-three miles from Fort Lincoln; and again, the wagon ruts are still visible today). They camped on beautiful tableland, buttes visible to west; overlooking the Knife River Valley, one mile west of Young Man's Butte. There was plenty of wood, water and grazing; lots of trees in the valley.

EVENING—When nearly dusk a party of Indians was observed, moving slowly west along a butte on a distant ridgeline, silhouetted against the darkening sky. They were too far away to go after; but heavy guards were posted.

The trail comes in from the left around Young Man's Butte then heads northwest and went into camp on a branch of the Knife River. Actually the command camped on the prairie with the creek below. West of the campsite is a farm. Near the road leading to the house is the grave of Sergeant Stempker, who died due to dysentery on the return of Custer's Black Hills Expedition. Benteen supervised the burial while the balance resumed their march to Fort Lincoln.[87]

Steamer "Josephine"—Major Moore again arrives at Stanley's Stockade (Glendive), unloads, and heads back.

Montana Column Trains—6 AM—The Maclay wagons broke camp, rolling eastward, and at 7:30 AM Lieutenant English (I/7I), accompanied partway by Lieutenant Roe (F/2C), started back to escort the contract-train of John W. Power—eighteen wagons—whose company had recently been discharged. When he met the new contract-train of E.G. Maclay and Company's Diamond-R, English was to release Power's wagons and escort Diamond-R's with the supplies from Fort Ellis. The Gatling gun and crew, commanded by Lieutenant Alfred B. Johnson; Barney Bravo; and two Crow scouts accompanied the wagons.

9 AM—The Maclay train reached White Beaver Creek where it halted for two hours. They found good water and grass and started out again at eleven AM.

NOON—The Maclay train crosses Middle Beaver and East Beaver creeks. With the exception of the creek crossings, the roads were good, but they had to double the teams when crossing streams. Wagon Master Carroll writes that "Quinton and Countryman" overtook them at East Beaver Creek, informing them Lieutenant Jerome had to go back to Fort Ellis.[88] (This must have been Lieutenant Quinton [C/7I] whose company was not on the campaign.)

7 PM—Finally, the Maclay wagon train makes camp.

Gibbon/Montana Column—Gibbon's command was about two miles below the confluence of the Rosebud and Yellowstone. The Indians, unbeknownst to Gibbon, were now camped about seven or eight miles up the Rosebud (according to Wooden Leg). Gibbon now sends out Lieutenant Hamilton (L/2C) to scout for Indians and Hamilton reports seeing two parties, fifty and seventy in strength. Unbeknownst to the troops, a large party of warriors—maybe as many as 200—had crossed the river and were in the hills north of the camp. These Sioux kill three of Gibbon's men who are out hunting. George Herendeen heard the firing and returned to camp to tell the news: privates Henry Rahmeir, H/2C, and Augustus Stocker, H/2C, the only one of the three who was scalped; and civilian teamster, Matt [or James] Quinn. Herendeen and four soldiers were also out hunting. The Indians were pursued and a trail of about forty was found, then another of about 150 to 200.

1:30 PM—The bodies of the three dead men were brought back to camp.

6 PM—A mackinaw from Benson's Landing arrives bringing a full load of eggs, butter, tobacco, and fresh vegetables: "Colonel" J.D. Chestnut, trader from Bozeman, and his crew of four. Prices were very steep: potatoes, eight cents a pound; butter, $1 a pound; eggs, $1 a dozen.

7 PM—The three men were buried while a Sioux war party lined the bluffs across the river, watching the ceremony. (It is interesting to note here, Lieutenant Bradley wrote in his diary of seeing an Indian with an immense war bonnet, shaking it defiantly at the troops ... and he was "about a mile distant" ... yet Lieutenant Charles De Rudio, when he described—at the Reno Court of Inquiry—the three riders on a bluff 1,000 yards away, was hardly believed.)

MAY 24, 1876—WEDNESDAY—*Military Correspondence & Intelligence Reports*—From the Assistant Adjutant General, Department of Dakota—"Forwards copy of telegram from Col. Gibbon, reporting that he leaves Fort Pease with his command on May 10th, 76."[89]

From the *Chicago Times*: "In all there are Cheyennes, Sioux, and others, some 3,000 ready to fight out this campaign against Gen. Crook. They have numerous allies and people well-informed place the actual hostile Indian camp at from 7,000 to 8,000 first class fighting men...."[90]

Dakota Column—4:10 AM–4:15 AM—The column breaks camp. Another bright, clear, very warm day and lots of rolling prairie ahead.

9 AM—The column crossed the survey line of the Northern Pacific Railroad.

2 PM [the reporter Mark Kellogg claimed it was three PM]—Terry orders camp made on the Green River, a branch of the Heart. The Green is about thirty feet wide, a foot deep, alkaline, swift flowing, and clear, with lots of different fish: *Green River, Camp 8*, about 1½ miles northwest of present-day Gladstone, North Dakota. The "May 24 campsite on Green River. Camp was established in the bend of the river. Trail seen!"[91] The column had made nineteen miles this day (now 102 miles from Fort Lincoln). The camp had good fishing, ample grazing, good water, bathing, good wood, and the area loaded with wild roses. Temperature in the mid-seventies, and as can be expected, the troopers did a lot of washing. The Ree scout Red Bear returns from Fort Lincoln with mail.

Gibbon/Montana Column—As for the Gibbon/Montana Column, at 2:30 AM, reports of Indian crossings kept the command alert. It turned into a very hot day and the column remained in camp with no incidents except a solitary Indian spotted a half-mile below the camp. He was chased.

Montana Column Trains—NOON—Without Lieutenant Jerome, the Maclay train started, making slow progress and only seven miles because of the difficult terrain.

2 PM—The train managed to get over a tough grade, having to repair the roads. They camped at dark.

MAY 25, 1876—THURSDAY—*Military Correspondence & Intelligence Reports*— From General George Crook—"States that he will have someone meet the 'Crows' at Reno. Reports Indians watching their movements."[92]

From General George Crook—"Wishes any information up to 30th inst. tele-graphed to him at Fort Fetterman."[93]

Dakota Column—4 AM–4:15 AM (Terry's diary has the column moving at 4:45 AM)— The column begins its march; a clear and mild day, 48°. "The country passed over was rolling, grassy plain, soft underfoot, and lush green as far as the eye could view. The grass was tall—sometimes as high as the horses' knees...."[94] They went through a series of halts again: 6:30 AM, halted, then resumed march at this time; 7:45 AM— halted in valley country with easy slopes; 8:15 AM march resumed; 9:30 AM—halted; 10:30 AM—march resumed; 11:20 AM halted to build a bridge. At noon a wash had to be bridged ... and the temperature rose: mid-day temperature was now about 74°.

2:40 PM—Custer selected a campsite near a high butte called Crow Ridge, along a tributary of the Heart, five miles north of present-day South Heart, North Dakota: *Crow Ridge, Camp 9*. The column marched almost twenty miles this day (122.32

miles from Fort Lincoln), the longest so far. This was another easy day and another excellent campsite.

Indian Village—The Indians were probably moving from their first Rosebud camp on this day or the next. At their second camp—twelve miles upstream from the first—Crow Indians were reported to have been seen. Later in the evening it was reported to have been an error. They stayed in this location only one day, then moved another twelve or fifteen miles to the Teat Butte camp.[95] The Teat Butte camp was probably their camp number three.

Gibbon/Montana Column—2 AM—Troops were again wakened to be on the alert for Indians. They too had a warm and sunny day ahead of them.

Montana Column Trains—The Maclay train had another hard day of travel, however, finally reaching the river at eleven AM. The road was rough, but good; then at 2:06 PM they began moving again, camping four miles below the old Camp Supply.

MAY 26, 1876—FRIDAY—*Military Correspondence & Intelligence Reports*—From Commanding Officer, Fort Ellis—"Relative to Crow Indian Scouts being induced to join Gen. Crook's command."[96]

Dakota Column—3 AM—Scouts depart the Terry-Custer camp with mail for Fort Lincoln. Shortly after dawn, other scouts arrive *from* Fort Lincoln with mail.

5 AM—according to General Terry—the column begins to move (other sources claimed 5:30 AM), "ascending a long and easy slope to an alkaline plain covered with cactus and prickly pears. Beds of red gravel interspersed the terrain…."[97] Once again several streams had to be bridged, causing delays. This turned out to be the hottest day so far, 79°, and muggy. The column eventually reached the highest elevation since leaving Fort Lincoln, 3,279 feet. They encountered many annoying plants: Devil's Club, hay-needles, prickly pear, cockleburs, and were nearing the badlands of the Little Missouri, red-topped, conical-shaped hills coming in sight.

Custer rode far in advance with Captain Thomas Weir's Company D. On the other hand, scout Reynolds, looking for Davis Creek, got lost, going about three miles too far, and had to backtrack. The stop-start began once more: 5:30 AM—Terry: column halts; six AM—column begins to move; 7:10 AM—column halts to build a bridge; 9:20 AM—Terry: column begins to move; 10:40 AM—column halts; one PM—column moves.

2:30 PM—The column finally pulls into camp. This was the ***Belfield, Camp 10***. Overall, for the day, they covered only twelve miles (and were now 134 miles from Fort Lincoln). This campsite was about 3½ miles south of present-day Belfield, North Dakota. There was plenty of grass, but no wood. Very warm with lots of mosquitoes and grasshoppers; heavy rainstorm that night.

Steamer "Far West"—On this day, the steamer "Far West," loaded with supplies, leaves Bismarck.[98]

Gibbon/Montana Column—As for the Gibbon column, it was more of the same, as well. At two AM the command again turned out on picket line in case of attack. And again, nothing. The day turned out to be very warm and dry. That evening, Gibbon told Bradley to prepare for a scout tomorrow to try to locate the Indian camp.

Premonitions must have been raging, for the troops witnessed a rather rare occurrence—the evening star—Venus—was seen. Yet it was still very puzzling: no Indians had been seen now for a couple of days.

Montana Column Trains—10 AM—Lieutenant Roe and his F/2C return to camp after escorting the John W. Power wagon caravan toward Fort Ellis. At this same time, the Maclay train was moving, and they spot the trader, Linas McCormick heading down the Yellowstone. The train passes Clark's Fork. Slightly before noon, the wagon train "noons," halting "where road leaves the river to cross a big prairie for eight miles."[99] At noon the train leaves halt and at six PM, having passed the mouth of Clark's Fork, the wagon train camps for the night about a half mile from the river having made another fifteen miles.

MAY 27, 1876—SATURDAY—***Military Correspondence & Intelligence Reports***—From the Governor of the Dakota Territory—"Asks if protection will be furnished a provision train which it is proposed to send to the relief of the Black Hills miners."[100]

Dakota Column—3 AM—Reveille.

4:30 AM—The command was on the march (5 AM—Terry's diary). The rain from the night before had done away with much of the dust, but an early fog obscured landmarks and the column got lost looking for the Davis Creek valley entrance into the badlands. This route would take them to the Little Missouri.

6:15 AM—First halt.

8 AM—The column was on the move again; 9:20 AM saw another stop, only now the badlands were in sight. As before, Custer was in advance with Company D (Weir) and the scouts, looking for the proper trail. Unsure, Terry sends Captain Otho Michaelis with fifteen men and Private McCue as the guide, south, to find Stanley's trail. Charlie Reynolds also scouts to the south; and the Indian escorts are sent out as well.

After fog lifted, at around one PM Custer spotted the Sentinel Buttes, thereby correcting his bearings, still looking for the Stanley trail from the Yellowstone Expedition of 1873. It was the only trail through the badlands. The day turned warm and clear with pleasant westerly winds (the days were getting much hotter and the horses were having some difficulty with wild cactus). Finally, the column reached the badlands, the so-called *Mauvaises Terres*.[101] At two PM the column entered the long narrow valley of Davis Creek. Some fifteen minutes later—around 2:15 PM–2:25 PM—after marching about seventeen miles and one mile into the valley, they went into camp (a more direct route would probably have been about seven miles)—the **Head of Davis Creek, Camp 11.** (Now about 151 miles from Fort Lincoln, though some of it was back and forth.) The camp was set up about six miles south and one mile west of present-day Fryburg, North Dakota. The grass was of very poor quality and there were some sparse cottonwoods, and because of the area, the water was highly alkaline.

> The general area of the May 27 campsite in the badlands. Sibley went through as well as Stanley. Once into the badlands the trail was definitely dictated by terrain. This was a harsh and brutal land. The campsite was near Davis Creek, but many of the wagons did not make it down to the valley until later on, some not even that night. It is a beautiful spot for a campsite.[102]

That evening, Custer had the band play for the troops. And in the *Army and Navy Journal* of this date, it was reported, "The Sioux are said to be at Blue Stone River, Montana, 300 miles from Fort Fetterman, with 3,000 lodges or 12,000 warriors. Three thousand warriors have left Cheyenne Agency to join Crazy Horse…."[103]

Gibbon/Montana Column—5 AM—By this time, ferried across the Yellowstone by Captain Clifford and his boats, Lieutenant Bradley sets out on another scout to see what has become of the Sioux camp (the Sioux seemed to have abruptly disappeared). Gibbon was extremely concerned the hostiles had possibly moved *east*. Bradley takes his mounted infantry (thirteen troopers), Tom LeForgé, and five Crow scouts, including Curley and White Man Runs Him—twenty, in all. They head south toward the Wolf Mountains, crossing some open country "which they found strewn with recently killed buffalo and laced by hundreds of pony tracks"[104]; Indian signs were abundant. Bradley wrote, by the signs it was apparent, "there must have been hundreds of mounted Indians here within a recent period. Near the mountains, where they had been compelled to travel close together to pass defiles, they had left a beaten track like a traveled road."[105] Approaching the lookout point from the earlier scout (fourteen miles out), they found the warrior trail seen by the Crow on the nineteenth. It led toward the lower Rosebud. From these signs Bradley concluded these warriors had been the vanguard of the "leisurely" movement of the entire village from the Tongue to the Rosebud.[106]

Peering through the mist, Bradley finds an immense 400- to 500-lodge Sioux camp (some eight to ten miles distant, up the valley) on the Rosebud—which was a surprise (Gibbon feared they may be moving east)—only eighteen to twenty miles from Gibbon's base camp below Rosebud's mouth. The camp appeared to be spread out over a distance of some two miles.[107] (Bradley and his "hard-riding infantry detachment had earned the sobriquet, 'The Shoo-flies.'"[108]) "'The fact that they had moved down within easy striking distance…' Bradley observed, 'seemed to prove that they held us in no awe.'"[109] Before Bradley could have each of his soldiers ascend the peak and peer into the valley to see the village—for verification—some of his scouts spotted villagers driving some ponies as if they had spied the Crow. Reluctantly, Bradley and his men withdrew and he led them on a hard ride back to the Yellowstone. Captain Clifford had boats waiting to ferry them across.

> I place Bradley's viewpoint [was actually a little] farther east in the range of hills in Rosebud Buttes. My reasoning is that from my viewpoint I can see all the way up the Rosebud for miles and almost all the way to the mouth of Rosebud Creek and the fringe of trees bordering the Yellowstone. It has a place at the bottom of the hill to hide the horses from view as well. I climbed all of the higher buttes and believe this is the one. From my butte I can see the cutback bluffs adjacent to the 7th campsite on Rosebud Creek, the June 22nd camp. From the site I can see about where the Indian trail would have entered the Rosebud valley en route to their first Rosebud camp! Bradley used the same lookout later on and looking up the valley could see that the Indians had moved over from the Tongue.[110]

Author/historian John Gray wrote,

> Obviously, such movements *(of the Sioux)* so near the Montana column meant it stood in little awe of the troops it had been raiding.… The information Bradley reported at this time was the most valuable Indian intelligence discovered during the campaign. It established the present location and direction of movement of the consolidated force of winter roamers.[111]

Bradley estimated the village at about 400 lodges and 800 to 1,000 warriors. Lieutenant Roe, however—who was *not* with this scouting party—later expressed the opinion there were between 1,500 and 2,000 warriors in this particular village.[112] Roe may have been correct for even Edgar Stewart claimed more and more Indians were joining, so the camp had to be growing over this period, and comments made after the Little Big Horn battle indicate the possibility this single camp was actually becoming multiple camps. It is extremely interesting to read Bradley's comments about the village and how it compared to what was seen in the Little Big Horn valley: Bradley thought the majority of the officers in Gibbon's command felt they could have whipped these hostiles, "…and prevented that tremendous aggregation of force a month later that made the massacre of Custer's command possible."[113] Some time between 11:30 AM and noon, Bradley returns to base camp with news. As usual, his report was greeted with skepticism.

At dark Gibbon sends a dispatch (mentioning Bradley's report as a "P. S.," since the report had been prepared prior to Bradley's return) with privates William Evans and Benjamin Stewart (both E/7I) and scout John Williamson, downriver to Terry (130–150 river-miles away; Bradley said the one trooper was Private James Bell, rather than Evans, but since Evans was awarded the Medal of Honor for his efforts, Bradley was obviously incorrect[114]; Gibbon verified it was Evans and Stewart[115]). Gibbon cleared this up in his October 1877, *American Catholic Quarterly* article, "Hunting Sitting Bull." After the debacle at the Little Big Horn, Terry and Gibbon were anxious to communicate with General Crook, especially since they had now heard of his defeat on the Rosebud. Gibbon asked for messengers and twelve men volunteered, including the intrepid Evans and Stewart, but this time Private Bell (E/7I) as well. Those three were chosen…. Sunday, July 9, 1876.[116]

Gibbon's decision not to attack the Sioux village—if he even fully believed Bradley's report—was based on several factors: his orders were to keep the Sioux south of the Yellowstone and attack only if *certain* of success. In addition, he was still smarting over his failure to get his force across the river several days earlier and the Yellowstone was even higher now; and he was extremely concerned about his supply train and even now was contemplating sending two more companies back to reinforce its escort, further reducing his offensive force. These reasons were all valid, but what is incomprehensible is Gibbon's failure to fully believe Bradley, follow-up at least, on his discovery, and report it to Terry like it was real and not just some ephemeral hope of his chief scout. Part of Gibbon's hesitancy to fully believe Bradley may have stemmed from the fact Terry had expected the Sioux to fight him on the Little Missouri. This belief had to have been communicated to Gibbon much earlier. At dark Gibbon sends captains Ball (H/2C) and Thompson (L/2C) down the north bank of the Yellowstone to the Tongue to check for any Sioux crossings and to provide moral support for the three couriers.

Montana Column Trains—Also at noon, the Maclay trains halted for lunch having been in harness for six hours and traveling twelve miles. By three PM they were on the roll again, and at 7:45 PM they camp just below Baker's Battleground, ten additional miles. All told, the trains made forty-one miles in two days. This area provided good grass for grazing.

11:30 PM—The train's mules pulled back in.

Indian Village—After only one night in the Teat Butte camp—their third on the Rosebud—the Indians moved again. Wooden Leg's camp numbers differ by one.

MAY 28, 1876—SUNDAY—*Military Correspondence & Intelligence Reports*—From Charles G. Wicker—"Relative to allowing provisions train to go to Black Hills by Pierre route."[117]

Dakota Column—4:25 AM—The column broke camp (4:45 AM—Terry's diary). Both Terry and Custer, knowing of reports of hostiles in the region of the Little Missouri, figured they might start seeing signs of the Indians fairly soon. As the command moved out, the advance guard moved two miles in front and Lieutenant Edward Godfrey's Company K brought up the rear.

5 AM—Lieutenant Maguire began building the first of eight bridges that day, within the Davis Creek valley of the Little Missouri badlands. It proved to be the hardest day—in terms of work—of the entire expedition as temperatures reached 80°, though considerably warmer in the canyon walls. By 5:45 AM they had reached the first crossing of Davis Creek: 3.95 miles. The second crossing was another: 1¾ miles; 6:45 AM—third crossing: 200 yards, forty minutes; 8:45 AM—fourth crossing; ten AM—fifth crossing ... 10:30 AM—seventh crossing. And finally, at 12:30 PM Terry ordered the troops into bivouac. *Davis Creek, Camp 12.* Seven miles traveled; 158 miles from Fort Lincoln. The camp was about mid-way down the canyon with fair grass and wood, but the water was too alkaline to drink.

> Good view of the May 28 campsite. The picture shows the last creek crossing where they lost a wagon. After crossing the trail they turned to the left and camp was established on a slight plateau bordered by the sinuous creek. Before the crossing of the creek near some sandstone bluffs is what is called Initial Rock. Troopers W.C. Williams and Frank Neely carved their names on the rock. Most likely they were on picket duty. Regarding the lost wagon: the front axel [sic] and wheels are in the carriage house at the Chateau de Mores. A few metal items are in the North Dakota Historical Society. The campsite is a lovely elongated site dictated by the curvaceous creek. It is bordered by multi-colored buttes to the south and scattered bluffs with prairie to the north.[118]

That afternoon Lieutenant Maguire, along with companies G (Lieutenant Donald "Tosh" McIntosh), K (Godfrey), and M (French) go out and build two more bridges to facilitate the next day's march.

Gibbon/Montana Column—Meanwhile, as a fine rain fell cooling the day, Gibbon, with a cavalry escort, makes a short foray downriver to examine the ground and at noon the Linas McCormick's boat arrived, bringing a cargo of vegetables, canned goods, tobacco, butter, cigars, and mail. The crew reported seeing no Indians downriver from Benson's Landing, but they did see the Diamond-R train below the Stillwater, two days prior.

Upon Gibbon's return he is handed a dispatch from Terry (dated May fourteenth at Fort Abraham Lincoln) ordering him to march for the stockade (Stanley's) above Glendive Creek, cross the Yellowstone, and move east to meet him. It is in this note

Terry tells Gibbon he expects to fight Sitting Bull on the Little Missouri: "…the hostiles were concentrated on the Little Missouri, and between the Missouri River and the Yellowstone… [March your column] … at once to a point on the Yellowstone opposite Stanley's Stockade."[119]

Stanley's Stockade was located about 130 miles downriver from where Gibbon was presently camped and Gibbon read Terry's note, wondering, if the Sioux were where Terry said—some 200 miles eastward—then why was Gibbon's column seeing so many Indians a mere eighteen to twenty miles away and on the Rosebud? Terry's note was two weeks old. "It is exceedingly unlikely that such a concentration is taking place, for the village opposite us is apparently working the other way, having already crossed from the Tongue to the Rosebud."[120] Gibbon's dilemma is simple: he has orders to move some 130 miles in the opposite direction from where he *knows* Indians are presently camped and other than the messengers he sent, has no way of informing Terry. Obviously, he is concerned the Indians will simply move farther away and then scatter. His solution is a short delay, hoping, in the interim, he would receive a note from Terry telling him to stay put. He decides to send Sanno (K/7I) and Roe (F/2C) with some wagons, back up the Yellowstone to speed along the Diamond-R wagons (with Lieutenant Kendrick's detachment). This will buy him some time.

Montana Column Trains—Kendrick (H/7I) and the Diamond-R train meet Lieutenant English and Second Lieutenant Alfred Bainbridge Johnson (I/7I) with thirty-seven men, one Gatling gun, and the John W. Power Co. train, six miles below Baker's battleground. According to Matthew Carroll, the Power train would be discharged after returning to Fort Ellis.[121] Since the train made only ten miles this day and had to make Pompey's Pillar the following day as there was no water at this location, English requested the train stay the night. Another heavy windstorm and more rain hit them at night.

Crook/Wyoming Column—A day prior to departure, Crook—concerned about enlisting scouts for his expedition—sends out two companies of cavalry to try to locate and recruit Crow and Shoshone scouts: Captain Frederick Van Vliet (C/3C) and Lieutenant Crawford (G/3C).

Indian Village—The fourth Indian camp was set up in the Greenleaf Creek area [R-34[122]], the Cheyenne occupying that confluence, with the Hunkpapa circle about a mile below. This was also the first camp where one of the Sioux circles camped on the west side of the Rosebud.[123] More Cheyenne joined them here, telling the Indians the soldiers were coming to fight them. They remained at this site for five or six nights.

MAY 29, 1876—MONDAY—*Military Correspondence & Intelligence Reports*—From Assistant Adjutant General, Department of the Platte—"Expedition leaves Fetterman today. Gen. Crook remains till evening to receive any dispatches, then goes to Camp."[124]

From General George Crook—"Reports all young warriors from Red Cloud Agency gone to join hostiles who are concentrating at mouth of Powder river."[125]

Telegram dated May 29, 1876, from Brigadier General George Crook, Fort Fetterman, Wyo., to Lt. Gen. Sheridan, Chicago, Ill.—

Egan encountered about six hundred warriors going north from Red Cloud Agency he has information of all young warriors going north from this agency leaving families to be protected can't you do something to stop this. Either warriors return or families join them. Indications are that we shall have the whole fighting force of the Sioux nation to contend with. Command marches today. I shall wait till towards evening and join Camp sixteen miles out hostiles are said to be concentrating at mouth of Powder River. George Crook, Brig. Gen'l.

Dakota Column—3 AM—Reveille.

4:45 AM—The troops break camp (this time agrees with Terry's diary).

6:20 AM—Terry, Custer, and the advance guard reach the Little Missouri (near what is now Medora, North Dakota), still in the badlands, choosing a campsite. The banks of the river were lined with groves of cottonwood, elm, and pine. The Sioux called it, "Thick Timber River." (Historian Edgar I. Stewart claimed this camp was not reached until May thirtieth.[126])

9 AM—The wagons and troops begin arriving at what was to be their campsite: *Little Missouri, Camp 13.* This would be a two-day camp. For the short day the troops had traveled some 6.4 miles, for a total of 165.87 miles from Fort Lincoln. That evening, Terry and Custer agree Custer should reconnoiter southwards, through the badlands, to see if he can pick up some sign of the Indians.

> The campsite of May 29 was established near some cottonwoods east of the Little Missouri River, and southwest of where Davis Creek entered the river. In 1976, on our Custer Trail re-ride we stayed at the Custer Trail Ranch at the base of a high bluff. It was almost directly east of the crossing of the Little Missouri and Custer Wash. Today the entire campsite area is a golf course.[127]

Montana Column Trains—5 AM—Carroll has his wagons rolling, his objective for the day being Pompey's Pillar, twenty-five miles away, but it was cloudy and raining. The train was now hauling some tents and bedding for English and his men. By 8:30 AM, the rain had ended, but heavy clouds remained, making the day cool for traveling.

11 AM—The train "nooned" in a dry camp.

1 PM—Carroll's Maclay train breaks a rest camp, heading for Pompey's Pillar.

7 PM—The train makes Pompey's Pillar and goes into camp, having traveled twenty-five miles.

Gibbon/Montana Column—Some time later in the morning, Gibbon sends Sanno (K/7I) and Roe, along with Jacobs, the regimental quartermaster, and all the wagons (twenty-four of them)—empty—back to lighten the contract-train and hurry it along. Gibbon's after-action report says Sanno and Roe were sent on the twenty-eighth, but this was the date they prepared to leave.

2 PM—The Ball/Thompson scout returns from the Tongue River area, having seen no hostiles. The three couriers sent by Gibbon arrive at Stanley's Stockade, but not finding Terry, proceed downriver where they encountered the "Far West." They rode that back to the supply camp.

That evening Dr. Paulding reported a "squabble" among the officers in which Bradley called an officer whose name he did not know and who claimed he had not seen the Sioux village, a "liar." ("Since he had accomplished more than all the others put together, he had a right to be miffed."[128])

Crook/Wyoming Column—Meanwhile, on the other "front," the Crook/Wyoming column Crook opens its "second" campaign … at noon. The command consisted of five companies of the 2nd Cavalry; ten companies of the 3rd Cavalry; three companies of the 9th Infantry; two companies (D and F) of the 4th Infantry (one source says three, but this is an error); thirty-three officers and 959 enlisted personnel. The column was accompanied by Captain William S. Stanton, Corps of Engineers. Crook took 103 wagons, each pulled by a six-mule team.[129] Unknown to anyone and disguised as a man, "Calamity" Jane was one of the teamsters. The column moved north from Fort Fetterman, along the Phil Kearney-Bozeman Trail route to the headwaters of the south fork of the Tongue River (Goose Creek) where a temporary camp was set up,[130] the same route followed in the March expedition. The column stretched out for more than four miles. After traveling twelve miles for the day, Crook camped on Sage Creek.

General P.H. Sheridan—In the meantime, General Sheridan wrote to General Sherman:

> As no very accurate information can be obtained as to the location of the hostile Indians, and as there would be no telling how long they would stay at any one place, if it was known, I have given no instructions to Generals Crook or Terry, preferring that they should do the best they can under the circumstances and under what they may develop, as I think it would be unwise to make any combinations in such country as they will have to operate in. As hostile Indians in any great numbers cannot keep the field as a body for a week, or at most ten days, I therefore consider—and so do Terry and Crook—that each column will be able to take care of itself and of chastising the Indians should it have the opportunity.
>
> The organization of these commands and what they can expect to accomplish has been as yet left to the Department Commanders. I presume the following will occur: General Terry will drive the Indians toward the Big Horn Valley, and General Crook will drive them back toward Terry, Colonel Gibbon moving down on the north side of the Yellowstone to intercept, if possible, such as may want to go north of the Missouri to the Milk River.

MAY 30, 1876—TUESDAY—*Military Correspondence & Intelligence Reports*—From Commanding Officer, Fort Laramie—"Telegraphs that about 800 or 1,000 Indians have left Red Cloud Agency to mouth of Powder river and 50 lodges from Spotted Tail also gone."[131]

Side Notes—The comment about Spotted Tail is quite interesting for it reinforces the reports of a smaller village on the eastern flats adjacent to the Little Big Horn River beneath Weir Point at the time of the battle.

Dakota Column—On this day, most of the troops of the Dakota column remained in the Little Missouri camp while Custer, four companies of cavalry (C, D, F, and M), and Lieutenant Charles Varnum and twelve Ree scouts, and a small train of five pack mules with forage would go out on a scout. George Custer's brother, Tom, who had been riding with the staff, their nephew Autie Reed, and Dr. DeWolf went along, as well. Custer was ordered to return by seven AM the following morning. At 3:30 AM there was reveille for the companies going out on the recon and at four AM they had breakfast. By five AM the Custer reconnaissance up the Little Missouri (south) begins.

Opposite: Dakota Column: Fort Lincoln to the Powder River.

Dakota Column
Terry-Custer, Fort Abraham Lincoln to the Powder River Depot

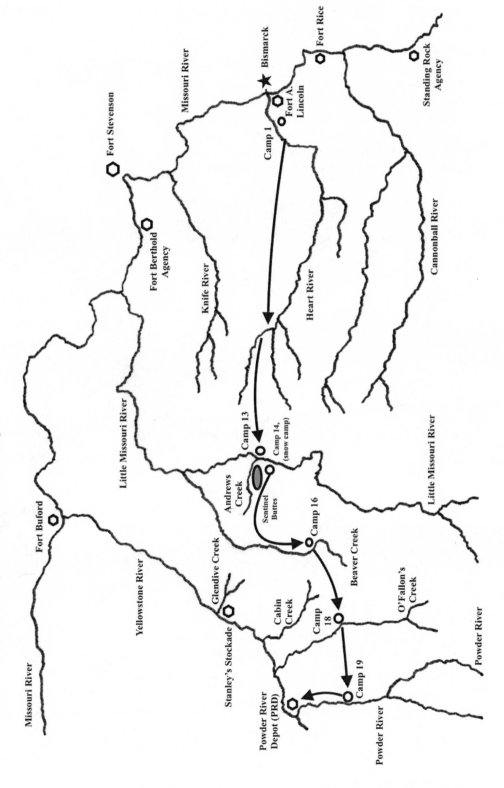

(Private William O. Taylor [Company A] claimed fifty miles, round-trip, though Taylor was not on this expedition and while many of his future references were off the mark, this one was fairly close to accurate.) The valley itself is about one mile wide, with badlands on both sides. The river meanders all over and the troops had to cross it some thirty-four times.

Terry's plan, as outlined to his sister, Fanchon ("Fanny"), in a letter begun May 23, 1876, was simple. He expected to move on the next day, head west,

> …go two or three marches west, halt and send out reconnaissance, right, left, and south hoping to find some trail leading to an Indian camp. If I do not, I shall move to the Yellowstone…. I had reason to hope that we should find the Indians here in force prepared to fight but now I fear that they have scattered….[132]

That afternoon Ree scouts arrived from Fort Lincoln bringing mail and dispatches, and Lieutenant Maguire was busy at work building a road at the river crossing. Terry, as well, reconnoitered the route with Captain Edward Smith (his Acting Assistant Adjutant General—AAAG). When Terry returned to camp, he sent Smith with First Lieutenant Eugene Beauharnais Gibbs (Aide-de-Camp—A-d-C) and three companies to help repair Maguire's road.

Rather early and as a surprise, Custer returns by six PM, well ahead of schedule: he had traveled about fifty-five miles and nary a sign of Indians. He conferred with Terry and they decided to move on to the Powder River country where the Indians had been in March 1876. That night there was a very heavy thunderstorm.

Gibbon/Montana Column—2 AM—Gibbon, still worried about the proximity of the Sioux, wakes his command.

3 PM—Scout John Williamson, and privates William Evans, and Benjamin Stewart reach Glendive depot (Stanley's Stockade), but find only Major Moore and his battalion of 6th Infantry.

DUSK—Two Crow scouts from Gibbon's command cross Yellowstone to again try to steal Sioux ponies. Quickly return after running into a war party of about thirty.

Montana Column Trains—6 AM—The Maclay train leaves the Pompey's Pillar camp, then, some time in late morning, after traveling about nine miles, the train "noons" on a small creek. That afternoon it rained. Later in the day, after making eighteen miles, the train camps on Sunset Creek, with "plenty of water in holes; wood and grass scarce…."[133]

Crook/Wyoming Column—George Crook, worried about Sioux activity in the region, dispatches two companies to reconnoiter west: Captain Meinhold (B/3C) and Captain Vroom (L/3C). They took four days rations and were to re-join the column at old Fort Reno.[134] Proceeding northwest, the main column traveled twenty miles, camping on the South Cheyenne River, "…a shriveled stream of muddy and alkaline water standing in pools."[135]

MAY 31, 1876—WEDNESDAY—*Dakota Column*—8 AM—The column breaks camp. The night had been wet and there was no dry kindling for fires, the troops eating a breakfast of hardtack and raw bacon … with muddy water. The river bottom was firm, hard gravel, but the banks were soft and it took almost an hour to get all the wagons across. Terry crossed the stream with the advance guard, eventually halting near Gable Butte. Lieutenant Gibbs reported from the rear that the wagons had cleared. Reno comes up front while Custer "played" wagon master. Terry moved out again with the advance. Custer then heads out on a "lark" with his entourage. The day was misty, with heavy, dark threatening clouds and a chilled wind blowing from the east. The day's temperature hovered between 58° and 65°. The column traveled through badlands: torturous gullies, ravines, canyons and finally onto a butte. The column got lost and had to backtrack, infuriating Terry, especially since Custer was nowhere to be found.

9 AM—Custer, now ahead of everyone, picked a bivouac site, and at 9:30 AM Terry halts: the odometer showing only 5⅓ miles. At 11:30 AM Terry moves on for about two miles when he received a message from Custer saying they were not on Stanley's trail. Terry backtracks.

2 PM—Terry camps some eight miles southeast of Sentinel Buttes (North Dakota), straddling a small branch of Andrews Creek: *Andrews Creek-Snow Camp, Camp 14.* The command had traveled between ten and twelve miles, 175 miles, total, from Fort Lincoln.

7 PM—A heavy, cold, freezing rain began; it then turned to sleet and by midnight it begins snowing.

> These are good photos of the two buttes that look at each other and the terrain marched through, but not of the campsite. The march left the campsite, headed south and due to high banks bordering the river to the west, crossed the river, and utilized a wash leading into the river, marched up that and with a lot of bull-work by the engineering companies finally extricated themselves and eventually made it to the top of a plateau and marched west. Due to the menace of bad ground and the ominous presence of Square Butte, the route was changed to the north. Eventually, the command headed down off the plateau and established camp on a branch of Andrews Creek.[136]

Gibbon/Montana Column—2 AM—Gibbon's troops took up their usual position on picket lines in case of surprise attack; cold winds were blowing. Shortly after daylight, Gibbon—anxious about the supply trains and Indians crossing to intercept them— sends Captain Wheelan's G/2C for another scout, sixteen miles upriver and back with LeForgé and five Crow, but found nothing along a rising rapidly rising Yellowstone River.

5 PM—Wheelan finally arrives back in camp and then, that night as well, the spring blizzard began: cold rain, sleet, then snow.

Montana Column Trains—6 AM—The Maclay wagons break camp, reaching the Yellowstone by 9:30 AM. Then at 10:30 AM Lieutenant Jacobs and Captain Sanno with his twenty-four empty wagons joins up with the Maclay train. Since the cargo transfer took most of the day, camp was established where they met. They loaded 459 sacks of grain on the Sanno trains and because of the fear of Indians the mules were kept in all night.

Crook/Wyoming Column—Crook's column made another twenty miles, then camped on the North Fork of the Wind River. It was this evening, while chopping wood for a campfire, Private Andrew Tierney accidentally shot himself, the wound proving mortal. He died in camp on June 7, 1876.

4

The Call of Trumpets

June 1 through June 21

JUNE 1, 1876—THURSDAY—*Dakota Column*—Because of the heavy snow, the troops remained in camp. ***Andrews Creek-Snow Camp, Camp 14.*** By 6:30 AM there was three inches of snow on the ground while the snow fell all day, finally stopping late at night. Terry writes that the assumption the badlands were only a four-mile strip along the river was erroneous. This was the worst part of the badlands, but they extended further on. Dispatches were sent to Fort Lincoln: Barking (Scabby) Wolf and Left Hand (a Dakota who eventually joined the Sioux at the Little Big Horn and was killed there) being used as messengers. By seven AM the snow began falling even harder.

> During the night of the 31st, it snowed. By three AM the next day, several inches of snow had fallen. The small creek had swollen. Wood was scarce and not easily obtained. The horses, mules, and beef cattle suffered for the want of grass. Charley Reynolds killed two Bighorn sheep on the trail to the campsite. Prior to leaving, the wagon train was moved across the stream, some during the storm. It was a miserable camp. Many of the men suffered and they no doubt hatched colds and sore throats. The reason they stayed so long in the camp was because the roads were terrible. Scouts and the chosen engineering companies looked for a good road. The doctors also pleaded their case that moving in this kind of weather would most likely sicken more men.[1]

***Steamer "Far West"*—**10 PM—The steamer arrived at Glendive (Stanley's Stockade), under the command of Lieutenant Nelson Bronson and his detachment of Company G, 6th Infantry, with additional supplies.

***Montana Column Trains*—**5 AM—Despite the snow, the wagon trains were moving, though the roads were very "heavy." Since the loads were lighter, however, they moved at a good pace and kept on the heels of the government wagons,[2] even though they had to double all the teams. As it was farther east, it was snowing and cold: a very unpleasant day. In the late afternoon or early evening, the wagon train went into camp, four miles below Fort Pease.

***Crook/Wyoming Column*—**5 AM—Crook's column, despite the wind and heavy snow, is on the march. (Later in the campaign, Crook changed marching times to six AM for the infantry and 7:30 AM for the cavalry.[3]) As the storm abated, Crook made camp on the Dry Fork of the Powder River. The command had traveled another twenty miles. As well, Captain Meinhold returned, finding no Indians, friendly or otherwise.

JUNE 2, 1876—FRIDAY—*Military Correspondence & Intelligence Reports*—From Lt. Col. Wesley Merritt, 9th Cavalry—"Gives disposition of troops for protection of routes to Black Hills and relative to young warriors who have left Agencies to join hostiles."[4]

From Commanding Officer, Camp Robinson—"Reports that at least 2,000 Indians left Red Cloud Agency since 10th ult."[5]

Telegram dated June 2, 1876, from Fort Laramie, Wyo., to Lieut. Gen'l Sheridan, Military Headquarters, Chicago, Ill.—

The following is the disposition of troops with regard to protection of routes to Black Hills two companies of infantry at Sidney two companies of infantry & one of cavalry at Laramie four companies of infantry at Robinson and one company of infantry & one cavalry at Sheridan there are two companies of infantry enroute to this post & the company of cavalry at Sheridan has been order to change stations with a company of Infantry from Robinson the two companies enroute here to take station on the Black Hills road one at the head of Sage Brush Creek sixty-two miles from here the other at the east end of Red Can[y]on about fifty miles from the above & forty miles from Custer also a company of Infantry is ordered from Robinson to take station at the Laramie road crossing of the running water. The cavalry is to scout the roads. The company at this post and the company at Robinson alternating. It is safe to say that a great ma[n]y Indians have left the Red Cloud Agency it is said there are not five hundred warriors remaining there some families have gone. It is hard to tell how many as the Indian agents are themselves but poorly informed & are interested in understating the number of Indians now on reservations are bitter against all who took part in last winter's expedition & there was no chance of Crook's inducing any of them to go with him this time. Captain Egan whose report you have seems positive that from seven hundred to a thousand warriors have left the two agencies. He also says some have gone from Missouri river agencies [?] it would be well if two more companies of Infantry could be sent here one for service at Robinson. The Black Hills road cavalry would answer better. I don't know what arrangements [*illegible, but it seems:* have been made] for the protection of the Sidney road to Sheridan. The post Commander here has sent to the post Commander at Robinson for all information as to Indians who have left agencies up to this time. I will await instructions from headquarters here. Merritt.

As an explanation,

[This] was set up to protect travelers on the Black Hills route. The Old Hat Creek Station and fort, established in 1875 by Captain James Egan, was located north of the Hat Creek Breaks on Sage Creek. Captain Egan mistakenly believed he was on Hat Creek in Nebraska. Egan, an Irishman, received a battlefield commission in the 2nd Cavalry during the Civil War, was wounded at Cold Harbor, and saw service in the West from the end of 1865 until at least the late 1870s, being stationed at various times at Fort Lyon, Colorado, Fort Sanders, Fort D.A. Russell, Fort Laramie, and in Montana. The fort burned in 1883. Subsequently, a new station was constructed a short distance to the west on Cottonwood Creek. The new station, still in existence, was a log, two-story, hip-roofed structure. Stations frequently would have all needed accommodations for travelers, including corrals, blacksmiths, feed for the horses, etc. The larger, more elaborate stations were referred to as "road ranches." The modern equivalent would be a truck stop with a motel. The Ecoffey and Cuny facility, started out as a road ranch but was converted to a hog ranch when there was a decline in business.[6]

Letter dated June 2, 1876, from Head Qts Camp Robinson, Neb., to Major E.F. Townsend, 9th Infantry, Commanding, Fort Laramie, W. T.—

Major:

I have the honor to acknowledge the receipt of your communication of the 29th ultimo asking for information as to the number of Indians that have left Red Cloud and Spotted Tail

Agencies. In reply thereto I would report that I can give no definite information on the subject but from the result of inquiries made at the Agency and elsewhere and from my own knowledge I believe that at least 2,000 Indians (1,500 Sioux and 500 Cheyennes) men women and children have left the Agency here for the North, since the 10th ultimo, containing among the number at least 500 warriors. I would report further that the Agent here claims that 12,000 Indians men women and children belong to his Agency.

I will report relative to the number of Indians that have left Spotted Tail Agency as soon as practicable.

I am Major, Very respectfully,
Your obedient Servant.
(Sgd) Wm H. Jordan, Captain, 9th Infantry, Commanding Post

Dakota Column—The Dakota column stayed in camp because of heavy snow and squalls. The dampness of the snow made the mud quite high.

Major Moore sends three messengers to find Terry and give him messages from Gibbon and himself. In all likelihood, these couriers were the peripatetic John Williamson (from Gibbon's column), and Charles Sargent and Crow Bear, the latter two Moore's men from Glendive.

By noon the snow had ended, but the weather was still cloudy. The snow on ground was rapidly disappearing and the ground drying as the temperature rose. Charlie Reynolds and Chief Wagon Master Charles Brown were sent out to examine the road. They report the road was good for 2½ miles, then bad for a short stretch, then good again over rolling prairie. Terry orders his train to cross the stream so they would be ready to move in the morning. At the same time, Terry sends Maguire out to check the bad part of the road.

Montana Column Trains—4 AM—The wagon train's mules were turned out by Carroll's teamsters. Then, at six AM the train breaks camp, enduring a very arduous trip, again having to double the teams to cross the creek. At 7:30 AM the train reaches the tableland. "[H]ad to double up a short, steep pitch, thence across bench to where Devil Froze Creek empties into the Yellowstone; thence down bottom, which was very wet and sluggish, camping on the bank of the Yellowstone...."[7] By mid-morning the snow had ceased and at 2:30 PM, after traveling sixteen tough miles, the train camps along the banks of the Yellowstone. Wood, grass, and water were good; plenty of elk and antelope located, as well.

Gibbon/Montana Column—Gibbon's column remains in camp this day.

Fort Leavenworth, Kansas—General John Pope receives telegram from Lieutenant General Phil Sheridan directing him to send eight companies of the 5th Cavalry under Lieutenant Colonel Eugene Asa Carr to Cheyenne, Wyoming Territory, ostensibly to police the agencies and to make sure no one leaves for Sitting Bull's encampment.

Indian Village—The Indians left their Greenleaf camp around this time. The next camp was where the Sioux held their sun dance, Indian camp number five.[8]

Crook/Wyoming Column—Facing a raw and cold day, Crook continued moving northwest: the Big Horn mountains could be seen on the far horizon; Pumpkin Buttes plateau could be seen in the east; and much farther east one could see dark vestiges of the Black Hills (with binoculars).[9] Finally, the column arrived at Fort

Reno: dilapidated and in ruins and it was this day when "Calamity" Jane was discovered with the wagon train.[10] Van Vliet returned in the afternoon having seen no sign of scouts. Concerned over the Indian scout issue, Crook sent out scouts Grouard, Pourrier, and Richaud to travel to the Crow Agency, 300 miles away through what was country probably infested with hostile Sioux. Before departing, they advised Crook to head for the forks of Goose Creek (near present-day Sheridan, Wyoming): fresh clean water and good grazing would be found there.

JUNE 3, 1876—SATURDAY—*Military Correspondence & Intelligence Reports*— From Lt. Col. Wesley Merritt—"Dispatches received. Leave for Red Cloud tomorrow morning. Nothing new."[11]

Dakota Column—5:15 AM—The column breaks camp, moving west (once again, Terry's diary: 5:45 AM). Temperature was 35° with heavy, biting, raw winds. "We passed through a most picturesque country. Our path was down a wide valley with peaks of naked earth and stone of the most fantastic forms bounding it on either hand...."[12] The snow had vanished in a fast and sloppy thaw, but the winds still cold and biting. The column's guides were unfamiliar with this country, but after about a six-mile march, they reached rolling prairie again, and the weather suddenly turned beautiful.

6:55 AM—The column halts for a brief rest and at eight AM arrives at a wooded ravine where they build fires.

9 AM—The column is on the move again.

10:05 AM—Three riders are spotted, riding hard, coming at them from the northwest. Terry sends Reynolds out to greet them. They were the couriers from Stanley's Stockade at Glendive with the dispatches from Gibbon and Moore. One of them was Gibbon's scout, John Williamson. These couriers probably traveled some forty-five miles before finding Terry. They carried a dispatch from Gibbon mentioning the killing of the three men by Sioux (May twenty-third). Also: Terry's supplies have reached the field depot; the Yellowstone afforded excellent navigation; the "Far West" was waiting to serve Terry; and the steamer "Josephine" had returned to Bismarck. There was no mention—at all—of Bradley's discoveries, other than a somewhat disingenuous reference reporting Sioux east of the Rosebud, south of Yellowstone and in great numbers. In essence, Terry had learned nothing of any real importance. Terry now changes his plans based on this intelligence and the intelligence gathered from Custer's reconnaissance of the Little Missouri. Terry made his decision and wrote his sisters: "Gibbon's dispatches coupled with the entire absence of any evidence that Indians had been on the Little Missouri for a long time past convinced me that the best policy would be to keep Gibbon opposite the Rosebud and make myself for the Powder River...."[13] Based on the dispatches, he figures the Sioux are—as Gibbon said—now south of Yellowstone and east of the Rosebud (this of course, was incorrect, based on the reports from Gibbon, who ignored Bradley's reconnaissance intelligence).

> Custer had spent May 30 scouting up the Little Missouri, where Sitting Bull's army was expected to make a stand.... Moore and his scouts had found no signs around the depot or on the trail to Terry's column; and now Gibbon had nothing to report from the upper Yellowstone. Terry could only draw the obvious conclusion that the hostile Sioux were still south

of the Yellowstone and east of the Rosebud. This error was the first consequence of Gibbon's concealment.[14]

Steamer "Far West" and the Steamer "Josephine"—Terry now orders Moore to move supplies from Stanley's Stockade at Glendive Creek to mouth of Powder River by steamboat and await Gibbon. He sends Williamson.

Dakota Column—Terry gives the scout a message to Gibbon to hold his position and not move farther down the Yellowstone. Furthermore, he orders Custer to move the column up Beaver Creek (south), cross, circle west to the head of O'Fallon's Creek, then descend O'Fallon's north to the Yellowstone; up the Yellowstone (west) to mouth of Powder. At this point to their left was the Powder River ridgeline; to their center were the badlands; and to their right was rolling country, then the Yellowstone bluffs. The traveling, however, was becoming a bit easier … and the temperature climbed to 59°.

> The part about the Powder River ridge to their left, the badlands at their feet, and the bluffs of the Yellowstone, etc., was written by Lieutenant Maguire, the Department of Dakota Engineering Officer. There is only one small hillock to the right of the trail where this vista can be seen. The trail ran to the left, the viewpoint to the left.[15]

This halt was for only ten minutes, and at 10:15 AM, the column begins moving again. Then, at 11:15 AM they halt until 1:10 PM. At 2:55 PM Terry orders another rest halt, and at 3:20 PM the column is once again on the move.

4:25 PM—After a march of about twenty-five miles (the longest march so far), they camp at junction of Beaver Creek and Duck Creek (Montana). This was the **Beaver Creek, Camp 15** (200 miles from Fort Lincoln), situated seven miles west and three miles south of present-day beach, North Dakota. As late as 1967 the site was still inaccessible. Beaver Creek was about thirty to thirty-five feet wide, one to six feet deep, and cold and clear (according to Lieutenant Maguire). Its banks had a thick growth of brush. Scouts found Stanley's bridging of the creek partially washed away; and Terry said there was no wood to repair it, yet there was plenty of smaller wood for fires; and the grazing was excellent. There were also plenty of mosquitoes making it difficult to sleep!

> The first campsite on Beaver Creek—the first campsite in Montana—is accessible. We visited in 1976 on our Custer Trail re-ride. South of the campsite is a butte named Red Top Butte, due to the red scoria rock on top. From the top of the butte a grand view of the campsite looking north is seen.[16]

Gibbon/Montana Column—2 AM—Picket positions were assumed again, but still no threat. The morning started very cold and icy and at five AM the wagon train leaves camp traveling two miles before reaching a bench-land. Captain Edward Ball's company (H/2C) starts upstream to go as far as Big Porcupine Creek to find the best place for wagons to cross and to build the necessary bridges, while Captain William Logan (A/7I) heads downstream to build bridges for a movement in that direction.

Montana Column Trains—12:30 PM—The wagon train reaches the Big Porcupine, crosses the stream, then waters its teams while still in harness. The roads remained heavy making it quite hard on the mules. They began looking for a camp for the night when Ball's command rode up and advised they were only sixteen miles from the main column. Having already traveled twenty-three miles, they all went into camp.

Crook/Wyoming Column—Crook departs old Fort Reno and despite the ground frost, the going was easy and signs of spring could be seen on the prairie. The next watering hole was thirty miles away. At noon purported Indian signal fires could be seen in the distance and cavalry was ordered to investigate: nothing came of it, however. That evening—Crook bivouacked on Crazy Woman Creek.

JUNE 4, 1876—SUNDAY—*Military Correspondence & Intelligence Reports*—

From Commanding Officer, Fort Fetterman—"Repeats telegram from CO. [*illegible name, but possibly Strombaugh*] relative to Snake Indians enrolled for service with Gen. Crook, and his reply that it will cost $400 to reach Gen. Crook from that point."[17]

In a letter dated June 4, 1876, from Headquarters, U.S. Military Station, Standing Rock, D. T., to the Assistant Adjutant General, Department of Dakota, St. Paul, Minn.—

Sir:

An Indian recently arrived from Cheyenne Indian Agency reports that a large war party, composing Indians from Spotted Tail's and Cheyenne River Indian Agencies, left the latter place with the avowed intention of going to Fort Berthold Agency to attack the Rees.

One of the party came into this agency last night, probably to obtain reinforcements. He reports the war party *seven days out* and at some distance below Standing Rock awaiting other reinforcements from Cheyenne.

The above information I have communicated by scout to the Commanding Officer of Forts Rice, Abraham Lincoln, and Stevenson, D. T.

I learn from reliable authority today, that Kill Eagle a prominent chief of the Blackfeet Sioux at this Agency who lately left with twenty (20) lodges, ostensibly to hunt, has certainly joined the hostile Sitting Bull.

Many of the young men belonging to this Agency have left the agency. Some on the pretext of hunting game, who are now probably with Sitting Bull. The principal chiefs remain here, and did they receive an adequate and proper supply of food, would I think continue here, disposed upon every consideration to keep the peace. But notwithstanding that the agent has officially reported and estimated for rations for over 7,000 Indians at this agency and he is required by U.S. statutes to issue to and report the number actually present, and that there has not been to exceed a monthly average of 4,500 the rations are so diminished as to cause partial distress and dissatisfaction.

The following memorandum of issues June 3rd was prepared on the statement of one of the most reliable Indians at this agency. A diminished quantity of flour and corn, a little coffee, usual quantity of beans, but the corn is not ground, and beef has not been issued for three weeks.

Bacon has not been issued for three months.

Pork has not been issued for three months.

Sugar and tobacco have not been issued for two weeks.

The corn is not available as food, yet an engineer and miller and mill are, but not used. Other items go to show that there is, besides the deliberate falsehoods uttered by this agent in his official report to the Commissioner of Indian Affairs as to the products of Indian labor, etc., last year, either gross maladministration or inefficiency, or both—as the supplies sent here for 7,000 certainly should be ample for 4,500 Indians.

Last year these Indians *starved* for *one* month.

In consideration of the organized expeditions against the hostiles—their relatives—should these agency Indians generally join the hostile camp it ought to be charitably attributed to the want of food two years in succession which they have been compelled to suffer, and which if issued to them, would keep them, as no other bond or attraction can, at these Reservation homes with confidence in the promises of Great Father.

Very respectfully,
Your obedient servant,
(Sgd) J.S. Poland, Captain, 6th Infantry, Commanding

Dakota Column—4:55 AM–5 AM—Terry and Custer were on the move, southward, along the east bank of Beaver Creek. At 6:15 AM the column halts for fifteen minutes and at 6:30 AM were on the march again. At 6:50 AM they halted to build a bridge across a wide ravine. At 9:40 AM the march resumed.

NOON—Halt at crossing of Beaver Creek. Terry now sends Reynolds and three men out front to search for water as Maguire and his "engineers" build a bridge across Beaver Creek. For a change the weather was clear and pleasant and the afternoon was very warm. The command had passed through a prairie dog town and was now in a grassy, rolling prairie with badlands peaks in the distance. Terry, however, becomes sick from the sun. Finally, at 2:15 PM the command begins crossing Beaver Creek and the column meets up with Reynolds. Reynolds reported no water within five miles, but other scouts discovered week-old Indian signs, probably hunters: three wickiups were found with leaves still green.

2:35 PM—Camp was ordered: *Beaver and Ash (Cottonwood) Creek, Camp 16*. The column had covered eighteen miles for the day (217 miles from Fort Lincoln). It was a site Stanley had used in his 1873 expedition and it would be the last comfortable camp for the entire expedition, with abundant grass, plenty of wood, and cold, clear and swift running water. As a side note, the most important prairie grasses for sustaining herds of horses and buffalo were blue stem, blue grama, and buffalo grass, some of which were encountered here and elsewhere.[18]

> The June 4 campsite was along Beaver Creek and adjacent to the west-flowing east fork of Beaver Creek. The reason Beaver Creek's south-flowing direction changes to the northwest at this point is due to high rolling prairie to the south and southeast. Plenty of wood and clear, cold water.[19]

Gibbon/Montana Column—5 AM—Captain Logan and A/7I march downriver to build bridges.

Montana Column Trains—6 AM—The Diamond-R train resumes its march downriver, traveling through a canyon. The day was warm and dry.

2 PM—Sanno/Roe and English reach Gibbon's camp with the Diamond-R contract-train, thus restoring Gibbon to full strength. The wagons were loaded with grain for the return trip. Gibbon now decides he must move his camp downriver.

Crook/Wyoming Column—Column marches about twenty miles and camp was pitched on Clear Creek.

> During the day's advance, Indian *sign* began to reveal a *significant* and unusual characteristic: pony tracks were everywhere in evidence, but the tracks of *dragging lodge poles* were not! Bourke observed: '...*men were slipping out from Red Cloud and Spotted Tail agencies and uniting with the hostiles, but leaving their families at home, under the protection of the reservations*.'... If the women, children and other non-combatants were being left behind, and the *warriors only*

were gathering, there could remain no doubt but that the Indians fully intended to fight the white man's armies.[20]

JUNE 5, 1876—MONDAY—*Military Correspondence & Intelligence Reports*—From Commanding General, Department of the Platte—"Repeat telegram from C.O. Fort Laramie relative to reports from hostile Camp and attack on mail carrier and that Gen. Merritt left [for] Red Cloud June 4th."[21]

From General W.T. Sherman—"Relative to appointment of a Commissioner to confer with Red Cloud and Spotted Tail with a view to release their rights to the Black Hills, and to protection of route thereto."[22]

From Commanding Officer, Fort Fetterman—"C.O. Fort Laramie telegraphs important Indian news to Gen. Crook and relative to enlistment of Snake Indians to co-operate with him."[23]

From 1st Lieut. Wm. Quinton—"Reports his inability to procure Crow Scouts required by Gen. Crook."[24] (*First Lieutenant William Quinton had been assigned to the 7th Infantry on May 3, 1870. He was born in Ireland and had been in the U.S. Army in one capacity or another since 1861. He was the commanding officer of Company C and not on the campaign as such.*)

Telegram dated June 5, 1876, from unknown/missing source [though it appears to be from General Sherman], Washington, D.C., to Gen. P.H. Sheridan, Commanding Div. Chicago, Ill.—

> Just came from conference with Sect'ys Chandler and Cameron the former says he thinks a bill will pass today appointing commission to confer with Red Cloud and Spotted Tail with a view to obtain the consent of the peaceful Indians to release their rights to Black Hills to emigrate to some other reservation. You can use the eight companies Fifth Cavalry as escort to these commissioners and being at the agencies they can exercise a supervision each [*sic;* such] as General McKinzie now does at Fort Sill whilst Crook & Terry are dealing with the hostiles. Meantime the old treaty to be respected & no intrusion on the reservation to be encouraged or permitted. No military protection promised on the Fort Pierre route on that from Sidney north only patrols on the road from Laramie lying mostly outside the reservation and this in the interest of humanity. Judge thinks our orders discriminate against Yankton whereas the.... [*remainder of telegram missing*].

Dakota Column—5 AM—On the move; heavy dew and a very warm day. The column advanced 1.88 miles and arrived at a ravine/creek that required bridging. They halted, bridged the gap, and then began moving over very fine country with rolling prairie and luxuriant grass. At seven AM they halted once more, but by 7:40 AM were on the move.

8:40 AM—Halt on edge of more badlands. Traveled 10.48 miles so far.

9:20 AM—On the move.

10 AM—Halt to repair road.

10:30 AM—Moved again, and headed south down Beaver Creek, for about ten miles (in three hours), then crossed Pennel Creek and turned west. Once again, they were following Stanley's 1873 trail. Heavy sagebrush, cactus, prickly pear, very alkaline, dry land; lots of rattlesnakes, leaving the grasslands behind. Mark Kellogg considered this the toughest day's march so far.

12:15 PM—Having traveled eighteen miles the main column halted at a creek for a brief rest, and were on the march again by 1:45 PM. Finally, at 2:20 PM they camped.

For the day the column made 20½ miles (237½ miles from Fort Lincoln), camping on Pennel Creek; thus, **Pennel Creek, Camp 17**. Willert called it **Cabin Creek,** the camp being near the headwaters of that stream. Grass was thin, almost no water except snow run-off, and virtually no wood. Two men from Benteen's company went out hunting this night, but did not return. It was believed the Sioux had taken them.

> The route to the June 5 campsite was at first south as it crossed Beaver Creek, extricated itself, and gradually climbed out of the valley. The march was over rolling country. Badlands with their deep gullies prompted the command to turn west and down a steep hill with its deep washouts and clay-like soil. In working on my book I searched all over for the route the command descended. There are modern day roads all over. While looking over my maps I met a guy … the former mayor of Baker, Montana. He told me he had made all of the roads in the area for the oil companies. I told him what I was about … and he mentioned that years ago there was a road homesteaders had used to get to their ranch. He took us to the place and my heart almost stopped … there it was! Not only did the mileage match, but it was all there like Maguire, Kellogg and others mentioned. It is my belief the homesteaders used Custer's route to the bottom. The route was dictated by watered ravines and high bluffs, many badlands formations. They crossed three tributaries of Cabin Creek, then established camp. The campsite of June 5 had a tributary of Cabin Creek to the north and another to the south. To the west a series of high bluffs were observed. Grass and wood [were] limited; water was found in pools, some of it alkaline. A north-running tributary of Cabin Creek is east of the campsite. A lot of fossils found![25]

Steamer "Far West"—1:05 PM—Begins the seventy-eight-mile trip up the Yellowstone from Glendive Creek to the proposed site of Camp Supply at the Powder River confluence. On board were Captain James W. Powell, the C. O., C/6I, and supplies. Gibbon's scout, John Williamson, was also on board.

Gibbon/Montana Column—3:30 AM—Reveille.

8:55 AM—Gibbon breaks camp.

1:45 PM—Gibbon goes into camp along the Yellowstone. Captain Thompson recognized the area as being about a half-mile from where he and Captain Wheelan had concealed their troops on May nineteenth, watching as the fifty Sioux attempted to cross the river. The campsite was beautiful and the afternoon weather was warm.

Montana Column Trains—9 AM the wagon train—loaded with about 8,200 pounds per team—pulls out of camp.

2 PM—After traveling about ten miles, the train makes camp at the foot of a big hill. They too were now on Stanley's road of 1873, and water, wood, and grass were excellent.[26]

Crook/Wyoming Column—The column passes Lake DeSmet and by evening, having traveled sixteen miles, Crook camps at the site of old Fort Phil Kearny, along Big Piney Creek, east of the ruined fort.

JUNE 6, 1876—TUESDAY—*Military Correspondence & Intelligence Reports*—From Assistant Adjutant General, Department of the Platte—"Col. Carr desires to employ Pawnees as Indian Scouts. Can authority be granted?"[27]

From Lt. Col. Sheridan—"Your dispatch about concentration at Powder river received."[28]

Lieutenant Colonel Michael V. Sheridan—Lieutenant General Philip Sheridan's brother—dispatched a message to Terry: "Courier from Red Cloud Agency reported... [on June 5, 1876] that Yellow Robe ... says that 1,800 lodges were on the Rosebud and about to leave for Powder River ... and says they will fight and have about 3,000 warriors."

Side Notes—This now clearly indicated the military expected a large number of Indians, willing to fight. Terry received this message *after* the Little Big Horn fight.

Dakota Column—4:35 AM—The column began its march, south and west, with a clear, cool, light breeze blowing. A shade over two hours later, they made their first halt—6:40 AM—then at 6:55 AM the march resumed. By seven AM the column had reached the south fork of O'Fallon's Creek.

Side Notes—No white men—except maybe some trappers—had ever been through this area.

Dakota Column—They had gone about ten miles when the command made the middle reaches of O'Fallon's Creek, but Charlie Reynolds misidentified it and the column headed south following the south fork of O'Fallon's rather than north along the main stream and towards Yellowstone. At 8:45 AM the advance resumed.

10 AM—The two men from Benteen's Company H who were missing the previous night, rejoined the column and at 10:10 AM, after having traveled sixteen miles, the command halted to welcome "home" the lost soldiers. At 11:05 AM the advance resumed.

NOON—They had reached the valley of O'Fallon's and twenty minutes later halted to water in a branch of O'Fallon's. By 12:30 PM the column realized its mistake in direction and made the necessary correction, finally making camp at 4:30 PM. This was the **O'Fallon Creek, Camp 18** (255½ miles since leaving Fort Lincoln). There was plenty of wood, but no grass and little water. Including the backtracking the column made between eighteen and twenty-two miles this day. This night, Terry changed his plans again, deciding to head west over the badlands directly to the Powder River.

Steamer "Far West"—9:15 PM—The steamer with Captain James W. Powell's C/6I, arrives at Powder River to set up new supply depot. At night the "Far West" brought the two couriers, Sargent and Williamson—at extra pay—five miles farther upstream with Terry's dispatches to Gibbon. There was a heavy lightning storm with high winds and heavy rains that night ... then a full moon as the rains cleared.

Gibbon/Montana Column—7:40 AM—Gibbon breaks camp, Bradley and his scouts out front, as usual. At eight AM the column reached the base of a steep plateau, taking the wagons several hours to climb it. Bradley halts to wait for the main column. By eleven AM the train finally makes the grade and is on the plateau. The column moves on for about three miles, then begins its descent to the river. At four PM, after continuing along the Yellowstone for about ten miles, Gibbon chooses a beautiful cottonwood-timbered area in which to make camp and at 4:30 PM the wagons pull into camp as well. It began raining slightly and then in the evening high winds arose, with lightning off in the distance ... and a slight rain.

Crook/Wyoming Column—Crook's column passes over Lodge Trail Ridge: Goose Creek was now only about twelve miles away. The column, however, like its Dakota counterpart, made a wrong turn, heading north following Prairie Dog Creek, away from Goose Creek. (Prairie Dog Creek is also known as Peno Creek.) They moved for eighteen miles before realizing their error. Then it poured. Unknown to Crook and his men, a party of Cheyenne—including Wooden Leg—spotted them, then followed for a day before returning to their camp on the Rosebud.[29] Captain Noyes, however, had been sent out earlier to scout the Goose Creek area. He did so and when Crook's column did not show up, Noyes went looking for the command. Noyes camped a short distance away so as not to spook Crook's pickets. They linked up the following morning.[30]

JUNE 7, 1876—WEDNESDAY—*Military Correspondence & Intelligence Reports*— From Lt. Col. Merritt—"Relative to about 2,000 Indians having left Red Cloud since May 10th a large proportion of whom are warriors."[31]

Telegram dated June 7, 1876, to Lieut. Gen. P.H. Sheridan, Military Hdquarters, Chicago, Ill.—

> Have just arrived and have opportunity to send dispatch by courier. Have seen Indian Agent and talked with Captain Jourdan. It is thought that from fifteen hundred to two thousand Indians have left the reservation. Since tenth of May a large proportion of those who have gone are warriors. The agent is inclined to underestimate those who have gone. I made proposition for him to call for certain young men I would name to show themselves when he admitted reluctantly that Red Cloud had informed him that some of his and other principal families had gone but that they were absent to recover stock stolen by Northern Indians. Some of the sons of principal chiefs are absent. The Indians here are not friendly in their feelings in fact they are generally hostile. The feeling at Spotted Tail is better though some Indians have left there. I will be able to send more definite information when I return to Laramie. Merritt.

Dakota Column—3 AM—Reveille. By 4:45 AM–4:50 AM they were on the road once more. Heavy mists, dark clouds hung overhead, but Custer guided the column this day, rather than Reynolds, risking the blame and more of Terry's ire at another wrong turn. He took his two brothers, Weir's Company D, and the scouts, up front. The day was once again a series of halts and advances: 6:45 AM—first halt; 7:10 AM, advance resumed; 8:10 AM—halt; 8:25 AM, advance resumed, having had to build a bridge; 10:35 AM, halted on a wooded ridge; 11:25 AM, advance resumes; 12:45 PM, halt to excavate a road; 1:30 PM, advance resumes; 2:50 PM, halt at a ravine. This was a constant stop-start day to cut roads.

3:30 PM—Finally, Custer and Weir arrived at the Powder River (Custer told Terry the day before, he would guide them to the Powder by three PM!). For the rest of the column, the advance resumed at 4:40 PM, and finally at 6:55 PM the Terry/Custer camp is established on the Powder River, twenty-two to twenty-four miles above its mouth and about four miles north of the present-day town of Locate, Montana.[32] This became known as the *Powder River, Camp 19.* The column had now traveled approximately 287½ miles since leaving Fort Lincoln. It was a long and grueling march this day, some 32.3 miles. Terry wrote his sisters, letter dated June second–twelfth:

> …it was through an extremely difficult country and over a ridge which must be more than 1,000 feet above both our starting point and the valley of the Powder. For the first time we met pine covered hills—long ridges wooded to their tops. We had at times literally to dig and 'pick' our way through….[33]

Side Notes—The area covered was the eastern face of the divide separating O'Fallon's Creek from the Powder River valley. The valley was at least a mile wide. There was adequate timber for fuel and the valley was covered in good grass. The river itself was about 200 feet wide and two to three feet deep, with a gravel bottom and some quicksand. Often called "the … 'filthiest stream of water in America' … 'too thick to drink and too thin to plow.'"[34] "… [F]our hundred miles long, a mile wide, and an inch deep."[35] Yellow water. First white man to see it was Lieutenant William Clark in 1806. The river got its name from the dark, powdery sand along its banks.[36] The camp was located "in a bend of the Powder, among cottonwood trees and sagebrush, near the tributary of Snow Creek."[37]

> Of all of the various marches toward the Little Bighorn the June 7 march from O'Fallon creek to Powder River was the most taxing on the troops, wagons, and animals. The Engineers and the various companies assigned were busy the entire route. The route, once they reached high bluffs, had to be hacked through the timber. There was much digging and picking done. Myself, brother Bob, and teacher friend Larry Larson, rode the entire Custer trail in 1976. On this day's march we met the landowner of the June 7 campsite, as well as the owner of the land we needed to travel over, Allie Bradshaw. They rode with us across Bradshaw's land. The land in 1976 was grazing land and had been in the family since the late 1880s. The land was virtually untouched by the plow or roads of any kind. The Dakota column's trail was accurately traced in the sod. We ate lunch near where the command did a lot of pick and shovel work. We traveled in the original ruts across the country, entered the pine covered hills, rode in ruts where pine trees now grow, and up to the divide where the wagons rolled and pioneering companies labored. Many of these sites were shown to us and mapped on the spot.
>
> The Powder River ridge does not run north to south prior to reaching the Powder. Powder River ridge is on the west side of the Powder. The divide many allude to actually runs east and west. It can be viewed from the top of Sheridan Butte north of the Yellowstone. Once committed to the route along the divide there was no turning back. In places the ridge followed is 100 to 250 feet high, with deep coulees and ravines on either side. The top of the ridge followed varied from 20 to 40 feet wide, often so short you cannot turn a wagon around. Wind-ravaged sandstone could be seen to the left of the trail. There is a small hillock where Lieutenant Maguire stood to the right of the trail where he wrote, "To our left was Powder River ridge, with its fringe of pine trees. At our feet was the bad-land formation, with deep, yawning chasms and its various-colored earths, fashioned into weird and fantastic shapes by the rains and floods … to the right there stretched out a rolling country backed in the distance by the Yellowstone bluffs, whose rugged outlines stood forth in bold relief." From Maguire's viewpoint the march gradually came down off the divide and made its way eventually to the bottom lands along the Powder. The trail can still be seen as pick and shovel work can be seen where the trail was cut through a small ridge. The trail continues, heads a creek, and skirts the side of bluffs to the bottom. The June 7 campsite was in a loop of the river south of where Snow Creek enters the valley from the east. The campsite was excellent. It had plenty of wood, grass, and water, though the water was gritty. The timber was all cottonwood of smallish or medium size.[38]

Dakota Column—9 PM—The last of the wagons and the rear guard reached camp. Then, at ten PM Terry sends out the Ree scouts, Goose and Stabbed, to the "Far West," to advise of his location on the Powder.

Gibbon/Montana Column—Earlier that afternoon the couriers Williamson and Sargent turned back a little below the Tongue River after spotting what they thought were hostile Sioux—but who were actually Bradley's Crow—the couriers losing their ammo and rations in their haste.

7:40 AM—Gibbon's column leaves its bivouac. The weather had turned cold and blustery, cloudy and dark, and the ground was covered with large cacti. About 7¾ miles from the previous camp they encountered a large, rock-strewn creek bed. A halt was made to smooth the road. Reaching another plateau—with magnificent soil and grass—they glimpsed the Tongue River stretched out in the southern distance. Lieutenant McClernand estimated they could see some twelve miles up the Tongue. To the east they could see the broken hills west of the Powder River. At eight AM the wagons break camp. They crossed three ravines, then went up a good grade onto the Stanley road. Hitting a spring, the wagons sank in the mud and Carroll had to double the teams to pull free. Finally, they reached a prairie "with the best grass I ever saw."[39] Descending to the river—and after traveling twenty-two miles for the day—Gibbon goes into camp at seven PM about two miles below the confluence of the Tongue and Yellowstone rivers, on the north bank, but he is extremely uncomfortable, especially with his communications.

    8 PM—The wagons make camp in a heavily timbered area, some two miles below the mouth of the Tongue River. For the day they had made 21½ miles. By nine PM Gibbon's camp was in pretty good shape and finally, around ten PM the troops were able to eat dinner.

> In three days, the column had covered only forty-one miles of the 130 miles downriver to Glendive Creek to meet Terry. The command, moreover, had been delayed nearly a full week. And, there was no way of knowing whether the three couriers had been able to contact Terry! Such was the cost of having no practicable communication system in the wilderness! Gibbon felt certain that Terry had already arrived at the Glendive rendezvous, and had been wondering why the 'Montana Command' had not put in appearance? Perhaps Terry was even now sending scouts upriver to make contact! And it was also remotely possible that Terry feared that his own dispatches had not gotten through to Gibbon![40]

Side Notes—It should be noted there is forty miles between the Tongue and Powder rivers. Also, the continuing warming weather and recent heavy rains caused the Yellowstone to rise and it was now "booming" and rushing onward. As the column would have to move inland, Gibbon advised Clifford to take two days rations as he moved his boats downriver, the main column probably not being able to reach the Yellowstone again during that period. That night, the Yellowstone rose six feet.

Crook/Wyoming Column—Crook, rather than admitting his navigating error, chose to continue down Prairie Dog Creek, traveling seventeen miles through torturous terrain until he reached the creek's mouth on the Tongue River and there he camped. Private Tierney died in this camp. At midnight voices were heard on the bluffs across the river. The courier, Ben Arnold, was sent to investigate. He could not make out what was being said or what language was being spoken, so he called out in Sioux and the parties vanished in the night. Crook was incensed because he believed the voices may have been Crow scouts ... he turned out to be correct.[41]

Carr's 5th Cavalry—Lieutenant Colonel Asa Carr's 5th Cavalry contingent begins arriving in Cheyenne: companies A, B, D, I, K, and M. They were from Brigadier General John H. Pope's Department of the Missouri: Kansas, Indian Territory, and Colorado, and were traveling on the Kansas Pacific Railroad through Denver to Cheyenne.

JUNE 8, 1876—THURSDAY—*Military Correspondence & Intelligence Reports*—From Department of the Platte—"Telegraphs report relative to Indians under Sitting Bull and Crazy Horse and also to report that Indians had met Custer's troops and had fought them all day many killed on both sides."[42] This is a misplaced entry though the June 8 date on the document is quite clear ... or it was an augury of the battle yet to come. See full telegram, below.

From Col. Merritt—"Reports return from Red Cloud. Nothing new. Asks if there are any instructions."[43]

Telegram dated June 8, 1876, from Omaha, Neb., to the Assistant Adjutant General, Headqrs Mil. Div. Mo, Chicago Ill.—

> Commanding officer at Laramie reports 'Hand' Indian courier from Red Cloud brings report that just before he left an Indian arrived from the mouth of Tongue river. Found there twelve hundred and seventy-three 1,273 lodges under Sitting Bull, Crazy Horse & others on their way to Powder River to fight Gen. Crook. On his return he met same band that Egan saw May seventeenth. They told him that they had met Custer's troops and had fought them all day. Many killed on both sides. No results reported. This occurred about eight days ago. He also reports Spotted Tail at Laramie yesterday who says his people are at home and will not go out and that many have left Red Cloud and other agencies on the Missouri River. R. Williams, Ass't Adjt General.

Dakota Column—On this day Terry begins preparing a major operation based on inferences from Gibbon's dispatches.[44]

6 AM—Williamson and Sargent arrive at the site of the soon-to-be-established Powder River Depot with their "harrowing" story of encountering "hostile" Indians. Then, by eleven AM the Ree scouts, Goose and Stabbed, sent out the night before (covering forty-four to forty-eight miles in about thirteen hours), return with dispatches from Captain Powell (and Major Moore) aboard the "Far West" at Powder River junction with Yellowstone. One dispatch reports a war party of about forty Sioux near the Tongue River, but this turned out to be a mistake. These Indians were the Crow spotted by Williamson and Sargent. Meanwhile, the main body of troops remains in the Powder River camp. Powell's note mentions that he has seen no hint of Indians.

> On reading this, why would Terry lead the 7th Cavalry far south and west, when the hostiles were nearby and due west? He may have recalled that Gibbon mentioned, as an afterthought, a village on the Rosebud.... Delayed he (Gibbon) must have been.... Had Gibbon found the Sioux and attacked? or been attacked? If not, he must be very close, and the boat was now available at the mouth of the Powder. By going down now, Terry could contact Gibbon in person, save time, get the latest information, and arrange a concerted action against a possibly known target.[45]

NOON—based on the Powell dispatches—and thinking the Sioux may be in the region of the Tongue and Powder Rivers, Terry abruptly changes plans and takes companies A and I of the 7th Cavalry and heads north to the mouth of the Powder. He alerts Marcus Reno to be ready for a long scout, but with no wagons, only pack mules. Apparently, Terry had a number of questions on his mind: where was Gibbon?; had Gibbon left the Rosebud?; what was the strength of the Sioux village on the Rosebud?; what was their strength around the Tongue?; could the wagons be brought to the new Powder River Depot (PRD) before hostilities began?; were there Sioux between Terry's camp and the Yellowstone?; had the "Far West" brought sufficient supplies?[46] At the camp, the troops made ready for the scout, breaking mules for packsaddles ("aparejos"), re-packing equipment, cleaning weapons, re-outfitting worn equipment, etc.

2 PM—On his way north Terry halts for ten minutes. The first six miles traveled were easy riding and it took 1½ hours along the flat, left bank (west) of the Powder—a fast walk. By 2:35 PM the terrain became considerably rougher and the troops forded the river to its right bank—four hundred feet wide—via an island, shallow on the west side, but too deep for wagons on the east. At 3:25 PM the troops reached a second ford, losing thirty minutes searching for a wagon road, and finding none. Not finding suitable terrain or crossings for the wagons, Terry re-crossed to the west side and marched on the left bank through extremely rough country to a point five miles from the mouth. After another long delay—almost an hour—they find another ford, also not practicable for the wagons. Then, to make matters even more difficult, it began raining at four PM.

8 PM—Terry finally reaches the "Far West" and is told by Powell of Williamson's error in mistaking the Crow for Sioux. Clifford and Brisbin also meet him and relate all that was going on with the Montana column. Apparently, Gibbon had instructed Brisbin to take the boat to the next campsite, but intentionally or not, Brisbin interpreted Gibbon's order to mean all the way to the Powder River Depot site. Gibbon was reported to be very hot about Brisbin's meeting with Terry. That evening—after dark—Terry sent a message to Gibbon, carried by George Herendeen and a Crow scout.

> I believe Terry rode to the mouth of Powder River to ascertain if all the supplies had been moved from Stanley's Stockade, to see if there were any hostiles between the command and the mouth, and to determine if wagons could follow the valley down to the mouth. One trivial item Terry overlooked when he wrote in his diary about the trip downriver is the banks of the river. Pretend you are in a boat going downstream … to your right is the right bank, left is the left bank. If you head upstream, the right bank is to your left, left to your right! The campsite of June 7 was located on the right bank of the river. Terry left heading downriver up to the mouth of the Powder and its junction with the Yellowstone. He took Keogh's and Moylan's companies with him. Terry's party crossed the river a total of four times and traveled 21.8 miles. Terry found out one crucial thing: the wagon train would have to find an alternate route to the mouth.[47]

Some time after dark—and after Captain Clifford arrived—Terry dispatched the scout, George Herendeen (see Montana column, below), with a message to Gibbon to remain in place wherever he was. Terry would travel on the "Far West" the following morning to meet him.

Gibbon/Montana Column—After breakfast on a cool and pleasant morning, Gibbon sends Bradley out ahead and Clifford loaded 10,000 rounds of ammunition into his boats, joined by Major Brisbin and Lieutenant Gustavus Cheney Doane. At 7:40 AM Gibbon's command moves out. As they moved along, Bradley's Crow scouts discover the sack of provisions and ammo dropped by Williamson and Sargent. Bradley correctly figures the sack belonged to couriers from Terry and he sends it back to Gibbon. Some time during the afternoon Gibbon sends Captain Clifford down the Yellowstone, ferrying the "Fort Pease" boats. Remaining on board were Brisbin, Doane, and now George Herendeen, and several Crow scouts. They arrived at the Powder River Depot, thereby "uniting" the two commands. It was now discovered the "hostiles" Williamson and Sargent had seen were actually Crow scouts. After having covered 10½ miles, Gibbon halts at three PM for two hours, then resumes his march at five PM traveling another six miles. Between 7:40 and eight PM, Gibbon, having moved a total of sixteen miles, pitches camp seventeen to eighteen miles below the Tongue, near the present-day town of Kinsey, Montana.

Despite bad roads, the trains, as well, made sixteen miles and camped on the Yellowstone. Gibbon's command is now 334.32 miles from Fort Ellis. At this location the valley is about three miles wide and fifteen miles long, with heavy grass. While the troops marched, Clifford's boats made good time and as they approached the Powder, the steamboat "Far West" came in sight, moored to the riverbank. Brisbin, Clifford and the rest are welcomed aboard and information is exchanged.

Crook/Wyoming Column—Crook remained in his Prairie Dog Creek-Tongue River camp, giving the men and animals a day of rest. During the day sixty-five miners joined the camp (they were to play a significant and unforeseen role several days later). Also, two couriers arrived bringing news from General Sheridan that 120 Shoshone scouts would be joining the command in a few days. The dispatches also told of warriors departing the Red Cloud Agency ... and the wires connecting to the Crow Agency had been severed.

Carr's 5th Cavalry—The 5th Cavalry has fully departed Kansas to bolster Crook's rear.

JUNE 9, 1876—FRIDAY—*Military Correspondence & Intelligence Reports*—From Col. Merritt—"Reports nothing important to communicate. The feeling among Indians left at Agency not good."[48]

From Assistant Adjutant General, Department of Dakota—"Forwards copy of letter from C.O. Standing Rock Agency rel. to a large war party of Indians moving to Berthold Agency with the avowed intention of attacking the Rees, and attributing disaffection to lack of supplies of food."[49]

Dakota Column—The troops remain at the camp on the Powder River.

Gibbon/Montana Column—2 AM—George Herendeen and the Crow scout ride into Gibbon's camp with orders from Terry to leave his command in camp and meet downriver on the "Far West" that morning ... that the Dakota column had reached the Powder. Furthermore, an Indian courier reported at Fort Laramie that there was a great throng of Indians at the mouth of the Tongue: 1,273 lodges under Crazy Horse set to be on its way to the Powder to fight Crook.[50] At seven AM Gibbon takes Ball (H/2C), and following Boyer, Bradley and his mounted infantry and Crow, heads downriver to meet with Terry. That morning the scout Tom LeForgé is thrown from his horse, breaking his collarbone.

Steamer "Far West"—SHORTLY AFTER 3 AM—Grant Marsh, the skipper of the "Far West," orders the boilers started in preparation for the trip upriver, and at four AM the steamer, with Terry aboard, starts up the Yellowstone in the pouring rain. The river was very high and the current swift. The steamer could only average about 4.2 MPH and it would take 6½–7 hours to reach Gibbon's camp.

11 AM—Finally, Terry and Gibbon meet on the "Far West," upriver from the

Powder. It took 1½ hours for the steamer to make its way to Gibbon's upriver rendezvous. Ironically—or maybe otherwise—Lieutenant Bradley, the best intelligence officer in the entire campaign, was sent back upstream and did not even attend the conference, Bradley and Ball reaching their camp by noon, the "Far West" not far away and in sight. At the conference, Terry orders Gibbon to backtrack and set up base at mouth of Rosebud, but it appears virtually none of Bradley's top-flight intelligence as to the location of the Indians was accepted at this conference, Gibbon only casually mentioning Bradley's recon and report of Sioux on Rosebud, never stressing its importance. Also, no one thought to question Mitch Boyer who could have provided full info about the size and movements of the Sioux village. Yet Terry's march from Fort Lincoln uncovered no significant indications of Indians while Gibbon's did. It appears Terry now believed the Indians *may be* in this vicinity. "However, he could not discount the possibility that, during the interval, the Indians may have moved!—perhaps east or west!"[51] Ultimately, Terry's plan indicated woefully defective knowledge of the location and size of the Indian village meaning Bradley's intel was virtually ignored. "Furthermore, Gibbon never did admit Bradley's findings."[52] Terry did, however, decide to retain the services of Mitch Boyer for his own command.

12:30 PM—Still struggling upstream, the "Far West" reaches Gibbon's bivouac. The conference ended and a reception was held for the officers. Then at one PM the steamer headed back downstream, tying up again at the mouth of the Powder River around 2:45 PM. Once there, Terry orders Captain Powell to advise Major Moore to transport—by steamboat—the remainder of the troops (Captain Daniel Hamilton Murdock's D/6I and Second Lieutenant George Brinton Walker's I/6I) and supplies from Stanley's Stockade at Glendive to Powder River Depot.

3:40 PM—Terry begins the arduous twenty-four-mile return to Custer's camp up the Powder River. Twenty minutes later, a heavy downpour began and lasted the whole trip to camp. Boyer led the way. Between four and 4:10 PM heavy thunderstorms struck, making it difficult for Terry and the troops. It rained the whole trip back, and through noon the next day. Rains had swollen the river so much the fords were considerably more difficult to cross. Between 9:50 and ten PM—guided by Mitch Boyer, who smelled the smoke of the campfires—Terry arrived back at camp.

Indian Village—According to Wooden Leg, the next Indian camp after the "sun dance" camp was across the Rosebud from Davis Creek. The Cheyenne set up on the stream's east side and the Hunkpapa were down by the Busby school. This would be Indian camp number six. They may have stayed here for only one night.[53]

Crook/Wyoming Column—Crook remained in camp, but at 6:30 PM bullets from the bluffs above struck the bivouac. Three companies of infantry (C, G, and H, 9th Infantry) were dispatched to deal with the threat, crossing the river and mounting the bluffs, but the Indians fled. Captain Anson Mills moved his battalion (A, M, E, and I/3C) up the Tongue and crossed, dismounting and scaling the bluffs. He spotted the Indians 1,000 yards away on the next bluff. Back at the camp, more firing was heard as additional warriors tried to drive off the livestock. These Indians were a small band of Cheyenne under Little Hawk, alerted to the troops' presence by Wooden Leg. A steady, cold rain fell during the night.

JUNE 10, 1876—SATURDAY—*Military Correspondence & Intelligence Reports—*
From Assistant Adjutant General, Department of Dakota—"Repeats telegram from
Gen. Terry reporting his arrival at Little Mo. river, that progress has been slow. No
signs of Indians seen."[54]

From Assistant Adjutant General, Department of the Platte—"States C.O. Fort
Laramie telegraphed depredations of Indians on Chugwater. Cav. in pursuit."[55]

Telegram dated June 10, 1876, from Omaha, Neb. to Assistant Adjutant Gen.,
Mil. Division Missouri, Chicago, Ill.—

> Commanding officer Laramie telegraphs war party of about fifty Indians ran off this morning
> twenty head of horses from Kelly's ranche [sic] on Chugwater. He has sent Egan after them and
> thinks a Company of Cavalry should be stationed in Chug Valley six Companies [F]ifth Cav-
> alry have reached Cheyenne. Have ordered them to march for Laramie as soon as can conve-
> niently be done. Commanding officer Red Cloud reports by letter has received orders from
> Commanding officer Laramie instructed by department Commander to send Company of Cav-
> alry and one Company of infantry with one months [sic] supplies to scout towards Black Hills.
> Thinks two companies of infantry left at Red Cloud insufficient to protect agency and post in
> case of outbreak liable to occur. No other news. R. Williams, Assistant Adjt General.

Telegram dated June 10, 1876, from St. Paul, Minn., to Adjutant General, Division
Missouri, Chicago—

> Following just rec'd Camp on Little Missouri May thirtieth, a[t] Bismarck June tenth. We
> reached this place yesterday today has been employed in scouting up the valley & making a
> road through the bad lands west of river contrary to all the predictions of the guides & scouts
> no Indians have been found here & there are no signs that any have been in this neighborhood
> within six months or a year. I intend to push on about two marches halt and again push a party
> well to the south hoping to find trails & if none are found I may halt once more for the same
> purpose before reaching the Yellowstone. We have had a great deal of hard work making a road
> yesterday & the day before we built thirteen bridges over Davis Creek our progress has there-
> fore been slower than I could have wished but the force is in excellent conditions few of the
> troops are sick and the animals have greatly improved since we left Lincoln. Signed Alfred H.
> Terry, Brigadier Gen'l.... Commanding officer Lincoln reports scout will start on return Sun-
> day morning telegrams for expedition should go through to Lincoln tonight—Ruggles, Asst
> Adj. Gen.

Dakota Column—It rained until eleven AM, and the Dakota column remained at the
Powder River camp. At noon—and based on this new intelligence and consultation
with Custer—Terry changed his plans to head south and west, and instead, ordered
Reno out on a scout as part of his new plan. (The Powder River Depot detachments
from Reno's companies were also probably made at this camp and accompanied
Custer, the next day, to the mouth of the river.) Since fifteen days elapsed since Bradley had seen the Indians on the Rosebud, Terry figured they could have gone anywhere. He discards his old plan to take the entire 7th Cavalry south and west in a
blind search for the Sioux and decides instead on a two-stage plan. The first stage
would be a recon by Major Reno far up the Powder River valley, back, and over to the
Tongue, down it to the rendezvous point. The second stage would be a two-pronged
attack on the Sioux village on the lower Rosebud. Custer would take nine companies of the 7th Cavalry up the Tongue, cross west to the Rosebud and descend it to
attack the village from above (south). Then Terry would take the three remaining
companies of the 7th Cavalry up to Gibbon's camp, take Gibbon with his four cavalry

companies and five infantry companies, cross the Yellowstone, head up the Rosebud
and attack the village below (north). Apparently, Custer saw little need for this scouting operation. He felt strongly, the Sioux were west, on the Rosebud and the scout
was a waste of time. On the other hand, some writers/historians believe Custer was
furious at not being selected to run this scout.[56] The reporter, Mark Kellogg, however, was clear on this point: "General Custer declined to take command of the scout
of which Major Reno is now at the head of, not believing that any Indians would be
met with in either direction. His opinion is that they are in bulk in the vicinity of the
Rosebud range."[57] Furthermore, "Terry explicitly and positively ordered Reno not
to move in the direction of the Rosebud, for fear it would 'flush the covey' prematurely."[58] As Terry, likewise, never expected Reno to encounter any Indians this was
merely a precautionary scout.

> Headquarters Department of Dakota
> In the Field, Camp on Powder River, M. T.
> June 10, 1876
> Field Special Order No. 11[59]
>
> ... 2. Major M.A. Reno, 7th Cavalry, with six companies (right wing) of his regiment and one
> gun from the Gatling battery, will proceed at the earliest practicable moment to make a recon-
> naissance of the Powder River from the present camp to the mouth of the Little Powder. From
> the last named point he will cross to the headwaters of Mizpah Creek, and descend that creek to
> its junction with the Powder River. Thence, he will cross to Pumpkin Creek and Tongue River,
> and descend the Tongue to its junction with the Yellowstone, where he may expect to meet the
> remaining companies of the 7th Cavalry and supplies of subsistence and forage.
>
> Major Reno's command will be supplied with subsistence for 12 days, and with forage for the
> same period at the rate of two lbs. of grain per day for each animal.
>
> The guide Mitch Bouyer and 8 Indian scouts, to be detailed by Lt. Col. Custer, will report to
> Major Reno for duty with this column.
>
> Acting Assistant Surgeon H.R. Porter, is detailed for duty with Major Reno. By command of
> Brigadier General Terry.
>
> Edw. Smith, Captain, 18th Infantry
> Acting Assistant Adjutant General

Terry's diary entry for June tenth makes no mention of Reno not proceeding to
the Rosebud: "Issued orders for Reno to make scout up the Powder to go to the forks
of the Powder thence to go to the head of Mizpah Creek thence down to the mouth of
the Mizpah and then by Pumpkin Creek to Tongue River."[60]

In brief, Reno's orders were to go up (south) the Powder to its forks (the mouth of
the Little Powder; near present-day Broadus, Montana; about seventy-seven miles),
thence across to the headwaters of the Mizpah (west), down the Mizpah (north) to its
junction with the Powder (near present-day town of Mizpah, Montana), then over to
where Pumpkin Creek runs into the Tongue River (west), and down (north), about
fourteen miles, to its mouth at the Yellowstone. This move to the Tongue was merely
the most direct route to the rendezvous and would have been *below* where the Sioux
encampment on the Tongue had been. The orders sanctioned no deviation, no precise purpose, and no instructions as to what to do if Reno were to run into any hostiles. The entire route was about 175 miles, and the plan was to cover it in six or seven
days, tying in nicely with Terry/Custer's arrival at the rendezvous on June sixteenth.

Reno was to take his right wing, two battalions, consisting of companies B, C, and I under Captain Myles Keogh, and companies E, F, and L under Captain George Yates. He would also take Mitch Boyer and eight Indian scouts (Ree: Forked Horn, Young Hawk, One Feather, and William Baker or Tall Bear, according to Willert.[61] Dakotas: *Caroo, Ma-tok-sha*, Whole Buffalo [*Pta-a-te*], and White Cloud [*Machpeya-ska*]; the Ree scout, Red Star, mentions only four names: *Caroo*, Forked Horn, Young Hawk, and One Feather.[62]) Chief-of-Scouts Charles Varnum did not accompany Reno on this scout, but the acting assistant surgeons, Dr. Henry R. Porter and Dr. James M. DeWolf did. Reno also took one squad of the 20th Infantry with one of the Gatling guns, under Lieutenant Francis X. Kinzie. Two condemned cavalry horses would pull the gun carriage. Also, Reno had a pack train of sixty-six mules (eleven for each company)—carrying twelve days rations—and five QM packers,[63] and he assigned one NCO and four privates for each company as "packers."[64]

Once this was done, Terry ordered First Lieutenant Francis Marion Gibson to take Company H and scout the west side of the Powder River, and Captain Weir to take his Company D to scout the east side, ostensibly to find an easy way to take the wagons downriver to the Yellowstone. "By nightfall, Weir's company had not returned. And as to the latter assignment, Terry scrawled testily into his brown notebook: '... Gibson did nothing.'"[65]

5 PM—Terry wrote in his diary Reno departed camp at this time. That evening Lieutenant Gibson returns without having found a good wagon-road. Weir does not return.

Major Reno's Scout—6:30 PM—After traveling eight miles along the east bank of the Powder, Reno makes camp (approximately four miles south of present-day Locate, Montana) between Meyer's and Horse creeks. James Willert claimed the column camped at ten PM, but given the start time this seems too late entirely.[66]

Gibbon/Montana Column—3:30 PM—Gibbon's cavalry heads back up-river, per orders, but does not go much more than a few miles because of the rains and swollen ravines. They reach a point about four miles below the mouth of the Rosebud. They remain in camp until the twenty-first.[67] Barney "Bravo" and six Crow accompanied the column. Because of the bad road conditions—very muddy—Gibbon delayed his own move for a day. Lieutenant Edward Godfrey, in the 1908, revised edition of his *Century Magazine* article, quoted from a June 10, 1876, letter: "The 2nd Cavalry officers were greatly disgusted; one company has to be mounted all the time; the C.O. selects very poor camps for cavalry and *their horses are in very poor condition*."[68]

Crook/Wyoming Column—As for the Crook-Wyoming column ... well, they remained at the Tongue River camp.

JUNE 11, 1876—SUNDAY—*Dakota Column*—3 AM—Since Weir had yet to return, Terry asked Custer to locate a suitable route. Custer was up immediately, preparing for the move downstream. He placed Godfrey's Company K in charge of the pack mules. Then at 3:30 AM reveille was sounded and at five AM Terry and Custer broke camp. Custer took one cavalry company and the Ree scouts and led out (5:50 AM, according to Terry's diary). Terry then takes the remainder of the 7th Cavalry north, down the Powder toward the Yellowstone. The countryside was the usual sagebrush, dry, alkaline earth, and the column and wagons were able to travel on several plateaus on the east side of the river making it much easier for them.

6:15 AM–8 AM—Successive halts were needed for road building. The column reached the plateau previously scouted and marched on it for three-quarters of a mile, then halted, the march resuming at 9:30 AM.

10 AM—Custer, with the advance, finds Weir, and a favorable high plateau the wagons would be able to cross. Then at 10:30 AM Terry halted the column near the head of a deep ravine. They managed to traverse the ravine and reach a high plateau beyond.

12:20 PM—The column halts again for a brief rest on a high plateau. That lasted about thirty-five minutes and at 12:55 PM the advance resumed, the command traversing yet another deep gorge. By early afternoon the heavy rains returned. Difficulties now began in earnest. At 1:55 PM they reached a creek and the column halted to make a road. By 2:45 PM the march resumed, only to halt again a little after three PM. The march resumed at 4:05 PM and finally, at 6:15 PM the Terry-Custer column arrived at the Yellowstone near the mouth of the Powder. The steamer "Far West" was there to greet them and the band struck up "Garryowen" to welcome all the arriving troops.

Side Notes—"Garryowen" is an old Irish quickstep (Gaelic for Owen's garden), traced back to about 1800. (It is definitely Irish, though some thought it was originally Scottish.) It was used by several Irish regiments, including the 5th Royal Lancers. It was George Custer's favorite military air:

1
Let Bacchus' sons be not dismayed
But join with me each jovial blade;
Come booze and sing and lend your aid
To help me with the chorus.

CHORUS
Instead of Spa we'll drink down ale.
And pay the reck'ning on the nail;
No man for debt shall go to gaol
From Garry Owen in glory.

2
We are the boys that take delight in
Smashing the Limerick lights when lighting;
Through the streets like spotters fighting
And clearing all before us.

3
We'll break windows, we'll break doors
The watch knock down by threes and fours;
Then let the doctors work their cures,
And tinker up your bruises.

4
We'll beat the bailiffs out of fun
We'll make the mayors and Sheriffs run;
We are the boys no man dares dun,
If he regards a whole skin.

5
Our hearts so stout have got us fame
For soon t'is known from whence we came;
Where'er we go they dread the name,
Of Garryowen in glory.

6
Johnny Connell's tall and straight,
And in his limbs he is complete,
He'll pitch a bar of any weight,
From Garryowen to Thomondgate.>

7
Garryowen is gone to rack,
Since Johnny Connell went to Cork,
Though Darby O'Brien leapt over the dock,
In spite of judge and jury.

Powder River Depot—The Powder River Depot was now officially established, located approximately six miles southwest of present-day Terry, Montana, and when the 7th Cavalry moved on several days later, the wagon train—with Wagon Master Charles Brown—was left there with the infantry companies under Major Moore: C and G/17I. Right now, however, this became the **Yellowstone/Powder River, Camp 20** (total distance traveled to date: 318.5 miles). Custer and his six remaining companies remained here until June fifteenth.

Major Reno's Scout—Between five and 5:30 AM, with Yates' Company F in the lead, Reno breaks camp and moves up the east bank of the Powder for six miles. He crossed to the west bank at a "well-known" ford, about 2.3 miles below the Mizpah, then forded the Mizpah, remaining on the west bank of the Powder. They moved some ten miles up the river's west bank and crossed Ash Creek. The command traveled another ten miles up the Powder before bivouacking, passing through groves of cottonwood trees bordering the river, while making painstakingly slow progress because of the rain-soaked ground.

At this point the river was about one hundred yards wide and two feet deep and along its west bank grew the ubiquitous cottonwood trees, plus sagebrush, prickly pear cactus, and "bunch" grass. High cliffs blocked any passage to the west.

Some time between 1:30 and three PM Reno made camp, having traveled twenty-six miles. Dr. James DeWolf noted the flats they had crossed were very soft and made for difficult riding. The column bivouacked between Ash Creek and the Powder, and below where Alkali Creek enters the Powder.

Gibbon/Montana Column—5:30 AM—Brisbin's cavalry resumes its march, and at 6:20 AM Gibbon's infantry and the wagon train begin the trek back up-river. At ten AM the infantry column approached "Sunday" Creek, about six or seven miles east of the Tongue confluence. The continuing rains had turned it into a "river." At noon the column halts to bridge the creek only to be rained on even more at one PM. By late afternoon—after more heavy rain—Gibbon calls it quits and goes into a bivouac. Naturally, the roads were very bad and a dry creek crossed by the trains a few days before had turned into a river; only one crossing was made by the trains and overall, for the day, they made only ten miles.

Indian Village—The Indians crossed the Rosebud–Little Big Horn divide—probably around this date—heading into what Wooden Leg called, Great Medicine Dance Creek, what we now call Reno Creek.[69] They camped along the creek, about two miles intervening between the western-most Cheyenne camp and the eastern Hunkpapa camp. The center of the camp was "where the present road crosses a bridge at the fork of the creek."[70]

Crook/Wyoming Column—Crook finally departs camp in the meantime sending a dispatch to Sheridan—dated the eleventh—telling him of the skirmish on the ninth. He also expressed his belief the Indians were located on either the Tongue River or the Little Rosebud.[71] His command moved back up Prairie Dog for eleven miles, then turned west. After seven miles more—and in a hailstorm—Crook's column reached Goose Creek … camping for the night.

Carr's 5th Cavalry—Six companies depart Cheyenne heading for Fort Laramie.

JUNE 12, 1876—MONDAY—*Military Correspondence & Intelligence Reports*—From Lt. Gen. P.H. Sheridan—"Arrived here on time. All very well. Carr left yesterday with six Co.'s."[72]

From the Army Adjutant General—"Furnishes copy of letter from W.D. [*War Department*] to Dep't of Int. rel. to operations against hostile Indians and asking that Military be allowed control over Red Cloud and Spotted Tail Agencies, and in regard to Fort Pierre route to Black Hills."[73]

Major Reno's Scout—5 AM—Reno breaks camp, a day proving to be one of the hottest since leaving Fort Lincoln. After riding about ten miles out, the column reached a broad creek called Blacktail where they discovered the remains of an abandoned Indian camp. Mitch Boyer walked among its ashes and Dr. DeWolf wrote in his diary: "'Twenty-six lodges … camped here about one week earlier … perhaps thirty families' … between 175 and 200 Indians. Their *trail sign suggested a westerly* departure … perhaps no more than 75 or 80 warriors…."[74] (in all likelihood summer roamers heading out to join the winter roamers). Continuing south, they discovered "several" other camps, at least a week old.[75] At about four more miles out, Reno reaches Stump Creek; and four miles farther, they camp around two PM–three PM. Reno is now nineteen miles short of the Powder's junction with the Little Powder River (as far as they were ordered to go) having made twenty-four to twenty-six miles.

Steamer "Far West"—12:30 PM—The "Far West" leaves the Powder River Depot and heads to Stanley's Stockade for more supplies, reaching Glendive at four PM.

Dakota Column—Terry and Custer remain at the depot. The troops bought supplies from the traders and sutlers: John Smith and James Coleman, items such as straw hats, canned fruit, and tomatoes.

Gibbon/Montana Column—2 AM—Reveille for the cavalry. Finally, on a clear, beautiful day, at nine AM Gibbon's column resumed its splintered march up the Yellowstone, following on the trail ruts of Stanley's 1873 expedition.

6 PM—Brisbin's cavalry goes into camp, some ten to twelve miles in advance of the trains and the infantry.

7 PM—Gibbon establishes a camp "on a flat about three miles north of the Yellowstone (probably in the vicinity of present-day Sheffield, Montana)."[76]

Montana Column Trains—5 AM—Matt Carroll and the wagon train depart camp: no grass or water. They take 3½ exhausting hours to climb the hill, then, for three miles, followed "a gravelly backbone and after a while came into Stanley's road."[77] A little later in the day Carroll's train came upon two springs with ash trees growing around them. They camped on the river bottom in a ravine where they found water, using sagebrush for fuel. The trains made sixteen miles this day and were now twenty-six miles from the Rosebud. At 11:30 PM the wagon train's mules, which had been put out, were brought back in.

Crook/Wyoming Column—Crook remains in the Goose Creek camp. The weather was turning milder and the area was beautiful, with clear cold water, luxuriant grasses, and plenty of wood.

General P.H. Sheridan—General Sheridan arrives in Cheyenne and confers with Merritt. Merritt reports, "the feeling among the Indians left at the agency is not good. The 5th Cavalry is not here too soon."[78]

Sheridan's travels to Fort Laramie and the agencies seem to be the result of a paranoia about the unseen rather than the unknown. The military hierarchy in Omaha and Chicago was receiving accurate and up-to-the-minute situational reports from these agencies, mostly from army commanders on the scene, not from the Indian agents whose veracity and support were questioned.[79]

JUNE 13, 1876—TUESDAY—*Military Correspondence & Intelligence Reports***—From Lieut. Gen. P.H. Sheridan—"Leave for Laramie this PM. All well."[80]

Steamer "Far West"—3 AM—The steamer departed Stanley's Stockade with the last of the supplies and Captain Daniel Murdock's D/6I. At eight PM it finally arrived (after bucking the upstream currents of the Yellowstone at an average speed of about 4.2 MPH, compared with a downstream speed of twenty-eight MPH!), completing the move from Stanley's Stockade at Glendive Creek to the Powder River depot. The "Far West" would accompany the column to the Tongue River and beyond.

Dakota Column—Terry and Custer remained at the Yellowstone/Powder River camp (the Ree referred to this camp as *Camp 20*[81]). While there, Custer had the 7th Cavalry crate up its sabers.[82] (Reno and the six troops on his scout crated theirs after they returned from their scout. Lieutenant De Rudio—and possibly Lieutenant Edward Mathey—retained his saber and carried it at the battle.) The troops, keeping busy, transferred supplies from the wagons to pack mules.

Major Reno's Scout—5 AM—"Following a 'trail breakfast' (hard tack, bacon and coffee…),"[83] Reno broke camp and proceeded about 13.4 miles along the west bank of the Powder River, as much as 5½ miles short of the forks (the Little Powder), before impassable bluffs forced him to turn west. Finding no Indians, Reno swung west, eight miles over the divide, to Mizpah Creek (a "rough crossing over a very crooked trail"). The last six miles of the day were down the Mizpah. At one PM Reno makes camp on the Mizpah, at the mouth of Ash Creek, near Wolf Creek, having traveled 24½ miles (James Willert uses Lake Creek as the camp area, slightly north of Tom Heski's Ash Creek). The branches of the Mizpah were almost all dry, with little water where they camped. James Willert wrote,

> The track followed was an old trail made by buffalo traveling between the Powder and Pumpkin Creek Valley. The Indians had used it as well. The trail was narrow and very crooked, difficult to pass through. Ravines were frequent and invariably steep…. The column had to proceed in single file much of the way. The Gatling gun and carriage had to be dismantled and the parts carried by the soldiers. The badlands extended over seven miles before pine-crested buttes were reached.[84]

Reno sends companies B (Captain Thomas Mower McDougall) and C (Lieutenant Henry Moore Harrington) north—down the Mizpah—about thirteen miles to scout for signs. Such a move "would have taken them to the vicinity of Hay Creek or Dick Creek…."[85]

10 PM—McDougall and Harrington return from their scout having found abandoned camps only.

Side Notes—This was now half of Reno's mission and he had followed orders precisely. It was here, however, Reno decided to disregard those orders and veer west towards Pumpkin Creek. It is a good bet Reno had spoken with Mitch Boyer and

learned of Bradley's discovery on the Tongue. The prescribed route in his orders—
moving to the Mizpah, then back over to the Tongue—would bypass that village.
Bradley had seen the Sioux about thirty miles above the mouth of the Tongue, but
Terry's orders would have taken Reno to the Tongue *below* that camp. Once there,
Reno could count the lodge-sites and return with some useful intelligence. Making
matters difficult, however, was the fact the 1872 map used on the campaign proved
useless in this vicinity. Several abandoned camps had been seen, but all of them were
quite small and were passed with little comment.

Gibbon/Montana Column—Brisbin's cavalry breaks camp early in the morning and
at seven AM Gibbon's split command resumes its difficult march. At one PM they
paused for two hours to build roads, and finally, at four PM, after thirteen miles of
soggy and arduous terrain, Gibbon goes into camp at the mouth of Coal Creek.

Montana Column Trains—7 AM—The wagon train also breaks camp, meeting soft
and muddy roads and another very hot day, the hottest day of the season to date. That
night the wagons camped at the foot of a long gulch along the Yellowstone, the trains
having made fifteen miles for the day.

Crook/Wyoming Column—Once again Crook remained in camp, increasingly nervous about the scout situation and the safety of the three he dispatched to the Crow
Agency. Crook now sends out Lieutenant Samuel Swigert (D/2C) and a detail to old
Fort Phil Kearny to try and locate the Shoshone scouts. Swigert returned with no
news.

JUNE 14, 1876—WEDNESDAY—*Military Correspondence & Intelligence Reports*—
From Commanding Officer, Fort Fetterman—"Rel. to the Lieut. Gen'l's dispatch
regarding the 5th Cav."[86]

Dakota Column—The Terry-Custer command remained at the Powder River Depot.
Determinations were being made as to troops who would be left behind. Terry also
issued orders for Custer with six companies of the 7th Cavalry and the "battery" of
Gatlings to move for the Tongue River at six AM the following morning. Custer was to
take twenty-five additional mules to replace any Reno might have lost.

Powder River Depot—The following would remain as security at the depot: HQ—
One officer, two enlisted men; Co. A—four enlisted men; Co. B—nineteen EM; Co.
C—nine EM; Co. D—eleven EM; Co. E—three EM; Co. F—eight EM; Co. G—sixteen EM; Co. H—two EM; Co. I—four EM; Co. K—twenty-one EM; Co. L—six EM;
Co. M—six EM; and the band—all fourteen members, all enlisted personnel; totals
one officer, 111 EM, plus the band. Most of these were recruits and they also included
those who still did not have horses (probably most of the original seventy-eight).
The band's horses were re-distributed, the fittest going to the troopers who needed
them the most. In addition to these men, there were several others who were listed
as "sick," "AWOL," or "detached duty": Company C—two; E—one; F—one; I—one;
M—one. The troops from the companies on the Reno scout were probably detached
before Reno left on the scout. Four Ree scouts were left at the depot as well, along
with seven more carried as "detached." One Dakota (Left Hand) left the command
at Powder River Depot as his enlistment was up (there are accounts claiming he was

eventually killed at the Little Big Horn when he joined the Sioux relatives and fought against the troops). All wagons would remain at Powder River, as well as some 900 mules. Except for a few of the officers', all tents were left there as well. Stationed at the depot besides those left by the 7th Cavalry, were Major Moore's three companies of the 6th Infantry: Powell's, C; Murdock's, D; and Walker's, I; and the two companies of the 17th Infantry: McArthur's, C; and Sanger's, G. Captain Baker's B/6I would remain on the "Far West."

Side Notes—Private William O. Taylor of Company A—who left us a diary—claimed companies B, G, H, and K had a large number of recruits, maybe as many as twenty-five apiece (obviously, he was wrong about Company H; Benteen, in his after-action report to Reno, said he had a large number of recruits in his *battalion*, companies D, H, and K). The writer and historian, Evan Connell, estimated the 7th Cavalry consisted of 30 percent recruits. That would equate to about 210 EM. (The actual number on the campaign with one year's service or less was 154, including those left at the Powder River Depot.) Archaeologist Douglas D. Scott estimated 22 percent, including new officers, making Connell's number too high. Scott cites Sills at 21.6 percent or 127 enlisted men of 588; and MacNeil with 20.4 percent or 118 of 577, battle strength. (The *actual* number of uniformed personnel at the battle was thirty-one officers and 576 enlisted troopers; 607 uniformed personnel.)

Steamer "Far West" and the *Steamer "Josephine"*—While all this was being determined, the troops continued to move forage from the two steamers.

Major Reno's Scout—5 AM—Reno breaks camp on another extremely hot day, and heads slightly north of west, up Hay Creek for twelve miles to a point a little northwest of present-day Coalwood, Montana. From there, he moved 8½ miles northwest (along present-day route U.S. 212) down S.L. Creek (an eastern branch of the Pumpkin) to the Pumpkin, one mile below the mouth of Little Pumpkin (two miles), about four miles south of present-day Volborg. Writer Tom Heski proposed a different route, since First Sergeant James Hill's diary differs from DeWolf's (above):

> Heski's on-the-ground research has suggested the column moved up Ash Creek five miles, then turned northwest by the head of Lake Creek, marched through timbered valleys to Camp Creek, paralleled the Pumpkin for 6.3 miles until bluffs obliged a crossing to the Little Pumpkin and camp was made 1.4 miles from that confluence.[87]

Dr. DeWolf wrote: "Crossed from Mizpah Creek … on west fork about twelve miles … to divide fair road divide some pines & ravines but not so bad as to Powder from O'Fallon's Creek … march up Pumpkin Creek from [*illegible*] mile to about 1 mile above forks fair day trails S or W."[88]

    1 PM—Reno makes camp, having traveled 22½ sweltering miles.

Gibbon/Montana Column—7 AM—Gibbon's 7th Infantry and the wagon train were guided by Lieutenant Bradley through a coulee and onto firmer ground and into a long valley … a cool and cloudy day, contrary to what Reno was enduring farther east. The roads were still very heavy and the wagons lost a couple of hours getting down a steep hill. By two PM they had camped some four miles east of the mouth of the Rosebud, near where the Indians had killed Gibbon's three men. It was the same area Brisbin's cavalry had camped at the night before. Gibbon now orders captains Thompson

(L/2C) and Wheelan (G/2C) to ride upriver to Fort Pease (a five-day jaunt) to see if Indians had crossed the river anywhere in between. They were to leave the following morning. According to Matthew Carroll, the wagons arrived at the camp at about this same time. They traveled thirteen miles for the day.

Crook/Wyoming Column—Crook remains in the Goose Creek camp as scouts Grouard and Richaud return—along with an old Crow Indian—relieving Crook's anxiety. "Big Bat" Pourrier and some 175 Crow warriors were ten miles behind them. It was also discovered at this time the voices chased by Ben Arnold were, in fact, a Crow scouting party of fifteen led by scout Pourrier. The older Crow informed Crook of the Sioux crossing the Yellowstone and raiding Gibbon's Crow scouts' pony herd (May 3). He also told Crook Gibbon was currently opposite the mouth of the Rosebud, and said "the Sioux were on the south side of the Yellowstone, believed to be somewhere on the Tongue, between the mouth of Otter Creek and the Yellowstone River."[89] Grouard told Crook from the signs he had seen, he believed the Sioux were on the Rosebud. The Shoshone Indians arrived as well, most carrying better weapons—.45-caliber Springfields—while most of the Crow had .50-caliber rifles. After "Retreat" (the bugle call) Crook called in his battalion commanders and issued orders: the wagons were to be left behind; every man was to carry four days rations (hardtack, bacon, and coffee) and 100 rounds of ammunition; no tentage; men would carry one blanket each; all infantrymen would ride a mule; and if a village were attacked, all food supplies would be preserved for later or if they continued to the mouth of the Rosebud to link up with Terry and Gibbon ... a lesson learned from the Reynolds–Powder River fiasco in March.

General P.H. Sheridan and *Carr's 5th Cavalry*—Sheridan—coming from Chicago—along with Lieutenant Colonel Asa Carr and six companies of the 5th Cavalry—A, B, D, I, K, and M—plus staff and others, arrive at Fort Laramie.

JUNE 10 TO JUNE 14—*Indian Village*—The Sioux had moved up the Rosebud valley (south), camping where Davis Creek enters the Rosebud, then moving up Davis Creek and crossing the divide into the Reno Creek valley. The Cheyenne camped on the east side of the Rosebud, just across from Davis Creek. The Sioux followed and camped downstream from the Cheyenne, while the Hunkpapa circle was just below the present Busby school. A council was assembled to discuss what should be done about the encroaching soldiers. The younger warriors wanted to attack, but the older men were more cautious as scouts were sent out to watch the soldiers. By now, the Indians were aware of Crook's column—remember the Cheyenne hunting party?—but had lost touch with Gibbon, probably thinking he was still moving eastward down the Yellowstone. The Indians had no idea Gibbon had returned to the Rosebud and the Sioux were completely unaware of Reno's movements and Terry's presence.

> This poor reconnaissance on the part of the hostiles was a usual habit with them—contrary to the popular notion—for they were not as reconnaissance-minded as some writers would have us believe. Indeed, their carelessness ... could have brought them defeat at Little Big Horn, had not their numbers compensated, for Custer, Terry and Gibbon were able to advance ... almost to the hostiles' village limits without detection....[90]

In all likelihood, the Indians crossed the Rosebud–Little Big Horn divide around June eleventh, having stayed in the Davis Creek/East-of-the-divide camp only one night, June tenth.

June 15, 1876—Thursday—*Military Correspondence & Intelligence Reports*— From Lieut. Gen. P.H. Sheridan—"Leave for Red Cloud today. Home on 22nd. Telegrams will reach me by courier."[91]

From Commanding Officer, Fort Fetterman—"Two couriers just in from Crook. His dispatches to Gen. Sheridan for'd by courier."[92]

From Gen. Crook—"Reports demonstration by Indians on his camp. Main camp of Indians supposed to be on Rosebud. Rel. to disposition of 5th Cav. Co's."[93]

From Brig. Gen. Geo. Crook—"Reports arrival of Indian Scouts, marches command tomorrow, and expects to strike hostiles within four days. Leaves 100 men to guard camp."[94]

Dakota Column—6 AM—Captain Fred Benteen had his wing ready to move and the command held a parade, the regiment passing in review. Benteen began the march, with six companies, scouts, and a train of pack mules, up (west) the south side of the Yellowstone towards the Tongue River to rendezvous with Gibbon, Reno, and Terry (when he reached there on the "Far West"). A little after six AM Custer joined Terry for a brief conference aboard the steamer. At seven AM Custer departed and set out to join his column. (It was at this time Lieutenant George "Nick" Wallace was chosen to keep the regimental itinerary.[95]) The column moved leisurely, but still made twenty-five miles, camping on the riverbank, *Yellowstone River, Camp 21*.

Steamer "Far West"—1:30 PM—Terry and Baker's B/6I begin moving up-river on the "Far West" to join Custer, but at 5:30 PM the steamer broke down after a fifteen mile up-river jaunt.

Side Notes—The terrain between the Powder and Tongue Rivers was pitted with ravines and gullies and in some areas the bluffs extend to the water's edge. Custer moved as much as four miles inland to avoid some of the more difficult terrain. Mark Kellogg wrote the, "country north of the Powder River, for a distance of twelve to fifteen miles, is very poor, low and causing hard marching, with a soil producing no grasses, only sagebrush and cactus." Kellogg also wrote, they passed through an abandoned Indian village, probably less than a year old, containing between 1,200 and 1,500 lodges.[96] He described the Yellowstone as resembling "yellowish clay at this point … cool and pleasant to the taste and is a larger body of water than that of the Missouri River above its mouth, but very much superior for purposes of steamboat navigation."[97] Kellogg: "The waters of the Tongue River are of a deepish red color, running swiftly, and not very palatable to the taste."[98]

Major Reno's Scout—5 AM—Reno breaks camp, traveling about ten miles, west, up a branch of the Little Pumpkin called Nameless Creek, by a broad valley, to a point three miles north of wooded Liscom Butte (elevation, 4,377 feet). From there, he moved northwest down Lay Creek to its junction with the Tongue (forty-four miles from its mouth and fifteen miles below—north of—present-day Brandenburg, Montana). Another three miles down the Tongue brought them to their campsite for the day. According to Tom Heski, the column marched westward, up Lone Tree Creek, and then turned northwest in pine-timbered valleys. They then crossed Foster Creek, passed through more badlands, crossed Foster's south fork and proceeded north along Lay Creek for 7.7 miles. Because of extremely bad badlands, the column was forced to head north by northwest down a wide valley to the Tongue River.[99] The day's march was very hard, through pine-covered hills, narrow trails that jammed the horses into one another, and through deep ravines where they had to unlimber the Gatling guns, unhitch the horses, and carry the guns by hand.

1 PM–2 PM—Having traveled twenty-five miles, Reno called it quits for the day. The camp was located about two miles below where Lay Creek enters the Tongue valley.

Side Notes—Tom Heski placed the campsite in Section 36, Township 3N, Range 45–46E, on the USGS map. The camp was located on the east bank of the Tongue. At this point the river was about seventy-five yards wide and two feet deep, water cold and sweet. Cottonwood and ash trees were abundant, along with wide meadowlands on both sides of the river.[100]

Summer Roamers—The Northern Cheyenne chief, Little Wolf, departed the Red Cloud Agency with 1,000 of his people, including 200 warriors. They headed northwest.[101] (Other sources—probably considerably more reliable—suggest Little Wolf had seven lodges!)

Gibbon/Montana Column—EARLY AM—Gibbon sends out Wheelan (G/2C) and Thompson (L/2C) to examine the north bank of the Yellowstone, from the Rosebud, westward to the mouth of the Big Horn, a total of about sixty miles; six Crow went with them.

Crook/Wyoming Column—Preparations were made to depart. Captain John Vincent Furey—the assistant quartermaster—would remain behind with about 100 men including teamsters and packers. About 175 infantrymen were given a brief lesson on mule riding. Strength totals for the command were as follows: Captain Henry Noyes' 2nd Cavalry Battalion: 269 men; Captain Anson Mills' 3rd Cavalry battalion: 207; Lieutenant Colonel William Royall's 3rd Cavalry battalion: 327; Major Alexander Chambers' infantry battalion: 175; Crow scouts: 176; Shoshone scouts: eighty-six; packers: twenty; Montana miners: sixty-five (remember those miners that had joined up earlier?); for a total of 1,325 personnel, red, white, civilian, and uniformed.

General P.H. Sheridan—5 AM—Sheridan departs Fort Laramie for Camp Robinson and the agencies. With him were his aides, "Buffalo" Bill Cody, and a seventeen-man escort from Company F, 9th Infantry Regiment.

JUNE 16, 1876—FRIDAY—*Military Correspondence & Intelligence Reports*—From the Commanding Officer, Fort Fetterman—"Snake Indians en route to join Gen. Crook."[102]

Steamer "Far West"—2:30 AM—Repairs are completed and she begins moving again, the day starting out very warm. At 8:20 AM the steamer reaches Buffalo Rapids and has difficulty negotiating them. In one spot, the water was only six feet deep. By 12:15 PM, however, they finally reach Custer's camp.

Dakota Column—After daylight Custer moves toward the Tongue River, reaching its vicinity early, and he decides to pitch camp there on the remains of an old Sioux winter campsite, two miles east of the Tongue, ***Vicinity of Tongue River, Camp 22.*** There they discovered the remains of a dead soldier. According to James Willert, this unfortunate fellow could have been either a missing trooper from the Custer fight with Sioux on August 4, 1873, or one of the Crook/Reynolds men from the March seventeenth Powder River battle.[103]

Major Reno's Scout—5 AM—Reno breaks camp, marching about eight miles down the east bank of the Tongue, to a point three miles above the Sioux camp spotted by Bradley and Boyer on May sixteenth. His scouts—including Mitch Boyer—had gone ahead and now reported back, describing the abandoned camp. Boyer confirms 400 lodges (i.e., 800 warriors). According to Heski, "the site of the Indians' camp of 16 May was probably eight miles northwest of Garland School, 'in a bend of the river.'"[104] John Gray said Reno was now only thirty-three miles from completing his mission, but it is here where he decides to violate his orders "drastically by moving to the Rosebud." Gray added, Boyer probably told Reno this was the same village seen on the Rosebud a week later and a village that large would have to move every few days. "By now it could be so far away that Terry's plan to strike it on the lower Rosebud would prove a fiasco."[105] Not only was the camp found, but,

> …a broad *lodgepole* trail was discovered—guiding *west* toward the Rosebud. This camp—Boyer probably advised Reno—would have been the village discovered May 16 by Lieut. Bradley, and the trail would probably lead directly to the May 27th village along the Rosebud.[106]

Reno now turned west for nineteen miles. According to Heski: the column forded the Tongue River (USGS map, Section 1, Township 3N, Range 46E) and headed west. They then turned southwest, and crossed the tributaries of Horse Creek, Six Mile Creek, and Miller Creek, continuously south and west.[107] The country was hilly with pine-covered hills and they crossed the tributaries of Cow Creek, Ranch Creek, Coal Creek and the headwaters of Cottonwood Creek and Dry Creek. That brought the command to a hill known as Gobbler's Knob, 4½ miles from the Rosebud valley (USGS map, Section 7, Township 2N, Range 44E).[108] Reno now began to move cautiously, sticking to ravines and avoiding ridges. His scouts were well out to the front and flanks.

8 AM—The command begins crossing the Tongue-Rosebud divide. Finally, at some time between two and 2:30 PM, Reno halts, 4½ miles short of the Rosebud (after traveling twenty-seven miles), and waits for his scouts to report back. Boyer immediately finds the old Sioux camp Bradley had discovered on May twenty-seventh (at John Gray's R-19 benchmark)—380 lodges. It was apparently abandoned on or around May twenty-ninth. The camp had been set up in such a way as to tell Boyer the Sioux had considered an attack likely. Young Hawk, one of Reno's Ree scouts, climbs Teat Butte and discovers the next Sioux camp (R-26) at the base of the Butte, abandoned May thirtieth. Boyer reports to Reno with news of both camps and a heavy trail leading up (south) the Rosebud valley.

8 PM–8:30 PM—Reno is on the move again, traveling eight miles down John Hen Creek: 4½ miles to the Rosebud (R-22¾), entering the valley probably not far from

where Sprague Creek enters the Rosebud from the west and Pony Creek enters from the east, and an additional 3½ miles, camping (R-26¼) at the upper end of the Sioux/ Teat Butte campsite.[109] Willert also estimated Reno's entry into the Rosebud valley twenty-two to twenty-three miles above the creek's mouth: where Sprague Creek enters from the west.[110] Boyer counted cooking fires, estimating the village contained some 360–400 lodges and as many as 800 warriors; several thousand Indians.

> Boyer is said to have counted 360 lodge fires arranged in nine circles, all within supporting distance of each other. There was evidence, also, to indicate that the pony herd had been driven inside the circles at night, showing that an attack was expected and that the hostiles were prepared to meet it.[111]

Dr. DeWolf wrote, "...find large trail week-old trail lodgepole...."[112] Exhausted— maybe by anxiety more than fear—Reno decides he has had enough for the day and camps at 11:30 PM.

Gibbon/Montana Column—The column and its trains remain in camp. The Crow scouts discover a heavy smoke up the Yellowstone and on its right (southern) side, in the vicinity of O'Fallon's Creek. There was speculation either Custer or Crook had attacked the Sioux, but Bradley felt it more likely hostiles were moving in that direction and had accidentally set the grass on fire. By evening it had died out.[113] Captain Henry Blanchard Freeman reported the same smoke in the direction of Sarpy Creek.[114] Freeman, however, corrected this sometime later, believing it to be from Reno's scouting column on or near the Rosebud. Even this proved incorrect.[115] Meanwhile, four soldiers from Wheelan's company (G/2C) return with First Sergeant John Ruth, who had become ill about twenty-five miles upriver: inflamed tonsils.

Crook/Wyoming Column—5 AM—Crook's column breaks camp and begins its march north, skirting the left bank of the Tongue to avoid difficult terrain. The route swung northwestward gradually, crossing the Tongue-Rosebud divide. At noon the column halted on the Spring Creek divide and scouts were sent out in search of Sioux. While the resting troops boiled water for coffee, the scouts spotted a large, grazing buffalo herd, also seen by Cheyenne Indians under Little Hawk, who were camped on Reno Creek. Another group of Cheyenne under Magpie Eagle, camped on Trail Creek, spotted the herd as well. Throwing insults at one another, the Cheyenne scattered and headed toward the Rosebud. Grouard reported the incident to Crook who believed the hostiles were located on the Rosebud (they were *not!*). Both Little Hawk and Magpie Eagle returned to the camps[116] to warn of soldiers on the upper Rosebud, setting the stage for the following day's events. At 7:20 PM Crook went into camp at the head of the south fork of Rosebud Creek, having marched thirty-five miles for the day. That night Crook told the Indian scouts he wanted them to go out, but except for one small party, they refused.

NIGHT OF JUNE 16 INTO THE 17TH—*Indian Village*—The Cheyenne under Young Two Moon(s), Spotted Wolf, and Two Moon(s) began moving up Trail Creek to the Rosebud. Sioux, under Crazy Horse, were moving up the south fork of Reno Creek and down Corral Creek to the Rosebud.

JUNE 17, 1876—SATURDAY—*Dakota Column*—4 AM—Reveille. It rained an hour or two earlier and the morning was cool and misty. At six AM Custer's column is moving out, riding briskly, Benteen in the lead. At 8:30 AM Custer reaches the Tongue River junction with the Yellowstone (near present-day Miles City, Montana), and pitches camp in a heavily wooded area on the Tongue's east bank: ***Mouth of Tongue River, Camp 22-A***.

Steamer "Far West"—8 AM—Started out for the mouth of the Tongue River, arriving at noon and mooring near Custer's camp.

Major Reno's Scout—8 AM—After a later than usual start, Reno breaks camp and continues his march up the Rosebud for 7½ miles (R-33¾), the Ree scouts preceding the column. Portions of the lodgepole trail seemed to be from one to two weeks old, some appearing fresher than others. There were no indications the Indians were in any hurry.

10 AM—Reno goes into a halt for several hours. This halt was probably between Pony Creek and Greenleaf Creek [R-34]. His troops examined an old entrenchment area where 149 prospectors from Bozeman held off a large party of Sioux on April 5, 1874. [Township 12, Section 13, NW ¼, Rosebud County.] The scouts examined the next Sioux campsite at R-34 (junction of Greenleaf Creek and the Rosebud), abandoned June fourth. They also had to assure themselves the heavy and deep trail continued up the Rosebud rather than southeast along Greenleaf Creek. During this halt, Reno took extra precautions to guard against discovery: no trumpets or loud noises and pickets were posted around camp. While Reno waited, Boyer, the only scout familiar with the territory, led the Ree up the Rosebud, and about 12¼ miles out reached the next Sioux camp at R-46. This was Sitting Bull's famous sun dance camp (abandoned June eighth).

Side Notes—When Custer's column reached this site on June twenty-fourth, Lieutenant Godfrey noted the size at 300–400 lodges. This is highly significant because it indicated to the soldiers the size of the winter roamers' village had remained fairly constant over the three weeks it spent traveling from the Tongue River to this point. Thus, Custer and his men may have had a false sense of the hostiles' size, even as late as the evening before the battle. The summer roamers had not joined yet, though it appears Boyer had other thoughts … so….

Major Reno's Scout—[*continued…*]—By this time Boyer had to have figured the *village* sites were up to several weeks old, but the *trails between those sites* were much newer, maybe only one week; the inference being the village of about 400 lodges (containing an estimated 3,000 Indians, maybe ⅓ to ½ of whom were warriors) had been more recently joined by other bands of Indians moving after the main body.

Edgar Stewart wrote, Reno reported finding, "a great Indian trail more than half a mile wide made by thousands of trailing lodgepoles."[117] Boyer continued up the Rosebud and at R-53, came to another oblique bend of the river, at a point where Lame Deer Creek joins from the southeast. Boyer, in all likelihood, scouted just enough more to ensure the trail did not leave the Rosebud at this point. In fact, it continued up the Rosebud. He turned back here, and when reporting to Reno, said the soldiers could overtake the Sioux in a day's march. John Gray stated these claims were made *not* based on a fresher campsite, but on fresher *overlay* trails that joined at Lame Deer Creek. It was probably somewhere near here as well, the Indian trail became "more than a mile wide, the earth so furrowed by thousands of travois poles that it resembled a plowed field."[118] "Along the way, they examined travois trails that appeared to be even fresher than the village sites. Clearly, other bands were moving after the main camp."[119] "If asked, [Boyer] could have added that the trail would probably continue to the Busby bend of the Rosebud (R-70), where it could turn south up the Rosebud, west toward the Little Bighorn, or north down Tullock's Fork."[120] Reno now decides to turn back, stating Custer had said to, "turn back if we found the trail."[121]

4 PM—Reno heads back downriver, covering another fifteen miles, going into camp at eight PM (R-18¾), about four miles below where he entered the valley.

Gibbon/Montana Column—Gibbon remained in bivouac.

Crook/Wyoming Column—3 AM—Stirring in the camp, fires lit, men preparing coffee. Everyone knew they were in the heart of Sioux country. The Rosebud Creek at this camp was a sluggish stream, no wider than twenty yards in any place and less than ten yards in most, with thickets of wild roses along its banks.[122]

6 AM—The column began to move, as always with Crook, the infantry first, then cavalry, then packs. They traveled less than three miles when the creek's north fork entered the main stream from the left. For the next 2¾ miles the creek flows eastward through a narrow valley; then switches back to a northward flow. The lead battalions were Mills (A, E, I, and M/3C) and Noyes (A, B, D, E, and I/2C).

8 AM—Crook ordered a halt to brew coffee and rest … and his Crow scouts warned him there were signs of Sioux in the area, so Crook dispatched pickets to the hills north of the camp. At this point the valley was a half-mile wide. To the south, bluffs rose 500 feet above the valley floor. North of the camp was a series of ridges 150–800 yards from the creek.[123] The main crest, now known as Crook's Hill, was about one mile north of the ridges and extended for about three miles, northwest to southeast.[124] "A spur ridge comes in one mile west of Crook Hill and runs at an acute angle southeast for one mile until its termination several hundred yards above the creek, a half-mile east of the west bend [of the creek]."[125] This is called Royall's Ridge today. Between Royall's Ridge and Crook's Hill lies a broad expanse known as Kollmar. "The head of Kollmar originates just over one mile west of Crook Hill. Kollmar parallels Royall Ridge and extends southeast for two miles before emptying into Rosebud Creek at a point midway between the west bend and the Kobold House."[126] Anson Mills occupied the right bank of the Rosebud opposite the Kobold House; Captain Van Vliet (C and G/3C) was in the center; Captain Henry (B, D, F, and L/3C) followed Van Vliet. Noyes was on the left bank, opposite Mills. After Noyes came Major Chambers' infantry (D and F/4I; and C, G, and H/9I). The packers and miners were in the rear and were not yet fully in camp.

Gunfire was heard to the north (where the pickets were), but nothing was thought of it, many believing the scouts were just having some fun. As it grew in intensity, others believed it was just firing at buffalo. Soon, the shots were heard spreading out.[127] A number of Shoshone and Crow scouts moved north and about eleven miles from the camp, ran into a small force of Sioux on Corral Creek. Pushing back the small band of Sioux, the scouts suddenly encountered larger bands and finally, they pulled back quickly, followed by several hundred hostiles. Sioux were not only in the north, but east and west of the valley.

At about 8:30 AM, near the head of the Rosebud (R-91), Sioux and Cheyenne warriors commenced their attack on Crook's Wyoming column, whipping him in an indecisive battle lasting most of the day. Crook was forced to retire with his wounded, camping along Goose Creek.

Side Notes—The Sioux village, having already left the Rosebud at its Busby bend, was camped west of the Little Big Horn–Rosebud divide. This was the camp on Reno Creek where the so-called "lone tepee" was later found (the Cheyenne were camped at the lone tepee[128]). Edgar Stewart claimed they used only half their force of warriors to attack Crook, the rest staying back to protect the camp.[129] Stewart also claimed the tribes had gone into the Little Big Horn valley, but finding game scarce, they moved back into the Rosebud valley, then later, back across into the Little Big Horn.[130] The camp was said to have contained 12,000 inhabitants.[131]

NOTE—Much of the description of the Crook-Rosebud fight was developed from Neil Mangum's excellent book, *Battle of the Rosebud: Prelude to the Little Bighorn.*

Crook/Wyoming Column—[*continued...*]—Captain Randall, Chief-of-Scouts, quickly formed his scouts on a skirmish line north of the camp and for the first twenty minutes of the fight, Randall's scouts and the pickets formed the only barrier between the Sioux and the rest of Crook's command, the Indians getting within 500 yards of the camp,[132] their main thrusts coming from the northeast and west.

Crook decided he needed to secure the bluffs to his south, as well as the high ground to the north. He sent Van Vliet to take the southern bluffs. Indians had the same idea, but Van Vliet ran them off: "...the top was a broad flat plain."[133] An excellent description of the Indians' tactics was provided by Captain Azor H. Nickerson, Crook's adjutant:

> The warriors dashed here, there, everywhere; up and down in ceaseless activity.... Our efforts were directed toward closing in with the enemy by a series of charges, and theirs to avoiding close contact until, by the nature of the ground, our forces began to get scattered, and then their tactics changed from the defensive to the offensive. Each separate detachment was made the objective of terrific onslaughts; the warriors charging up to them, careening on their horses, and firing from behind them, while exposing as little of their own persons as possible. All the time they were whooping and yelling, hoping thereby to strike terror into the hearts of their adversaries and if possible, stampede them.[134]

The Indians "'were extremely bold and fierce,' said the reliable Lieutenant Bourke, who took notes during the fighting, 'and showed a disposition to come up and have it out hand to hand.... They advanced in excellent style.'"[135] Crook's left rested near where the Rosebud's north fork joins the main creek; this was the west bend of the Rosebud. Captain Guy Henry's battalion was ordered to occupy and hold a low hillock south of the Rosebud, some 300 yards east of the west bend. This—with Van Vliet's positioning—secured Crook's left and rear. Crook now ordered captains Burrowes (G/9I) and Burt (H/9I) to take the ridges to the immediate north; and captains Cain (D/4I) and Luhn (F/4I) and Captain Munson (C/9I), west of the others, were ordered to move forward, northward, as well, as skirmishers. The miners and packers were on the infantry's left flank.[136] Dispositions had to be made rapidly, for large numbers of warriors charged in quickly on the infantry.

Strips of red cloth had been issued to the scouts to differentiate them from the hostiles.[137] By a little past 9:30 AM Crook had stabilized his command and had driven the Indians back. He was spread out over three miles, however, and this concerned him. The miners and packers got into the fight and at this time held the northwestern edge of Crook's defense at Packers Rock. Some men held the southern edge of the ridge. These latter men were facing west looking at the broad Kollmar Creek valley. Crook was on the ridge's southwest crest along with three companies of Mills' cavalry. Three infantry companies occupied the center of Crook's Hill, and to the infantry's right was Noyes' 2nd Cavalry along a long sloping ridge leading to a gap.

Royall, with five companies of cavalry—B, D, F, I, and L/3C—charged the warriors, but his position in the Kollmar valley separated him from the rest of Crook's command. Elements of Captain William Howard Andrews' I/3C under Second Lieutenant James E.H. Foster got too far out front and Andrews had to order him back, both officers realizing Foster's peril. At ten AM, Royall now concentrated his command at the head of Kollmar Creek, one mile west of Crook's Hill, at the eastern end of a series of rocks and ledges.[138] Andrews was at the western end of what is known today as Andrews Point. One of the officers wrote:

> Nothing had been accomplished by our repeated charges except to drive the Sioux from one crest, to immediately reappear upon the next…. Nothing tangible seemed to be gained by prolonging the contest. When we took a crest, no especially advantage accrued by occupying it, and the Sioux ponies always outdistanced our grain-fed American horses in the race for the next one.[139]

Indians recognized Royall's precarious position and about 500 warriors converged on him from the west, north, and south. The troops' carbines, however, kept them at a distance. Some time between 10:30 and eleven AM Crook ordered Royall back toward the main body, but Royall sent only one company, Captain Charles Meinhold's B/3C. It was around this time when Crook figured the only reason the warriors were fighting this hard with this many was their camp was nearby. *This, of course, was incorrect.* Crook now ordered Anson Mills to search out the village down the canyon.

In all likelihood, seeing this, the Indians interpreted Mills' departure as the beginning of a general retreat. The Indians would severely press a retreating force and they attacked Royall furiously. Royall now tried to re-join Crook's force to the east, but he had waited too long, and Indians drove a wedge between Royall and Meinhold. Seeing this, Royall decided he could only move south to a long ridge south of Kollmar, so he sent his held-horses first; then endured fierce charges … without a casualty. Royall's second position was at the western edge of the ridge's crest. Andrews (I/3C) and Vroom (L/3C) were posted to the north slope, facing their first position which was now occupied by the warriors. Henry (D/3C) and Reynolds (F/3C) were to occupy the south slope, arriving just ahead of warriors attempting to outflank the command. In the meantime, another force of warriors charged down Kollmar, splitting Crook and Royall, and wound up in the camp area the troops had just occupied. Only Van Vliet's arrival stemmed the attack (see 11:30 AM), the warriors backing away from Van Vliet's cavalry.

Around 10:45 AM, and as the Indians moved back up Kollmar, they were attacked in the flank by the Crow and Shoshone scouts under Randall and Bourke. The warriors pulled back in confusion, but rallied, and fighting became hand-to-hand. Finally, the warriors were forced to pull back. At eleven AM—Scouts returned to their position after driving off the Sioux. By this time, however, the Sioux were pressuring Royall from three sides. Crook now ordered his infantry to advance on the Indians occupying Conical Hill, the higher ground forming the northwestern extension of Crook's Hill. The companies of captains Avery Billings Cain (D/4I), Gerhard Luke Luhn (F/4I), and Samuel Munson (C/9I) advanced, Cain on the left—his flank anchored by the edge of the bluffs—Luhn in the center, and Munson on the right, his flank bordered by the edge of the plateau. The Indians pulled off Conical Hill; the infantry occupied it momentarily and then withdrew.

At 11:30 AM Van Vliet (C and G/3C) arrived, taking up the slack from the departed Mills. Again, Crook sent a messenger to Royall to pull back. Royall, however, was sorely pressed and had only about 150 dismounted cavalrymen (not counting horse-holders). As the troops backed away in preparation to mounting, they came under tremendous Indian fire from three sides. Royall sent Lieutenant Henry Rowan Lemly—his adjutant—to Crook with an urgent plea for assistance. Realizing his error of sending off Mills to hunt for the village, and knowing he had underestimated the Sioux, Crook sent his adjutant—Captain Azor Howitt Nickerson—to Mills with a message to return. He then sent infantry to help extricate Royall. Royall ordered Vroom to drive back marauding Indians, in the hope of buying some time for others to reach their horses. The fighting became so serious around Vroom that Royall had to send Captain Guy Henry to extricate Vroom. In a brief span, Vroom lost five killed and three wounded. Four of Royall's companies formed a 325-yard skirmish line atop this ridge, now called Royall's third position. Estimates of Indian strength ran 500–700 warriors. Indians were so close to the skirmishing troopers that the firing singed the warriors' horses.[140] Suddenly, Captain Henry went down, shot in the face. As the Sioux approached Henry's prostrate body, soldiers and Crow and Shoshone scouts rushed to his rescue, driving back the Sioux. At this time, as well, the troops saw their opportunity to rush for their horses in Kollmar. Indians continued to pour fire at the retreating troopers, but the infantry now rushed to their aid: Captain Andrew "Andy" Sheridan Burt (H/9I) and Captain Thomas Bredin Burrowes (G/9I). They arrived at a small knoll about 600 yards north of Kollmar, northeast of Royall's position, and just about the time the cavalrymen were breaking for their horses. The Crow and Shoshone scouts, however, formed a defensive line and more than anyone else—except possibly Burt and Burrowes' commands—were responsible for saving the bulk of Royall's command.[141] In the meantime, warriors from Conical Hill nearly overran the packers, miners, and troops on Packers Ridge, but were also driven off.

1 PM—Royall's beleaguered command had finally reached the safety of Crook's Hill. The return of captains Mills and Henry E. Noyes' battalions—eight companies, about 350 men—saved Crook's command on the Rosebud.

The warriors reassembled near Conical Hill, ready for another assault, when Mills re-appeared. Mills' route took him in a counter-clockwise route down the

Rosebud, then to an approach east of Conical Hill. He had approached an area of the valley only about 150 yards wide with bluffs of some 400 feet on either side and his scouts refused to proceed, afraid of a Sioux ambush. This fear was heightened further with the appearance of thirty to forty warriors. Mills ordered Captain Alexander Sutorius (E/3C) to chase them, which he did. By now Nickerson had arrived with Crook's message to return.

At 2:30 PM Mills had returned to the main command and the battle had basically ended. After the battle, Crook ordered the Indians pursued, but they broke and scattered. Crook persisted, however, and led his cavalry downstream until reaching the bottleneck Mills had faced. The scouts refused to go on—fearing an ambush—and Crook turned back. At four PM Crook returned to the battlefield from his downstream foray, posting infantry on Conical Hill. At seven PM he withdrew his infantry, putting the command in the camp they maintained at the start of the battle.

That evening Crook held a council and proposed a night march to locate the village for a dawn attack. Again, the scouts refused and Crook, loath to advance without their assistance, decided to return to Goose Creek to replenish stores, send for reinforcements, rest his troops, and attend to his wounded.

Various estimate of casualties poured in, and according to Lieutenant John Bourke, Crook suffered fifty-seven killed and wounded,[142] but the "killed" number is clearly inflated: 3rd Cavalry (Lieutenant Colonel William B. Royall)—nine killed, fifteen wounded; 2nd Cavalry—two wounded; 4th Infantry—three wounded.[143] Overall, ten killed outright; four mortally wounded.

Crook reported—and these numbers are invariably correct—nine uniformed killed; one Indian (Shoshone) scout killed; twenty-one wounded. These came from the following: 3rd Cavalry: nine killed, sixteen wounded, including Captain Guy Henry; 2nd Cavalry: two wounded; and 4th Infantry: three wounded. General Phil Sheridan in his November 25, 1876, report, said thirteen Indians were left dead on the field; and Crook's losses were nine enlisted men killed; and one officer, twenty-three enlisted personnel wounded.[144] Thomas C. MacMillan (a correspondent): concurred with Bourke (who clearly must have changed his estimates): one officer and ten enlisted men "dangerously wounded"; thirty others slightly wounded. Scout Frank Grouard claimed: twenty-eight soldiers killed in action; fifty-six wounded, obviously exaggerated number.

Crook realized the formidability of the Indians and when Sheridan implored him to "hit them again!" Crook replied, "How do you surround three Indians with one soldier?" Crook estimated he was out-numbered by three to one, which was as clear an exaggeration as the excessive casualty numbers. It appears, however, Crook understood and admitted to being over-confident prior to the battle and he admitted to underestimating both the size and formidability of the Indians. "They had nearly caught [Crook] by surprise. Their numbers had been far greater than anyone had suspected, or believed… [Crook's] troops had fired 25,000 rounds this day to keep the warriors at bay."[145]

During the fighting, the Indians supposedly carried off all but thirteen of their dead. The Blackfeet Sioux chief, Kill Eagle, claimed four Indians were killed and left on the field and twelve died in camp. He said there were as many as 400 wounded and they had 180 horses killed.[146] Historian James Willert estimated 2,000 Indians attacked Crook.[147] Edgar Stewart estimated the Indian force at between 1,000 and 1,500,[148] the lower end probably very close to the truth. Author James Donovan estimated, "…at least seven hundred warriors…."[149] (It should be noted here, Donovan is quoting Dr. Charles Alexander Eastman [born February 19, 1858—died January 8, 1939], a full-blooded Santee Dakota Sioux physician and writer, educated at Boston University, who always seemed to have a tendency of *under*-estimating warrior numbers, a proclivity equally egregious to history as the troops *over*-estimating the numbers they were forced to fight. Neither practice serves us well.)

The warrior Standing Bear said, "…I was not in that fight. There were *many* [emphasis added for reference later in the 7th Cavalry's trek up the Rosebud Creek] who were not." Also, it appears neither Gall nor Crow King were there. If correct, that would mean many more warriors would have joined the village in the Little Big Horn valley *after* the Crook fight. In a very cogent remark, James Donovan wrote, "Never before on the plains had such a large force of Indians attacked an even larger force of soldiers, or fought with such cohesion and tenacity, and that knowledge would almost certainly have altered Terry's plans."[150] Lastly, Wooden Leg made the following estimates of Indians killed at this battle: Cheyenne: one (Black Sun); Cu Brulé: one; Minneconjou: one; and other Sioux: approximately twenty.

JUNE 18, 1876—SUNDAY—*Military Correspondence & Intelligence Reports*—From Lieut. Gen. P.H. Sheridan—"Telegraphs return from Red Cloud; all quiet there. Crook awaiting Indian Scouts at Reno."[151]

From Major J.J. Upham, 5th Cavalry—"Has sent Company to Chug Springs."[152]

***Dakota Column*—**Custer remains in camp, **Mouth of Tongue River, Camp 22A**, and during the day Lieutenant Maguire somehow measured the width of the Yellowstone at this location and found it to be 426 yards across. The troops while-away the time, fishing, rock collecting, and bathing in the river.

***Major Reno's Scout*—**5:30 AM—Marcus Reno breaks camp and travels the 18¾ miles down the Rosebud, plus another one to 1¼ miles down the south bank of the Yellowstone—east—to a point, opposite and within three miles of Gibbon's camp. The day was very hot. Between noon and two PM Reno orders camp in a nice area with plenty grazing for the horses—all their grain had been consumed and the grazing on the scout had been very poor.

***Gibbon/Montana Column*—**In the meantime, Gibbon's alert scouts report the approach of Reno's column. Gibbon, not knowing it was Reno, assumed it was Terry and tried to get a note to him across the raging Yellowstone. Two Crow scouts—one of them Jack Rabbit Bull—swam the river with the note. While it was difficult for Reno and Gibbon to communicate (because of the river), Reno did manage to inform Gibbon that he had seen no Sioux, the two commands apparently communicating by Army signals. With all this, Gibbon wrote Terry he thought the Indians were either near the headwaters of the Rosebud or the upper Little Bighorn. Never once—despite later protestations—did any of them think of the *lower* Little Bighorn.

> Gibbon would express this uncertainty as to the hostiles whereabouts at this time: "…As it was, we were still groping in the dark in regard to the location of the hostile camps, and had every

reason to believe that the Sioux (,) with their women and children (,) were solicitous only to avoid us."[153]

At this point, Gibbon obviously knew Terry's attack plan had to be changed, and he gave his note to Reno to give to Terry. Gibbon remains in camp. The wagon master, Matthew Carroll, wrote in his diary that scouts came in this evening reporting a large Indian camp supposed to be on the Big Horn.

Side Notes—It is extremely interesting here that lieutenants Bradley and McClernand both wrote Reno's scout had proven the Sioux and Cheyenne were now encamped on the Little Big Horn/Big Horn rivers. Whether these thoughts were included in their diaries *at the time* or were inserted later—after things had become clearer—is uncertain, though Willert writes both of them apparently edited their works *after* the battle. Referring to Mitch Boyer's discoveries, Lieutenant Bradley wrote in his diary:

> Boyer ... counted 360 lodge fires, and estimated that there were enough beside to make the number of lodges about 400.... The lodges had been arranged in nine circles, within supporting distance of each other, within which the Indians evidently secured their horses at night, showing that they considered an attack not unlikely and were prepared for it. A well-defined trail led from the site of the village across the plain toward the Little Big Horn, and it is now thought that the Indians will be found upon that stream.[154]

This may be the very first indication there was no separation between circles, a factor that increased the size of the population without increasing the length of the village ultimately seen on the Little Big Horn River. This must be considered one of the root causes of Custer's defeat, a situation he was *not* prepared for.

Indian Village—The Indian camps moved this morning, reaching the Little Big Horn and turning south, camping along the east side of the river.[155] The Indians never camped in a straight line during this period. The form of the land and the streams determined the tribes' locations. The only protocol was none would camp ahead of the Cheyenne or behind the Hunkpapa.[156] They stayed in this location for "six sleeps,"[157] meaning they moved again in the morning of June twenty-fourth. Five Arapaho warriors joined the camp during this period, as did more Cheyenne. The Cheyenne and Sioux camp was now located "along the east bank of the Little [Big] Horn River, and south of the confluence of 'Medicine Dance Creek' (Reno Creek, etc.)...."[158]

Crook/Wyoming Column—Crook begins his move to Goose Creek. After traveling twenty-two miles, Crook pitched camp near the divide separating the Tongue River valley from the Little Big Horn valley. Shortly before nightfall, Crow scouts informed Crook they are departing, but will return in fifteen days. They never do.

General P.H. Sheridan—Sheridan and his entourage arrive back at Fort Laramie from Camp Robinson and the agencies. Sheridan orders Carr with eight companies of the 5th Cavalry....

> ...up the Black Hills road to the intersection of the Powder River trail and from there proceed westward, scouting as long as supplies allowed. Sheridan anticipated that the actions of Generals Terry and Crook, who were operating on the lower Powder River and south fork of the Tongue River, respectively, could well drive the Indians toward the 5th Cavalry....[159]

It was suspected war materiel was being trafficked on the Powder River trail and thus part of Carr's mission was to patrol that area.[160] As noted earlier, a man named Boucher, living near the Spotted Tail Agency, was known to be an arms trafficker.

JUNE 19, 1876—MONDAY—*Military Correspondence & Intelligence Reports*—From Assistant Adjutant General, Department of Dakota—"Repeats telegram from Gen. Terry dated June 12th reporting his arrival at junction of Powder & Yellowstone rivers and giving disposition of troops of his command."[161]

From R. Williams, Assistant Adjutant General—"Order restoring District of the Black Hills. Supplies and horses for Col. Carr, Commander."[162]

From the Commanding Officer, Fort Fetterman—"Dispatches for Gen. Crook will leave by 5 PM."[163]

From Capt Gilliss, AQM [Assistant Quartermaster]—"Has arranged for teams to be at Little Bear Creek and Pole Creek."[164]

***Side Notes*—**Captain James Gilliss had been the Army's Assistant Quartermaster since August 10, 1864, headquartered in Washington, D.C. He was promoted to major and Army Quartermaster on January 22, 1881; lieutenant colonel, Deputy Quartermaster General, February 11, 1894; and colonel, Assistant Quartermaster General, October 15, 1897.

***Military Correspondence & Intelligence Reports*—**Telegram dated June 19, 1876, St. Paul, Minn., to Adjutant General, Division Missouri Chicago—

> The following just received—Camp at junc't of Powder and Yellowstone Rivers June twelfth eighteen seventy-six—Reached Powder River at a point twenty-four 24 miles above here late the seventh inst. No Indians east of Powder. Reno with 6 companies seventh cavalry is now well up the river on his way to the forks whence he will cross to come down Mispah Creek & thence by Pumpkin Creek to Tongue river where I expect to meet him with the rest of the cavalry fresh supplies. I intend then if nothing new is developed to send Custer with nine companies of his regiment [from] the Tongue & thence across to and down the Rosebud while the rest of the seventh will join Gibbon's who will move up the Rose Bud. Have met Gibbon & concerted arrangements with him. Troops and animals in fine condition signed Alfred H. Terry Brigadier General. Ruggles, Assistant Adjutant General.

***Major Reno's Scout*—**4:30 AM—Reno breaks camp and heads down the south bank of the Yellowstone to join Terry at the mouth of the Tongue River. The trail was so rugged and the day so very hot, it took four hours to go the first 9¾ miles. Meanwhile, Custer remains in camp at the mouth of the Tongue River. After pausing for a much-needed break, Reno again began moving at three PM through torturous terrain. Finally, at four PM he decided his troops and horses had enough and he camps on the south bank of the Yellowstone, on a plateau in the badlands above the river and eight miles above Terry and Custer on the Tongue, having covered thirty-three brutal miles that day. The total reconnaissance was 240½ miles. Once in camp, Reno sends a courier to Terry with Gibbon's note and his own report. The courier was probably Mitch Boyer, since he was the only one who knew this territory (another Indian scout may have accompanied him; Willert claimed Reno sent two Indian scouts[165]). In his report, he made no effort to predict where the Sioux *are,* though he does say where they are *not.*

At sunset Boyer, with the two reports, reaches Custer at the Tongue/Yellowstone camp. While Terry was very upset Reno was not only late (he was expected back on June sixteenth or seventeenth) and had "flagrantly disobeyed" his orders, he also realized Reno had saved them all from extreme embarrassment and a serious fiasco on the Rosebud. Custer was even more furious at Reno: "Had [Reno] pursued and overtaken the village, this error would have been forgotten; but instead, he counter-marched to the rear ... to report his blunder."[166]

Side Notes—This is one of the most significant and most overlooked phenomena of the entire campaign: Custer's ire at Reno. If Custer would have been mollified had Reno, with only six companies, attacked the village, he must have believed Reno could have whipped the Sioux. It appears Custer was *not* convinced the Indians were significantly stronger when the 7th Cavalry found them on the Little Big Horn, than they were when Reno found their encampments on the Rosebud. Therefore, Custer must have been *very* confident when he set out to attack them with his entire regiment. It also tends to emphasize Custer's hubris regarding the obvious signs he would be seeing along the Rosebud. Despite the opprobrium aimed at Reno—feigned or otherwise—Terry immediately set about devising a new and more flexible plan and ordered his aide, Captain Robert Hughes up to Reno's camp to tell him to stay there and he would be joined by the rest of the column. When Hughes returned to the Tongue River camp after speaking with Reno, he briefed Terry, who then called a strategy meeting with Custer, Benteen, and other officers. The strategy meeting was faulty, however. Regardless of Reno's first-rate information, some of Custer's concerns were valid. The general area and direction of march of the Indians seemed fairly well known at this point, yet the army—and by extension, Terry, Gibbon, and Custer—was wrestling with incomplete and inaccurate maps.

> The official army map—that drawn in 1872, and used upon this 1876 campaign—showed the two valleys [the Powder and Mizpah] as miles apart, and hence, Terry's design that the detachment should scout down the Mizpah to almost its confluence with the Powder, but *actual view* from atop the Powder *divide* had revealed ... a considerable distance down that valley, and if hostiles had been camped anywhere down along the Mizpah, their *smoke sign* would have been plainly visible. But no such indications had been observed.... Should the detachment proceed, as per Terry's orders ... [o]r should the Mizpah be *presumed empty* of any hostile camps, and the detachment move west to the valley of the Pumpkin and Tongue beyond?[167]

Terry's maps were based on the mapping of an expedition led by Captain William Franklin Raynolds and Lieutenant Henry Maynadier in 1859–1860. Wherever the expedition went, the map was platted with *fair* accuracy, but where they could not survey, they guessed, adding dotted lines as conjecture. The guesses were inaccurate and misleading. Rosebud Creek on Terry's map was only accurate for twenty miles up; the remainder platted was a *probable* course.

> Reno's column had followed the Indians' broad trail about twenty miles further up the valley and the stream had veered to the southwest. Since the trail of the hostiles was following the stream—and the extension of dots on the map angled upon a line almost due west, the direction appeared to suggest that the Indians were headed either toward upper Tullock's Creek, or, across the Little Chetish or Wolf Mountains to the upper valley of the Little Big Horn River.[168]

Terry used what is referred to as the "Hancock Map," taken from the field surveys of Raynolds and Maynadier and approved by the army cartographers under Major

General Winfield Scott Hancock's name, and issued in 1872. The Hancock Map is a "skeleton" map, showing only water-courses and is devoid of any topographical features. "There is no attempt to record contours, ridges, mountain ranges, or even rough shading to reveal their approximate locations."[169] Mountain ranges are noted, but only by name, not by feature. Hughes claimed Terry used only the Hancock Map, but there was another map approved some time in 1876—exact date unknown. This was the Gillespie Map, "entitled 'Yellowstone and Missouri Rivers,' prepared by Major G.I. Gillespie, Chief Engineer of the Military Division of the Missouri…. If [the map was published] early in 1876, Terry possessed the chart for his field campaign against the hostiles."[170] Because of this uncertainty, there were no assurances the Indians were not moving west, south, or even east.

Gibbon/Montana Column—The troops remained in camp all day, and by early evening Wheelan and Thompson return. They found no sign of the Sioux north of the Yellowstone, but they had decided to probe the region just south of the confluence of the Big Horn and Yellowstone: "the Crow scouts with them '… *reported seeing large fires in the direction of the Little Horn (Valley)…*'; moreover that the Crow Village had moved westward!"[171] Lieutenant Bradley felt this westward movement of the Crow village indicated the Sioux were likewise headed in that direction.

> The Crow village which some weeks ago was on the Big Horn seems to have disappeared from that country—another indication that the Sioux are heading in that direction. It is pretty well demonstrated that they have no intention of crossing to the north side of the Yellowstone, as they would not have passed so high up the stream for that purpose.[172]

The fact the Indians were *not* moving northward, but were still moving south and possibly west, were building large campfires, and making no effort at concealment, certainly indicated by this time they were not afraid of the soldiers, nor fearful of an attack, despite the defensive nature of their village encampment.

Indian Village—The Indians had moved down Medicine Dance Creek (Ash/Reno Creek), but did not cross the Little Big Horn. Instead, they….

> …entered the valley by skirting the east bank of the river, where it angled across the valley from its channel along the western hills. The Little Horn … sources are in the Big Horn Mountains… [and the river] etches obliquely across the valley floor to continue its northward course beneath the valley's eastern bluffs. The Indians had moved into the valley above this oblique channel, and had thus avoided having to ford the river.[173]

The Cheyenne were camped to the south, heading *up* the valley, for this was their original intent. It was only after they were there awhile, that the decision was made to move *down* the valley. Indian scouts tracked Crook's forces *away* from the Indians, so they felt the threat from the soldiers was subsiding. This clearly indicates the Sioux and Cheyenne were unaware of the Terry/Custer column and reinforces the contention they were caught "napping" when Custer hit them.

Crook/Wyoming Column—1 AM—Crook's nervous pickets fire on unknown objects. A recon was sent out, but nothing was found. Later in the day Crook's command reaches Goose Creek and the Shoshone scouts depart.

General P.H. Sheridan—Sheridan, along with the Fort Laramie commander, Major Edwin Franklin Townsend, leave Fort Laramie for Cheyenne.

JUNE 20, 1876—TUESDAY—*Military Correspondence & Intelligence Reports*—From the Army Adjutant General's Office—"Furnishes copy of letter transmitting to Int. Dep't copy of dispatch from Col. W. Merritt relative to affairs at Red Cloud Agency."[174]

From the Commanding Officer, Fort Fetterman—"Reports detention of dispatch from Gen. Crook by the Courier by the direction of the Correspondent."[175]

From R. Williams, Assistant Adjutant General—"Dispatch from Laramie rel. to Little Wolf Cheyenne Chief having left Agency with 1,000 of his band."[176]

From Lt. Col. E.A. Carr—"Report lack of Commissary Supplies at Laramie."[177]

From Lt. Col. E.A. Carr—"Proposes to take the Company at Sage Creek. Asks for another Company of Infantry."[178]

From R. Williams, Assistant Adjutant General—"Courier arrived at Fetterman from Gen. Crook."[179]

From Commanding Officer, Fort Fetterman—"Courier from Gen. Crook—Crows and Snakes have joined."[180]

Telegram dated June 20, 1876, from Fort Fetterman, To Gen. [*unclear if it was Sheridan or Sherman*] [*illegible*]… "The dispatch from Gen. Crook was held back until this morning by the courier and without my knowledge the courier informed me that he was employed by the correspondence [*sic*] and it was by the…" [*Remainder missing.*]

Dakota Column—Terry's new orders directed Custer to take the remaining six companies of the 7th Cavalry, Lieutenant Low's Gatling battery, the pack train, and the Ree scouts, up to Reno's bivouac, assume command and proceed to the mouth of the Rosebud. It was another very hot day, maybe the warmest yet.

8 AM—Custer leaves the Tongue River camp to join Reno, heading south along the east bank of the Tongue, looking for a suitable ford. About two miles upriver, he crosses the river and leads a brisk march toward Reno's camp, eager to chew Reno's butt for disobeying orders. He arrives at 11:30 AM. Custer administers the requisite tongue-lashing to Reno, though Terry's arrival smoothed things over somewhat. The former was furious Reno could not report the exact number of Indians and the precise direction they were heading instead of "guessing." [Ironic, since Custer, as well, would soon fail to compute the "exact number" of Indians.] Some time in here is when Reno's six companies had their sabers crated up. The troops now looked like tough, hardened veterans, with faded uniforms, trimmed beards, and they spent some time relaxing and cutting hair, cleaning, morale high and anxious: their quarry was within reach.

12:30 PM—Terry, on the "Far West," arrives at Reno's camp and another conference was held on board the steamer.

3:45 PM—Terry starts up the Yellowstone, on the steamer, to join Gibbon at mouth of the Rosebud. He takes the entire Gatling battery with him to spare them the rugged march up to the Rosebud.

4 PM—Custer resumes his march up the Yellowstone to Gibbon's camp (four miles below mouth of Rosebud): the Rosebud is approximately seventy miles from the mouth of the Powder River, and at 8:30 PM, he goes into camp, *Yellowstone, Camp 23,* about fourteen miles west of Reno's former camp. That evening doctors

Porter and DeWolf, lieutenants Harrington and Hodgson, go out pistol shooting: Porter came out best, DeWolf next. Long after they returned to the bivouac area, Lieutenant Godfrey and his K Company, the rearguard, finally arrive at the camp. It was eleven PM.

Steamer "Far West"—9:15 AM—The "Far West," loaded with supplies, heads up the Yellowstone to Reno's camp.

9 PM—The vessel is at its mooring spot alongside the 7th Cavalry's encampment.

Indian Village—The Sioux and Cheyenne remained in their camp on the east side of the Little Big Horn, up-valley from Reno Creek. Scouting parties had spotted fresh signs of antelope downriver near where the Little Big Horn flows into the Big Horn, so their plans to move up the valley were changed. Other scouts, tagging Crook, reported his column was moving farther away. No scouts were in the vicinity of the Yellowstone or lower Rosebud; the last time the Indians had seen any soldiers along the Yellowstone, those soldiers—Gibbon's column—were moving *downriver*. They had pulled in their scouts, so had no idea the troops had reversed course and were now headed back upstream and into the Rosebud valley. This, obviously, was a grave error.

Gibbon/Montana Column—Remained in camp all day. Train issued rations and took inventory: 48,000 pounds of stores.

Carr's 5th Cavalry—Companies C and G arrive at the regiment's camp along the Laramie River, one mile east of Fort Laramie. They joined companies A, B, D, I, K, and M, bringing the complement to eight companies.

JUNE 21, 1876—WEDNESDAY—*Dakota Column*—6 AM—Custer marches the 7th Cavalry west towards the Rosebud Creek, and at 8:35 AM, Terry, on board the "Far West," arrives at Gibbon's camp, immediately ordering him to send the remainder of his command up to the mouth of the Big Horn, picking up his "road-workers" along the way. Terry also assigns six of Bradley's Crow scouts to Custer: Half Yellow Face, White Swan, White Man Runs Him, Hairy Moccasin, Goes Ahead, and Curley, all chosen by Boyer. In addition, Terry hires George Herendeen to scout for Custer, ostensibly to reconnoiter the Tullock's Fork and valley and then to meet Terry at the mouth of the Big Horn. He assigns Boyer to Custer. Then, at 9:30 AM Terry, Gibbon, Brisbin, Boyer, and the six Crow, steam up the Yellowstone for mouth of the Rosebud.

Gibbon/Montana Column—6 AM—Gibbon, anticipating the change in Terry's plans, sends three companies (H, E, and K, 7th Infantry) under Captain Freeman, up the north bank of the Yellowstone to do some roadwork and build bridges.[181] The Big Horn confluence was some sixty miles away. Gibbon now had at his command: A, B, and I/7I, and F, G, H, and L/2C; and the Diamond-R supply train contingent. Lieutenant Bradley, with his mounted infantry and Crow scouts, leaves to scout the van for Gibbon's column, very upset at losing Boyer and six of his best Crow scouts.

9:30 AM–10 AM—Gibbon's column starts up the north bank of the Yellowstone for Fort Pease and the Big Horn River.

Side Notes—Some time prior to ten AM Terry writes his June twenty-first report to Sheridan. In it, he mentions his plan to send Gibbon (and himself) to the mouth of the Little Big Horn and Custer up the Rosebud and across to the *headwaters* of the Little Big Horn, and *down* that river. This is similar in concept to his Rosebud plan: a quasi-pincer movement. Terry wrote:

> No Indians have been met with as yet, but traces of a large and recent village have been discovered 20 or 30 miles up the Rosebud. Gibbon's column will move this morning on the north side of the Yellowstone for the mouth of the Big Horn, where it will be ferried across by the supply steamer, and whence it will proceed to the mouth of the Little Horn, and so on. Custer will go up the Rosebud tomorrow with his whole regiment and thence to the Little Horn, thence down the Little Horn. I only hope that one of the two columns will find the Indians. I go personally with Gibbon.

It is also interesting to note here, Terry never said anything about a "pincer" attack, any plan of having the two columns meet. This was probably "in accordance with Sheridan's idea that it was an absurdity to expect cooperation in such an open and broken country, especially since each column was believed able to take care of itself if it met the Indians."[182] Apparently, however, he used the phrase, "double movement."[183] This is also an insight into Terry's thinking and plans for Custer's route, and the use of the discretion he would grant his subordinate.

Steamer "Far West"—11:45 AM—The "Far West" arrives at the mouth of the Rosebud to await Custer's arrival.

7th Cavalry—NOON—Custer finds a good place to camp, two miles below the mouth of the Rosebud and about sixteen miles from his previous camp, **Yellowstone/Rosebud, Camp 24**, and by 12:30 PM whatever tents they had were pitched.

Terry-Gibbon Column—Terry and Gibbon now steam back down two miles to the Custer bivouac: "…the better point selected by Custer for his camp."[184]

2 PM–4 PM—A strategy conference was held on board the steamer: Terry, Gibbon, Custer, and Brisbin (notice the absence of Major Reno and Lieutenant Bradley).

The Crow report to Custer (in his "big" tent near the river's edge), who in turn, has them report to Lieutenant Varnum. Not long after the camp was established, a mackinaw boat pulled into the south bank of the river. It was probably this boat that had the merchants from Bozeman. They sold fresh eggs and many other things, including straw hats, and they sold them much more cheaply than the traders and sutlers that had latched onto the column in its westward march. This is where Reno bought a straw hat for 25¢.

Side Notes—Gibbon's scouts had recently reported seeing smoke from the vicinity of the Little Big Horn valley, so it was assumed the Sioux were somewhere in that area. In an article published in the *Los Angeles Times* on November 8, 1884, Jim Brisbin wrote, "The Indians had left the Rosebud and gone no one knew exactly where, but we had a pretty good idea, through our Crow scouts. The Sioux were on the big bend of the Little Horn."[185] (In reality, they were well below the big bend.) Terry believed the Indians were at the *headwaters* of either the Little Big Horn or the Rosebud. Much of Terry's thinking, however, may have had to do with his maps. The Rosebud was not platted all the way to its headwaters and his map had the creek swinging southwest. If the Indians followed the creek—as Reno's scout indicated they had—it was reasonable to assume the hostiles would cross the Wolf Mountains and head to the valley of the Little Big Horn. Because of the melting snowfields of the Big Horn Mountains, it was thought *if* the Indians were in the Little Big Horn valley, they could only be approached from two ways:

> ...the Indian position could only be approached from the north or east. If a concentrated attack were made from the north, a line of escape was left open to the eastward.... Terry's plan was for Custer's column... "to occupy this eastward line and so cut off escape in that direction before the Indians were disturbed, while Gibbon's column closed in from the north."[186]

Because of the disparity in troops and distances (Gibbon's column, with its infantry, would be slower; Custer said he could move thirty miles a day; and Gibbon was sixty miles from the Big Horn), it was decided, if Custer reached the Little Big Horn valley by June twenty-fifth, he would have to lay low and mark time for a day until Gibbon's command could reach the area. Terry wrote Sheridan telling of his desire Custer *bypass* the Indian trail if it led west into the Little Big Horn valley, and continue south (Custer should send scouts along the Indian trail). This way, Custer could ensure if the hostiles had moved *south,* up the Little Big Horn valley, or south and then back east, Custer would intersect them. If they had moved west and Custer were to follow their trail and the Sioux had turned south, Custer would find himself between Gibbon and the Sioux, merely forcing another chase and negating Terry's "trap." Terry wanted to bring the infantry into the fight. When Custer said his 7th Cavalry could win the fight without any support, Terry said, "I will not have the infantry out of the fight!"[187]

The idea was not a simultaneous attack, but an attack where one force—Gibbon's—would act as a blocking force, and the other force—Custer's—driving the Indians into the anvil. If the Sioux had moved south, it was figured they would run into Crook. Lieutenant Bradley wrote:

> ...a combined movement between the two columns in the neighborhood of the Sioux village about the same time and assist each other in the attack, it is understood that if Custer arrives first he is at liberty to attack at once if he deems prudent. We have little hope of being in on the death, as Custer will undoubtedly exert himself to the utmost to get there first and win all the laurels for himself and his regiment.[188]

Both Terry and Gibbon emphasized to Custer the importance of adhering to this plan, but apparently, Custer was rather disconsolate about it. If the Sioux had not turned west and gone into the Little Big Horn valley, but had continued south, then Custer was to pursue them and send messengers back to inform Terry. Colonel John Gibbon wrote:

> Hence it was agreed that Custer, instead of proceeding at once into the valley of the Little Big Horn, even should the trail lead there, should continue on up the Rosebud, get closer to the mountains, and then striking west, come down the valley of the Little Big Horn, "feeling constantly to his left," to be sure that the Indians had not already made their escape to the south and eastward. General Terry, applying a scale to the map, measured the distances, and made the calculation in miles that each command would have to travel.[189]

There was some thought the Sioux may have been camped on Tullock's Creek, "a broad valley, running oblique to the Yellowstone, whose western terminus touched the lower Big Horn River, and whose eastern opening emerged somewhere near the valley of the Rosebud.... [T]he plat was accurate on Terry's official map."[190] Gibbon would explore the lower reaches, Custer the higher. In his *American Catholic Quarterly* article, Gibbon states his assignment was: "...and up [the Little Big Horn River] to co-operate with Custer's command."[191] Because of his knowledge of that area, George Herendeen was transferred to Custer.

As seen earlier, this area had been scouted and platted by Captain William Raynolds and Lieutenant Henry Maynadier in 1859–1860. When Maynadier explored the region up Tullock's Creek from the mouth of the Big Horn, he platted a creek whose source was unknown, then inserted dots connecting this creek with the lower course of the Rosebud. "There was no certainty that this linkage was valid."[192]

Raynolds described Tullock's creek in his journal, beginning with the last paragraph of his September first entry:

> [Thursday, September 1] ... Bridger reports that our route to-morrow will be into and down the valley of Tullock's fork, a branch of the Big Horn, which we are approaching, and as I propose that Lieutenant Maynadier shall go up that stream, I gave him his orders that he may make his arrangement to leave us when we strike the creek. The grass at our camp to-night is tolerably good.
>
> Friday, September 2—The road this morning continued up the valley in which we had encamped, thence along the ridge for about a mile, and then turned down a small creek that flows into O'Fallen's or Tullock's fork of the Big Horn. We reached the latter stream at about noon after a march of seven miles.
>
> At this point Lieutenant Maynadier and party separated from us, ascending the fork, while we continued down to the Big Horn, arriving at that river after a further advance of seven miles, and pitching our tents upon its right bank. The division of the party was a necessary step, and we separated in excellent spirits and with mutual and fervent good wishes.
>
> The road to-day has been very poor, and until we reached the valley of Tullock's creek the hills were so steep that it was barely possible to cross them. West of the ridge gully after gully intercepted our progress, and at times we were forced into the bed of the streams, where the sand or stones formed serious obstacles. These circumstances, added to the delay occasioned by the separation of the parties, made the day a very laborious one, and we were in the saddle between nine and ten hours, although the distance traveled was less than 15 miles.
>
> One of our horses escaped this morning, and was pursued by Mr. Wilson and one of the men, who have not as yet returned. In all probability they were compelled to return to Fort Sarpy, in which case they will have over 50 miles to travel, and cannot get back before to-morrow afternoon.
>
> Dark clouds have filled the sky in the northeast all day, and a cold north wind blowing this evening rendered a fire necessary for comfort, and eventually culminated in a storm, which has prevented observations and caused serious personal discomfort.

That is in Chapter Two of the journal. The following is Raynold's first in-depth mention about the Little Big Horn River from his September sixth entry.

> About noon the mouth of the "Little Big Horn" came in sight. Here the river takes a wide sweep off to the east, coming back again beyond, and as our route would thus naturally lead some distance from the stream, a halt was ordered, as we were in possession of the three great requisites for camping—wood, water and grass. Though we had been in the saddle but six hours, and in that time had stopped to butcher buffalo, the distance traveled today was 13.86 miles.
>
> Our camp is two or three miles below the mouth of the Little Big Horn. The Indian name of the Big Horn is Ets-pot-agie, or Mountain Sheep river, and of the Little Big Horn, Ets-pot-agie-cate, or Little Mountain Sheep river—the trappers' names for most of the streams in this country being translations of the Indian titles.

He mentions it a bit more in his September seventh entry but not until September twelfth does he enter the Little Big Horn valley itself. In addition,

The 1860 part of the 1859–1860 Raynolds Expedition was star-crossed due to the requirement of the Secretary of War that Raynolds make solar eclipse observations from British territory north of today's Montana on July 18. They left Fort Pierre in early spring with LT Maynadier splitting off to travel and survey down the Wind River and Big Horn River to meet up at Three Forks in June. Captain Raynolds had the famed Jim Bridger as scout and an entourage of Ferdinand V, with Hayden's scientists studying the plants, geology, and paleontology of the area. Their goal was to survey an area the size of Great Britain in two summers. The first summer they were on the Missouri River from Fort Pierre to the Yellowstone confluence. Their reports of the numbers of buffalo seen were absolutely astounding. Luckily they had not had Indian troubles, probably largely due to Bridger's experience and reputation. He was the most recognizable and respected white-eye of the era. The expedition ran into huge amounts of snowpack in the upper Wind trying to find a pass Bridger knew onto the Yellowstone Plateau. The incredible legends of that plateau, now Yellowstone Park, had the scientists drooling to be the first to explore and describe the area. Raynolds had been a desk jockey and pilot-light builder up to this assignment and had never been west of the Mississippi, but he had Hayden with several years experience geologizing in many of the territories of the West and, of course, he had the old "Blanket Chief," Bridger. In fact, much of Raynolds' map was drawn from Bridger's amazing memory of the rivers and mountains. Raynolds' half of the operation was plagued by the heavy snows that were slow to melt that year. They abandoned the idea of getting to the Plateau from the southern ramparts after several abortive attempts and a near mutiny by the scientists trying to reach the Plateau. They finally crossed the Snake River at Jackson's Hole and came west and over Teton Pass, then through Pierre's Hole, and up the Henrys Fork. Once they reached the Missouri drainage Raynolds ran into the same problem Maynadier had all along: swollen and nearly impassable rivers from snowmelt. They rendezvoused near Three Forks, late and out of food and had to head for forts Benton and Union on the Missouri missing the eclipse. The nation was in turmoil when they returned east to the firing on Fort Sumter, the scientists without funding, and Raynolds re-assigned to map-making in the South for the Union Army. Hayden was a doctor and became a surgeon and then ran and designed Union "field hospitals." The map was not completed until after the war.[193]

Brisbin wrote a letter to Godfrey in January 1892, saying,

…that at General Terry's request he traced the routings of the troops on the map and placed pins to show their probable places en route; that Custer turned to the right and left the Rosebud just twenty miles short of his furthermost point on the Rosebud routing.[194]

In a footnote, Graham seems to indicate his belief Custer "is given discretion" in these orders, "when so nearly in contact with the enemy, etc."[195] Obviously, in Terry's report afterwards, he noted the trail should have not been followed, but Custer should have proceeded up the Rosebud.[196]

7th Cavalry—Custer refuses Lieutenant Low's Gatling battery as too slow and cumbersome—condemned cavalry horses. Instead, the battery was ordered to join Gibbon's column, report to Captain Edward Ball, and take thirteen mules, injured with Reno's march, with him. According to Brisbin, Custer accepted Low's battery initially then changed his mind, probably having asked Reno his opinion.[197]

Custer's orders anticipated the Sioux to be on *upper* reaches of the Little Bighorn. He was ordered to move up the Rosebud to its headwaters, and once there, he was to swing west, cross the Little Big Horn–Rosebud divide, and aim for the upper reaches of the Little Big Horn River, all the while feeling out towards his left to make sure the Sioux did not escape to the east. Once at the upper Little Big Horn, he was to head down the valley towards the blocking position at the mouth of the river established by the Terry/Gibbon forces. The latter column—smaller, slower, less mobile, and with fewer scouts—was expected to be in position by June twenty-sixth, *thus some emphasis on Custer going up to the headwaters of the Rosebud to give Terry the time to enter the Little Big Horn valley.* With that imbedded in the planning, Custer was to drive the Sioux towards the blocking position. Importantly—and the genesis of arguments for more than 140 years—he was given almost total discretion in his execution of the plan. At this particular time the scouts placed the Indian strength at some 5,000 warriors, while Custer and a few others anticipated 1,000 to 1,500. It appears most officers felt even that number was too high.[198]

Side Notes—In an extremely good synopsis of what was expected of Custer, Neil Mangum wrote:

> If the trail veered west to the Little Big Horn as expected, Custer was to ignore it and continue south up the Rosebud before turning west and descending the Little Big Horn—unless he saw sufficient reasons to change the orders. The rationale for not directly following the Indian trail across to the Little Big Horn was to minimize the possibility of detection, and reduce the chances of "scattering" the enemy. Indians were notorious for scattering into small bands and melting into the countryside to avoid major confrontations and to elude pursuers, much the way partisan rangers, such as those under John Singleton Mosby, had done during the Civil War. Terry expressed to Custer the necessity of preventing the Indians' escape by advancing far enough south before turning west. Custer's positioning on the headwaters of the Little Big Horn River would enable him to intercept fleeing warriors, give battle, or at least drive them north, down the valley, into Gibbon's column marching up the Little Big Horn.[199]

It is time now to determine just how many men, accouterments, and supplies General Terry and George Custer would be throwing at whatever enemy forces the 7th Cavalry would encounter. Based on detailed studies of the 7th Cavalry's regimental and company returns of May, June, and July 1876, it appears Custer's total strength was as follows:

- 607 uniformed personnel—thirty-one officers, 576 enlisted men.
- Five scouts and quartermaster employees—Mitch Boyer, George Herendeen, Charlie Reynolds, Bloody Knife, and Boston Custer.
- Two interpreters—Isaiah Dorman and Fred Gerard.
- Thirty-four enlisted Indian scouts—twenty-four Ree, six Crow, four Dakota.
- Two civilians—Autie Reed and Mark Kellogg.
- Five civilian packers.
- Total: 655.

Few people pay much attention to the number of packers attached to Custer's column, but authors Kenneth Hammer and Vern Smalley listed twelve. There is testimony at the Reno Court of Inquiry (January–February 1879) that the number was probably closer to six, yet we can only account for five by name and some accounts allude to that specific figure. Twelve pack mules were assigned to each company (historian Bruce Liddic claims 175 mules accompanied Custer's column[200]; James Willert also used 175 mules[201]). In the *Army and Navy Journal,* it was reported Custer took

185 pack mules.[202] In addition, according to the Ree scout, Red Star, five mules were assigned to the scouts.[203]

Fifteen days rations of hardtack, coffee, and sugar, and twelve days rations of bacon were allotted; 24,000 rounds of reserve ammunition were carried on the twelve strongest mules (two boxes of 1,000 rounds, each, per mule); 100 rounds of carbine and twenty-four rounds of pistol ammo were issued to each man, individually. All this was to last for the duration of the final push, estimated to be fifteen days. In addition, twelve pounds of oats were issued to each man for his individual horse and an extra supply of salt was issued in case they were forced to eat horsemeat.

Some time after four PM officers call was sounded and the 7th Cavalry's officers assembled in and around Custer's tent for a briefing. His manner was curt; his emphasis was on locating and pursuing the Indians, and he blamed Reno for possibly alerting them. He also dissolved his wing and battalion commands established earlier when leaving Fort Lincoln. This all came as somewhat of a surprise.[204] And, of little surprise, shortly after seven PM a short, but fierce, hail and thunderstorm hit. An omen?

That evening many of the officers and men sang songs: "Larboard Watch" (Reno and Lieutenant John Carland, B/6I), "Shenandoah," "Annie Laurie" (the war song of the Crimean War), and "Loreena":

> *The year creeps slowly by Loreena,*
> *The snow is on the grass again,*
> *The sun's low down the sky, Loreena,*
> *The frost is where the flowers have been,*
> *But the heart throbs on as warmly now*
> *As when the summer days were night;*
> *Oh, the sun can never dip so low*
> *As down affection's cloudless sky.*

Other favorites were "Bonny Jean," "Fairy bell," "Over the Sea," "Lightly Row," "Little Brown Jug," "Mollie Darling," "Captain Jinks," "Drill Ye Tarriers," "The Man on the Flying Trapeze," "Dinah's Wedding," "La Paloma," "Grandfather's Clock," "Little Footsteps, Soft and Gentle," "The Good-Bye at the Door," "Jeannie With the Light Brown Hair," "Susan James," "*Soldaten Lieder*," "The Blue Danube," and "Doxology." Another favorite, composed by the bandleader, Felix Vinatieri, was "The Mosquitoes of Dakota Waltz." A verse from "Captain Jinks":

> *I joined the Corps when twenty-one,*
> *Of course I thought it capital fun,*
> *When the enemy comes, of course I run,*
> *For I'm not cut out for the Army.*

After the brief storm, the night was dark and cloudy with no moon and just a few stars with a slight sprinkle. It was this evening or night when Custer and his obstreperous captain, Fred Benteen, got into something of a tiff. A group of officers— including Custer and Benteen—sat around discussing the campaign and Benteen mentioned he hoped he would be better supported than he was at the Washita. The exchange between the two men became rather heated.[205]

Indian scouts sat around singing and dancing their death dances. It was truly an

Stream Map

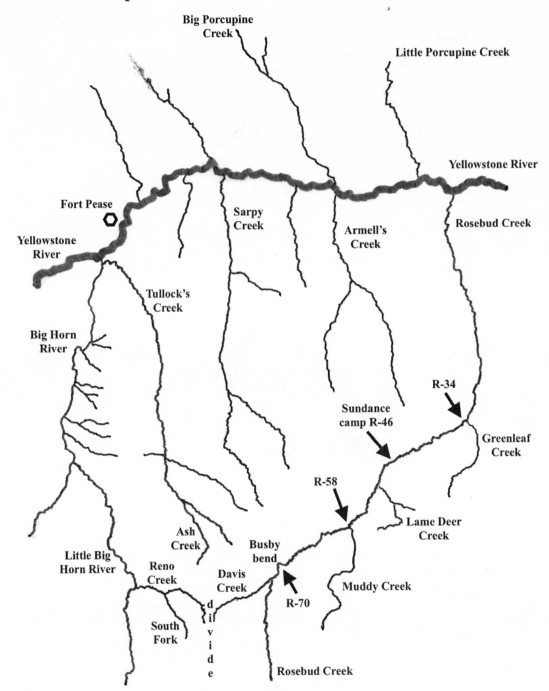

Rosebud Creek and Yellowstone tributaries.

evening and night of gloom and apprehension. And as was their wont, a high-stakes poker game took place on the "Far West," finally breaking up around two AM: Tom Custer, Jim Calhoun, Captain William Crowell (6th Infantry), Grant Marsh, and others. Apparently, Crowell won several thousand dollars (one source claimed $6,000).

George Custer, Boston Custer, Autie Reed, and Walter Burleigh (owner and clerk of the "Far West") were there as well, all attended to by Private John Burkman, Custer's striker.

Gibbon/Montana Column—As for Gibbon's column, these troops marched about nineteen miles and established a bivouac around seven PM, a short distance below the mouth of the Great Porcupine. They picked up Freeman's three companies of the 7th Infantry (E, H, and K) who were building roads in advance of the column. That heavy hailstorm hit them as well, and a short shower ended their day. At midnight Lieutenant Low's Gatling gun battery caught up to Gibbon's bivouac.

Crook/Wyoming Column—EARLY MORNING—Crook began evacuating his wounded from the Goose Creek camp to Fort Laramie.

Part II

Hour-by-Hour

"What we omit from a single *hour* is lost to eternity."
—Johann Christoph Friedrich von Schiller

5

Prelude

Thursday, June 22–Saturday, June 24

Lieutenant Colonel Edward S. Luce, letter to Charles G. DuBois, dated February 26, 1953. Charles G. DuBois Historical Collection.

"A cavalry horse walks four miles per hour; trots eight miles per hour; gallops twelve miles per hour, and the extended gallop or charge is sixteen miles per hour. Normally in good weather a troop would average about 9½ miles per hour. They generally start off for the first ten minutes, then halt about two minutes ... then trot for about twenty minutes, gallop for some ten, come down to a trot and then a walk."[1]

Cavalry marches from Colonel Emory Upton's 1874 *Cavalry Tactics*: "...[T]he formation would march initially for one hour, at which point the column would halt for ten to fifteen minutes to adjust tack (saddle, bridle, saddle girth, etc.). The troopers would then remount and the column would resume the march for another hour. After the second hour, the troopers did not rest, but rather dismounted and led their horses for twenty minutes. The cavalrymen then re-mounted and the column moved forward at the trot (a rate of speed of seven to eight miles an hour) for twenty minutes. The column then slowed—but stayed mounted—to a walk (3¾ miles per hour). At the end of this third hour—and at the end of each succeeding hour—the column would halt for five minutes. This pattern of dismounted walk, trot and walk was maintained, along with short gallops to allow the horses to stretch (nine to eleven miles per hour), was designed to conduct a march of six hours per day, during which the column would cover twenty-five miles."[2]

June 22, 1876—Thursday—*7th Cavalry*—After 2 am—Custer remained awake writing letters in his tent: one to his wife and a second, an anonymous correspondence to the *New York Herald*. In both, he iterated a common theme: Reno may have alerted the Indians by his unauthorized scout and the major should be court-martialed because he disobeyed Terry's orders. The *New York Herald*, July 23, 1876:

> In the opinion of the most experienced officers it was not believed that any considerable, if any, force of Indians would be found on the Powder River; still, there were a few, including Major Reno, who were convinced that the main body of Sitting Bull's warriors would be encountered on Powder River. The general impression, however, is, and had been, that on the headwaters of the Rosebud and Little Big Horn rivers the hostiles would be found.[3]

4 am—Troops of the 7th Cavalry heard the melodious sounds of reveille. Sunrise was at 5:18 am (4:21 am, local time) and the day was dawning gloomy and cloudy,

7th Cavalry Map

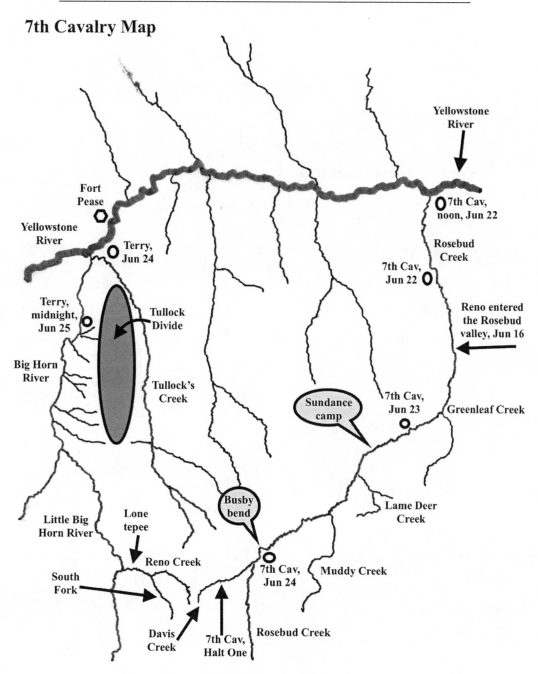

7th Cavalry: June 22 to June 25.

with a chilly west wind, but a good, solid breakfast was had by all: coffee, bacon. Then, at eleven AM, Custer receives his official marching orders.

Camp at Mouth of Rosebud River
Montana Territory, June 22, 1876
Lieut. Col. Custer, 7th Cavalry

Colonel:

The Brigadier General commanding directs that as soon as your regiment can be made ready for the march, you will proceed up the Rosebud in pursuit of the Indians whose trail was discovered by Major Reno a few days since. It is, of course, impossible to give you any definite instructions in regard to this movement, and were it not impossible to do so, the Department Commander places too much confidence in your zeal, energy, and ability to wish to impose upon you precise orders which might hamper your action when nearly in contact with the enemy. He will, however, indicate to you his own views of what your action should be, and he desires that you should conform to them unless you should see sufficient reason for departing from them. He thinks you should proceed up the Rosebud until you ascertain definitely the direction in which the trail above spoken of leads. Should it be found (as it appears almost certain that it will be found) to turn towards the Little Horn, he thinks that you should still proceed southward, perhaps as far as the headwaters of the Tongue, and then turn towards the Little Horn, feeling constantly, however, to your left, so as to preclude the possibility of escape of the Indians to the south or southeast by passing around your left flank. The column of Colonel Gibbon is now in motion for the mouth of the Big Horn. As soon as it reaches that point it will cross the Yellowstone and move up as least as far as the forks of the Big and Little Horns. Of course its future movements must be controlled by circumstances as they arise, but it is hoped that the Indians, if upon the Little Horn, may be so nearly enclosed by the two columns that their escape will be impossible.

The Department Commander desires that on your way up the Rosebud you should thoroughly examine the upper part of Tullock's Creek, and that you should endeavor to send a scout through to Colonel Gibbon's column, with information of the result of your examination. The lower part of the creek will be examined by a detachment from Colonel Gibbon's command. The supply steamer will be pushed up the Big Horn as far as the forks if the river is found to be navigable for that distance, and the Department Commander, who will accompany the column of Colonel Gibbon, desires you report to him there not later than the expiration of the time for which your troops are rationed, unless in the meantime you receive further orders.

Very respectfully, Your obedient servant,
[Signed] E.W. Smith, Captain, 18th Inf., AAAG

Side Notes—It is interesting to note here in any discussion of whether or not Custer disobeyed his orders, Terry wrote in his official report:

> Custer ... should proceed up the Rosebud until he should ascertain the direction in which the trail discovered by Major Reno led; that if it led to the Little Big Horn it should not be followed; but that.... Custer should keep still further to the south before turning toward that river, in order to intercept the Indians should they attempt to pass around his left, and in order, by a longer march, to give time for Colonel Gibbon's column to come up.[4]

It is also very important to remember while Terry was under no illusions of a "coordinated attack," per se, he desired and hoped for the two columns to be able to co-operate, "so that either of them which should be first engaged might be a 'waiting fight' give time for the other to come up."[5] Another interesting point regarding Custer's orders can be seen in a dispatch from Sheridan to Lieutenant Colonel Eugene Carr commanding the 5th Cavalry regarding the defeat of Crook's force:

> When your command reaches the crossing of the Powder River trail by the Custer City road, halt there, or at some convenient place covering the trail, until further information of the Indian affairs is received from Gens. Crook or Terry, unless you acquire such reliable information as would warrant you in going on to carry out the written instructions which I gave you at Fort Laramie....[6]

Note the discretion. Similar discretion can be found in a dispatch from Terry to Gibbon (see Gibbon's instruction, February 10, 1876). This appears to have been a common practice, probably brought about by the inability to communicate quickly.

Shortly before he died, James Sanks Brisbin wrote Godfrey a letter disputing the copy of Terry's order in Godfrey's *Century Magazine* article. Brisbin claimed after Custer's death, Terry placed Brisbin in charge of all cavalry for the campaign. That gave Brisbin access to Terry's various orders. In his January 1, 1892, letter Brisbin copied, verbatim, from Terry's original order to Custer:

> "You should proceed up Rosebud until you ascertain definitely the direction in which the trail above spoken of leads." (*Terry had already referred to the trail Reno followed*). "Should it be found, as it appears to be almost certain that it will be found, to turn toward the Little Big Horn he thinks" (*that is, the Department Commander thinks*) "that you should still proceed southward, perhaps as far as the headwaters of the Tongue River, and then" (*"then" underscored in order*) "turn toward Little Big Horn, feeling constantly, however, to your left, so as to preclude the possibility of the escape of the Indians to the South or Southeast by passing around your left flank. It is desired that you conform as nearly as possible to these instructions and that you do not depart from them unless you shall see absolute necessity for doing so." (*The absolute necessity mentioned here meant following the Indians alone or attacking them alone with your meager force*).[7]

When Graham checked this version against the official records at Fort Snelling, Minnesota, Brisbin's version proved to be incorrect. The question arises as to where Brisbin got this copy. He died, however, shortly after Godfrey received his letter.

PLEASE NOTE—From this point on all sub-references to columns or units not specifically part of the 7th Cavalry and the Indians engaging the regiment, will be highlighted in *italics*. Direct participant quotes will remain in italics.

7th Cavalry—12:10 PM—Custer and the entire 7th Cavalry paraded before Terry, Gibbon, and Brisbin—in a column of fours—with the regimental trumpeters playing "Garryowen" (as best trumpeters could play it!) while Gibbon's men cheered. As each company reached the reviewers, its officers went up to Terry, saluted, and the general spoke a few words to each of them. When the review was over, they started out for the Rosebud Creek valley (south). (Verified by Wallace, Godfrey, and Herendeen.) As the parade ended Gibbon wrote, "I made some pleasant remark. Warning [Custer] against being greedy, and with a gay wave of his hand he called back: 'No, I will not'...."[8] Colonel William A. Graham quoted Gibbon: "Now, don't be greedy Custer, as there are Indians enough for all of us!"[9]

Side Notes—Gibbon's remark, like so many others associated with Little Big Horn adventures, has been taken out of context in myriad ways, all to the detriment of George Custer's reputation and intentions. We see a perfect example of that in the television version of Evan Connell's book, *Son of the Morning Star*. Instead, however, of applying the "No, I will not!" phrase to Gibbon's supposed admonition of "there are Indians enough for all of us!" being twisted into "saving some for them for us," we see Gibbon's own words as he wrote them:

> The pack-mules, in a compact body, followed the regiment; behind them came a rear-guard, and as that approached Custer shook hands with us and bade us good-bye. As he turned to leave us, I made some pleasant remark, warning him against being greedy, and with a gay wave of his hand he called back, "No, I will not," and rode off after his command. Little did we think

Campaign Map
Terry-Montana Column

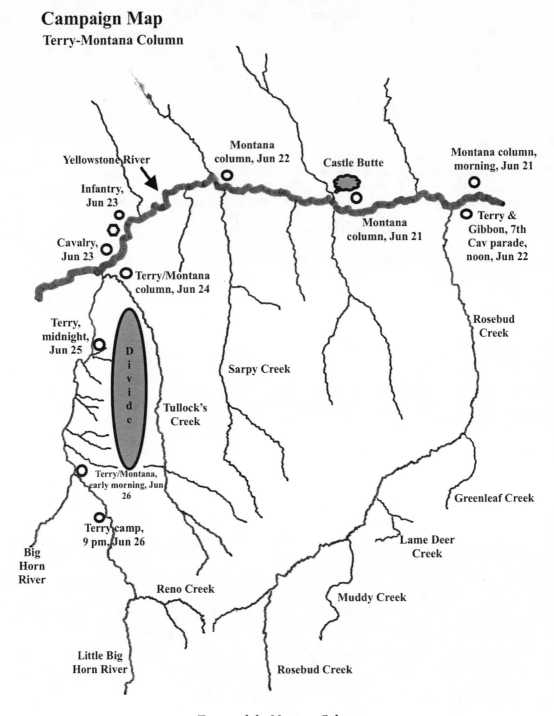

Terry and the Montana Column.

we had seen him for the last time, or imagine under what circumstances we should next see that command, now mounting the bluffs in the distance with its little guidons gayly fluttering in the breeze.[10]

7th Cavalry—Godfrey wrote, as the parade ended, the command moved out in a column of fours, each company followed by its pack mules.[11] According to Captain Benteen, it was shortly after the parade when Custer issued the order breaking up the wings and battalions.[12] This was verified by Major Reno at the 1879 inquiry,[13] and alluded to by Lieutenant Godfrey: battalion formations were abolished on June twenty-second when starting the move up the Rosebud. Each company commander was made responsible for his own company regarding grazing and watering of horses.[14]

12:40 PM—At this time, the 7th Cavalry left its supporting elements, left its department commanding general, left its well-wishers, and reached the mouth of Rosebud Creek, beginning a march into legend, and giving its descendants and followers a mystery to hang on to and ponder for years to come. Three days later it would etch its legacy into memories more hardened than the finest gems ... but for now it was simply a walk into the mist.

Lieutenant Nick Wallace described the Rosebud as a narrow creek, about three or four feet wide and three inches deep! The mouth, however, was broad, and high bluffs ranged to the west, sage-covered hills to the east. The narrow creek snaked through the eastern flats.

> It was a clear running stream, from three to four feet wide, and about three inches deep; bottom gravel, but in many places water standing in pools. Water slightly alkaline.... We had plenty of wood and water, and grass for our animals. During the greater part of the march the trail followed the high ground, or second bottom, where the soil was poor, the grass thin, and crowded out by sage-brush and cactus. In the lower part of the valley the soil appeared to be good, the grazing fair, the bottom timbered with large cottonwood. Small willows grew thickly along the banks in many places. For the first eight miles the hills sloped back gradually, but near camp were more abrupt, and covered with stones and cactus. Several deep ravines were crossed during the day. The only serious obstacle to a wagon-train would be the numerous crossings of the bends of the Rosebud. Weather clear, but not unpleasantly warm. No game visible. Plenty of fish in the creek.[15]

As the column moved on, it was forced to stop to re-tie packs on the mules, sloppily done in the early morning, probably because most of the packers were hung-over ... and the soft rains persisted. After a short while, the command crossed to the west side of the creek (left bank), and at one PM Custer sent the Ree scouts out in advance—though their fear of the Sioux kept them remarkably close to the column—with Soldier leading one group and Bob-tail Bull leading another. Because the valley narrowed sharply, Custer was forced to cross and re-cross the creek, causing problems with the pack mules as they struggled through the foliage-hidden creek bed. Plus, some nervousness permeated the command: Custer was still very concerned Reno's unauthorized scout up the valley had alerted the hostiles and that they were watching the column. Standing operating procedure in those days was the Indians would allow the soldiers to get only so close to their village and then they would attack, allowing time for the village to slip away. George Wallace continued....

> ...the trail followed the high ground, or second bottom, where the soil was poor, the grass thin, and crowded out by sagebrush and cactus. In the lower part of the valley the soil appeared to be good, the grazing fair, the bottom timbered with large cottonwood. Small willows grew thickly along the banks in many places....[16]

As the column moved farther up the valley, the terrain became more difficult.

Terry-Gibbon Column—3 PM—General Terry, aboard the "Far West," dispatched six Ree with mail to the Powder River Depot. He also requested Major Moore send additional supplies upriver on the "Josephine." And by now a heavy, cold wind was blowing out of the north.

4 PM—The "Far West" leaves the mouth of the Rosebud and heads upriver toward old Fort Pease. Terry, Gibbon, and Brisbin were on board.

7th Cavalry—4 PM—Custer ordered camp be made near the base of a steep bluff on the west bank of the creek, about twelve miles from where they started, ten miles up the Rosebud. Wood, grass, and water were in adequate supply.[17]

ABOUT SUNSET—8:50 PM—A 7th Cavalry officers conference was called by Custer, but oddly enough, it was not a cheery get-together.[18] During the talk a flare-up occurred between Custer and Benteen: Custer questioned the loyalty of some of his officers and said they were grumbling behind his back to Terry. Benteen challenged Custer to name names, but Custer said Benteen was not one of those in question (there is some evidence—read: innuendo—it may have been Keogh), and the tensions cooled. Custer became very conciliatory after that. Uncharacteristically, Custer even called for suggestions. He told his officers of his estimates of the size of the Indian force: the Indian Office in Washington estimated 3,000 persons, translating to 850 warriors. That tied in with Boyer's earlier estimate of 400 lodges equaling 800 warriors. Custer figured another 500 *might* come out of the agencies for the summer, making a maximum range of some 1,300 to 1,500. "This figure was an underestimate, for General Sheridan's attempts to control the agency Indians with heavy garrisons would drive out exceptionally large numbers of summer roamers. That was what Custer did *not* know."[19] In addition, Custer announced the suspension of all trumpet calls and officers' watches were synchronized. Lieutenant Godfrey wrote that watches were compared to ensure they were set on "official time."[20] This was the only instance of comparing watches mentioned in any of the journals.[21] Godfrey also said, "We did not have the local time, our watches were not changed."[22] Stable guards were to wake the troops at three AM; and they were to march at five AM. Benteen was designated Officer-of-the-Day for the following day.[23] Oddly too, Custer gave great discretion to the troop commanders, saying the only thing to come out of his headquarters would be,

> …when to move out of and when to go into camp. All other details, such as reveille, stables, watering, halting, grazing, etc., on the march would be left to the judgment and discretion of the troop commanders; they were to keep within supporting distance of each other, not to get ahead of the scouts, or very far to the rear of the column.[24]

Godfrey claimed Custer showed a lack of self-confidence. "His manner and tone, usually brusque and aggressive, or somewhat rasping, was on this occasion conciliating and subdued."[25] As lieutenants Wallace, Godfrey, and McIntosh were walking away, Wallace made the comment, "Godfrey, I believe General Custer is going to be killed…. I have never heard Custer talk in that way before."[26] Godfrey made the necessary preparations and gave the necessary orders to his company. During this routine, he came to the bivouac area of the scouts and met up with Mitch Boyer, Bloody Knife, and Half Yellow Face. Boyer saw him and—apparently at the suggestion of the Crow—asked Godfrey,

"Have you ever fought against these Sioux?" The following conversation ensued: Godfrey: "'Yes,' I replied. Then he [Boyer] asked, 'Well, how many do you expect to find?' I answered, 'It is said we may find between one thousand and fifteen hundred.' 'Well, do you think we can whip that many?' 'Oh, yes, I guess so.' After he had interpreted our conversation, he said to me with a good deal of emphasis, 'Well, I can tell you we are going to have a ----- big fight.'"[27]

Side Notes—Author/historian John Gray does not mention the flare-up between Benteen and Custer, but does say Custer encouraged his officers to cooperate; Gray does mention Benteen's testiness, however. Willert brings it up, saying Benteen was the only person to have ever mentioned it and neither Godfrey nor Gibson—both of who wrote of the meeting—ever brought it up.

Gibbon/Montana Column—6 AM—*Captain Ball ordered Gibbon's cavalry on the march. They were to head to Fort Pease as rapidly as possible. The infantry was to follow as soon as it could.*

7 AM—Bradley's scouts and Freeman's infantry started their march, soon passing the cavalry whose trains got stuck in mud.

5 PM—After traveling some twenty-two miles over bad roads, the wagons camped along the Yellowstone, below the cavalry. The plan was to continue to old Fort Pease where the boats would join up and ferry the cavalry over the Yellowstone. At 5:30 PM Freeman, Ball, and Bradley go into camp along the Yellowstone, the infantry and cavalry in sight of one another. They had traveled about twenty-nine miles. And by now the cavalry decided to resume its trumpet calls.

Steamer "Far West"—*After traveling only about seventeen miles against a strong current, the "Far West" moors. It was 8:15 PM and the rain had stopped. The day's chores, however, were not over as the steamer needed to take in wood.*

Carr's 5th Cavalry—EARLY MORNING—*Seven of the eight companies of the 5th Cavalry depart Fort Laramie. There were more than 350 effectives.*

JUNE 23, 1876—FRIDAY—*Military Correspondence & Intelligence Reports*—From the Acting Assistant Adjutant General, Department of the Platte—"Repeats telegram received from Capt. Nickerson A. D.C. reporting fight with Indians on Rosebud Creek. Nine men killed and twenty-one wounded."[28]

From Gen. Geo. Crook—"Reports fight with Indians on Rosebud Creek."[29]

From the Acting Assistant Adjutant General, Department of the Platte—"Repeats telegram from Ge. Crook, directing five companies of infantry to join his command."[30]

From the Acting Assistant Adjutant General, Department of the Platte—"Reports the sending of 3 Co's of Infantry in accordance with Gen. Crook's directions."[31]

From the Acting Assistant Adjutant General, Department of the Platte—"Company H, 3rd Cav. ordered to North Platte Bridge."[32]

From the Acting Assistant Adjutant General, Department of the Platte—"Notes receipt of dispatch and orders given in accordance therewith."[33]

From the Commanding Officer, Fort Laramie—"Telegram from Flagler to Gen. Carr the only one rec'd. Detachment will start at 4 PM."[34]

From the Commanding Officer, Fort Laramie—"Notes the receipt of two telegrams for Gen. Carr."[35]

From the Commanding Officer, Fort Laramie—"Gen. Carr will probably receive 1st telegram before he reaches Sage Creek. Capt. Montgomery will take second in the morning."[36]

7th Cavalry—3 AM—The stable guards moved throughout the camp waking the troopers. Their breakfast consisted of black coffee and fried bacon cooked over small fires dug into the earth, and at five AM the regiment departed camp. On what would prove to be another very hot day—unlike the day prior—Custer led out, followed by two sergeants, one carrying the regimental standard, the other carrying Custer's personal flag. Godfrey mentioned it was the same flag Custer carried in the "Rebellion."

The column continues up the Rosebud, crossing and re-crossing, for about thirty miles. Benteen's H and two other companies brought up the rear, behind the recalcitrant mules,[37] now re-organized into one command following the main column. (Time verified by Wallace, Godfrey, and Herendeen.[38]) It appears SOP dictated each company would detail four to six men, each day, for duty with the pack train.[39] Lieutenant Wallace wrote,

> All were ready at the appointed time, and the command moving out we crossed to the right bank of the Rosebud. The bluff being very broken, we had to follow the valley for some distance, crossing the Rosebud five times in three miles; thence up the right side for about ten miles. There we halted, to allow the pack train to close up. Soon after starting, crossed to the left bank and followed that for fifteen miles, and camped on right bank at 4:30 PM, making a distance of over thirty miles. The last of the pack train did not get into camp until near sunset. About five miles from our last camp we came to the trail made by Major Reno, a few days previous, and a few miles farther on saw the first traces of the Indian camps. They were all old, but everything indicated a large body of Indians. Every bend of the stream bore traces of some old camp, and their ponies had nipped almost every spear of grass. The ground was strewn with broken bones and cuttings from buffalo hides. The country passed over after the first few miles was rolling, and a few deep ravines the only obstacle to hinder the passage of a wagon train. Soil poor, except along the creek. Grass all eaten up. Plenty of cottonwood along the creek. During the last five or six miles of the march, the cottonwood timber was gradually replaced by ash and a species of elder. The valley was about one-fourth of a mile wide, and for the last fifteen miles the hills were very steep and rocky, sandstone being present. The country back from the hills looked to be very much broken. The hills were covered with a short growth of pines. No game seen during the day; weather warm and clear.[40]

The lead party probably consisted of Custer, Bloody Knife, Boyer, Herendeen, and Half Yellow Face.[41]

Side Notes—In a different context, James Willert mentions Godfrey not being a part of Benteen's three-company, bring-up-the-rear assignment. Yet when the divide was crossed on June twenty-fifth, Benteen was assigned companies D, H, and K, the latter being Godfrey's. This is merely another example of Custer's proclivity for doing whatever he wanted, assigning whatever company he wanted, whenever he wanted to do so.[42]

7th Cavalry—[… *continued…*]—Meanwhile, at 7:40 AM, the main players cross the Rosebud to its right bank, and the column passes the first Sioux camp (eight to nine miles), and Custer remarks to Charles Varnum, his Chief-of-Scouts, "Here's where Reno made the mistake of his life. He had six troops of cavalry and rations enough for a number of days. He'd have made a name for himself if he'd pushed on after them."[43] Benteen said the village was "immense." This was the camp below (R-19) where Reno entered the valley (R-22¾).

Side Notes—Now begins one of the more perplexing series of antinomies reasonable, experienced, and intelligent men succumbed to. Lieutenant Godfrey was perplexed by the "numerous stands of brush, whose crowns had been joined to form a kind of overhead framework." At first, the troops thought it was to protect the Indians' dogs, but it was later learned—and Wooden Leg also told Marquis—these were wickiups housing young, single warriors who had joined the main camp.[44]

Seeing this, let us review what we know about these Indians. To reiterate: the Indian Office in Washington, D.C., had told Custer they estimated the winter roamers at 3,000 persons, i.e., 850 warriors. That tallied with Boyer's estimates of villagers on the Tongue and Rosebud Rivers, i.e., 400 lodges, 800 warriors. Based on all this, Custer figured 1,000, plus another 500 coming out of the agencies, the so-called "summer roamers." What Custer did not know, however, was Sheridan's attempts to control the agencies with larger garrisons (the 5th Cavalry) drove exceptionally large numbers of Indians out of the agencies. These summer roamers joined the winter roamers; but what about the telegrams Terry sent to Sheridan, first 2,000 lodges, then 1,500, versus what Custer was seeing now? How did he ever reconcile the vast discrepancies in these numbers? So let us look once again at the post-battle census ordered by General Sheridan. At the Spotted Tail Agency: instead of 9,610, there were 2,315; at Red Cloud: instead of 12,873, there were 4,760; at Cheyenne River: instead of 7,586, there were 2,280; at Standing Rock: instead of 7,322, there were 2,305. The totals: instead of 37,391, there were 11,660.[45] Again, even these lower numbers—whether pre- or post-campaign—have been largely discounted by modern scholarship as inflated, but this does not reconcile what was being seen on the ground with Terry's and Sheridan's reports, and it does not excuse the complete ignorance of educated and experienced soldiers to what they were seeing.

7th Cavalry—[*… continued…*]—At one of these first Sioux encampments, the Ree scouts discovered ancient pictographs (they mistook for new) Bloody Knife interpreted to mean: "Do not follow the Dakotas into the Bighorn country … for they will turn and destroy you."[46]

The targets of the campaign—their whereabouts long a mystery—were now coming into focus. Having traveled another eight miles, at 10:20 AM the column passed the second Sioux camp (Teat Butte, twenty-six miles up the Rosebud: R-26) on the creek's right bank. They go another two miles and at eleven AM halt for the pack train to catch up. At 11:30 AM, they leave the halt and head up the creek's right bank. Then, at 1:30 PM the column crosses Greenleaf Creek and reaches the third Sioux camp—the Greenleaf site (thirty-four miles up the Rosebud), and six miles farther up from the halt. (Wooden Leg claimed this was the fourth Indian camp on the Rosebud. *See May twenty-eighth.*)

These last two camps were no more than fourteen miles from the first and the trail kept widening. *Everyone assumed the camps were simply consecutive locations of one village and not possibly separate villages, all ultimately moving in the same southerly direction.* Reno worried about this, but apparently was the only one who did, writing in his autobiography:

> I was chastised by General Terry for going to the Rosebud. I do not think his discomfort was so much with me as with the fact that the information I brought forced him to change his plans. Custer also condemned my actions, saying that I ran too much risk of being discovered. Both seemed to hint that I was "glory hunting," when in fact I had neither the ammunition nor the supplies to have taken on the hostiles. What I really did was to prove that Terry's plan was futile and by forcing him to revise the plan saved him a great deal of embarrassment. One of the most important bits of intelligence was never known to us. *The signs we found were all signs of the winter roamers only; the summer roamers had not yet joined them. This fact caused everyone to grossly underestimate the ultimate size of the village we would encounter on June 25 at Little Big Horn.*[47] [Emphasis added.]

Varnum wrote: "We struck not only the trail of the Indians but the entire valley of the Rosebud appeared to have been a camp, where they had moved along as the grass was grazed off."[48] Custer would spur his command forward, usually leaving Benteen and the pack train and the last three companies well behind. This was more than thoughtless, because Custer himself—prior to advancing up the Rosebud—cautioned his commanders not to lag behind.

> The trail in some places was at least 300 yards in width and deeply worn. The scouts said it had been made by about 1,500 lodges and since there were doubtless other trails, they agreed that it proved that enormous numbers of Sioux, Cheyennes, and Arapahoes had left the agencies to join Sitting Bull. But the officers, misled by the report that there were only [500] to 800 warriors in the hostile bands, missed the significance of the trail entirely and persisted in believing that these large camps—they were from ⅓ to ½ a mile in diameter—were a succession of camps of a single band, rather than what they were, the single camp of several large bands together.[49]

As the command moved on, the valley narrowed to about a quarter of a mile in width, bordered by steep, rocky hills covered in pine. It was along this stretch that Reno turned back. Wallace wrote, the "country back from the hills looked to be very much broken."[50] It was ideal country for an ambush.

Between 4:30 PM and five PM the column moved up the right bank of the creek another nine miles. Custer now ordered the regiment to pitch camp on a broad, sage plain. The camp was located near the present-day junction with the Colstrip Road; Willert said where Lee Coulee enters the Rosebud Valley. They had traveled thirty-three miles for the day,[51] forty-three miles from the mouth of the creek. (The halt time was verified by Wallace[52]; Godfrey claimed it was "about five PM."[53]) The camp was perfumed by the pleasant summer aromas of plum, crabapple, and wild roses. Ash and elder covered the creek banks rather than the more common willow and cottonwood. To the west, rugged pine-covered bluffs; to the east, less rugged cliffs of sandstone, topped with pine. Edgar Stewart claimed the column was under constant surveillance by the Sioux and Cheyenne,[54] but based on what happened on June twenty-fifth, this is difficult to believe. In addition, there is little to no evidence to support Stewart's claim.

At Sunset (approximately 8:50 PM) the last of the pack train arrived in camp. Benteen was guided into the bivouac area by the adjutant, First Lieutenant William Winer Cooke. As they rode in, Benteen told Cooke he had devised a way of better dealing with the pack train and asked Cooke to tell Custer. Cooke refused, telling

Benteen he better inform Custer himself. Benteen was hesitant, but did so the following morning. The incident points out the reticence of the officers to tell Custer of anything new, indicating Custer's self-sufficient attitude. That evening seems to be when Custer's personal guidon blew down repeatedly, interpreted by some officers as a bad omen. Godfrey was the one who kept putting it back up. Both Edgar Stewart and James Willert claimed the incident occurred while the command was checking out the sun dance camp the following morning.[55]

Side Notes—According to Wooden Leg, there were six Indian camps along the Rosebud. The famous "sun dance" camp—yet to be encountered—was number five and the Busby/Mouth-of-Davis Creek camp was the sixth and last *along the Rosebud*. A seventh was in Davis Creek valley; the eighth, along Reno Creek; the ninth and tenth in the Little Big Horn valley. This particular Indian camp was the one Bradley had seen on May twenty-seventh, and it was estimated to be in the range of 350 to 400 lodges in size. Was this the camp seen by Lieutenant Bradley?

Indian Village—The Indians prepared to move downriver as even more joined them. They would move the next morning. (On June 28, 1876, three days after the battle, Captain Edward Ball [H/2C] tracked the Sioux *up* the Little Big Horn valley and discovered another, very large Indian trail leading downriver.)

> Our trail … was from a quarter to half a mile wide at all places where the form of the land allowed that width. Indians regularly made a broad trail when traveling in bands using travois. People behind often kept in the tracks of people in front, but when the party of travelers was a large one there were many of such tracks side by side.[56]

Gibbon/Montana Column—6 AM—The wagons leave camp, but because of the heavy rains recently wagons had difficulty crossing creeks, though they were aided by the day becoming very warm and drying out the roads. Shortly after the wagons departed—at 6:05 AM—Lieutenant Bradley's mounted scouts left their bivouac area. That afternoon Brisbin's 2nd Cavalry command arrives at Fort Pease, about two miles above the old trading post, and establishes a bivouac.

5:30 PM—The wagons, having made twenty-two miles, and 7th Infantry camp one-half to one mile below Pease. There, they find plenty of fresh meat in the camp, but the boats had not arrived as yet. Indians were seen across the river, but wagon master Carroll believed they were some of the Crow scouts.

Steamer "Far West"—8:40 PM—The "Far West," with Terry and a now very sick Gibbon, ties up about eight miles below Fort Pease and fifteen miles below the Big Horn–Yellowstone confluence.

JUNE 24, 1876—SATURDAY—*Side Notes*—From this point on, the times are based on my timing studies and in certain cases are accompanied by the work of others, primarily to show differences and discrepancies … and duly noted. It is important to understand others' timings are based on local sun time, while my research has determined the command was actually operating on headquarters, St. Paul time, some fifty-seven minutes later. This difference is reflected in *my* times. According to the U.S. Naval Observatory, sunrise was at 4:21 AM, MST (local).

It is also important to note an organizational change in our event presentation. For June twenty-fourth and June twenty-fifth, events will be shown in chronological order, unlike earlier when "tags" for various columns were isolated and presented as a whole. To show the relationship of events to each other we now follow a strict time sequence, a sequencing showing these interrelationships of time and space.

Military Correspondence & Intelligence Reports—From the Assistant Adjutant General, Department of Dakota—"No dispatch rec'd here from Lt. Gen'l to Gen. Terry. Have instructed C.O. Fort Lincoln to be on look out for it."[57]

From the Assistant Adjutant General, Department of Dakota—"Lieut. Gen'l's dispatch to Gen. Terry received."[58]

From the Commanding Officer, Fort Laramie—"I do not understand dispatch of today. I did not send telegram about Gen. Crook's dispatch."[59]

From Lt. Col. E.A. Carr—"Rel. to hiring of two guides who report hostile Indians on Powder river."[60]

7th Cavalry—4:30 AM—Five Crow scouts ate their breakfast and left to scout the route of advance.

5 AM (headquarters/St. Paul, Minnesota, watch time)—The 7th Cavalry leaves camp, moving up the right bank of the Rosebud, riding hard. Half Yellow Face and Boyer rode with Custer. The air was cool, crisp, and invigorating with a brisk headwind blowing from the south. From Lieutenant Wallace,

> After we had been on the march about an hour, our Crow scouts came in and reported fresh signs of Indians, but in no great numbers. After a short consultation, General Custer, with an escort of two companies, moved out in advance, the remainder of the command following at a distance of about half a mile. We followed the right bank of the Rosebud; crossed two running tributaries, the first we had seen. At 1 PM the command was halted, scouts sent ahead, and the men made coffee. The scouts got back about four, and reported a fresh camp at the forks of the Rosebud. Everything indicated that the Indians were not more than thirty miles away. At 5 PM the command moved out; crossed to left bank of Rosebud; passed through several large camps. The trail now was fresh, and the whole valley scratched up by the trailing lodge-poles. At 7:45 PM we encamped on the right bank of Rosebud. Scouts were sent ahead to see which branch of the stream the Indians had followed. Distance marched today, about 28 miles. Soil in the valley very good, and in many places grazing very fine. Timber scattering, principally elder and ash. Hills rough and broken, and thickly covered with pines. Weather clear and very warm.[61]

Captain George Yates was designated OD (Officer-of-the-Day),[62] thereby making Company F the pack train escort for the day, while Company M was the rear guard.[63] The Crow scout Curley—generally riding with the advance—soon returns to the main column. He tells the command, "Evidences of deserted camps continued to be found along the valley; but, interestingly, none appeared to be significantly larger than those already examined."[64]

Steamer "Far West"—4:30 AM—*The "Far West" passes Bradley's camp.*

5 AM—"Far West" arrives at old Fort Pease. On board were the following, most of them forming the crew:

- *Grant Marsh, captain and pilot*
- *Walter Burleigh, owner and clerk*
- *Dave Campbell, pilot*
- *Ben Thompson, first mate*
- *George Foulk, chief engineer*

- *John Hardy, engineer*
- *Reuben Riley, ship's steward*
- *James M. Sipes, a sometimes-barber*
- *Buford, kept the daily log.*
- *James Boles (?)*
- *Approximately thirty deck hands.*
- *Also aboard were the "Post Traders" for the expedition, John Smith and James Coleman, along with a fellow named Hall (nothing known about him other than he was an "experienced western farmer"[65]). George Morgan, who was married to a Crow woman and was the man who translated what Curley said when he came aboard after the Custer battle, was also on the vessel.*

Gibbon/Montana Column—6 AM—*Gibbon's infantry and Bradley's scouting command leave their bivouac.*

7th Cavalry—Meanwhile, back on the Rosebud, at 6:10 AM, the four Crow scouts reached Lame Deer Creek [R-53¾] where they find fresh trails of summer roamers joining the main trail. Godfrey wrote they "passed a great many camping places, all appearing to be of the same strength." Then, in one of the more telling admissions of error, he remarked,

> One would naturally suppose these were the successive camping-places of the same village, when in fact they were the continuous camps of several bands. The fact that they appeared to be of nearly the same age, that is, having been made at the same time, did not impress us then.[66]

7 AM—Custer tells George Herendeen to get ready to take Charlie Reynolds and scout Tullock's Creek, but Herendeen tells him it is too early yet, the gap leading to the creek's headwaters is still farther ahead. Boyer concurs. Then, a few minutes later—probably just about 7:10 AM—to everyone's surprise, "the *first* of the campsites to be of *considerable size and dimension* was encountered. This had been the place of the Sun Dance celebration of the Indians"[67] [R-46, Gray], the fourth Sioux camp. (According to Wooden Leg, this would have been the fifth Sioux camp.) While others disagree, John Gray claimed this was the first camp encountered this day and it became the command's first halt, around 6:30 AM. The exact timing of the discovery of this "sun dance" camp is uncertain. What *is* certain is the camp was located at Deer Medicine Rocks. In our timeline, we use an arrival time for the regiment of 7:10 AM, and ten miles from the camp of the twenty-third, basically in agreement with Gray. Gray placed the halt distance at one mile above the camp at R-47, four miles for the day, so far. This is located several hundred yards west of the state highway now paralleling Rosebud Creek. Willert claimed it was "a short distance below the valley which today guides to the small settlement of Lame Deer."[68] A scalp was found on a willow twig and someone brought it to Custer. Herendeen identified it as belonging to Private Stocker (H/2C), one of the three men killed from Gibbon's command a number of days earlier (May twenty-third). Godfrey claimed this was found in the sun dance camp.[69] The "sun dance" camp was much larger than the others and Godfrey remarked, "It was whilst here that the Indians from the agencies had joined the hostiles' camp."[70] (It was located near the Deer Medicine rocks; this being the location for the incident is verified by Paul Hedren.[71]) As the site was being examined,

Custer's personal flag—which had been stuck in the ground—blew down. Lieutenant Godfrey picked it up and stuck it back in, but it blew down again. Lieutenant Wallace considered it an omen of Custer's demise, though he apparently kept it to himself at the time. The sun dance pole itself was probably in excess of thirty-five feet high and troops discovered a sand pictograph (in a sweat lodge), the Ree and Crow scouts interpreted to mean "many soldiers plummeting towards an Indian village." They also found an iconograph—three red stones in a row—meaning a Sioux victory, as well as a cairn of rocks with the skull of a buffalo on one side and the skull of a cow on the other, with a stick aimed at the cow. "This meant the Sioux would fight like bulls and the whites would run like women."[72] All these things indicated just how confident the Indians were.

Side Notes—Distances of importance are: sun dance site to Lame Deer Creek: 1.8 miles. Another seven miles to Muddy Creek; 8.8 miles total, from the sun dance site.[73]

Gibbon/Montana Column—*7 AM—The infantry and Bradley join with the cavalry command, the latter being issued six pack mules per company, while four per company were issued to the infantry.*

~7:30 AM—Captain Thaddeus Sandford Kirtland's B/7I was left behind to guard the bivouac, wagons, and supplies while the rest of the column started up the Yellowstone. Two of the Gatling guns were also left behind at Fort Pease.[74] At the same time, Matthew Carroll's wagon train arrived at Ball's cavalry camp, two miles above Pease.

7th Cavalry—7:10 AM—The Crow scouts return reporting fresh tracks, "but in no great numbers."[75] (Willert has the discovery of the sun dance camp shortly *after* this halt for the Crow's report. He says it was shortly before the command halted for lunch, so probably late morning. Primary evidence suggests otherwise, therefore my estimate of an earlier discovery.) "...Three or four ponies and of one Indian on foot."[76] The scouts also told Custer the trail was fresher ten miles ahead.

> The tracks of the ponies and that of the lone Indian constituted the first evidence of the recent presence of Indians on the trail. It did not signify much, but it was enough to put Custer on the alert, hold a short conference with his officers and personally lead an advance guard of two companies.[77]

Custer calls his officers together for a quick briefing.

7:30 AM—The regiment moves out, marching at a fast walk, up the creek's right bank. Custer moved out in front with the scouts and two companies, the remainder of the regiment following about one-half mile behind. They moved at a fast walk. The regiment was required to march on separate trails to keep the dust clouds down and soon slowed down, moved slowly up the right bank (the east bank). Custer sends the four Crow ahead again. Lieutenant Godfrey wrote,

> The march during the day was tedious. We made many long halts so as not to get ahead of the scouts, who seemed to be doing their work thoroughly, giving special attention to the right, toward Tulloch's Creek, the valley of which was in general view from the divide. Once or twice smoke signals were reported in that direction. The weather was dry and had been for some time; consequently the trail was very dusty. The troops were required to march on separate trails so that the dust clouds would not rise so high. The valley was heavily marked with lodge-pole trails and pony tracks, showing that immense herds of ponies had been driven over it.[78]

More and more pictographs were discovered on the sandstone out-cropping.

9:20 AM—The Crow, trotting at six miles per hour, reach the abandoned Sioux camp at East Muddy Creek [R-58]. This would be the fifth Sioux camp (Wooden Leg does not account for this camp), and at 9:40 AM after studying the campsite head back to the column to report.

10:30 AM—The column passed Lame Deer Creek (six miles; R-53¾, Gray), basically where Boyer had turned back to the column when he was on Reno's scout. The Crow scouts return, now reporting of the abandoned campsite at East Muddy Creek [R-58]. At the same time, George Herendeen spotted an Indian trail that diverged up Lame Deer Creek and he follows it. It continued to diverge and he turned back to report to Custer.

Terry-Gibbon Column—10:30 AM—Terry orders a reconnaissance up Tullock's Creek valley, expecting his scouts to run into Herendeen, who he believed was probably on the way down the valley. Then, once Terry finds out what was going on with Custer, he could further develop his plans.

Side Notes—The best description of the Tullock's area—the valley and the divide between the Big Horn River and Tullock's Creek—comes from Roger Darling's outstanding book, *A Sad and Terrible Blunder*, and is outlined below.[79] The divide itself runs almost directly north-south:

> At its northern tip, the range begins its rise near the mouth of Tullock's Creek on the Big Horn River, at the very site of Terry's June 24th camp. Extending 28 miles southward, the range ends abruptly at a vast elevated plateau, dissipating as a gently rolling descent into the Little Big Horn Valley. At its greatest east-west bulge, Tullock divide is only 13 miles wide.
>
> Tullock's Creek, a placid stream meandering through a mile wide valley, constitutes the eastern boundary. Although gorges and deep winding ravines emerge from the divide ridgeline hovering hundreds of feet above and to its west, this initial ruggedness of the eastern drainage surface gradually smoothes itself into gentle pastures and rangeland by the time it descends to the creek bed. In consequence of this natural topography, Tullock Creek valley has offered an ideal trail for movement through the region since prehistoric time.
>
> The Big Horn River which marks the divide's western boundary and drainage outlet is not so hospitable to man's uses. The river's eastern bank is a continuous cliff from Tullock Creek mouth to near the Big Horn–Little Big Horn River forks, while just to its west stretches the broad fertile valley, the Big Horn Valley, taking its name from the river. For nearly the Tullock divide's entire length, sharp, steep-curving coulees gouge that western slope from the higher elevations to the river's edge. Hundreds of feet deep in places, these channels claw into the softer earth and scattered patches of sandstone moderating only occasionally to form manageable trails for human passage down their courses.... Where these streams slice through the cliff face, they create the few access points to the river water.
>
> Between Pocket Creek and the Big Horn forks to the south, the elevated plateau stretching between them is cut by North and South Cottonwood Creeks, Nine Mile, and Dry Creeks. These channels are deep, occasionally mistaken for rivers when they flow full of water for miles from their headwaters at the ridgeline. Whereas north-south human movement over the eastern, more tempered ground of Tullock Creek is easy, these cleavages of the divide's western drainage do not absolutely preclude, but place severe obstacles in the way of such transit.
>
> The narrowness of the 28 mile ridgeline is notable. The first third of its entire length, a linear 9 miles, constitutes a steady rise from Tullock Creek mouth southward to Tullock Peak, 800 feet above the valley floor. Along this route the ridgeline is often indistinguishable as such. Meandering across wide patches of rangeland, randomly splattered with prickly yucca and

sumac plants, scrub pine, ponderosa forests, and massive sandstone outcroppings, the ridgeline loses its identity. The diverse plant growth coupled with a gently rising surface gives the top-most region the deceptive appearance of soft, rolling hills. Occasionally, the huge sharp ridge spine reappears as a narrow path a dozen feet wide negotiating between huge rocks and trees. As one nears Tullock Peak, broad panoramic vistas of both Tullock and Big Horn Valleys come into view; even the Yellowstone River to the north and Big Horn Mountains to the far south are clearly seen....

Tullock Peak is not a distinctive mountain top. A family of three, adjacent, curving hills forms a small plateau, a bowl-like depression at it center. Looking south from this elevation, Holmes Peak is clearly seen eight miles away.

The intervening terrain constitutes the second, or middle third of Tullock divide, an abrupt and distinct departure from the more gentle northern third. Holmes Peak is a prominent, elongated ridge wall stretching east and west. Butte-like in appearance, its western edge drops off abruptly. Higher than Tullock Peak, Holmes rises 1,000 feet above the valley floors. What little definition there is of the ridgeline stops at Tullock Peak. Between Tullock and Holmes it disappears entirely and is replaced by a labyrinth of coulees forming the headwaters of Rough and Pocket Creeks. The waters draining this maze eventually blend into Pocket Creek which slices through the cliffs at the Big Horn River. Direct human passage through this middle third region of the divide is all but impossible.

The final southern third of the divide stretches from Holmes Peak to the headwaters of Dry Creek. Here, another discontinuous upheaval of rocky heights creates the headwaters of North and South Cottonwood Creeks and various other streams cutting the high plateau. That ridge-line definition which disappeared between Tullock and Holmes Peaks does not reestablish itself here either. Any north-south traveler through this more mountainous portion of the divide is forced to move well below the upper ridges and along the smoother surfaces of the river cliff tops.

The linear distance is twenty-two miles from Tullock Peak to the forks of the Big Horn River.[80] Then at 10:35 AM Terry begins sending a detachment of Indian scouts to the right bank of the Yellowstone, instructing them to scout Tullock's Creek. At eleven AM twelve Crow scouts were ferried across the Yellowstone and ordered to scout Tullock's Fork until they found "a Sioux village on a recent trail."[81]

Indian Village—MID-MORNING—The Indians dismantle their village, preparing to cross to the west side of the Little Big Horn River, and begin moving downstream, the Cheyenne leading, the Hunkpapa bringing up the rear.

7th Cavalry—NOON—The 7th Cavalry's advance is continued. Herendeen—Godfrey, as well—spots an Indian trail of lodge poles diverging up a tributary valley leading to Lame Deer Creek. Herendeen reports this to Custer. Custer sends out scouts, some to summon Varnum, and when he reported in Custer instructed him to check out Herendeen's diverging trail. Varnum protested his scouts could not have missed any such trail, but he went out to check anyway. Varnum claimed Custer told him it was Lieutenant Godfrey who reported the diverging trail.[82] Custer also assigns Lieutenant Luther Hare to assist Varnum at this time.

Terry-Gibbon Column—NOON—*Gibbon's command begins ferrying across the Yellowstone to the east bank of the Big Horn confluence, aiming for Tullock's Fork, a tributary of the Big Horn.*

7th Cavalry—1 PM—Custer orders a halt to await Varnum's return. This was the second halt of the day, at East Muddy Creek [R-58], the fifth Sioux camp location (some five miles more; halt time verified by Wallace). Varnum and his scouts follow the diverging trail and discover it was merely a branch-off from the main trail and it swings west, re-joining the main trail, but there was plenty speculation as to why the trail had diverged. While Varnum is out and the troops resting, Custer sends out the Crow to scout the advance. It was probably here the Indian trail became "more than a mile wide, the earth so furrowed by thousands of travois poles that it resembled a plowed field."[83] Historian Charles Kuhlman claimed this halt was at the "sun dance camp,"[84] but this was incorrect. "The assemblage was a straggling one, since the hostiles did not move in 'Indian file' but in a wide, irregular column, each family traveling by itself, and the group was spread out probably one mile wide and over three miles in length."[85] Despite the cumbersome formation, they could move with remarkable speed, covering as much as fifty miles a day. John Gray never mentioned, specifically, Connell's huge trail, but he did write,

> …everyone noted puzzling changes in the Indian trail…. Instead of a single heavy trail with old campsites a day's journey apart, there were now multiple trails in various directions and small scattered campsites, some growing fresher and fresher. These were, in fact, converging trails left by summer roamers coming out to join the winter roamers.[86]

Gray goes on to explain why this was of such concern to Custer and why he spent the next four hours bivouacked, while he sent scouts scurrying hither and yon. This is also an extremely important point when considering Custer's actions and strategy during the battle: "Every officer on the frontier knew only too well that Indians shunned pitched battles and were so mobile and elusive as to be frustratingly difficult to corral. Thus, the overriding fear was that the village would break up and scatter."[87]

While resting and relaxing, the troops made coffee and prepared a meal. In the meantime, after about a twelve-mile trot over two hours, out and back, Varnum reported Herendeen's trail did diverge, but it eventually *re-*joined the main trail. He also reported the trail became fresher by the mile and the signs indicated an *immense* force of Indians.

> Lame Deer Creek joins Rosebud Creek…. Near the junction of the two streams, the crossing of Lame Deer is mandatory. Rosebud Creek skirts the high banks on the left bank, making travel on the right bank more accessible due to the opening up of the valley on that side. The vast Indian trail heading up Rosebud Creek all but obliterated any good crossing of Lame Deer Creek. Therefore, if any of the bands of Lakota traveling near the end of the vast assemblage wanted to cross Lame Deer Creek, they most likely would have turned and headed up Lame Deer Creek a short distance, crossed the creek, and instead of following the creek back down to the Rosebud, would have cut across country picking up the main trail again farther on…. [T]he deviant travois trail left Rosebud Creek, traveled southeast up Lame Deer Creek about 0.7 miles from the Rosebud, crossed the creek, thence skirting bluffs to the south eventually wound its way back to the trail again. This deviation most assuredly followed the 'short cut,' or tribal road for a short distance before rejoining the main trail.[88]

Heski feels the reason Custer halted was to wait for Varnum to return. He states, "Another reason for the halt … was the remains of another village site a few miles west of Muddy Creek." Herendeen said the halt was for two hours, between one and three PM:

> …the command started ahead on the large trail again, which became fresher as we advanced. We passed over places where a number of camps had been pitched quite close together from

which we wrongly inferred that the Indians had been traveling very slowly and moving only for grass … these camping places represented the village of separate bands or tribes simultaneously encamped and not successive camps by any one band.[89]

Indian Village—That afternoon the Indians' move downstream begins. Most accounts claim they were preparing to move again, either the same day or the day after Custer struck, making this only a temporary camp.

7th Cavalry—4 PM—The Crow scout White Swan returns and reports finding a fresh camp at the forks of the Rosebud, some ten to twelve miles farther south. Heski feels this was an indication the hostiles were no more than thirty miles away.[90]

> … [W]hat the Crows reported during the second halt [this one] brought [Custer] up sharply; for here was something wholly unexpected, something that might call for action radically different from what was contemplated in his orders. The Crows had been over the trail made, evidently, only a day or two before by a large body of Indians coming from the agencies to join the camps on the Little Big Horn. They had not followed the Indian trail down the Tongue, i.e., the course taken by the rest during their spring wanderings, but had crossed over to the Rosebud a little above the site of the Sundance lodge, where, as related in the report of Wallace, the troops struck it soon after resuming the march at five o'clock.[91]

Varnum also reported the diverging trail linked up again with the main trail, up the Rosebud and farther westward. He told Custer,

> …the trail sign indicated a force of immense size ahead, that the trail was fresher by the mile, that a "…fresh camp…" had been found "…at the forks of the Rosebud…" some ten or a dozen miles west, and that the hostiles, at this time, were probably "…not more than thirty miles away…."[92]

Terry-Gibbon Column—*4:15 PM*—*The ferrying of Gibbon's command is completed. Their march up the Big Horn begins. Brisbin tells Terry scouts Muggins Taylor and Henry Bostwick have found a good crossing of Tullock's. Terry immediately orders the troops to advance, and assuming he will be hearing from Herendeen, orders a bivouac to be found along Tullock's Creek. While Barney Prevo accompanied this group, Bradley headed out and finds a suitable site about one mile up the creek from its mouth into the Big Horn.*

> *5 PM*—*Gibbon's troops begin their move to Tullock's Fork—a tributary of the Big Horn—though without Gibbon and Kirtland's B/7I. They are to camp on lower Tullock's Creek. And John Gibbon is still sick on board the "Far West."*

7th Cavalry—5 PM—The 7th Cavalry resumes its march up the Rosebud, now across to the narrow, sage covered left bank of the valley, passing "…through several large camps. The trail was now fresh and the whole valley scratched up by trailing lodgepoles."[93] Custer sends out flankers—Varnum took the left front; Hare took the right front—to check for diverging trails, again worried about the village breaking up. "He said he wanted to get the whole village and nothing must leave the trail without his knowing it."[94] Only *converging* trails were found, however, but Custer and his officers never grasped the meaning, always thinking the trails moved away. "The fresh side trails represented agency Indians finally joining the large camp."[95] The column is now moving very slowly as several more campsites were found, and a number of halts were made, ostensibly to check what they found, but equally, to keep down the dust.

The trail was heavily marked by lodge poles and pony herds, and Herendeen was impressed greatly by the fact the village sites seemed so close to one another.

Terry-Gibbon Column—5:30 PM–6 PM—The Montana column goes into bivouac on Tullock's Fork, about a mile above its mouth, at the foot of a perpendicular wall of rock. The distance from this camp to the staging area at the fork of the Big Horn and Little Big Horn rivers is thirty-seven miles via Tullock's Creek valley, then westward.[96] *Terry, his staff, the headquarters contingent, and an escort leave the "Far West" and head up the Big Horn, while Gibbon, still very sick, remains on board the vessel. Dr. Williams is with him.*

7th Cavalry—6:30 PM—In one of the strangest episodes of the entire campaign, Custer and his lead elements reach the gap in the western hills leading to the head-waters of Tullock's Creek. Herendeen tells Custer, but the latter only kept moving forward and Herendeen simply remained in the column. No trails went in the direction of Tullock's.

> But Custer—Herendeen recalled—only looked at him, said not a word, and finally the civilian scout reined back to once again take his place in the moving column. Herendeen was unable to fathom Custer's curious behavior at this junction, but Custer's reason should have been obvious—the hostiles *trail* continued up the Rosebud Valley, but *where did it lead?*[97]

Godfrey wrote that smoke signals were reported—once or twice—from the direction of Tullock's Creek valley, but even that seemed to make no impression on Custer (and they proved ultimately to be nothing).[98]

Terry-Gibbon Column—7:30 PM—The Terry-Gibbon column has arrived at camp on lower Tullock's Creek, having been delayed by repacking mules. No word yet from Custer and Terry expresses visible disappointment.

7th Cavalry—8:20 PM—The sun is behind the mountains to the west, creating shadows in the valley and giving one the impression of sundown and at 8:31 PM civil twilight ends and it has become too dark to read. According to the U.S. Naval Observatory, civil twilight ended at 8:42 PM, MST, in today's time zones, the discrepancy accounted for based on one's precise location.

    8:42 PM—Custer orders the command into camp at the Busby bend (present-day town of Busby, Montana, approximately seventy miles from the Yellowstone), on the right bank (twelve miles; and twenty-seven miles for the day; Godfrey claimed twenty-eight miles). (Time established by Wallace and verified by Godfrey as "about sundown…"; nearly sundown in Chicago would have been 6:30 PM.) It was here Varnum had discovered the fresh camp. This would be the sixth Sioux camp discovered by the regiment, bringing it in line with the Wooden Leg figure.

Indian Village—The following shows the primary Sioux and Cheyenne camps:

- "Bradley camp"—R-7—May 27.
- 1st camp—R-19, where Custer made the remark to Varnum.
- 2nd camp—Teat Butte, R-26.
- 3rd camp—Greenleaf Creek, R-34.
- 4th camp—Sundance camp, R-46.
- 5th camp—East Muddy Creek, R-58.
- 6th camp—Busby bend, R-70.

7th Cavalry—PVT Windolph wrote the troops "…went into camp at sundown. In late June up here in the Northwest country that means around nine o'clock."[99] It appears Windolph was also operating on St. Paul (headquarters) time. This would tie it in with Heski's comment. Heski goes on to say that around seven PM in June, the sun is behind the Wolf Mountains, creating shadows in the valley. If there are no clouds, you can still see objects until about ten PM.

This Indian camp was approximately two miles below and opposite the (upper) Rosebud forks, specifically, Davis Creek. On the right was a high bluff and between this bluff and the river was a level, grassy plateau (about 200 yards wide) covered with wild roses. The camp was located in the freshly abandoned summer roamer campsite. George Herendeen stated: "About four o'clock we came to the place where the village had been apparently only a few days before, and went into camp two miles below the forks of the Rosebud [i.e., Davis Creek]. The scouts all again pushed out to look for the village…."[100] Heski explains the time difference—Herendeen's four PM versus the 7:45 PM—by saying Herendeen probably arrived at the bivouac site earlier with the scouts. Another explanation may be the fact Fort Ellis was apparently operating on San Francisco time and Herendeen had come from that area and was conceivably still using that time reference. At this site, scout Charlie Reynolds began distributing his personal belongings to several of the troopers obviously fearing he would not survive. He did not.

Indian Village—Somewhere around this time two Cheyenne warriors from Little Wolf's party of seven lodges that had left the Red Cloud agency to join the Sioux— Big Crow and Black White Man—spot the troops in this camp. That evening the Cheyenne village held a dance, a social affair. Similar dances were being held in each of the Sioux circles.

> The Cheyenne location was about two miles north from the present railroad station at Garryowen, Montana. We were near the mouth of a small creek flowing from the southwestward into the river. Across the river east of us and a little upstream from us was a broad coulee, or little valley, having now the name Medicine Tail coulee.[101]

There were only six main Indian circles: Cheyenne, Minneconjou, Oglala, Sans Arc, Hunkpapa, and Blackfeet Sioux. The Brulé, Assiniboine, and Waist and Skirt (Santee) stayed in their own groups, but close to another circle.[102] The Santee camped next to the Hunkpapa; the Brulé, part by the Oglala, part by the Blackfeet. The general order was Cheyenne, Sans Arc, Minneconjou, Hunkpapa along the river, while the Oglala were away from the river and southwest of the Cheyenne and Sans Arc. The Blackfeet were also back from the river and between the Oglala and Hunkpapa, nearer the latter. All the camps were east of the 1930 highway and the railroad. Wooden Leg, in his discussions with Thomas Marquis, broke down the size of the village as follows: the Cheyenne: 300 lodges; Blackfeet: 300 or a few less; Sans Arc: more than 300; Minneconjou: more than the Sans Arcs; Oglala: more than the Sans Arcs; and Hunkpapa: 600 lodges….[103] Overall, this would seem to equate to more than 2,000 lodges and clearly would be too many.[104] (Wooden Leg said there were no whites or mixed breeds in the camp.[105])

According to archaeologist Douglas Scott, the camps were configured as follows:

the Hunkpapa circle was the southernmost. Then, just below and slightly northwest was the Blackfeet circle. The Minneconjou circle was northeast of the Blackfeet and close to the river. Due west of the Blackfeet was the Brulé circle and right next to the Brulé, slightly north and west, was the Oglala. Near the river and at the mouth of Medicine Tail Coulee was the Sans Arc circle; and near the river, just to the north and west of the Sans Arc—but still across from the Medicine Tail ford—was the Cheyenne circle.[106]

Terry-Gibbon Column—8:45 PM—*The twelve Crow scouts returned reporting seeing only buffalo about six miles up Tullock's Creek. An arrow had wounded one of the buffalo and the Crow thought this was momentous news. In reality, they were afraid to go any farther ... and there was still no news from Custer. Terry now sends orders to the "Far West" to enter the Big Horn River at noon tomorrow (the twenty-fifth) and head to the mouth of the Little Big Horn by noon the day after (the twenty-sixth). Meanwhile, Lieutenant Bradley expresses disappointment and disgust, for the Crow had only gone about ten miles—or less—in eight hours, bringing back no worthwhile intelligence other than a wounded buffalo, probably hurt by a Sioux hunting party, so now Terry decides to send Bradley up Tullock's Creek in the morning. He also—inexplicably—chooses Lieutenant McClernand to pick the trail for the column to move up the Tullock's Creek valley.*[107]

7th Cavalry—8:45 PM—As darkness was falling the three Crow scouts returned to report the Sioux had turned west and crossed the divide to the lower Little Big Horn valley. They were not sure which direction the hostiles were heading, however. Custer went over to their camp and had a talk with them. (Varnum claimed five Crow were at this meeting, Half Yellow Face still out somewhere.) Herendeen probably now wondered if Custer would send him down Tullock's Creek, but again, Custer gave no sign that was what he wanted to do. Instead, Custer decided to send the Crow out again, to follow the trail until they could locate the village or they had traveled until noon of the following day. The command would stay put until the scouts reported back. Even though Terry's orders had suggested Custer by-pass the trail if it led west toward the Little Big Horn valley, Custer felt it better to camp this night *on* the trail until he could be certain of where it went and then make his decision. The Crow scouts now made a suggestion they ride to a promontory (the Crow's Nest) where they could view the Little Big Horn valley when it got light. This way they could give Custer reliable information without having to ride all night and into the valley. Custer accepted this suggestion and instructed Varnum to go with them. He also would send Boyer, Reynolds, and eight or ten Ree.

> The prospect of an *earlier* awareness as to the hostiles' position—if they should be in the Little Big Horn Valley—now prompted Custer to cancel his earlier plan to stay the night in his present position ... and to proceed in a *night march* ... toward the divide.[108]

Custer told Varnum to leave around nine PM, so the meeting was probably held a bit earlier than this. Custer said he would move the command at eleven. John Gray felt this was the final proof Custer still had not known, even by the time he reached the Busby bivouac, the Sioux had crossed the divide to the Little Big Horn. Yet the trail was so fresh it became obvious the Sioux had to be on the *lower* Little Big Horn and

Village Map
Wooden Leg's Camp Sites

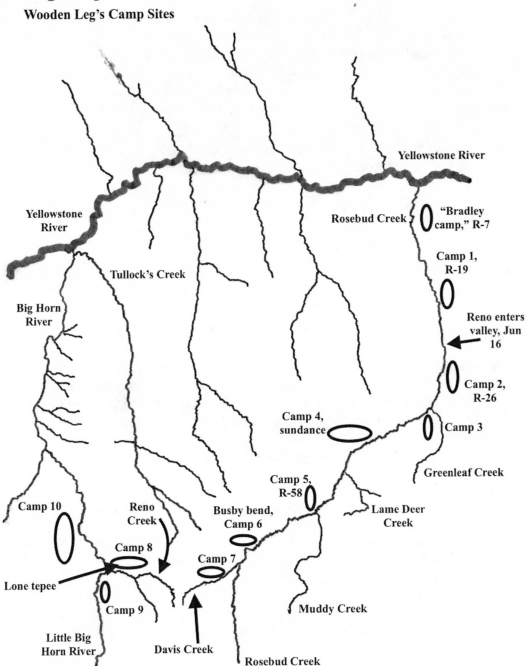

Yellowstone River

Yellowstone River

Rosebud Creek

"Bradley camp," R-7

Camp 1, R-19

Reno enters valley, Jun 16

Big Horn River

Tullock's Creek

Camp 2, R-26

Camp 4, sundance

Camp 3

Greenleaf Creek

Camp 5, R-58

Camp 10

Reno Creek

Busby bend, Camp 6

Lame Deer Creek

Camp 8

Camp 7

Lone tepee

Camp 9

Muddy Creek

Little Big Horn River

Davis Creek

Rosebud Creek

Indian Village: Rosebud Creek to the Little Big Horn.

had not yet gone to its upper reaches. "The unexpected news brought by the Crows that the Sioux were probably on the lower, rather than the upper, reaches of the Little Big Horn posed a serious problem that demanded a weighty decision from Custer."[109] Terry's plan was a flexible one, but of all the scenarios envisioned, a Sioux encampment on the *lower* Little Big Horn was the one the plan could least accommodate.

Custer's orders were to scout the upper reaches of the Rosebud, cross the divide to the *upper* Little Big Horn, move north, down that river, and drive the Sioux north into Terry's blocking position, which he was to reach on the twenty-sixth. It was only the twenty-fourth, however, and Terry would be a good thirty miles from his blocking position. Custer's choices were to continue south along the Rosebud, risking detection and losing track of the village, or to cross the divide from the Busby camp at night and hide out for a day while Terry moved into position. This latter plan meant Custer's scouts could still keep track of the village and Custer would still have the element of surprise, still attack from above, and still block escape routes to the east.

> Custer could follow Terry's recommendation by marching up the Rosebud tomorrow and starting down the Little Big Horn the next day, thus preserving the timing. Even if these marches were made at night, however, he would leave a trail as readable as a poster, and discovery would warn the village to flee and scatter. He would also lose track of the village and at best have to search for it again; at worst it could escape undetected back to the Rosebud and eastward or down the Bighorn and attack Terry's weaker force on the march.[110]

9:20 PM—Lieutenant Varnum and his scouts (fifteen men, total) leave camp for the Crow's Nest (approximately 11¾ miles away). It was already dark and Varnum had probably traveled as many as seventy miles this day, checking out every possibly Indian trail, especially those leading off to the left or east. He brought with him about fourteen others, including his orderly, Private Elijah Strode, Mitch Boyer, and Charlie Reynolds. In addition, there were the five Crow—White Man Runs Him, Curley, Goes Ahead, Hairy Moccasin, White Swan, and six Ree—Forked Horn, Black Fox, Red Bear, Strikes The Lodge, Red Star, Bull. Varnum says he took "about a dozen Rees...."[111] (In an April 14, 1909, letter to Walter Camp, Varnum claimed eight or ten Ree.[112])

9:22 PM—Nautical twilight ends—full darkness begins; nighttime.

9:25 PM—Shortly after Varnum's departure Custer called for the officers to get together, ordering everyone to report to his tent. Because of the deep, dark night, however, there was great difficulty finding the meeting and Benteen missed it, Keogh finally telling him of the plans. At 9:25 PM–9:30 PM, Lieutenant Godfrey says he and Lieutenant Hare lay down to take a nap,[113] but as they had just settled in, they were called for the officers' conference with Custer. Custer informed them of the Indians' probable location and that there would be a night march—leaving at eleven PM—to cross the Rosebud-Little Big Horn divide so as to not be seen. They would find a place to hide during the following day so the situation could be studied, and then an attack would be planned for June twenty-sixth. It was clearly dark at this time for Godfrey describes the difficulty he and Hare had locating Custer's bivouac area.[114]

The plan would be to lay low on the twenty-fifth, scout the area, find the actual location of the village, and make plans for the attack. They would then make another night march to the village and attack the morning of the twenty-sixth. "Reno wrote in his July 5th report, Custer notified the assembly it was necessary to cross the divide at night as 'it would be impossible to do so in the daytime without discovering our march to the Indians.'"[115] "Reno also stated Custer said, 'beyond a doubt the village was in the valley of the Little Big Horn.'"[116] According to Lieutenant Winfield Scott Edgerly of Company D, "[T]he Indian's village has been located in the valley of the Little Big Horn and the object (of the night march) being to cross the divide between the Rosebud and the Little Big Horn before daylight."[117] And Custer "told the officers they would have the fight of their lives."[118] Apparently, Fred Gerard had told Custer he could expect to find 2,500 to 3,000 warriors. Gerard claimed to have told Terry there would be as many as 4,000 warriors if all those who had left the reservations united.[119] The meeting was short and sweet and several officers sang a few songs for Custer: "Little Footsteps Soft and Gentle"; "The Good Bye" ("The Good-Bye at the Door"); "Doxology"; "Annie Laurie"; "For He's a Jolly Good Fellow"; and "Tenting Tonight."

Side Notes—9:30 PM–10 PM—Some authors claim Varnum and the scouts left for the Crow's Nest at this time. Willert estimated they moved about three miles per hour, figuring twelve miles between the Crow's Nest and the Rosebud.

9:45 PM–10 PM—Tom Heski has Varnum leaving for the Crow's Nest at this time.[120] He claimed there was a total of fourteen men.[121]

10 PM—Author Bruce Liddic has Varnum leaving for the Crow's Nest and Custer calling his officers together.

According to the U.S. Naval Observatory, the *waxing crescent moon* (twelve percent of the disk illuminated) set at 10:44 PM, MST.

11 PM—Original kick-off time, but the move may have been delayed. Author Vern Smalley claims eleven PM was the time the command began to move and cites the following witnesses: Godfrey: 11:30 PM; Herendeen: eleven PM; Benteen: eleven PM, sharp; Gerard: about 11:30 PM; Moylan: about eleven PM; Reno: eleven PM; Hare: eleven PM; De Rudio: eleven PM; Wallace: near one AM (in 1877); and Wallace: eleven PM (Reno Court of Inquiry, 1879).[122]

We resume....

7th Cavalry—10 PM—The troops were awakened for the night march, and at precisely eleven PM were on the move. Benteen wrote:

> We were to move at 11 o'clock that night, at which hour we did move, however, there was an hour and a half consumed [11 PM–12:30 AM], in getting the pack train across Mud Creek [Rosebud flood plain below confluence of Busby and Rosebud Creek]. Colonel Keogh had charge of the packs [rear guard escort] on that move and the column remained impatient on [the] other bank of the creek while Keogh was superintending crossing the pack train.[123]

As the column was assembling, Fred Gerard sat with Custer and claimed Half Yellow Face and Bloody Knife told Custer (apparently Reno, as well), he could not cross the divide before daylight without being discovered by Sioux scouts. It appears, however, this occurred around two AM near "Halt One" and not here and at this time. This is extremely important for obvious reasons that should become apparent as we continue on.

Lieutenant Godfrey believed the night march began at 11:30 PM.[124] He also quoted Private Giovanni Martini (H Company) as saying the same time. Lieutenant Wallace, in his report, claimed they left at one AM, but Heski disputes that saying

Wallace may have been referring to the time the packs cleared the Rosebud.[125] God-frey mentions nothing, however, of the departure time in his *Century Magazine* arti-cle, "Custer's Last Battle 1876," and it should be noted time discrepancies here are clearly the result of variable cueing.

11:48 PM—The crescent moon (about twelve percent) set.

6

To Armageddon

Sunday Morning, June 25

Military Correspondence & Intelligence Reports—From Commanding Officer, Fort Fetterman—"Reports that Courier was employed by Correspondent to bring dispatches."[1]

Telegram dated Fort Fetterman, Wy., June 25, 1876, to M.V. Sheridan, ADC, Division Headquarters, Chicago, Ill.—"I find that Courier was employed by Correspondents to bring dispatches and by Genl Crook to return with mail and the delay may have been an arrangement between them will report fully by mail. Coates, Comd'g."

Telegram dated Camp on Old Woman's Fork, June 25, 1876, to Ass't Adjt General, Military Division of the Missouri, Chicago, Ills—

> Lieut. Genls dispatch received. I took this road because it brings me on the trail a day or two farther west with camp of South Cheyenne near Powder River trail. We are all ready to push out should we delay much will need more supplies. Old Antoine Sadue and old Duval engaged as guides at five dollars per day. They are the only men to be found who have been on the trail. They say eighty lodges of Cheyennes under Little Wolf went on Powder River trail twelve days ago—sun dance was to be over today when it is said many Indians will go on war path. I have engaged two guides and ten scouts all told had to send in different directions for scouts at last moment and more came in than were expected. Please approve or disapprove; all will be useful. Crooks village of Indians may scatter and come this way but are likely to discover and avoid me. Will look out sharp and strike if possible. Have sent Stanton with scouts & a Company to examine trail etc. Carr.

7th Cavalry—As the column was assembling before the eleven PM jump-off, Fred Gerard sat with Custer and claimed Half Yellow Face and Bloody Knife told Custer (apparently Reno, as well), he could not cross the divide before daylight without being discovered by Sioux scouts. This, however, occurred not at eleven PM, but at two AM and the latter is the time mentioned by Reno in his report to Captain E.W. Smith (Aide-de-Camp and the Acting Assistant Adjutant General), dated July 5,1876. This makes more sense than reports the conversation took place at the Busby bend camp. James Willert wrote it was well after one AM when Custer queried Half Yellow Face if they could reach their goal this night. It was then the scout told Custer they would not reach the divide until *after* daylight. Custer asked the Crow if it would be possible to move the command across the divide in daylight without being spotted by the Sioux. Half Yellow Face said no.

Regardless, Custer ordered Gerard to make sure his scouts followed any left-hand trails—no matter how small—to make sure no Indians had escaped, while Half Yellow Face was tasked with guiding the column. Captain Myles Keogh's Company I (replacing Benteen and H Company) was assigned to bring up the rear of the packs, but there was considerable delay caused mostly by trouble getting the mules across Mud Creek, and finally by 12:30 AM the last of the packs was across the creek.

The Busby camp was about 11½ miles from the divide, up a gradual climb from 2,340 feet to 4,000 feet elevation. The bottom along Davis Creek had occasional areas of timber and the going was rather difficult. Godfrey claimed it was extremely dark and tough going. Some men even had to grab hold of the tail of the horse in front so they would not lose their way, and there was a lot of choking dust, "whistling or hallooing." The night was calm with a slight breeze. "We could not see the trail, and we could only follow it by keeping in the dust cloud … a slight breeze would waft the cloud and disconcert our bearings; then we were obliged to halt to catch a sound from those in advance…." The troops followed the rattling of the equipment—canteens, tin cups—in front of them, yet despite the darkness and difficulty, the column moved quickly and according to Benteen, "the gait was a trot … kept up for perhaps eight or ten miles" (about 6½, actually).

Side Notes—Oddly enough some historians claim the route to the divide was up Thompson Creek—off of the Rosebud but just to the south—and not Davis.

> [T]here is a possibility that the regiment followed Thompson's Creek for a short distance, then turned up the dry bed of Little Thompson Creek, which comes in from the north, and followed it to its source near the summit of the divide. From that point there is an easy pass over to the headwaters of Davis Creek, so that the regiment would have crossed the divide at the same place regardless of the route taken to get there…. Goes Ahead claimed that the last bivouac was made near its mouth; old-timers … of the vicinity still point out the spot where they say the ashes of Custer's campfires were visible for many years afterwards; the only water in the vicinity that is heavily impregnated with alkali is on that route….[2]

This has been rejected, however. White Man Runs Him told Hugh Scott Custer came through a pass to the head of the north fork of Upper Reno Creek. This pass followed up Davis Creek from the Rosebud. This is incorrect: it was Davis Creek, start to finish.

Steamer "Far West"—*At about the same time Keogh was struggling getting the mules across Muddy Creek, the "Far West" was entering the mouth of the Big Horn River to head upstream.*

7th Cavalry—2 PM–2:30 AM—having traveled eleven miles at a speed of some 2.13–2.36 miles per hour, including smoking halts—the exhausted Charlie Varnum, along with his small entourage, arrives at a small "pocket" just below the Crow's Nest hill; while Varnum catches some sleep, several of his scouts wait there for light. The Crow's Nest was about 4½ to 4¾ miles from Halt One, the regiment's first halt; and it was about a 4,400-foot elevation. The terrain from the future Halt Two site(s) to the "pocket" where Varnum and his scouts rested was "smooth-level and a little rising" (Fred Gerard).[3] The hill itself was described as a….

> …rounded oval hill directly southeast of where the great trail crossed the divide, a half-mile or less from the Camp Marker. This hill is exactly on the divide, and from it about everything of note that could be seen from the higher peak was observable from its summit. A few pine

trees are growing on it, and were in 1876, forming a slight screen from observation from the Reno Creek Valley. It was easily ascended, especially from the trail where it crossed the divide, and from the little branch of Davis Creek that had its beginning 40 rods [220 yards or 660 feet] southeast.[4]

"'...[W]e do not know precisely which hill, but in all probability it was the fourth peak south of the pass which connects the valley of Davis Creek with that of Sundance or Reno Creek.'"[5]

Tall grass carpeted the slopes of the divide below the... [Crow's Nest], and the ravine that marked the headwaters of Davis Creek was cloaked in ... pink and white wild rosebuds.... From the north bank of this tributary, the terrain sloped upward several hundred yards to a stand of pine trees, from which vantage ... certain observations could be made across the brow of the divide toward the Little Horn Valley. The divide was directly west of the slope, and to the south, dipped sharply into a broad ravine which formed the source of the south fork of the tributary known today as Reno Creek.[6]

The ride to the Crow's Nest was rugged, ending in a small pocket and a climb to the summit. It took about 5½ hours in the pitch-black night to reach this point: 2.14 miles per hour for the 11¾ miles. They stopped a couple of times in the dense undergrowth along the stream so the Crow could have a smoke. Varnum, Boyer, and White Man Runs Him led the horses into the pocket. Most of them—including Varnum—slept, waiting for it to get light enough to ascend to the summit. Two Crow—Hairy Moccasin and White Man Runs Him—begin climbing to the top rather than sleep.

2:15 AM—Having traveled 6.2–6.7 miles at 1.9–2.1 miles per hour, Custer halted the column on Davis Creek: Halt One (note how close the column's speed comes to the speed) Varnum and his scouts traveled in the dark, cloudy night. It is still dark when the regiment halted as Lieutenant Wallace claimed they arrived when "it was too dark to read my watch," implying it was before 3:34 AM, when civil twilight began. (Heski claims it gets light in Montana in June around three AM.)

3:40 AM—The two Crow scouts—Hairy Moccasin and White Man Runs Him—first spot the Indian encampment from atop the Crow's Nest. They scurry back to tell the others.

Side Notes—3:41 AM—(United States Naval Observatory)—2:44 AM, LOCAL SUN TIME—Nautical twilight begins—the end of full darkness. At 3:45 AM there is light on the horizon.

Terry-Gibbon Column—4 AM—Lieutenant Bradley—on orders from Terry—sends six Crow scouts up Tullock's Creek on an advanced scout to look for Herendeen.

4:30 AM—Bradley and his mounted infantry leave for a scout up the creek.

Side Notes—4:31 AM, HEADQUARTERS TIME; 3:34 AM, LOCAL SUN TIME—Civil twilight begins—reading still impossible.

Terry-Gibbon Column—4:45 AM—Captain-Dr. John Winfield Williams—who had been left aboard the "Far West" with Colonel Gibbon—arrives in Terry's camp. Then, at five AM Carroll's trains leave camp. "Went up to Tullock's Fork four miles, thence to backbone between it and Big Horn. Arrived at Big Horn River after making twenty miles."[7] Carroll watered his animals, then moved another three miles before "nooning." The road was still bad, however, and the battery of three Gatling guns had a lot of trouble.

7th Cavalry—4:47 AM–4:57 AM—Varnum was awakened by his scouts—probably Mitch Boyer—for a climb to the peak. Varnum manages the climb to the Crow's Nest peak, reaching its slope at about 5:15 AM, and he and the scouts study the Sioux village—or what they think may be the location of the village—and two tepees along Reno Creek, one of which was partly wrecked or knocked over. The Ree scout Red Star joins the group. Varnum, however, had trouble seeing the village, his eyes inflamed from the loss of sleep and hard riding in the dust. Varnum and his scouts also spot smoke from the troopers' breakfast fires, the Crow being very angry with this.

5:10 AM—SUNRISE—The regiment begins making breakfast. Godfrey wrote, "After daylight some coffee was made…."

Terry-Gibbon Column—5:30 AM—Terry orders Gibbon's command up Tullock's Creek toward the Tullock forks, with the intention of then heading for the mouth of the Little Big Horn River. This march would be some twenty-two miles over what Terry called "the most difficult country which I have ever seen." Terry would push the cavalry and the Gatling gun battery an additional thirteen to fourteen miles so the scouts could enter the Little Big Horn valley on the twenty-sixth.

7th Cavalry—5:40 AM—The Crow spot two Sioux warriors about 1½ miles in front, west and parallel to the divide, but moving in the direction to where the trail crossed the divide. Varnum wrote that one Indian was riding a pony and leading another horse on a long lariat, a boy following. They were now afraid the Sioux would turn right and cross the divide at the gap, thus discovering the advancing troops by the breakfast smoke. Author/historian Greg Michno wrote that Indians had gone out to hunt and look for some lost horses, but were seen and chased by "white scouts" who tried to kill them. One of the Indians outran the pursuers and reported back to the camp by noon.

This was one of two parties of Indians Varnum spotted. Others were believed to have been east of the camp that morning: Deeds (One Hawk), a young Hunkpapa boy who was subsequently killed somewhat later near the Little Big Horn River; Brown Back (probably Oglala); and Black Bear, an Oglala.

5:57 AM–6:10 AM—Varnum wrote this and the possibility of a village sighting in a note for Custer, handed it to Red Star and directed him and fellow-Ree, Bull, to deliver it to Custer. Shortly after the Ree departed, Varnum and his scouts, "saw two Sioux about one mile and a half west, moving down Davis Creek toward the soldiers' camp, and six other Sioux to the northeast over on Tullock Fork." Varnum said, "About five o'clock I wrote a note to the General and sent it off by the Rees, telling him the information I got from the Crows."[8] As the scouts trudged back to the command, Bull lagged because of problems with his horse. Red Star, however, claimed, "he urged his horse on for he had the note."[9] He did not lose track, however, of his comrade.

6:20 AM—Varnum led a dismounted sortie against the two Sioux. He took Boyer, Reynolds, White Swan, and one other Crow to chase the Sioux down and kill them, but as they set out they were called back. The Indians had changed direction. Varnum described these exploits in a letter to Walter Mason Camp, dated April 14, 1909:

After sending off the Rees we saw one Indian riding a pony & leading another at the end of a long lariat & some distance behind, an Indian boy on a pony. They were evidently hunting stray stock and were perhaps a mile off toward the Little Big Horn and riding parallel to the ridge we were on. There was a gap in the range to our right and the Crows thought they would cross there & soon discover Custer. By this time smoke could be seen in a ravine towards the Rosebud showing where Custer was. The Crows were mad that he lighted fires. Boyer said that White Swan, who seemed to be a sort of leader, wanted us to try & cut him off & kill them where they crossed the range so they would not discover the troops. Boyer, Reynolds & two Crows with myself started off dismounted to do so. After, perhaps, a half mile of hard work through very broken country, where we could see nothing I heard a call like a crow cawing from the hill and we halted … we started back. I asked Boyer what was the matter but he did not know. On our return we learned that the Sioux had changed their course away from the pass but soon after our return they changed again and crossed the ridge. We could see them as they went down the trail towards the command and could then see a long trail of dust showing Custer was moving but we could not see the column. Before it came in sight the Sioux stopped suddenly, got together & then as suddenly disappeared, one to the right & one to the left, so we knew that the Sioux had discovered our approach. About this time… [6 or 7 Sioux] rode in single file along the crest of a ridge forming a divide of the stream running into the Rosebud and in the direction of that stream. That they would soon discover Custer's command we knew and watched them accordingly. The crest where we were was higher than they were and as they rode along the crest, reflected against the sky their ponies looked as big as elephants. They rode leisurely but soon, all of a sudden, they disappeared and soon afterward one black spot took their place. They had evidently ran off to alarm their camp, leaving one man to watch the column. The command came in vision about this time and we watched it approach the gap where it halted. I rode down towards the column & soon met the Genl. He said, "Well you've had a night of it." I said yes, but I was still able to sit up & notice things. Tom Custer & Calhoun then came up to us & Custer was angry at their leaving the column & ordered them back. I told the Genl. All I had seen, as we rode back towards the Crow nest hill and we climbed the hill together. Custer listened to Boyer while he gazed long & hard at the valley. He then said "Well I've got about as good eyes as anybody & I can't see any village Indians or anything else," or words to that effect. Boyer said, "Well General, if you don't find more Indians in that valley than you ever saw together you can hang me" Custer sprang to his feet saying, "It would do a damned sight of good to hang you, wouldn't it" and he & I went down the hill together…. We rejoined the command and he sent for the officers to assemble and I hunted for water & grub, as I had had none since about 8 o'clock the night before.[10]

6:40 AM—Varnum has returned to the Crow's Nest.

Terry-Gibbon Column—6:30 AM—Nine miles up Tullock's from camp and moving at a speed of some 4½ miles per hour, Lieutenant Bradley orders a halt to await further orders. The men brew coffee and there were absolutely no signs of Indians. By now, Terry was extremely concerned that he had had no word from Custer. The distance to the Little Horn confluence was still almost forty miles and he had promised Custer he would have Gibbon's command there by June twenty-sixth.

6:35 AM–6:45 AM—2½ miles; less than three miles per hour, on average, the column had marched only two miles due to increasingly more difficult terrain, though the difficulty is questionable, especially in light of what happened next. Terry calls a halt. He decides to leave the Tullock's Creek valley and head to the tableland above, sending a squad of cavalry to tell Bradley. According to Roger Darling, Muggins Taylor, who had caught Terry's ear, precipitated this move. While the route up the creek's valley did not appear to be that difficult, the easy sloping terrain up toward the ridge's spine was deceivingly easy, only to turn into a nightmare a little farther along the ridge. Taylor had never been in this area and had no firsthand knowledge of the terrain. The advance had been for only about one hour and had covered only between two and three miles.

6:55 AM—Terry's advance resumed. Brisbin, Lieutenant Doane, and Muggins Taylor led the column toward what was believed to be tableland above the valley, only to discover the whole area was badlands. Terry wrote, "Turned to the right to gain the summit of the dividing ridge between Tullock's and Big Horn."[11] *Captain Robert Patterson Hughes, Terry's Aide-de-Camp and brother-in-law, blamed Custer for Terry's move out of the Tullock's Creek valley and into the brutal badlands separating the creek from the Big Horn River. Had Custer sent Herendeen down the valley as instructed—on June twenty-fourth—Hughes felt Terry would have simply moved up Tullock's Creek, then made the easy move toward the Indian village, basically following Captain Ball's route of a couple months earlier. Terry would then have been in position to assist in the battle. At 7:55 AM Terry's column halts for a break.*

7th Cavalry—6:55 AM—4½ miles; at six miles per hour—Red Star, carrying Varnum's note from the Crow's Nest, arrives at Custer's Halt One and reports to Bloody Knife. At 7:05 AM, Isaiah Dorman—the interpreter for the Dakota scouts—spotted the courier who was settling down for something to eat. At 7:08 AM Dorman told Custer's striker, Private John Burkman, to wake Custer, and the Ree interpreter Fred Gerard, and go to the Ree camp.

7:10 AM—Back at the Crow's Nest Varnum's scouts sight the two Sioux crossing the divide. The Sioux, however, changed their course away from the divide, but then changed again, moving in the direction of the gap.

7:12 AM—Burkman wakes Custer.

7:20 AM—Red Star hands Custer Varnum's note. Fred Gerard, Bloody Knife and others were already there. From the newspaper article by George Herendeen published July 7, 1876, Bismarck, D. T., and republished in the *Army and Navy Journal*, July 15, 1876: "About daylight we went into camp, made coffee, and soon after it was light the scouts brought Custer word that they had seen the village from the top of a divide that separates the Rosebud from Little Horn River." After absorbing the news, Custer rode back to saddle his horse Vic, and spoke briefly with Bloody Knife and a few officers. Bloody Knife was morose and cautioned against attacking because the size of the trail leading away from the sun dance site indicated many more Indians than originally thought. Custer may now have thought about sending Herendeen back to scout Tullock's, but since it was a fifty-mile hike, he probably thought it was useless at this point. Willert claimed Custer decided to cancel the eight AM move order and remain in camp all day, moving out when it became dark, position his troops, and launch a surprise attack in the early morning of June twenty-sixth. Custer decided to go to the Crow's Nest and gathered Red Star, Gerard, and other Ree and began to move off. An officer asked Custer if he still wanted the regiment to move and Custer said, no; but he *never* formally countermanded his order.

~8 AM—Custer mounted and rode to each of the companies, telling them to be ready to march. Godfrey remembered Custer gave orders to be *ready* to march at eight AM. Trumpeter-Private Giovanni Martini—a Custer orderly that day—confirmed this.

7:50 AM—At about six to eight miles per hour, Custer and others, leave for Crow's Nest. He took Red Star, Bob-tailed Bull, Little Brave, Bloody Knife, Fred Gerard, Tom Custer, and Lieutenant James Calhoun. Author Vern Smalley lists Red Star, Bob-tailed Bull, Little Brave, Gerard, and an orderly-trumpeter; also, Bloody Knife. Furthermore, Smalley claims Custer made a second trip and this time took his brother Tom, but there is absolutely no evidence for such a second trip to the Crow's Nest itself, but there is evidence of a second trip to the *divide*. Bruce Liddic writes that Bull and Private Martini were part of this group as well. There is some evidence Adjutant Cooke joined the party.

Side Notes—As for the regiment, Godfrey said, "We started promptly at eight o'clock...."[12] Based on Varnum's letter to Walter Mason Camp it appears Custer led the command himself and the eight o'clock departure was closer to 6:30 AM local sun time (7:27 AM, headquarters time). Herendeen: "...Some time after this [night bivouac] the scouts came back and reported that the location of the Sioux camp had been found. We moved forward again and about 9:00 AM [ten AM–10:30 AM] were halted where Custer thought the command would be concealed."[13] Godfrey confirms an eight AM departure time from Halt One, saying they traveled about ten miles[14]— uninterruptedly—stopping around 10:30 AM. Private Theodore Goldin: "...About eight o'clock, the command moved out and marched steadily for perhaps two hours, when we found ourselves well-sheltered in the ravine at the base of the divide, halted, and remained concealed for some time."[15] Captain Myles Moylan: they remained at Halt One until somewhere around eight AM and then moved forward. Moylan did not know who ordered the move.[16] Moylan described the country as rolling. "The country marched through was the valley of this dry fork ... and on either side, at a distance of half a mile in some places to a mile and a half in others, were high, broken hills."[17] Moylan said they halted around 10:30 or eleven AM. He was not sure. "I don't know that I know the time, I don't give that time as definite."[18]

7th Cavalry—8:15 AM—So with all this, we can figure the command left Halt One at about 8:15 AM and headed for the Crow's Nest area at a speed of 2.3 miles per hour.

8:05 AM—Varnum saw the two "Sioux" (he believed them to be Sioux) spotting Custer's party, or at least its dust. These two "Sioux scouts" were *not* Sioux, however; they were Cheyenne from a hunting party under Little Wolf. And none of this group was involved in the afternoon's battle, not joining the camp until after the engagement. Varnum watched the Indians moving down the east side of the divide, stopping suddenly (spotting the trail of dust raised by Custer's small party) and then disappearing. He figured they had spotted Custer's approach. Shortly, Varnum spots a party of seven Sioux riding single file eastwards along the crest of a spur ridge, parallel to Davis Creek. They disappeared suddenly, and then only one took the place of all seven. Varnum figured they had spotted the column or its back-trail and ran off to inform the village, leaving one man behind to watch. John Gray and Tom Heski indicate these Sioux were agency Indians—Black Bear and his party from the Red Cloud Agency—heading back, thus posing no alarm-threat for the village. They did, however, meet some Cheyenne coming out from the agency. They were watching and trailing the troops.

8:30 AM—Varnum spots Custer's party—having traveled four miles at six miles per hour—mistaking it for the "regiment"—approaching Halt Two; Varnum begins his descent to the "pocket."

> On divide ... there is a ridge running east and west at right angles to main divide. This spur ridge runs toward Rosebud, and Custer came along south of this ridge. The seven Sioux were going eastward along this ridge. There were two lodges at the lone tepee—one standing up and another had been broken down.[19]

8:35 AM—½ mile, approaching at six miles per hour—Custer arrives near the Crow's Nest, having averaged about 4¾ miles per hour. Varnum rides down to meet him, though in his book Varnum claims this occurred about ten AM. (Remember, Varnum's times are admittedly inaccurate.) Custer now sends Tom Custer and Calhoun back to the camp, though Varnum does not mention Calhoun being with Tom Custer.

8:55 AM—Custer reaches the top of the Crow's Nest. Among the Ree on the hilltop are Red Star, Bull, and Black Fox.

Side Notes—James Willert has Custer reaching the base of the Crow's nest at 9:30 AM, never explaining why it took him 1½ hours to get there. Willert makes a case for Custer never having made the arduous climb to the Crow's Nest, but having viewed the valley "from the higher ground rising to the north of Davis Creek ... his party mov[ing] to that position."[20] W.A. Graham claims Custer arrived at the Crow's Nest after ten AM and stayed there over an hour, again, never explaining the timing. Most writers feel he *did* stay for more than an hour. Knowing the personality of the man and his quandary regarding attacking or waiting, a casual walk from Halt One to the Crow's Nest—after hearing the momentous news of discovering the village—hardly makes sense. One must consider the distance between the two points—four miles—and a reasonable speed considering the circumstances. As it is, a six-miles-per-hour trot is quite understandable.

7th Cavalry—Custer had to have spent some time up at the Crow's Nest checking out the terrain and the approaches to the village. He was not in a hurry at this point, already having decided to mount an attack the following day and also knowing he had to be very close to the hostiles. His main concern now was to make sure he had not been spotted. Varnum informs him of all he had seen and that they had probably been spotted. Custer cannot see any sign of a village, but Varnum, by now convinced, assures him it was there, and Boyer said he would "find more Indians in that valley than you ever saw together," or else "you can hang me." "It would do a damned sight of good to hang you, wouldn't it?" (While some attribute the comment to Varnum, he claimed it was Boyer who made this remark.[21]) Charlie Reynolds also tries to convince Custer the camp is there and finally, the general agrees ... grudgingly. Varnum: "The column arrived at the trail-crossing of the divide about ten AM, and Custer came at once to where I was, I riding out to meet him. We climbed the bluff and the Indians tried to show Custer what they saw."[22] Willert says this was not the Crow's Nest.

Side Notes—While atop the Crow's Nest, the scouts tried to convince Custer that there was a huge horse herd, likening an undulating mass in the distance to "worms." After the battle, as the village headed south up the valley, the soldiers remaining on Reno Hill estimated the size of the Indians' pony herd to be between 20,000 and

28,000 horses. Author Gregory Michno, using 1,500 warriors, claims there were probably only 12,000 horses. That's eight horses per warrior, a fairly low estimate. On the other hand, if one doubles the number of warriors to 3,000, then 15,000 horses (five per warrior) would not be unreasonable based on Michno's reasoning. Using eight per warrior would make it 24,000 horses, right in between the soldiers' estimates. At five horses per warrior, 4,000 warriors would equate to 20,000 horses, in my estimation a more likely number and a figure jibing with the low end of what the troops on Reno Hill thought. Michno says one study claimed it took three horses to haul an average-sized tepee plus belongings. Figure close to 1,500 tepees and that totals 4,500 more horses. Two thousand lodges—almost a preposterous number—would equate to 6,000 more horses and 6,000 "lodge" horses plus 20,000 warrior horses would equal 26,000 horses. What appears to be exaggerated is the size—in area—these horses occupied, especially since many of them were nowhere near the higher foothills to the west, but were, in fact, north of the Cheyenne rings, some four miles farther down the valley from where the scouts saw "worms." The McElfresh map shows this herd.

7th Cavalry—White Man Runs Him, a Crow (the Ree did *not* want to attack) tells Custer he should attack, that the Sioux have spotted his dust and the campfires. Willert wrote:

> To [the Crow], when the enemy was near-at-hand, attack was the only justified action. The decision of Gibbon to march against the hostile's village [on May seventeenth] had pleased them, but the abrupt cancellation of the projected assault had confused and displeased them.[23]

Custer refuses to believe they have been spotted: "That camp has not seen us."[24] Ironically, Custer was probably correct. Custer is reported to have told Half Yellow Face through an interpreter, "This camp has not seen our army, none of their scouts have seen us.... I want to wait until it is dark and then we will march, we will place our army around the Sioux camp."[25] Custer states he will carry out his original plan of waiting out the day in hiding and attacking early on the twenty-sixth. The Crow scouts and the Ree, Red Star, apparently pretty much convinced Custer he had indeed been spotted and he should attack this day rather than take the risk of the Sioux attacking him. If he waited the warriors would come out to fight him to give the women and children time to escape, and then everyone would scatter. Willert: "If the hostiles' village was ... alerted to the presence of the regiment, it would not be long before the warriors would swarm out to attack, to give their non-combatants opportunity to slip away.... Custer could not afford the risk."[26]

Terry-Gibbon Column—8:35 AM—Terry's column resumes its march toward the mouth of the Little Big Horn and sometime between nine and ten AM the cavalry squad Terry had sent joins up with Bradley and informs him of Terry's decision to cut across the Tullock-Big Horn divide. At 9:40 Terry halts his column, then, at ten AM continues his march.

The Curtiss Episode—8:35 AM—Regiment: ¾ mile—Sergeant William Curtiss (F/7C) informed his company commander, Captain Yates—some claim he told Keogh, while Moylan clearly overheard it—some personal items had fallen from one of the pack mules, farther back on the trail. Yates sends Curtiss with four other enlisted men to look for the lost pack. Custer was told of this upon his return from his trip to the Crow's Nest. A minute or so later—8:36 AM—Captain Keogh informs Captain Yates of the missing pack ... or vice versa since Keogh was Officer of the Day. Yates instructs Curtiss to take four men and retrieve the pack.

8:37 AM—at 6 MPH—Curtiss takes four Company F troopers with him: James Rooney, William A. Brown, Patrick Bruce, and Sebastian Omling. (Only Curtiss and Rooney survived the battle: they were assigned to the pack train.)

8:43 AM—The Curtiss group finds three Cheyenne rifling through Curtiss' pack, probably fairly near Halt One. After the troops chased off the three Cheyenne, the Indians made their way back to spy on the command when they reached Halt Two. These Indians were part of Little Wolf's party of seven lodges that had left the Red Cloud agency to join the Sioux (see earlier "briefs"). Two of them may have been Big Crow and Black White Man, the Indians who had spotted the regiment in its Busby camp the day before. These three Cheyenne came across a small party of seven Oglala—six men and one woman—led by Black Bear. The Sioux were from the Red Cloud Agency and had been looking for horses stolen by some of the Indians joining Sitting Bull. They were hiding, watching Custer's column in Davis Creek when the Cheyenne met them: Black Bear, Owl Bull, Medicine Bird, Blue Cloud, Kill Enemy In Water, Knife, and Knife's wife. These seven Sioux were probably the ones seen by Varnum from the Crow's Nest. They tried to warn the village, but could not circle around quickly enough and only arrived there after Custer was dead.

8:44 AM–8:50 AM—Curtiss' detail runs off the Indians and secures the loose equipment.

8:58 AM—8 MPH—Curtiss turns and begins his trip back to the column.

9:16 AM—2.4 miles, 8 MPH—Curtiss and detail arrive back at the column and notify Yates of their findings.

7th Cavalry—10 AM—3½–4½ miles; 2.3 MPH—The regiment halts in a timber-covered ravine on Davis Creek, ¾ mile from the summit of the divide, for conceal-ment, 3¾ miles from previous halt and 10¾ miles from the Busby camp. This was Halt Two, and would have probably covered as many as three separate ravines, all close together. In all likelihood, this would have been the concealment halt had Custer stuck to his original plan of attacking on the twenty-sixth. When the troops arrived near the Crow's Nest, they moved into what Tom Heski has named McDougal Ravine, named after Keith McDougal who found artifacts in the area. The ravine—as Halt Two is commonly referred to—is one removed from the ravine outside the Crow's Nest pocket, not far from the Crow's Nest. Custer and the scouts watched as the column arrived at this rest-halt, less than one mile away. Author Vern Smalley calls attention to the precision of Wallace's time—as the column arrived—saying it "was one of the few times [Wallace] looked at his watch and immediately jotted down what he saw."[27] Wallace: 10:07 AM; Moylan: about 10:30 AM–eleven AM; Hare: ten AM; Godfrey: 10:30 AM.

After watching the regiment approach, at 10:05 AM Custer, Varnum, and the scouts leave the Crow's Nest. Curtiss, as well, arrives back at the halt-site, having reported chasing off the Cheyenne to Yates. Captain Moylan: "While at the second halt at the foot of the divide … a Sergeant returned on the trail some miles for the purpose of recovering … some clothing of his that had been lost from a pack mule the night before."[28] Tom Custer and Lieutenant Calhoun ride out to tell Custer of Curtiss' findings, and at 10:10 AM Custer arrives back down in pocket where the horses are kept. They meet the Custer party coming down from the Crow's Nest. Apparently, some troops must have followed them: "Tom, who in the devil moved these troops forward? My orders were to remain in camp all day and make a night attack on the Indians, but they have discovered us, and are on the run."[29] There is controversy about this move and whether or not Custer actually ordered the column forward before he left for the Crow's Nest. Bruce Liddic seems to think he simply forgot to countermand his march order. He writes, "Gerard also recalled Custer ordered his Adjutant, First Lieutenant William Cooke, to keep the command in camp until he returned."[30] Godfrey recalled Custer telling people to be ready to move.

10:15 AM—After chewing out Tom Custer and Calhoun, George Custer calls for an officers call, and at 10:16 AM Lieutenant Cooke informs Custer of the Curtiss lost pack incident.

10:20 AM—The officers are all gathered alongside a small knoll occupied by Company C troopers. Private Peter Thompson (Company C) watched Custer and some officers talking on a small knoll in the Davis Creek valley.

Herendeen tells Custer the head of Tullock's Creek was just north of where they were, but Custer said there was no longer any need to scout there, for the Indians were to the front. Herendeen agreed. In Custer's mind, this also obviated the need to send any scouts to Terry, for Terry could have done nothing anyway if Custer attacked as quickly as he wanted to. Herendeen could never have reached Terry in time. Besides, if Indians were on the back trails, a messenger would probably not have succeeded in getting through. Fred Gerard was at this meeting and agreed with Herendeen's recollections. Boyer and other scouts warn Custer of the size of the Sioux encampment, but size was not what worried Custer; his overriding concern was the Sioux would break up and scatter.[31] Godfrey called him "possessed" about this possibility.

Side Notes—Custer was forced to improvise on the run because of this lack of precise intelligence and because of the time pressure he felt he was under fearing the Indians might flee. It also explains archaeologist Richard Fox' idea—though one must doubt he figured it actually developed this early—that much of Custer's movement on the battlefield was an intelligence gathering mission prior to his anticipated attack. In later years Godfrey also made a point to Walter Camp that fighting Indians "was an inexact science," "dispositions… [had] to be 'made in the dark,'" and, "In Indian warfare the rule is 'touch and go.'"[32] It was at Halt Two when company commanders were instructed to leave six men and one NCO with the packs. This number is verified by Godfrey—a company commander—in his narrative.[33] Lieutenant Edward Mathey (Company M) is put in charge of packs. And because he was the first to comply with giving seven men to Mathey for the packs, Benteen was given the honor of leading the advance. Author and historian Roger Darling notes some of Benteen's friends within the regiment felt Custer was annoyed at Benteen's promptness and this led to his sending Benteen on the "wild-goose-chase" to the left, thus keeping him out of the fight, but this sounds rather odd. Captain Tom McDougall's Company B, being the last to report, was assigned to guard the pack train: two officers, 134 troops, five civilian packers, and two scouts: 143, total. Many writers use six packers. McDougall claimed it was about eleven AM when he was told to take charge of the packs. According to Private John Maguire (or McGuire) (Company C):

> There was a detail of a Non-Commissioned Officer and seven men with each company's pack mules. Officers say one NCO and six men. Besides these though, were strikers, cooks, headquarters details, and men leading officer's extra horses to the number of two-three per company, or [thirty] additional men. Besides that, there were eleven men, citizen packers, or roughly 125 men, all armed, with McDougall's company B. McDougall's company plus the additional 125 or so men was larger than either Benteen or Reno's command.[34]

There is also a story in Liddic's, *Vanishing Victory* that Varnum gave Custer another report indicating a small camp of Indians—sixty or so tepees—was moving downstream. According to Liddic, this was a group camped in the area of the lone tepee and headed for the larger village in the Little Big Horn valley.[35] The obvious inference was the soldiers had been spotted and this group of Indians was on its way to warn the main camp. Another inference was the village was already beginning to break up and scatter. Varnum made sure this report was relayed to Custer, so Varnum must have still been on the Crow's Nest while Custer headed back to Halt Two.[36] There may also have been the feeling they might soon be surrounded or the Indians might attack. Liddic brings up a valid point regarding Custer's plans: he had no precise intelligence as to either the size of the Indian force or its exact location, and therefore, could not make a definitive attack plan. (He was roundly criticized by several officers at the Reno Court of Inquiry for not informing them of any attack plans.) If this theory is correct, it eliminates many scenarios regarding Custer's so-called "attack" at Ford B. In reality, Custer was forced to improvise on the run because of this lack of precise intelligence and because of the time pressure he felt he was under fearing the Indians might flee.

7th Cavalry—10:22 AM—George Herendeen wanders off some 500 or 600 yards up a dry creek and spots what he thought might have been a deer or an Indian. Three minutes later—10:25 AM—Boyer sees Herendeen and asks him about what he has seen. Boyer tells him he saw three Indians with three or four loose horses. They moved rapidly off in the direction of the village.

10:35 AM—Boyer tells Custer what he and Herendeen have discovered. It was probably this report, on top of everything else, that convinced Custer to attack immediately rather than wait a day. This report is further confirmation for Custer and at 10:40 AM he tells of his plan to attack. Officers' call ends; Custer has decided to attack the village immediately, though he is still uncertain of its precise location and its size. Not a single officer disagreed with his decision once they learned the Indians had seen them, but the Ree scouts did not like the idea of attacking the Sioux: "*Otoe Sioux*," they cried, "*Plenty Sioux; too many Sioux.*" Custer had sat with several of them, including Bloody Knife, but seemed to pay them no heed; he was in a reverie of his own. At some point—precisely when is debatable ... and moot—Boyer tells Custer they will meet more Indians than they can handle. Custer responds by telling his scout he can stay behind if he was afraid, but Boyer said he would go wherever

Custer went, neither of them however, would leave the valley alive. Apparently, Boyer and Reynolds had ridden somewhat out ahead and having quickly returned, reported the village was much larger than expected. Bloody Knife understood their talk and glanced at the sun, signaling with his hands, knowing his end was near. Scout Billy Jackson read Bloody Knife's hands, choking up with emotion.

10:40 AM–10:55 AM—Assignments are made and Tom McDougall and Company B were assigned to accompany the pack train, "to take charge of the pack train and act as rear guard." This was "on the divide between the Rosebud and the Little Big Horn."

10:50 AM—Someone—Boyer or Reynolds—convinces Custer to take one more look at the Little Big Horn valley using De Rudio's field glasses. There is another school of thought claiming Custer made a second trip to the Crow's Nest and this was when he borrowed De Rudio's Austrian-made field glasses. Hare's statements to Walter Camp bear this out: "Custer had been out ahead with scouts viewing valley of the Little Big Horn…. [The column] lay concealed less than one-half mile from the divide for more than an hour. During this time Custer again went to Crow's Nest to look at Indians."[37] Hare did not actually see Custer return, but heard he did. De Rudio agreed and said Cooke came to him and asked to borrow his field glasses. Varnum was certain a second trip to the heights of the Crow's Nest by Custer was never made.[38]

Terry-Gibbon Column—10:50 AM—Terry halts; Gatling gun battery breaks down. Terry decides to head directly for the Big Horn River—seen to the west—rather than continue along the ridgeline toward Tullock Peak. The infantry is now in quite bad shape, blisters from the difficult terrain and shortage of water beginning to wear down the men. Terry sends scouts down Eckman Coulee—though not far—and chooses this route to the river. The column's descent begins shortly before Bradley reaches Terry. At 11:20 AM Terry's column resumes march.

7th Cavalry—10:51 AM—Custer agrees to go to the divide ridge in another attempt to see the village, and calls for his horse, taking a small party with him to the top of the divide.

11 AM—¾ mile; 6 MPH—Custer reaches the top of the divide, just 100 yards or so, from where the column is to cross.

11:10 AM—Custer spends some time looking into the Reno Creek valley and the LBH valley. Finished, he turns and heads back to his regiment.

11:18 AM—¾ mile; 6 MPH—Custer arrives back at Halt Two. Convinced or unconvinced, he orders his command to get ready to move.

11:19 AM–11:44 AM—And finally, taking a few minutes for final arrangements, the command readies to move.

11:30 AM—At ten MPH, and increasing speed, Lieutenant Charles Albert Varnum, his orderly Private Elijah Strode, and the Ree scouts lead out, become the first to cross the divide, and head to the left front. Lieutenant Luther "Luke" Hare takes the Crow and heads off to the right….

11:45 AM—The 7th Cavalry leaves the Halt Two site, and begins its fifteen-mile approach to the Sioux village and its ride to destiny.

PART III

Minute-by-Minute

"For every *minute* you are angry you lose sixty seconds of happiness."
—Ralph Waldo Emerson

7

Taps

The Battle of the Little Big Horn, Sunday,
June 25, 11:50 AM to 5:45 PM

THE 7th Cavalry started out in a column of fours, a fifty- to sixty-foot interval between companies. George Wallace wrote, "grass short, soil poor, hills low. From the crest to the Little Big Horn the country was broken and the valley narrow ... some timber along the little stream we followed down," while Godfrey concurred, "a rough, broken country of considerable elevation, of high, precipitous hills, and deep, narrow gulches."

11:50 AM–NOON—A TROT AT 6 MPH—Custer begins crossing the Little Big Horn–Rosebud divide. The only thing we can surmise about the order of march was Benteen's Company H was in the lead, followed by Tom Weir's D. After this, evidence intimates only that Donald McIntosh's Company G was ninth; Godfrey's K, tenth; and Tom McDougall's Company B last.

NOON—Custer halts the column, its rear already below the top of the divide.

NOON–12:10 PM—Between 12:05 PM–12:07 PM—They halt on a gentle curving slope, about one-quarter to one-half mile west of the divide. At this point Custer assigns battalions. Custer and his adjutant, Lieutenant Cooke, go off to the side, break the regiment into battalions, and inform Benteen to move off to the left with companies H, D, and K.

- Edgerly maintained throughout the years, that Custer gave Keogh (C, I, and L) and Yates (E and F) their battalion assignments at this time as well.
- Myles Moylan, at the Reno Court of Inquiry in 1879, stated Keogh had three companies.
- Reno is assigned Companies A, G, and M, plus scouts.
  - ◊ Company A: two officers, 39 EM;
  - ◊ Company G: two officers, 35 EM;
  - ◊ Company M: one officer, 46 EM;
  - ◊ Totals: five officers, 120 EM.
  - ◊ Attachments to battalion HQ:
  - ◊ Four officers: Reno; one Company A (Varnum), one Company K (Hare), one Company B (Hodgson, adjutant)
  - ◊ Eight EM: Strode (A), Trumble and Mask (B), Abbotts and Pendtle (E),

Davern (F), Penwell and Clear (K). [SGT Kanipe eventually joined Reno after seeing Benteen and supposedly delivering the message to McDougall, but is not counted in Reno's original strength.]

◊ 34 others: two from Regimental HQ (the contract surgeons, Porter and DeWolf); three QM scouts; two QM interpreters; 21 Ree, four Dakota, and two Crow.

◊ This totals **171** officers, EM, and scouts. Thirteen Ree scouts and the four Sioux did not join in the fighting. The pack escort (McDougall) and Benteen, each had one Ree scout assigned.

- Benteen takes H, D, and K: 116 officers and EM.
  ◊ + One Ree scout = **117** total
  ◊ Company D: two officers, 43 EM;
  ◊ Company H: two officers, 37 EM;
  ◊ Company K: one officer, 31 EM.
- Keogh gets C, I, and L: **128** officers and EM.
  ◊ Company C: one officer, 42 EM;
  ◊ Company I: two officers, 37 EM;
  ◊ Company L: two officers, 44 EM.
- Yates takes E and F: **79** officers and EM.
  ◊ Company E: two officers, 38 EM;
  ◊ Company F: two officers, 37 EM.
- HQ: **18** officers and EM, including attached orderlies (three for Custer, one for Lord) and the four Crow scouts. This includes CPT Tom Custer as his brother's titular aide-de-camp.
  ◊ HQ attachments: Hughes (K), Martini (H), Dose (G), CPL Callahan (K).
  ◊ Custer's battalion: **225** officers and EM (including scouts and civilians).
- McDougall with his Company B was placed in overall command of the packs, which included LT Mathey and seven men from each company, plus strikers, orderlies, horse-minders, and cooks not with their assigned companies. Total number assigned to packs and pack escort: **142** including two officers, one Ree, and five civilian packers.
- Godfrey recalled that the whole mule train was an embarrassment. The mules were badly used up and the packers were new and had inadequate equipment.
- Actually or possibly assigned to the packs: *Company A* (2): Franklin and Ionson; *Company B* (3): Campbell (?), Carey (?), and Stowers (?); *Company C* (8): SGT Hanley, Bennett, Fowler, Jordan, Mahoney, McGuire, Mullin, and Whitaker; *Company D*: None known; *Company E* (9): SGT Riley, Miller, Spencer, Berwald, James, Kimm, Lange, Liddiard, and McKenna (?); *Company F* (10): SGT Curtiss, Gregg, Howard, Hunter, Lefler, Lyons, Myers, Pickard, Reiley, and Rooney; *Company G* (4): SGT Brown, CPL Hammon, Campbell, and McEagan; *Company H* (1): Adams; *Company I* (9): SGT DeLacy, Braun, Jones, Kennedy, McNally, McShane, Owens, Ramsey, and Cooney; *Company K* (4): (according to LT Hare, Company K had only one NCO and five privates with the packs) SGT Rafter, Burkardt, Raichel, and Robers; *Company L* (13): SGT Mullen, Abrams, Banks, Brown, Burkman,

Etzler, Logue, Marshall, McHugh, Moore, Rose, Stoffel, and Sullivan; *Company M (3)*: SGT McGlone, SAD John Donahoe, and Henry Harrison Davis.

- Author Bruce Liddic contends Custer originally wanted to take Company D with him instead of giving Weir's unit to Benteen. Benteen strongly objected, however, claiming Company D was one of the strongest in the regiment and Custer relented.
- Benteen was issued his orders off to the side and out of earshot of all but the HQ staff.
- If Benteen found any Indians trying to escape up the valley of the Little Big Horn, he was to intercept them and drive them back in the direction the village was supposed to be. Furthermore: he was to proceed to "a line of bluffs four or five miles away"; to send an officer [he chose Gibson] and six men, in advance, ride rapidly, pitch into anything he might find and send back word at once.
- These "bluffs" actually turned out to be hills, the "first line" of which was really only 1.3 miles away, a serious miscalculation of distance. This miscalculation was probably due to the visual distortion from being higher up on the divide.
- Benteen supposedly asked Custer: "*Hadn't we better keep the regiment together, General? If this is as big a camp as they say, we'll need every man we have.*" Custer responded, "*You have your orders.*" The precise location of Benteen and Custer when this was said is in dispute, some believing it was at the officers call, others at this divide separation.
- Benteen: "*We had passed through immense villages the preceding days.... We knew there were eight or ten thousand on that trail.*"
- Benteen wrote to his wife on July 2, 1876: "*I was ordered ... to the left for the purpose of hunting for the valley of the river—or anything I could find.*"
- In a second letter, dated July 4, 1876, he wrote: "*I was ordered ... to the left, in search of the valley ... and to inform Custer at once if I found anything worthy of same.*"
- In his official report of July 4, 1876, Benteen wrote: "*The directions I received from ... Custer were, to move with my command to the left, to send well-mounted officers with about six men who would ride rapidly to a line of bluffs about five miles to our left and front, with instructions to report at once to me if anything of Indians could be seen from that point. I was to follow the movement of this detachment as rapidly as possible ... the ground was terribly hard on horses, so I determined to carry out the other instructions, which were, that if in my judgment there was nothing to be seen of Indians, Valleys, etc., in the direction I was going, to return with the battalion to the trail the command was following.*"
- As Benteen left on his mission, he passed by Reno and told him his orders were "*to sweep everything before him.*"
- Godfrey: "*Benteen's battalion was ordered to the left and front, to a line of high bluffs about three or four miles distant. Benteen was ordered if he saw anything to*

send word to Custer, but to pitch into anything he came across; if, when he arrived at the high bluffs, he could not see any enemy, he should continue his march to the next line of bluffs and so on, until he could see the Little Big Horn valley."

- The understanding of Custer's orders and Benteen's mission was clear and this understanding was re-iterated by Edgerly sometime after the battle: "*The idea I had was if they ran out of the village we would strike them on the left; and if to the right, then some other part of the command.*"
- In addition, Benteen wrote to his wife on July 2, 1876, "*Custer divided the 7th Cavalry into three Battn's—about fifteen miles from an Indian village, the whereabouts of which he did not know exactly.*"
- LT Gibson wrote in recall, after Benteen had been ordered to scout "*to the left about five miles to see if the Indians were trying to escape up the valley … we were to hurry and rejoin the command as quickly as possible.*"
- If Custer's order to Benteen to scout to the left had any military legitimacy, then it was because Custer needed to know the precise location of the Indians and prevent them from fleeing south.
- While Benteen was apparently pleased at his initial assignment, he became miffed when Custer modified his orders by first sending Chief Trumpeter Voss and then Sergeant Major Sharrow with orders to keep ridge hopping until he could see into the Little Big Horn valley.
- Benteen did not understand Custer's rationale at the time, nor did Custer explain his intentions.
- On August 8, 1876, Benteen wrote the *New York Herald*: "*Before I had proceeded a mile in the direction of the bluffs I was overtaken by the Chief Trumpeter and the Sergeant Major with instructions from General Custer to use my own discretion, and in case I should find any trace of Indians at once to notify General Custer.*"
- By the time Benteen moved towards Reno Creek down Valley Three, he had already traversed two tough ridgelines, LT Gibson had mounted a third (Ridge C), and there was at least another large ridgeline past C before Benteen's command could enter the Little Big Horn valley. [Valley Three and Ridge A used only as reference points.]
- Benteen even agreed Custer was correct in not having a formal plan at this point because he did not know the Indians' precise location or their size.
- Benteen, at the Reno inquiry stated, "*When I received my orders from Custer to separate myself from the command, I had no instructions to unite at any time with Reno or anyone else. There was no plan at all. My orders were valley hunting ad infinitum.*"
- Benteen: "*I received orders through the sergeant-major of the regiment that if I saw nothing from the second line of bluffs, to go on into the valley, and if there was nothing in the valley, to go on to the next valley.*"
- Godfrey estimated that within the seventy-two-hour period from June twenty-second to this point, the regiment had marched 113 miles. Obvious implication: tired men, tired horses. "*We were tired and dirty and hungry.… Our horses hadn't had a good drink of water since the day before.*"

12:04 PM—*Pack Train*—⁴/₁₀ of a mile; 6 MPH—Boston Custer turns back toward the packs to change horses.

Side Notes—12:05 PM was the last official time recorded by Lieutenant Wallace.

12:08 PM—⁴/₁₀ of a mile—Boston Custer reaches the packs, stops, and speaks briefly with CPT McDougall.

12:08 PM—**Speed varying**—The pack train, driven by LT Mathey and CPT McDougall, having crested the divide, pauses right behind the main column.

12:10 PM—*Benteen Battalion*—At 6 MPH—Benteen breaks off from regiment to scout to the left.

12:12 PM—At 10 MPH—*Custer-Keogh-Yates Battalions* and the *Reno Battalion*—Custer and Reno leave the divide halt and start the descent of Reno Creek (also known as Sundance, Ash, or, oddly enough, Benteen's Creek), Custer down the creek's right bank, Reno down the left bank.

- The march interval between companies was probably about sixty feet.
- Varnum sends Hare off to the right front of the advance while Varnum takes the left front.
- Hare: the six Crow, Boyer, Herendeen, and his orderly, PVT Elihu Clear.
- Varnum: PVT Strode, the Ree, the four Dakota, and Isaiah Dorman. Varnum had to have begun losing the Ree, piecemeal, after the divide, for they rode ahead of Custer and Gerard nearby.
- CPT Moylan thought they left the divide halt about 12:30 PM.
- Custer moves down right bank of creek
- Reno moves down left bank of creek, columns 100–200 yards apart.
- Godfrey: "*The Indian trail followed the meanderings of this valley.*"

12:13 PM—.15 miles from separation; 10 MPH, increasing to 12 MPH, varying down to 4–6 MPH—Custer sees the "line of bluffs" he has sent Benteen to are nothing more than a series of rounded hills, covered in places with brownish sage and grass, a rolling mountain pasture. Figuring Benteen will not be able to find a promontory from which to see the valley, he dispatches CTMP Voss to tell Benteen to go to the "second line of bluffs" if he discovers nothing at the first. This is supported by Benteen's testimony at the Reno inquiry [the RCOI].

- Custer's rate of march was anywhere from four MPH—or even a little less—to a quick gallop of up to twelve MPH. Apparently, Custer did not want to outdistance Benteen. Scouts with reports were riding in and out all the time. Varnum and his scouts were out to the left front of the advance: "*From every hill where I could see the valley I saw Indians mounted.*" Varnum reported his observations several times. He saw the main village and more Indians than he had ever seen before: "*It was impossible to get a good view of [the village] unless one got out on the valley floor because of the bends in the river and the timber around on the left bank.*"
- Hare and his scouts remained out to the right front of the advance.

12:13 PM—.15 miles from separation; 7 MPH—CTMP Voss leaves the column and heads to Benteen.

12:13 PM—*Benteen Battalion*—³⁄₁₀ of a mile from separation; 6 MPH—Benteen's column is moving toward the first line of ridges.

*12:15 PM—**LT Bradley's Scout**—After a hard ride up West Burnt Creek, then Haystack Coulee, LT Bradley reaches the ridgeline along the top of the Tullock's divide.*

12:16 PM—*Benteen Battalion*—⁶⁄₁₀ of a mile from separation; 6 MPH—At this time Benteen is still advancing toward the first line of ridges.

12:17 PM—Benteen's men see Custer's columns moving at a high rate of speed.

12:18 PM—Voss reaches Benteen on the lower slope of the first "bluff." Benteen had gone about one mile when Voss overtook him. Ascending these hills, Benteen and many of his men see the Custer column about one-half mile away.

- At the RCOI, Benteen testified that the rugged terrain kept forcing him to move more and more to his right. Godfrey brings up this same point in his narrative: "*The obstacles threw the battalion by degrees to the right until we came in sight of and not more than a mile from the trail.*"
- Godfrey also mentioned that the horses were "*jaded by the climbing and descending,*" and many fell behind.

12:18 PM—*Pack Train*—Pack train leaves divide halt on Custer's trail. Its van moved at a fairly constant three miles per hour walk. McDougall's Company B, with a few extra horses, brought up the rear, making sure things were closed up and policing any stragglers.

- After changing horses and as the packs begin to move, Boston Custer heads for the front of the main column, now some distance away and moving more rapidly.
- The packs had gone a little over a mile when LT Cooke came back to tell LT Mathey to keep the mules off the trail as they were creating too much dust. Cooke came back a little while later to tell Mathey he was doing a good job keeping the dust down.

12:18 PM—*Benteen Battalion*—Voss: ⁶⁄₁₀ mile from Custer; Benteen: ¾ mile from separation; 7–8 MPH—CTMP Voss reaches Benteen with Custer's message: "*[I]f I found nothing before reaching the first line of bluffs, to go on to the second line with the same instructions.*" [Benteen]

12:18 PM—*Custer-Keogh-Yates Battalions* and the *Reno Battalion*—.83 miles from Voss separation; .97 miles from divide separation; 10 MPH down to 6 MPH—Custer's column is advancing between two small knolls and approaching the waters of Reno Creek. He slows to a trot so Voss can catch up, but still concerned that his orders to Benteen are not specific enough, Custer dispatches SGM Sharrow with additional instructions.

12:18 PM—.97 miles from divide separation; 8–10 MPH—SGM Sharrow leaves the column and heads to Benteen.

12:18 PM—8 miles from the divide crossing; 10 MPH–6 MPH—Having just passed the morass, Varnum, Strode, and the Rees have moved down Reno Creek and now begin to swing more toward the left, mounting the higher bluffs on the south and west side of the South Fork-Reno Creek confluence. Their speed decreases sharply.

12:19 PM—12 MPH—Voss turns from Benteen and heads back to main column.

*12:20 PM—**Terry-Gibbon Column**—Terry's column halts. Terry sends Bradley off to the left to scout a ridge to look over the Little Big Horn.*

- *Bradley would go as far as Tullock Peak before turning back. While he could not see into the Little Big Horn valley from the peak, he did spot black smoke in the distance.*

12:24 PM—*Benteen Battalion*—⁶⁄₁₀ of a mile additional (1⅓ miles from separation); 6 MPH slowing to 4 MPH—Benteen reaches the forward part of the plateau (**Plateau A**) formed beyond the hills of the "first line of bluffs," 1.8 miles from the separation point with Custer.

- Pack train now about two miles behind Custer.

12:24 PM—*Custer-Keogh-Yates Battalions* and the *Reno Battalion*—1.43 miles from divide separation; 6 MPH—Custer's column is moving along Reno Creek as CTMP Voss re-joins it.

12:24 PM—1 mile; 10–12 MPH—Voss reaches the head of Custer's column on the main trail along Reno Creek.

12:26 PM—*Benteen Battalion*—Sharrow: 1.2 miles; Benteen: 1.95 miles from divide separation; Sharrow: 10 MPH; Benteen: 5–6 MPH—Benteen, now with Gibson and the six troopers at the far edge of the first plateau (Plateau A), receives a message from SGM Sharrow, again from Custer: if he saw nothing from the second line of bluffs, proceed into the valley and if nothing was there, proceed to the next valley. Benteen now waits while the rest of his battalion catches up, then proceeds to obey his orders.

- The terrain past this first plateau became more difficult—the west side was a near vertical descent—but only because his orders gave him no discretion in detouring from this direction or speed, i.e., there were easier ways to go other than those necessarily taken by Benteen.
- The difficulty of the terrain was beginning to take a toll on the horses.

12:27 PM—10–12 MPH—Sharrow starts back for the main column.

12:38 PM—1.9 miles from meeting Benteen (3.14 miles from divide separations); 12 MPH, increasing to 14 MPH along Reno Creek—Sharrow reaches Reno Creek. The tail-end of Custer's column can be seen far up ahead. Sharrow increases his speed.

12:40 PM–1:25 PM—± 1 mile; 3 MPH (average speed, 4 MPH)—Benteen, having descended the first line of bluffs was now ascending the steep, winding sides of the second plateau (Ridge B) when he and some of his men observed Custer's column and Smith's Gray Horse Troop (E) at the gallop. Benteen: *"The last I saw of the column was the Gray Horse Troop at a dead gallop."* Men in Benteen's column heard cheering and shots being fired; all verified by Godfrey: *"During this march on the left we could see occasionally the battalion under Custer, distinguished by the troop mounted on gray* *horses, marching at a rapid gait. Two or three times we heard loud cheering and also some few shots....*"

- Benteen's order of march was H, D, K.
- The speed of movement was rapid, Godfrey recalling, "*that many of their horses were getting exhausted by the climbing and descending.*"
- This puts Custer on Reno Creek, about 3½ miles from the separation point, because Benteen would only have been able to see up the valley he had, or was traversing, about a mile of Reno Creek from near the top of the second plateau.
- Distance from Benteen's first stop to the second ridge: 1.2 miles (three miles, total, from the separation point).
- At the top of this second ridge/plateau, Benteen and Gibson observed a third ridge, just as high, with a rugged west slope of broken peaks and cliffs.
- They still could not see into the Little Big Horn valley.
- At this point, Benteen and some of his officers were extremely irritated with the increasingly fruitless assignment. Benteen appeared fine until Sharrow gave him Custer's second set of instructions; now he thought they were on a wild goose chase.
- Benteen now orders Gibson and the six troopers to the next ridge across the valley, while he himself decides to take the remainder of the battalion into the valley, heading slowly north, awaiting Gibson's report.
- Benteen has figured Gibson might now be able to see the Little Big Horn; he was correct.
- LT Edgerly recalled Gibson went to the tops of various bluffs four times in six miles.

12:41 PM—*Custer-Keogh-Yates Battalions* and the *Reno Battalion*—**6.9 miles; Average: 10+ MPH, with speeds varying from 6 MPH to bursts of 15 MPH**—forty-one minutes from crossing the divide—Main column (Custer/Reno) reaches the confluence of No-Name and Reno creeks. Custer is moving with his five companies abreast—left to right—E, F, L, I, C. Reno is in a column-of-fours, Company A in the center.

12:42 PM—**10+ MPH down to as low as 6 MPH**—As the commands move down Reno Creek, varying speeds between rapid bursts and slower canters, a number of the Ree scouts begin to fall behind. These include Strikes The Lodge, Rushing Bull, Soldier, Bull, White Eagle, and Red Wolf.

12:43 PM—**7.3 miles; 10 MPH**—Custer passes the morass.

- Custer sends Cooke back to Reno informing him to take the lead. Custer's column would follow to the right and rear.

12:45 PM—**Declining gait, down to a walk**—The fast pace of the advancing column now begins to take its toll on some of the troops' horses. Company C trooper Private James Watson begins falling behind.

12:45 PM—***Terry-Gibbon Column***—*Terry's column resumes march.*

12:47 PM—*Custer-Keogh-Yates Battalions* and the *Reno Battalion*—7.9 miles; 10 MPH—forty-seven minutes from crossing the divide—Command reaches confluence of South Fork and Reno creeks.

12:48 PM—12 MPH, increasing to 14 MPH—LT Hare, seeing Custer right behind him, increases his speed to move farther ahead.

12:52 PM—3.4 miles since reaching Reno Creek; 15 MPH—SGM Sharrow reaches No-Name Creek.

12:53 PM—2.3 miles; 3.9 MPH since leaving Reno Creek—Varnum and Strode—having lost the Rees along the way—reach a high elevation mark (3,405, grid square 13, U.S. G.S. topographical map) where they halt, looking into the Little Big Horn valley. From this height, they can see up the valley as well as down and part of the Indian encampment.

12:57 PM—9.8 miles from the divide crossing; Increasing to 12 MPH—The regiment enters the "flats." Reno is called to the creek's right bank.

12:57 PM—*Reno Battalion*—Reno trots to flats (at 6 MPH); Reno is called to the right bank and Custer moves behind him, and slowing to a walk; 2¾ miles from the lone tepee. These flats were formed by the North Fork (or Custer Creek) joining Reno Creek. At the far end, where the two streams joined, the ground rose up forming a small butte.

- The Crow scouts (Half Yellow Face, Curley, White Man Runs Him) who had moved forward onto this butte, report two Sioux warriors who spotted them and the large dust cloud raised by the command. These two Sioux—in all likelihood the Sans Arc warriors, Two Bears and Lone Dog—rode to the ridgeline leading to Reno Hill and began warning the village by riding in circles. The Crow kill one of them, Two Bears. Another party, of which Brown Back and the boy Deeds were a part, came afoul of the scouts and Deeds was killed. This occurred near where Reno crossed to the west bank. What is clear here is there were a number of Indian parties ranging in size from two to considerably larger, that were outside the village—hunting, looking for stray horses, etc.—and several men warned the village of the on-coming soldiers.

12:57 PM—*Custer-Keogh-Yates Battalions*—Company F detail moving to 14 MPH—Seeing a tepee up ahead, LT Cooke orders a detail from Company F to move ahead and check it out.

12:57 PM—(9 MPH)—Varnum and Strode—alone atop the high ground lookout point overlooking the lone tepee—watch as the regiment enters the flats. They begin moving toward the flats.

- In his August 24, 1919, interview with White Man Runs Him, General Hugh L. Scott asked the Crow scout a number of questions while they were in the vicinity of the lone tepee. A note accompanying the interview says, "*Located nine miles down the north fork of Upper Reno from Custer's point* [Crow's Nest]. *On a flat near where Upper Reno forks into the south and north streams.*" This clearly refers to a tepee near Ford A and not the one traditionally referred to in books some five miles east of the river.

1:01 PM—10.11 miles from the divide crossing; 8.54 MPH, average, from the divide approach—Custer, now riding ahead of Reno and the rest of the command, reaches the lone tepee/dead warrior tepee.

- Brennan's (Company C) horse gives out around this time.
- The tepee contained the remains of Old She Bear, a Sans Arc warrior, mortally wounded in the battle with Crook. He died the night before Custer's men found him. Custer had an argument here with several of his Ree: he had instructed them to move on, to stop for nothing. Instead, they stopped to desecrate the Sioux death lodge. In signs, he told them that if they were not brave enough, he would take away their weapons and make women of them. They replied that if he did the same thing to his scared soldiers, it would take a very long time. They laughed at him and told him they were hungry for battle.
- Reno's command is now moving ahead of Custer's.
- White Man Runs Him said the lodge was set afire by the soldiers.
- These scouts were Boyer, Herendeen, and at least four of the Crow, including Curley. LT Hare may also have been among this group.
- They watched as Sioux drove ponies toward their village.
- These Indians had been warned by Indians Varnum had seen from the Crow's Nest.
- This latter group had departed the area of the lone tepee and was approaching the main village.
- Lieutenant Hare said they had seen some forty or fifty hostiles as they approached the tepee. The Sioux were on a rise between him and the river, and from the fact they disappeared almost immediately Hare concluded they had also seen the soldiers. This rise was the higher of the buttes between the lone tepee and Ford A. The lower hill was between the river and the higher butte. It would also make sense this higher hill was the one the scouts and Gerard climbed. This apparently gave everyone the impression the Sioux were beginning to run away.
- Scouts now beginning to report many Sioux apparently set to run away; also see some in Little Big Horn valley.
- These were some of the scouts on the bluff near the lone tepee.
- Custer asks the Crow, Half Yellow Face, what all the dust in the distance was. The scout's reply was, "*The Sioux must be running away!*"
- Herendeen tells Custer the Indians are running.
- There may have been as many as 100 Indians reported by Fred Gerard. Gerard was with LT Hare on these bluffs, about fifty yards to the right of the tepee. Gerard said he could "*see the town, the tepees and ponies.*" Furthermore, Gerard estimated the Sioux to be "*about three miles away, on the left in the bottoms.*" Hare recalled seeing "*forty or fifty between us and the Little Big Horn. They evidently discovered us, because they disappeared at once.*" It may have been this group of Indians, who, instead of heading back into the village, took the bluffs across Reno Hill, eventually causing Custer to veer off from the main column rather than following behind Reno.

- Custer orders Reno to lead out at a trot while he would follow directly behind.
- The regiment did not stop at this site.
- Gerard and Herendeen both testified they heard Custer give an order directly to Reno. Herendeen stated he was standing right beside the lone tepee when "Custer told Reno to lead out and that he (Custer) would be with him."
- Custer heads down right bank of Reno Creek.
- Weather: the temperature on this day was estimated to be in excess of 100° [there is no direct confirmation of that, though measurements were taken on the "Far West" and proved to be in excess of 90°] and there was a slight northern breeze blowing. "The day was sultry, cloudless and windless ... as both the Indians and the officers ... say. What little movement of air there was, was from north to south, as Gerard remembered it from the drift of the smoke where Reno had first fought in the valley, and where the Indians had fired the grass after the retreat of the troops."[1]

1:01 PM–1:05 PM—Fred Gerard rides to the bluff, sees the two Sioux and other Indians in the valley running ponies. Gerard waves his hat, signaling Custer and shouting, "*The Indians are running like devils!*" The tepee's location was just east of where North Fork joins Reno Creek. PVT Davern, Reno's orderly, claimed there was a tepee 1½ to two miles from the river [precisely, 1.7 miles] and that an order was given there. *This makes the most sense of any account of the lone tepee's location and where Reno received his "attack" order. There was no "warning" or "move out" order issued by anyone.* SGT Culbertson (A) testified that Reno's command left Custer about three-quarters of a mile from the Little Big Horn River near a tepee. *This verifies Davern's account.* SGT Kanipe who went this way possibly as many as three times that day, remembered only one lone tepee.

1:02 PM—7 MPH—Gerard rides off the knoll and joins Reno's column heading toward the LBH River in search of a ford. A number of his Rees precede him.

1:02 PM—Several scouts, seeing a Hunkpapa youngster named Deeds and another warrior, kill Deeds as he tries to signal a warning to the village. Goes Ahead is the one who kills him.

1:03 PM—Custer issues his attack order to Reno, via LT Cooke, stating the whole regiment, or "outfit," would support Reno.

- LT Cooke issues the attack orders to Reno: "*Custer says to move at as rapid a gait as you think prudent, and to charge afterward, and you will be supported by the whole outfit.*" LT Wallace: "*The Indians are about two miles and a half ahead, on the jump, follow them as fast as you can and charge them wherever you find them and we will support you.*" Dr. Porter: Reno asked if he would be supported, "*if the general was coming along,*" and Cooke answered yes, the general would support him. PVT Davern: "*Gerard comes back and reports the Indian village three miles ahead and moving. The General directs you to take your three companies and drive everything before you.*"
- Cooke's relayed orders lead to a significant misunderstanding. In Reno's post-battle discussions, he relates his belief that these orders led him to understand Custer would support him directly, i.e., be right behind him.

- While they disagreed on the exact wording, Reno and Dr. Porter—at the Reno inquiry—essentially agreed on Cooke's orders to attack.
- LT Cooke: "*The Indians are about 2½ miles ahead, on the jump. Custer says for you to take as rapid a gait as you think prudent and charge them afterward, and you will be supported by the whole outfit.*"
- Davern heard LT Cooke order Reno to charge: "'*Gerard comes back and reports the Indian village three miles ahead and moving. The General directs you to take your three companies and drive everything before you.' Those I believe were the exact words.*" "*Colonel Benteen will be on your left and will have the same instructions.*"
- In a letter to the *New York Herald* six weeks after the battle, Reno denied Davern's comment about Benteen being on the left. Martini remembered the orders to Reno, but said the reference to Benteen was that Custer "*would have Benteen hurry up and attack in the center.*"
- Both Herendeen and Gerard remembered Custer giving the order directly to Reno.
- LT Wallace agreed Custer told Reno to take the scouts, but Wallace said Custer transmitted the attack order through Cooke.
- Hare and Kanipe remembered Custer speaking with Reno *after* Cooke issued Reno the orders. It is likely—based on Custer's actions after Reno pulled ahead, he told the major to have Hare and scouts precede his column to avoid any possibility of ambush.

1:03 PM—LT Hare, coming off the knoll, is ordered by Custer to take a mounted detail from Reno's battalion and proceed toward the river ahead of Reno to hunt for Indians.

1:04 PM—*Reno Battalion*—10–12 MPH—LT Hare approaches CPT French for a detail to scout ahead. French orders his first sergeant—John Ryan—to cut out ten men to accompany Hare.

1:05 PM—10.3 miles from divide crossing; 8.16 MPH from divide approach—sixty-five minutes from divide crossing—Reno's command separates from Custer.

1:05 PM–1:09 PM—⁶⁄₁₀ of a mile from separation; 9 MPH—Reno moves toward the river. Formation is M, A, G, column-of-fours.

1:06 PM—*Custer-Keogh-Yates Battalions*—1.2 miles from lookout point; 11.5 miles—total—from divide crossing; 9 MPH (average speed from divide: 7.2 MPH)—Varnum and Strode reach Custer, who instructs them to go with Reno. LT Wallace tags along.

1:06 PM—Varnum, now with Custer, reports for the last time. He writes, "*probably two miles from the river, I saw squadron of three troops passing the head of the column at a trot. I asked where they were going and the Genl. said, 'To begin the attack.' I asked instructions and he said to go on with them if you want to. Lieutenant Hare and I and my whole party started at the trot. Lieutenant Geo. D. Wallace, a ... dear friend ... was riding at the head of the column with the Genl. ... I called back to him, 'Come on Nick, with the fighting men. I don't stay back with the coffee coolers.' Custer laughed and* *waved his hat and told Wallace he could go and Wallace joined me."* At the RCOI Varnum claimed this was about one mile from Reno's crossing point. Varnum's location when he saw this movement was probably at a 3,405-foot elevation, south of Reno Creek and about 1.7 miles southwest of the lone tepee. Custer told LT Wallace, the acting topographical officer, he could go with Varnum and Hare.

• Varnum said Custer was at the head of his column, moving at a walk, while Reno's column was moving out at a trot.

1:07 PM—⅙-mile from separation; at 5 MPH—Custer has slowed his column to a fast walk to put distance between him and Reno. Reno's command passes by and Custer proceeds toward the river, only 1.6 miles away.

1:08 PM—Custer instructs CPT Yates to send the NCO and four or five EM forward to act as an advance scout. These would be the same men Cooke ordered forward moments earlier.

1:09 PM–1:16 PM—*Reno Battalion*—1.1 miles from separation; 9 MPH—Reno skirts behind Middle Knoll, re-crosses the stream, and takes a dry creek bed to the river. His lead elements reach the river. Running into Reno Creek was another creek called North Fork, about one-half mile from the flats. At this point, Reno crosses to the left bank of Reno Creek at a trot, still following the Indian trail, LT Cooke riding with him.

• Reno instructs his men to keep their horses *"well in hand."* [Herendeen]
• Varnum, with eight to ten Indians overtakes Reno, but the column forces him aside. As soon as Reno passed him, Varnum was joined by LT Hare.

1:13 PM—*Custer-Keogh-Yates Battalions*—⅔ of a mile from separation; at 5 MPH—Custer is now ⅔ of a mile from the separation point and one mile from the river.

1:13 PM—Some Ree scouts, having trouble with their horses, ride with Custer's column, trying to catch up. These scouts are Soldier, Bull, and White Eagle.

1:13 PM—*Reno Battalion*—1½ miles from start; 10–12 MPH—LT Hare and the Company M detail reach the Little Big Horn. Seeing Indians ahead, Reno shouts for the men to wait and re-join their company. Hare crosses the river; the detail waits for Reno and French.

1:13 PM–1:14 PM—1.7 miles from knoll and lone tepee; 7–8 MPH—Fred Gerard, riding to the left and out front of Reno by eight or ten feet, reaches a small knoll next to the river [Cooke's Knoll] crossing at Ford A. He halts about fifteen to twenty feet from the river's edge.

1:14 PM—*Custer-Keogh-Yates Battalions*—The Ree scout, Stab—who had been with Benteen's column—we believe—initially—rides up to Soldier and the others. He rides on ahead, to follow Custer's column up the bluffs.

1:14 PM—Two more Company C troopers—Brennan and Fitzgerald—fall out.

1:15 PM—*Reno Battalion*—1.7 miles, total, from separation; 8–10 MPH—Reno, slightly ahead of his command and just behind Gerard, reaches the river.

1:15 PM—Gerard is informed by several of his Ree scouts that the Indians are coming back up the valley to confront the troops.

1:16 PM—**1.7 miles, total, from separation; a speed of about 7.5 to 8 MPH, an occasional lope**—Reno reaches Ford A, here, about twenty-five to thirty feet wide (Varnum) and crosses to left bank of the stream. Order of march: Company M behind Reno; Company A was in the middle; Company G was in the rear. As Reno enters the river, Gerard informs him of the turn of events. Reno ignores him.

- Gerard pauses, then turns back and meets LT Cooke. Gerard informs the adjutant of the Sioux moving up the valley. Cooke turns immediately and heads back to Custer.
- Varnum said the crossing began about ten or fifteen minutes after the two forces separated.
- PVT Taylor recalls it being fifty to seventy feet wide, two to four feet deep, and icy cold.
- Reno changes his front from a column-of-fours to a column-of-twos to cross the river.
- Company M crossed first, then A, then G.
- Troops and some scouts spot the Sioux "attacking."
- Gerard was now *east* of the crossing on a small knoll—no longer ahead of Reno—and was informed by several scouts who had ridden upstream along the river's high bank to get a better view and who looked north over the treetops, that the Sioux were not dismantling their village but were actually coming out to meet the soldiers.
- Reno is in the river at this time.
- This news is contrary to what Custer and his officers were expecting.
- Gerard claims he told Reno this news, but Reno denied he ever spoke to Gerard about it, stating, "*the scout 'had no right to speak to me officially.'*"
- Reno had absolutely no use for Gerard and had once dismissed him for stealing government items at Fort Lincoln.
- Gerard decides Custer needs to know this and starts back when he sees Cooke near this same knoll.
- Not seeing Custer's column behind, Gerard reports to Cooke (probably within eighty yards of the river), that the Indians are *not* scattering, but are attacking.
- Cooke says, "*All right, I'll go back and report.*"
- This report caused Custer to take the back trail rather than support Reno directly.
- Godfrey: "*In all our previous experiences, when the immediate presence of the troops was once known to them, the warriors swarmed to the attack, and resorted to all kinds of ruses to mislead the troops, to delay the advance toward their camp or village, while the squaws and children secured what personal effects they could, drove off the pony herd, and by flight put themselves beyond danger, and then scattering made successful pursuit next to impossible.*"
- Gerard turns and gallops off toward the ford.

- There is the story of PVT Theodore Goldin, detailed as an orderly to Cooke, going back to Reno with a note from Cooke, written as the command was on the bluffs before Reno Hill, the gist of which was, "*Crowd them as hard as you can. We will soon be with you.*" Goldin claimed to have ridden back—maybe five or six miles and crossing the river—delivering the note to Reno (who denied ever receiving it). The problem with the story rests more with Goldin's overall credibility than with anything inherent about the tale itself. While there is no other independent verification of Goldin's story, Walter Mason Camp seems to have believed it.
- Author Larry Sklenar wrote that Goldin was dispatched about one mile after Custer began his move *north* from the flats, maybe one-quarter mile from Reno Hill.[2] He also felt McIlhargey and Mitchell would have reached Custer as he was crossing Reno Hill. Also, "*Custer's column was easily more than a mile from the river when he diverged sharply to the right, the trail later drew nearer the river, but, at the time I was turned back we must have been in the neighborhood of a mile from... (Reno Creek).*" W.A. Graham, meantime, thought Goldin a complete liar, calling the story Goldin's "*'Paul Revere ride' to Reno.*"
- Cooke accompanied Reno to the Little Big Horn (Myles Keogh was with Cooke).
- Godfrey said Keogh and Cooke rode all the way to the ford and observed Reno's battalion crossing [Since Godfrey was not there, this had to have been hearsay].

Side Notes—Custer and the HQ detachment would remain with the left wing, i.e., Yates', throughout the entire battle. Keogh led the right wing across Luce Ridge, Nye-Cartwright Ridge, and onto Calhoun Hill (coordinates—45° 33'50.08" N latitude; 107° 25' 7.86" W longitude), while Custer, after viewing the situation from the heights of Luce went with Yates' left wing, down the ridges and Medicine Tail Coulee, to scout Ford B (coordinates—45° 32' 49.79" N latitude; 107° 24'59.21" W longitude). This would define the role of the left wing—including the headquarters contingent—as the active one.

Reno Battalion—Some claim Reno halted to water his horses. Herendeen tells Reno the Sioux are not running. Reno crossed at Ford A into an area of underbrush and timber that was variously said to be between fifty to 200 yards wide and difficult to traverse.

1:16 PM—1.7 miles, total, from separation; 5–7 MPH—Reno begins crossing the Little Big Horn at Ford A, his formation changing to column-of-twos. SGT Miles O'Harra positioned to keep troops moving. Some pause, briefly, to water.

At this same time LT Cooke leaves Gerard to report to Custer. Cooke stayed long enough to watch two companies ford the river; Keogh left earlier. Herendeen also informs Reno of Indians moving up the valley, and Reno, thinking Custer is right behind him, sends his striker, PVT McIlhargey (I), to tell Custer the Sioux were as thick as grass. The battalion was still crossing the river.

- A number of Ree were on a little knoll or rise just east of the crossing, discussing the Sioux to their front.
- McIlhargey remained with his company—Company I—and was killed with Custer.
- Gerard runs into McIlhargey, "hurrying east."
- Reno would send another messenger—PVT Mitchell—to Custer a few minutes later.

1:19 PM—*Custer-Keogh-Yates Battalions*—**Cooke: 850 yards from previous knoll; Custer: 1 ± mile from separation from Reno; Cooke: 10 MPH; Custer: 5–6 MPH**— As Custer is passing alongside Middle Knoll, Cooke intercepts him and informs him of Gerard's report. They are one-half mile from the Little Big Horn River.

- Custer hears Cooke's report and makes the fatal decision to try to get to the northern end of the village. He swings his command to the right and orders a gallop, **at 9–10 MPH.**
- Custer probably felt the Sioux "attack" was simply a delaying action.
- This 90° turn occurred about one-quarter mile from Ford A.
- Varnum claimed when he re-joined the column after riding down Reno Creek, Reno was passing by Custer and Varnum reported to the general. "*That was about a mile from where Major Reno afterwards crossed the Little Big Horn.*"
- After the battle, SGT Kanipe said the battalion turned north immediately after spotting a group of one hundred Indians on the northern high bluffs. Walter Mason Camp also recorded this, though the figure was sixty to seventy-five Indians, north of Reno Hill. Kanipe claimed to have made the report to 1SG Edwin Bobo (C), who in turn, reported it to LT Henry Harrington, and so on, up to Custer. There is no independent verification of these Indians, and since Bobo and Harrington were killed with the Custer command, the report is now considered bogus (especially since the reputed location cannot be seen from the area of Reno Creek).
- Curley claimed Custer's turn occurred about 1¼ mile from Ford A, and the command went to the north fork of Reno Creek, crossed it, and turned westward along the ridge.
- Curley described Custer's trail, "*directly across the country, on the crest of a long ridge, running to the bluffs and coming out to a point about five hundred feet north of the Reno corral.*"
- Terry in his official report said Custer's trail passed "*along and in the rear of the crest of bluffs on the right bank for nearly three miles.*"
- Gerard, at the Reno inquiry, thought there might have been two reasons why Custer veered off to the right: (1) when Custer heard the reports of the Indians coming out to meet Reno, Custer might have changed his plans; and (2) Custer saw a large trail—larger than the one followed by Reno to Ford A— that swung around the eastern side of the small knoll he had seen when riding with Reno.
- PVT Martini reported seeing this same trail and knew it was a lodge trail, meaning women and children.

- Lodge trails usually led to easy river crossings and Custer obviously had to know this.
- Godfrey wrote, as Custer's command rode on the bluffs, the two commands—Custer's and Reno's—could not see each other. This is hearsay, but Godfrey obviously got it from officers who rode with Reno. It also jibes with Martini's comments at the RCOI about Custer moving his command inland from the bluffs.
- According to Walter Mason Camp's research, Custer's command was in a squadron formation, a company front in a column of twos, moving at a trot and gallop all the way up the bluff. This would be ten horses across fifty feet of frontage, about twenty horses per column (200 feet deep): Yates: E, F; Keogh: L, C and I.
- Custer's column is now spotted by Standing Bear, who is on or near Weir Peak with several other Minneconjou and some women who were digging turnips. He had heard an alarm.
- Boyer and the four Crow rode on ahead of Custer to view the valley from the bluffs. After they reached the bluffs, Custer ordered them to the high hill just north of where Reno entrenched.

1:20 PM—*Reno Battalion*—**5–7 MPH**—The last of Reno's battalion has crossed the river.

- Varnum, Hare, *et al.*, allowed Reno's column to pass, then re-joined it as Reno's first company reached the ford. Varnum and Hare have crossed the river by the time the first company completes its crossing.

1:20 PM–1:21 PM—*Custer-Keogh-Yates Battalions*—**335 yards; 9–10 MPH**—Lead elements of Custer's command reach North Fork and pause to water their horses. Custer slows to a walk (3¾ MPH) to get to North Fork; halts to water less than one-half mile from the flats. North Fork forms one side of the flats.

- Custer orders two Crow—Half Yellow Face and White Swan—to scout ahead to the rising ridge leading to Reno Hill. These two, because of a misunderstanding, depart to follow Reno instead of heading to the high ground. The misunderstanding was probably caused by Varnum's attempt to gather in the scouts to go with Reno.
- Boyer sees the mistake and leads the other four Crow to the ridge to see the village for Custer.

1:21 PM—*Reno Battalion*—**7–8 MPH, speed increasing**—Reno pushes his troops on; early river crossers that stopped to re-cinch are now re-mounted. After the three companies crossed the river, Reno reformed his battalion into a column of fours and having no response yet from McIlhargey's message, sends his cook, PVT Mitchell (I), to tell Custer the Sioux are forming and not running and that they were in overwhelming numbers. Both men remained with their company and were killed with Custer.

- According to Dr. Porter, the horses were excited, vigorous, and in good condition.

- Reno wrote in his report a few days after the battle, "*I crossed immediately and halted about 10 minutes or less to gather the battalion, sending word to Custer that I had everything in front of me and that they were strong.*"

1:21 PM–1:26 PM—*Custer-Keogh-Yates Battalions*—Custer's command waters its horses.

1:22 PM—*Reno Battalion*—**.48 miles to the open valley (840 yards); 10–12 MPH, varying in stretches**—Reno begins his move into and down the Little Big Horn valley. He moved the battalion from a column of fours into a line, companies A and M, left to right, with G behind as a reserve. Company G is then brought into line on the left. Reno orders, "*Left into line, gallop—forward, guide center.*" Reno's frontage now became about 120 yards, Company G to Company M (left to right); Herendeen was some 100 yards farther to the left.

- At **10–12 MPH**—CPT French instructs 1SG Ryan to take men and ride in skirmish formation along the river's timbered edge to ferret out any Indians he found there. These men were probably sergeants White and O'Harra; CPL Scollin; and privates Newell, Meier, Thorpe, Galenne, Braun, Gordon, Turley, Wilber, Neely, and Klotzbucher, making it two sets-of-four.
- As Reno begins his move down the valley, a number of Ree scouts move with him on the command's far left. These scouts include Young Hawk, Goose, Red Star, Strikes Two, Little Sioux, Bob-tail Bull, Forked Horn, Red Foolish Bear, Boy Chief, Little Brave, One Feather, Billy Jackson, and Red Bear. Bloody Knife is with them, as well, as is the Dakota scout, Whole Buffalo.
- "Reno did not, and indeed could not, know that his commander had apparently changed his original plans and was at that moment riding just on the other side of the bluffs that line the eastern bank of the Little Big Horn. Major Reno had been ordered to pursue an enemy who was believed to be running away and to attempt to bring him to battle. He was doing just that."[3]
- Varnum corroborates the forming of the battalion during the RCOI: "*...I turned my head around and glanced back to see the cause [Indians to the front had stopped their circling and turned backward], and I noticed a battalion deploying from column into line....*"
- LT Wallace: "*Companies A and M were formed in line with the Indian scouts under Varnum and Hare ahead; and my company [G] in rear in line as a reserve.*"
- 1SG Ryan: "*...Company M, on the right and LT McIntosh's company [G] on the left, and CPT Moylan's [A] in the rear.*" This is the formation going down the valley.
- Varnum rode to Reno's far left about seventy-five yards in front of the battalion.
- The valley opened wider as the troops moved downstream.
- The Indians in front of the moving soldiers numbered about forty or fifty (LT Hare) and were firing and raising as much dust as they could, trying to obscure the village. Hare was toward the left of the line.
- This dust-raising tactic was merely a stall to allow the non-combatants to

gather what they could and flee. The huge dust screen hid their movements and concealed the number of Indians who were starting to come out of the village. The fact Reno could not see much beyond the wall of dust probably contributed to his dismounting.

- The troops started out at a trot, then after about a mile, moved to a slow gallop.
- The move—never called a "charge"—was for fully two miles before Reno ordered a dismount.
- Varnum: "*I have always stated the distance to Major Reno's skirmish line was about two miles … and from there it was about 800 yards to where the nearest tepees were in a bend of the river. Then the main bulk of the village was below that. There must have been quite a solid lot of tepees in that bend.*"
- Varnum also said he thought it was about fifteen to twenty minutes from the time Reno finished crossing the river to when he ordered the skirmish line.
- Taylor says they started out at a fast walk, then moved to a trot, and when they saw the puffs of smoke and heard the "pinging" of bullets, were ordered to charge.
- As Reno brought G Company into line, "the battalion did not break its fast gallop down the valley, riding faster than some of the troopers had ever ridden before."
- No large number of Indians were coming out to attack the galloping soldiers.
- Herendeen: "*…as we advanced down the valley, fires commenced springing up in the timber. We kept right on, facing a little point of timber that came out on the prairie.*"
- CPT Moylan: "*we could see Indians coming out of the dust mounted. They were so numerous.*"
- Varnum rode down the valley with Hare and Wallace. "*We put our spurs to our horses and crossed the river with the command and then pulled out ahead, with the scouts, guides, etc. The valley was full of Indians riding madly in every direction. We advanced rapidly down the valley, the Indians retiring before us for about a mile, Wallace, Hare and myself riding together.*"
- "*LT Hare also joined, and with the scouts and attackers we rode to overtake Reno which we did as he was fording the stream and came out into the open valley ahead and covered the advance with my scouts, Lts Wallace and Hare, Charlie Reynolds, Herendine [sic], Boyer [sic] and Fred Gerard and Bloody Knife, with myself, leading but spread out across the front.*"

1:23 PM–1:34 PM—½ mile so far; 12 MPH—As Reno's command moves rapidly down the valley, several of the men sight a figure they thought was Custer on the bluffs overlooking the valley. This is now one-half mile from the North Fork of Reno Creek.

- By the time Gerard re-crossed the river he saw Reno's battalion moving down the valley several hundred yards ahead.

1:24 PM—The Ree scouts, Soldier, Bull, and White Eagle follow after Custer's command.

1:25 PM—*Benteen Battalion*—**4⅛ miles from separation; average speed: 3.3 MPH**—After climbing three to four ridgelines, Benteen turns his command down No-Name Creek to return to the main trail. Benteen arrives at upper No-Name Creek—in the valley—and begins his turn down it, 3¾ miles from the divide halt.

- Gibson reaches a high promontory on the third ridge (Ridge C) and finds the upper reaches of the Little Big Horn valley empty.
- Benteen realizes Custer had been correct: the view of the Little Big Horn was invaluable and proved the Indians were down the valley, not up.
- Benteen: "*I knew the Indians had too much sense to go any place over such a rugged country—that if they had to go in that direction they had a much better way to go.… I had an idea that General Custer was mistaken as to there being.… Indians in that vicinity; and as there were no Indians there.… I thought my duty was to go back to the trail and join the command.*"
- Benteen, in a letter to his wife: "*I went up and down those hills for 10 miles … the horses were fast giving out from steady climbing—and as my orders had been fulfilled, I struck diagonally for the trail the command had marched on.*"
- Gibson ascended four different bluffs, scanned the upper Little Big Horn valley with his field glasses and signaled Benteen that there were no Indians in that direction.
- PVT Windolph remembered the country as quite rugged and very hard on the horses.
- Benteen's ride down No-Name Creek was along its right bank and was quite easy.
- Godfrey: "*Benteen very wisely determined to follow the trail of the rest of the command.…*"

1:25 PM–1:50 PM—**(2.9 miles to travel to the main trail); at 7 MPH**—Benteen's battalion begins its move down No-Name Creek.

1:26 PM–1:27 PM—*Custer-Keogh-Yates Battalions*—**300 yards; at 8 MPH**—Finished watering (five minutes), Custer's command mounts the bluffs, rapidly, and is seen by some of Reno's troops.

1:27 PM—**10 MPH**—Mitch Boyer, the four Crow—and Black Fox it appears, as well—leave Custer's command a couple minutes early to head up the bluffs.

1:27 PM–1:29 PM—**670 yards, total, from watering; 8 MPH**—Custer's command continues to mount the bluffs and after about 300 yards, swings off on a slight right angle for another 600–700 yards.

1:28 PM—*Reno Battalion*—**1 mile from crossing at Ford A; 12 MPH**—Several Ree scouts including Red Star, Strikes Two, Little Sioux, and Boy Chief break away from the advancing troops to chase three Sioux women and two or three children hiding in the timber-line and trying to make it back to the village. They kill at least two of the women and the children—Gall's family—and then spot some twenty-five or thirty Sioux ponies. They herd the horses across a ford. They see One Feather and Pta-a-te (aka, Whole Buffalo, one of the Dakota scouts). Red Bear continued to ride with the troops down the valley.

*1:30 PM—**Terry-Gibbon Column**—Terry's column reaches Big Horn.*

1:34 PM—*Custer-Keogh-Yates Battalions*—Another ¾ of a mile; 9 MPH—Custer's command continues to mount the hills, more inland and out of sight of Reno's men, but with Custer closer to the bluffs.

1:35 PM—*Reno Battalion*—Approximately 2½ miles from Ford A crossing—Reno orders his command to dismount and form a skirmish line.

- Hodgson ordered Company G to dismount; Reno ordered M and A to dismount.
- CPT French orders 1SG Ryan to take ten men to clear the timber. Once it was safe, the horse-holders moved into the woods with the horses.
- Reno's halt takes place in the middle of a prairie dog village and was apparently precipitated by out-riding vedettes signaling back that there was a ravine ahead. At the speed the troops were moving, stumbling into that ravine would have been catastrophic.
- Bruce Liddic wrote: "The ravine was actually a small unnamed tributary which emptied into the Little Big Horn from the west. Today, this small tributary is the present irrigation canal located east of the defunct Reno Battlefield Museum."
- In 1876, this ravine was about five feet deep and ten feet wide.
- What is interesting here is Liddic's assertion the vedettes signaled back about the ravine is not corroborated by Varnum's RCOI testimony. In his book, Varnum discusses heading down the valley on three separate occasions and never once mentions anything about the column being warned or halted by any outriders. He did say, however, that he and others had been working their way toward the left side of Reno's charging line, so unless the ravine extended a good deal further out toward the bench lands, Varnum may not have seen it, while riders on the right side of the line did spot it. Varnum does say, however, that the ravine was there, but he did not know of it at the time.
- The Indian village began about 300 yards north of Reno's right flank. Varnum claimed it was closer to 800 yards.
- Moylan said the beginning of the village was about 300 yards away. LT Wallace said the streambed angled northward to about 100 yards of the encampment.
- Varnum claimed there were only a few shots fired before Reno ordered the men to dismount and that when they were "*[a]t the left toward the bluff.... LT Hare I think fired a few shots.*"
- This is also when Varnum spotted Custer's command, though he did not know what companies Custer had taken. "*[A]bout the time Major Reno's command dismounted in the bottom, just as I joined it from the left and front, looking on the bluffs across the river to our right. I saw the gray horse company ... moving down along those bluffs.... It was back from the actual edge of the bluffs. The head and the rear of the column were both behind the edge of the bluffs in a sort of hollow, and I just happened to catch sight of about the whole of the gray horse company. I think they were a little farther down [the river] than*"

where we struck the bluffs we came upon them." They were moving at a trot.

- Company G on the right; horses moved into timber. Company A in the middle. Reno pulled part of G from the right, bringing it into the timber.
- According to James Willert, it was about this time when Reno ordered CPT French to send ten Company M troops into the timber to clear the area and prepare a spot to secure the horses. Liddic talks about the ten Company M men skirting the timber and river as the command moved down the valley.
- Varnum, in his RCOI testimony stated: *"Captain Moylan said the Indians were getting in on his left, and the horses were not covered by the skirmish line, and they would probably get in there."*
- Reno halted without any real contact with the Indians and Varnum claimed the nearest Indians were still 500 yards away.
- Despite all the critics who condemn Reno for stopping and not charging through the village, LT Hare believed they could not last another five minutes if Reno had continued and not a single man would have made it through the village. Hare believed Reno's order to halt was *"the only thing that saved us."* Most of the battalion officers agreed with Hare, though it seems French was not among them.
- It was estimated that between fifty and 500 Indians faced them.
- Reno: 500–600.
- Wallace: 200+, all in or near the ravine, 500 yards from where the troops dismounted. After the troops dismounted, he noticed many more arriving.
- Varnum: the valley was full of Indians, riding in every direction. Once on the skirmish line, *"[t]here was a very large force … soon after the command was dismounted, and there was a large force circling around us all the time, and passing around to the left and rear."*
- *"I don't think the entire force of the village was attacking us in the woods. I don't think the entire force of the Indians was ever attacking us because after we got on the hill we could see parties of Indians a long way off…. I judge the main fighting force of the village was against us there after we dismounted."*
- SGT Culbertson: few Indians until they reached the area of heavy timber and dismounted. Few near the troops; 250 altogether.
- Gerard: less than 100 warriors in front of the skirmish line.
- Hare agreed with Gerard. No more than fifty Indians until they dismounted, then hundreds *"moved down to the left and rear."* Two hundred continuously in Reno's front. Between 400 and 500 hostiles emerged from *"out of a coulee about 400 yards in front … and moved to our left and rear."*
- Herendeen: (on the extreme left of the line and about 100 yards in front) didn't see any Indians in the immediate front of Reno's line. They were all downstream until the troops dismounted. No more than 200 Indians.
- Dr. Porter: 75–100 Indians 800–900 yards away; maybe fifty confronting the troops; a good many more downriver.
- 1SG Ryan: 500, coming from the direction of their village.

- From its right near the edge of the timber by an old dry channel of the river, the line extended only a short way into the valley.
- According to LT Wallace, only about seventy-five men manned the line.
- If the normal five-yard interval were maintained, the line would have stretched about 375 yards from the edge of the timber into the valley.
- According to SGT Culbertson of Company A, the line was about 200–250 yards long.
- Company M moved farther west, toward the hills, splitting the skirmish line into two separate lines. The configuration was Company M to the far western side of the valley; a part of Company G on the far right (the remainder taken into the timber by Reno) abutting the timber; and Company A to G's left, a gap between A and M.
- Bobtail Bull was the last man on the left of the line.
- Fred Gerard believed the foothills to be at least 1,000–1,200 yards beyond the left end of the line.
- Gerard, Herendeen, and Reynolds were about 100 yards to the left and behind the skirmish line, in a small swale.
- Varnum: "*There was very heavy firing going on on both sides.... The heaviest firing of the Indians was toward the right of the line ... there were about 400 or 500 Indians in front of the line. There may have been a great many more.*"
- Varnum: "*It is almost impossible to estimate the strength of mounted Indians. There was a large force there soon after the command was dismounted, and a large force circling around all the time and passing to the left and rear.... I don't think there were less than three or 400 Indians in Reno's immediate front, and there may have been a great many more ... up the valley the whole country seemed to be covered with them. How many the dust concealed it is impossible to estimate.*"
- Dr. Porter: "*The Indians were circling back and forth and coming nearer in squads and firing more rapidly as they came.... There were many more [hostiles] down the river....*"
- Reno's men see Custer's battalion, on bluffs, now disappearing down toward Cedar Coulee.
- PVT Newell (M): saw Custer's troops on the bluffs as they charged down the valley.
- Varnum saw Custer's troops going on the bluffs about the time the skirmish line was formed. "*I saw the gray horse company moving down along the bluffs. I only saw it momentarily. It was back from the edge of the bluffs and the head and rear of the column were behind the edge of the bluffs.*"
- Godfrey: "*Some of Reno's men had seen a party of Custer's command, including Custer himself, on the bluffs about the time the Indians began to develop in Reno's front. This party was heard to cheer, and seen to wave their hats as if to give encouragement, and then they disappeared behind the hills.... It was about the time of this incident that Trumpeter Martini left Cooke with Custer's last orders to Benteen....*"
- Godfrey goes further in explaining the note to Martini: "*From this place....*

Custer could survey the valley for several miles above and for a short distance below Reno; yet he could only see a part of the village; he must, then, have felt confident that all the Indians were below him; hence, I presume, his message to Benteen. The view of the main body of the village was cut off by the highest points of the ridge, a short distance from him."

- Godfrey goes on: *"Had he gone to this high point he would have understood the magnitude of his undertaking, and it is probable that his plan of battle would have been changed."*

- Godfrey: *"He could see … the village was not breaking away toward the Big Horn Mountains. He must, then, have expected to find the squaws and children fleeing to the bluffs on the north, for in no other way do I account for his wide detour to the right. He must have counted upon Reno's success, and fully expected the 'scatteration' of the non-combatants with the pony herds. The probable attack upon the families and the capture of the herds were in that event counted upon to strike consternation in the hearts of the warriors, and were elements for success upon which General Custer fully counted in the event of a daylight attack."*

- James Willert quoted some veterans as saying the men were cool and calm, Reno, French, and Hodgson being the only ones standing, walking the line, urging the men on and telling them to fire low.

- Indians began to turn the left end of the line.

- Reno: *"We were in skirmish line under hot fire for 15 or 20 minutes."*

- Indians begin flanking skirmish line on left. Hodgson reports this to Reno who places Hodgson in charge of the line while he checked out the woods.

1:35 PM—6–8 MPH—1SG Ryan orders the other M Company flankers to clear the woods, PVT Morris claiming to be among them, though this appears to be a dubious claim. *"Ryan, in charge of the detail, gave the command, Double time! when we were close to the wood, and then, As skirmishers, march! We entered the woods, skirmished them to the river, saw no Indians in the woods and immediately returned."*

1:36 PM—Reno's troops begin deploying.

- Edgar I. Stewart: "Earlier, some of the warriors had seen dust clouds in the east … and later some of them had noticed soldiers about two miles east of the camp. They had seen Custer's command riding along the eastern ridges toward the lower end of the camp as though on dress parade…. [W]hile the Indians seem to have been aware of the earlier division of the regiment, they claim to have had no suspicion of an attack from the south. … It was apparently this huge dust cloud [being made by Reno] rolling rapidly down the valley toward them which interrupted the hostiles' speculation regarding the identity of the soldiers across the river and first warned them of their danger…. [W]hile most of the warriors rushed in the direction of the pony herd, a few went out to face Reno, some on foot and the others on ponies that, luckily, had been picketed in the village… [P]robably not more than one-fourth of the available fighting strength rode upstream to oppose the major's detachment…."

- In his report to the Assistant Adjutant General, Department of Dakota, St. Paul, MN, dated July 24, 1876, CPT J.S. Poland, Commanding Officer, Standing Rock, claimed he found out from seven Sioux who had returned from the battle, that the attack on the village came as a surprise. Furthermore, as the Indians were driving Reno's command up the bluffs, word came that more soldiers were attacking downstream. This also was a surprise.
- PVT James Wilber of Company M claimed about ten troopers, including himself, 1SG John Ryan, PVT Roman Rutten, and PVT John H. Meier, actually got among the Hunkpapa tepees. PVT William E. Morris was another. None of these men were killed during the battle.

1:38 PM—*Custer-Keogh-Yates Battalions*—1+ miles from watering; 9 MPH—Custer's command is approaching Reno Hill after picking up speed as the terrain evens out.

1:38 PM—1½ miles from watering; 10–12 MPH, slowing to 7–8 MPH—Custer's scouts—Boyer, the four Crow (Goes Ahead, Hairy Moccasin, White Man Runs Him, and Curley), and it appears the Ree, Black Fox, as well—riding slightly ahead of Custer, are crossing over Reno Hill and beginning to slow as they swing left and approach the edge of the bluffs.

1:40 PM—*Reno Battalion*—Five minutes from dismount—Skirmish line is deployed and begins moving forward. A gap begins to form between Company M and Company A as M moves toward the western foothills and A begins to swing more to its right.

1:40 PM—500–600 yards (.284 miles) from entering the timber; 4 MPH—6 MPH—5 minutes from dismount—The other half of the Company M skirmishers—at least Meier and Wilber, but probably SGT White as well—have reached the first of the Indian tepees and begin setting them on fire.

1:40 PM—A number of the Ree scouts deploy with Reno's troops, almost all of them on the left. Red Bear said the Sioux were lying down, and "no one was riding around on horseback."

1:40 PM (to 2:10 PM)—1 mile; 5 MPH, average—Ree scouts have captured a number of Sioux ponies and have herded them across the river and up a small coulee coming off the bluffs. They run into the tail-end of Custer's command and are fired upon by some trailing soldiers who mistake them for Sioux. The scouts now include Rees, Red Star, Strikes Two, Little Sioux, Boy Chief, One Feather, Bull-Stands-In-Water, and the Dakota, Whole Buffalo. (They will meet several others who did not cross the river with Reno, including the Rees, Soldier, Bull, White Eagle, Stab, and Billy Cross; and the Dakotas, White Cloud, Caroo, and Ma-tok-sha.)

1:41 PM—*Custer-Keogh-Yates Battalions*—PVT Peter Thompson of Company C drops out of formation as his horse begins to break down. He is on the northern side of Reno Hill. The rest of the command passes him by.

- As Thompson dismounts to tend to his horse, the F Company advance scouts pass him by; **at 10 MPH.**

1:42 PM—*Reno Battalion*—Varnum sees Gray Horse Troop on bluffs. **Sighted 500 yards downstream from Reno Hill.** Varnum writes that he saw the Gray Horse Troop as Reno was dismounting: "*Suddenly the Indians began advancing towards us and looking back I saw that the troops were dismounting to fight on foot. My scouts had disappeared. We rode back to the line of troops which rested its right on the timber which bordered the stream. Across the timber, on the other side of the stream, was a high bluff and looking up I saw the gray horse Troop E in column…. As I joined [A Company] I happened to look towards the high bluffs on the other side of the river and saw the gray horse Troop E, in column, going down stream. The conformation of the ground on the bluff was such that I could see only that much of the column.*"

- Varnum rather pinpoints his sighting of the Gray Horse Troop as being about one-quarter mile below (north) of where Reno's command occupied the hill. At the RCOI, Reno himself asked Varnum: "*Did I understand you to say that a prolongation of the skirmish line across the river would strike the point where you saw the gray horse company?*" Varnum's reply was yes.
- Gerard sees Custer's men about one-half mile below Reno's entrenchment area.
- Gerard estimated it would have taken Custer fifteen to twenty minutes to reach this point from where Gerard had last seen Cooke.
- LT Godfrey—who was not there—wrote: "*On this ridge…. Custer and staff were seen to wave their hats, and heard to cheer just as Reno was beginning the attack; but Custer's troops were at that time a mile or more to his right. It was about this time that the trumpeter was sent back with Custer's last order to Benteen.*"
- As Custer returned to his command, he moved it forward a bit, closing in on Cedar Coulee. He halted, but a number of the troopers saw the village, and in their excitement rode past Custer. Custer halted them, saying, "*Boys, hold your horses, there are plenty of them down there for us all.*"

1:42 PM—*Custer-Keogh-Yates Battalions*—(⅔ of a mile across the river and into the village); (5 MPH)—The Hunkpapa warrior, Iron Cedar, on or near Weir Point, sees Custer's column approaching near the bluffs to the south. He turns immediately and heads down the bluffs to warn the village of more soldiers.

1:44 PM—1+ miles; 7–8 MPH—Custer cautions his excited troops as they move toward the head of Cedar Coulee. The command begins to slow its pace considerably. "Hold your horses in, boys, there are plenty of them down there for us all."

1:45 PM—*Reno Battalion*—Distance unknown, but probably 500–600 yards and back.; 6–8 MPH—Having been split in two, the first group of Company M flankers have rapidly cleared the timber and have returned to their unit. PVT Morris claimed to be part of this group, though that claim is unsupported.

1:46 PM—*Custer-Keogh-Yates Battalions*—The scouts, now mingling around Custer and watching Reno's command, are told by Custer to proceed to the high ground north—Weir Peaks. Boyer, Goes Ahead, White Man Runs Him, and Hairy Moccasin turn and head toward Weir.

1:46 PM—*Reno Battalion*—**At 6–8 MPH**—The Company M flankers who had reached the village were now concerned about being cut off and begin to head back into the timber area.

1:47 PM—Reno leaves the general area where he is with Moylan and heads into the timber, taking LT McIntosh and a group of Company G troops with him. Moylan is forced to spread his command farther apart to cover the gaps. Hodgson is told to keep Reno informed.

1:47 PM—LT De Rudio arrives in timber.

1:47 PM—*Custer-Keogh-Yates Battalions*—It is not unreasonable to assume if SGT Daniel Kanipe was sent back with a message for CPT McDougall and the packs, he would have been sent about this time, from approximately the southwestern shoulder of Sharpshooters' Ridge.

- Kanipe started back along the trail, but when he saw the dust being rolled up by Benteen and the pack train, he cut across the backcountry directly toward them.
- About this time Custer orders five men from Company F forward to form a reconnoitering flank in front of the battalion.

1:48 PM—**Approximately 2½ miles from Middle Knoll**—Custer passes Reno Hill (another one mile), approaches Sharpshooters' Ridge and the top of Cedar Coulee. He moves to the edge of the bluffs. Thirteen minutes from Reno's dismount—Custer arrives at elevation point 3,411. His troops slow even more and head for the depression of Cedar Coulee.

- Troops are ordered into a set of fours.
- Custer sees the village for the first time and it was here where Custer uttered the comment about, "*we've caught them napping!*"
- Godfrey: "*On the battlefield in 1886, Chief Gall indicated Custer's route to me, and it then flashed upon me that I myself had seen Custer's trail. On June 28, while we were burying the dead, I asked Major Reno's permission to go on the high ridge east or back of the field* [appears to be SSR] *to look for tracks of shod horses to ascertain if some of the command might not have escaped. When I reached the ridge I saw this trail, and wondered who could have made it, but dismissed the thought that it had been made by Custer's column, because it did not accord with the theory with which we were then filled, that Custer had attempted to cross at the ford, and this trail was too far back, and showed no indication of leading toward the ford.*"
- If Gall watched as Custer descended Cedar Coulee into Medicine Tail Coulee, he did so from one of the knolls north of Weir Peak or from Weir Peak itself.[4]
- Godfrey also believed Custer never went to Ford B, but continued on across the ridges to behind (east of) Calhoun Hill. Godfrey's theory, however, does not account for the cartridge cases found along Luce/Nye-Cartwright.
- Benteen never suspected that Custer saw him from there. Benteen said: "*When that order was sent to me by Custer, he couldn't tell within ten miles of where I might be found from the nature of the order I had received from him.*"

- Some of Reno's men see Custer's battalion near Reno Hill.
- This could also be where Gall first spotted Custer's column.
- Varnum spotted Custer's column. "[H]e first *'saw E Company about a quarter of a mile, some little distance like that, from the point where Major Reno was when we struck the hill.'"*
- Custer passes Sharpshooter Ridge at a "*not very fast trot*" and enters Cedar Coulee, disappearing from view (another one-half mile).
- Gerard says "a fast trot" and "raising dust."
- There is also no testimony among the Crow that they were with Custer while moving along the bluffs' edge and on Weir Peak.
- Goes Ahead: Custer "*rode to the edge of the high bank and looked over to the place where Reno's men were….*"
- Hairy Moccasin: "*…we could see the village and could see Reno fighting….*"
- It is here Martini claimed Custer saw the village "asleep." Bruce Liddic feels this should not be taken literally and that Martini—an Italian immigrant— misunderstood the phrase "we've caught them napping," for, "they're asleep." While Liddic views catching the village unprepared or quiet as incredible, he goes on to say Curley supported Martini's story. The four Crow scouts and Boyer looked at the village and Boyer wondered aloud that maybe the Indians were out "campaigning somewhere."
- Martini said they could see nothing of Reno's command from here, even though they were looking for it.
- Kanipe said they had seen Reno earlier, "*moving at full speed down the valley.*"

1:48 PM–1:56 PM—Custer and two others—in all likelihood, LT Cooke and CPT Tom Custer—atop elevation point 3,411, watch the action in the valley below.

- Another quote from Custer, *via* Martini: "*We will go down and make a crossing and capture the village.*" Custer shouted it to the entire command.

1:49 PM—*Reno Battalion*—De Rudio reaches the spot in timber where he is to see Custer.

1:49 PM—Reno, with a number of his Company G troops, reaches the timber.

1:50 PM—Varnum—hearing Company G is going to charge through the timber— leaves skirmish line for woods.

1:50 PM—*Benteen Battalion*—8⅛ miles from east of divide; 5.3 MPH—7 MPH— Boston Custer, beginning to pick up speed, approaches the morass and sees Benteen's command.

1:50 PM—2.9 miles from turn; 7.1 miles, total; Benteen's scout before turning: 4.2 MPH—Benteen's column reaches the confluence of No-Name Creek and Reno Creek, one-quarter mile above mouth of No-Name Creek. The packs are seen about one mile up Reno Creek. A single rider—Boston Custer—is seen coming toward them. Benteen arrives at Reno Creek.

- This is an additional 4.2 miles of marching. This is approximately 5.4 miles east of Ford A.

- Benteen sights pack train, ¾ miles above, along Reno Creek.
- Boston Custer meets Benteen.
- At this point, LT Mathey estimated that the pack train was spread out two to three miles from front to rear and fairly well scattered.

1:50 PM—*Pack Train*—**6.25 miles from the divide; 4.01 MPH**—The head of the pack train reaches a point about one mile above No-Name Creek.

1:51 PM—**1,150 yards, including the river; 5 MPH**—Iron Cedar, having swum the river, reaches the Hunkpapa village and seeks out Gall.

1:51 PM—*Benteen Battalion*—**12 MPH**—Now at a full gallop, Boston Custer passes Benteen's battalion, waving as he goes by.

1:53 PM—*Custer-Keogh-Yates Battalions*—**¾ of a mile (1,350 yards); 7–8 MPH**—Boyer and the three Crow—Goes Ahead, Hairy Moccasin, and White Man Runs Him—arrive at Weir Peaks.

1:53 PM—*Reno Battalion*—De Rudio sees Custer at 3,411.

- LT De Rudio, leading several troopers into the timber to head off an attack by Indians on the right end of the skirmish line—and Reno, as well—spot Custer, Cooke, and another man (Boyer?) waving their hats from Weir Peak. "*It was on the highest point on the right bank, just below where Dr. DeWolf was killed … he was about 1,000 yards from where I was.*" De Rudio said he could see Custer, Cooke, and one other person, and could identify them because they wore buckskin pants and a blue shirt.

1:54 PM—*Benteen Battalion*—**¼ to ½ of a mile from the turn; 6 MPH**—Benteen's battalion begins arriving at the morass. Benteen arrives at the morass and stops to water horses; this is another one-half mile.

- Godfrey uses the phrase, "*Sometime after getting on the trail we came to a water-hole, or morass, at which a stream of running water had its source.*"
- Boston Custer trots on.
- The morass is thought to be about one mile east of where South Fork runs into Reno Creek.

1:55 PM—As the leading Rees reach the hills above Reno Hill, they are fired on by some troopers lagging behind Custer's rear. The Ree scout, Stab, is among those shot at and he joins others with the stolen ponies.

1:56 PM—*Benteen Battalion*—**725 feet from the head of the column; 7 MPH**—The last of Benteen's battalion arrives at the morass.

1:56 PM—*Custer-Keogh-Yates Battalions*—Custer leaves 3,411.

- White Man Runs Him: Custer "*did not leave that place until Reno had started fighting.*"
- Curley: "*Custer made a brief survey of the situation and turned and rode to his command … just saw Reno going down the valley but did not see him come back.*"

1:56 PM—*Reno Battalion*—½ mile from the village; 6 MPH—Company M flankers who fired the tepees have made their way back into the Reno timber area and seek out other troops and their company.

2 PM—*Custer-Keogh-Yates Battalions*—675 yards from 3,411 (⁴/₁₀ of a mile); 6 MPH—Custer arrives at top of Cedar Coulee; instructs Cooke to send messenger.

2 PM—(6 MPH)—Curley and Black Fox turn to head back down to Reno Creek.

2 PM—*Terry-Gibbon Column*—*Terry sends Brisbin's cavalry up the Big Horn about 1½ miles to "Mission Bottom." They unsaddle and rest.*

- *Author Roger Darling has Brisbin's cavalry reaching the Big Horn River at this time. If correct, the cavalry did not stop to rest at the Eckman Coulee–Greene Coulee bottoms before moving on and crossing a high hill immediately to the south.*

2:01 PM—*Custer-Keogh-Yates Battalions*—Cooke writes note; hands it to Martini. He was instructed to bring it to Benteen and also told to come back to the command if there was no danger, otherwise he was to stay with his company: "*Benteen, Come on. Big village. Be quick. Bring packs. W.W. Cooke. P. S., Bring pacs* [sic]."

2:02 PM—Martini heads back with the note.

- On his ride to deliver the note to Benteen, Martini saw Reno in action "*from the same ridge from which…. Custer saw the village.*"
- Martini: "*…the last I saw Reno's men they were fighting in the valley and the line was falling back.*"
- Martini claimed they could not see the river from their lookout point (the river runs too close to the bluffs in that area and cannot be seen from either 3,411 or Sharpshooters' Ridge; it can, however, be seen from Weir Peak).
- Walter Camp: Martini told him he left the command about half way down the coulee, contrary to what Martini testified at the Reno Court of Inquiry in 1879.
- Authors Stewart, Willert, and Dustin, as well as Weibert: Martini left at the junction of Cedar and Medicine Tail Coulee. This is incorrect.
- Author/historian John Gray: Martini left at the head of the coulee (Cedar) before the command entered it. Kuhlman: Martini left after 300 yards down the ravine. These are, in essence, correct estimates. Gray *categorically* rejects any claim Martini was sent back from Medicine Tail Coulee. He also rejects Martini's claim he witnessed Custer's retreat from Ford B. *We absolutely agree.*
- Martini testified that about the time the command had executed the column-left a little below the ridge and almost to the head of the ravine, he was ordered to Benteen.
- Author Vern Smalley quotes various Martini testimonies and concludes he was in Cedar Coulee, near its head, some 500–600 yards from where Custer's men saw the Indians from the bluffs. This agrees with Gray and Kuhlman. Martini's testimony changed over the years and in 1910 he told Walter Camp he left with the message when he was half way down Medicine Tail Coulee. Smalley believes Martini fabricated this "new" location so he could claim to have seen Custer retreating from the river.

- Martini was ordered to follow the trail back to Benteen. Martini recalled he traveled south about 600 yards and arrived on the same ridge from which he had seen the village with Custer not ten minutes earlier. This is from his RCOI testimony.
- Moved no slower than a trot and ran into hostiles, but managed to escape. His horse was wounded. Apparently, these hostiles were the same ones who fired at the Ree herding the horses.
- Martini saw Reno engaged.
- Custer had not yet reached MTC.
- By this time, Custer's strategy appears fairly clear: gather the fleeing inhabitants of the village and by this method render the warriors helpless. It was evident to Custer the Indians were pulling their usual strategy when attacked: flight under cover of rear-guard action. At this point in the battle, Custer is gleeful, figuring he has them where he wants them.

2:02 PM—250 YARDS; 6 MPH—Curley and Black Fox pass over 3,411.

2:05 PM—At 2½–4 MPH—Custer reaches the head of his column; begins move down Cedar Coulee. He slows because of the terrain.

2:05 PM—An additional 500 yards (.3 miles); 6 MPH—Curley and Black Fox are passing over Reno Hill.

2:05 PM (1:53 PM–2:12 PM)—The three Crow continue to watch the fighting in the valley.

2:05+ PM—½ mile down the coulee, five minutes at 6 MPH—Custer reaches bend of Cedar Coulee and halts.

- Boyer, Goes Ahead, Hairy Moccasin, and White Man Runs Him preceded Custer to Weir Peaks. There Boyer saw Reno's advance, but did not see many warriors in the village.
- In 1909 and 1913 interviews, Curley claimed the other three Crow went beyond Weir to bluffs farther downstream before leaving.
- Goes Ahead claimed Curley joined the Ree, Black Fox, prior to reaching Weir Peaks.

2:06 PM—675 yards from near the head of Cedar Coulee; Now, 6–7 MPH—Martini reaches 3,411; sees Reno's troops fighting on the skirmish line in the valley. He continues on without pausing.

2:07 PM—1 mile; 3 MPH—Kanipe, at a walk, is seen by the Ree who are still milling around the hilltops with the captured Sioux ponies. He is overtaken and passed by the Ree pony captors and stragglers, Stab, Little Sioux, Soldier, and others.

- Stab apparently told the others they should follow Custer's trail, but when they got near Sharpshooters' Ridge, they saw the Sioux starting to move around them.
- The Ree—according to Little Sioux—were pushing these horses up the bluffs about the time of Reno's retreat. Curley claims he saw this movement, thereby negating any claims that he rode with Boyer to Calhoun Hill.

2:07 PM—*Reno Battalion*—Reno and Hodgson reach the edge of the prairie; Moylan explains the situation and points out the Indians turning Company M's flank. Reno orders a pullback to the "brow" at the edge of the timber.

2:07 PM—*Custer-Keogh-Yates Battalions*—Boyer, seeing Custer's command moving down Cedar Coulee, releases the three Crow scouts and moves off Weir Point, heading for the front of Custer's column in Cedar Coulee.

2:07 PM—*Benteen Battalion*—At 7 MPH—CPT Weir, impatient at the watering delay, moves his Company D forward without Benteen's permission. Godfrey said, "Weir became a little impatient at the delay of watering and started off with his troop, taking the advance, whereas his place in column was second. The rest of the battalion moved out very soon afterward and soon caught up with him."

2:08 PM—At 7–9 MPH to start, catching up with Weir—Benteen's column begins leaving the morass as the pack train begins arriving. Godfrey mentions no time here, just that the packs were arriving.

- Benteen claimed this halt was less than fifteen minutes. Godfrey claimed the delay at the morass was between twenty and thirty minutes. Edgerly testified they were there only eight to ten minutes.
- CPT Weir led out from the morass. Benteen—with his orderly—raced ahead and retook the lead. He would now be a few hundred yards ahead of his battalion.
- Firing was heard in the valley.
- Windolph (H) heard firing before they left the morass. PVT Morris (M) said PVT Moller (H) told him they heard heavy firing as they were watering the horses.
- Godfrey: "*While watering we heard some firing in advance…. After we watered we continued our march very leisurely…. Weir became a little impatient at the delay of watering and started off with his troop, taking the advance, whereas his place in column was second. The rest of the battalion moved out very soon afterward and soon caught up with him.*"
- PVT Windolph: Godfrey's statement is not supported by comments from Windolph, who, after hearing firing in the valley, said, "*We all knew we'd be in a fight before long…. We were trotting briskly now, and there was a good deal of excitement. Horses seem to know when they are heading into trouble the same as men do and some of the mounts were anxious to run away, tired as they were.*"
- Benteen: "*I pushed rapidly on, soon getting out of sight of the advance of the train, until reaching a morass, I halted to water the animals, who had been without water since about eight PM of the day before. This watering did not occasion the loss of fifteen minutes, and when I was moving out, the advance of the train commenced watering from that morass. I went at a slow trot until I came to a burning tepee…. We did not stop.*"
- The order of march was now D, H, K.
- Godfrey: "*We heard occasional shots and I concluded the fight was over—that*

[we] had nothing to do but go up and congratulate the others and help destroy the plunder."

- Some of Mathey's pack mules, dying of thirst, smell the morass and make a break for the water. A number of them got stuck and it took CPT McDougall's men about thirty minutes to free them while Mathey had continued on with the rest.

2:08 PM—*Reno Battalion*—thirty-three minutes from dismount—Skirmish line begins pulling back.

- This area of timber had once been the bottom of the river. It was within a thousand feet of the village, most of the timber young and was filled in with a thick growth of underbrush. It was lower than the ground on which the lodges stood and was behind a dry loop of the river, several feet below the prairie. It afforded the troops some measure of protection. The timber was on a rise some thirty feet above the river bottom.
- Company G moved first after Moylan reported to Reno that Indians were infiltrating the timber alongside the river.
- Indians in the timber were threatening the right flank and the horses.
- Company A moved towards the right to cover the gap left by G, further lengthening intervals between men and weakening the line.
- Only one or two casualties at this time.
- Gerard and Reynolds enter the woods, behind the troopers.
- Varnum: "*I met Charlie Reynolds and Fred Gerard … and asked how things were going. They said things looked mighty bad. Fred Gerard had a half-pint flask of whiskey and said, 'Let's take a drink. It may be our last.' … Before I could do so, men were falling back into the timber and calling out, 'They are going to charge.'*"
- As the skirmish line pulled back, maintaining its rate of fire the Indians maintained their distance of hundreds of yards away.
- Some of the Company M troops turned and started for the woods, but CPT French stopped them and told them to fall back slowly, facing the Indians.

2:09 PM—Varnum reaches end of timber; sees the line is moving back and is in the process of establishing a skirmish line on the "brow."

- Sometime in here, Varnum says, "*When I had been on the line ten or fifteen minutes I heard someone say that 'G' Company was going to charge a portion of the village down through the woods, or something to that effect.… I rode down into the timber to go with the company that was going to charge the village.*"
- Varnum describes the timber he went into: in the timber there was an opening—a glade—from where you could see the stream, probably the downstream side of it. He assumed a detached part of the village was on the other side of the river and that was what they were going to attack. Reno was there with G—or a part of it—and Reno asked Varnum to return to the line and then report how it was faring. "*In the timber there is a little glade or opening, and I know in riding in on to this opening I could see the stream in one direction, so we must have been near the stream, and I could see the line of the*

opening in front, and supposed there was a detached portion of the village on the other side of the stream, and that is where they were going."

- Varnum, on his way out of the timber, met Hodgson and they spent a moment or two discussing Hodgson's possibly wounded horse. Hodgson went back to report to Reno, and when Varnum got to the edge of the timber he saw that the entire command had pulled back from the skirmish line to the cut bank at the edge of the timber.
- Varnum now saw Moylan at the far end and Moylan yelled out that the horses were at his end and the Indians were trying to swing around his left. This indicates A was on the left, G on the right, and M in the middle.
- Company A was now desperately short of ammo. Varnum brought the company's horses forward so the men could reach their saddlebags.
- It was after this that Varnum moved to the right side of the line in the timber and met up with Charlie Reynolds and Fred Gerard.
- The woods in front and around the soldiers were heavily timbered with dense underbrush. Behind them, the woods opened into a glade or grassy place. The horses were held in this "park-like" area. All this time, the Indians are infiltrating Reno's positions.

2:09 PM—3½ miles from passing Benteen; 12 MPH—Boston Custer passes the lone tepee.

2:10 PM—*Pack Train*—1¼ miles additional; 3.8 MPH—Lead mules of the packs begin reaching the morass. Mathey orders the men to push on without stopping.

2:10 PM—*Scouts*—By now, Ree scouts have captured a number of Sioux ponies—twenty-eight—and have herded them across the Little Big Horn and up a small coulee coming off the bluffs. As they were doing so, they ran into the tail-end of Custer's command and were fired upon by some trailing soldiers who mistook them for Sioux. The scouts now include Rees, Red Star, Strikes Two, Little Sioux, Boy Chief, One Feather, Bull-Stands-In-Water, and the Dakota, Whole Buffalo. Stab has already joined them, and they are soon joined by several others who did not cross the river with Reno, including Rees, Soldier, Bull, White Eagle, Strikes The Lodge, and Billy Cross; and Dakotas, White Cloud, Caroo, and Ma-tok-sha.

2:10 PM—*Warriors*—Gall and Iron Cedar head off to swim the river and climb the bluffs to watch for the soldiers on the east bank.

2:10 PM—*Custer-Keogh-Yates Battalions*—6 MPH down to 5 MPH—Martini, in the vicinity of Reno Hill, sees the Company C stragglers. He does not stop but begins to slow. His horse has been wounded, but he is unaware of it.

2:11 PM—*Reno Battalion*—250–300 yards; some running, 5–6 MPH—Last of Company A's men reach the "brow," forming a skirmish line with Company G.

2:11 PM—(⁸⁄₁₀ of a mile); 12 MPH—Company M, now fully mounted and harassed on its flank, makes a break for the timber line, supported by A and G's covering fire.

2:11 PM—*Warriors*—Crazy Horse, followed by a considerable number of his warriors, begins arriving as Company M breaks for the timber.

2:11 PM—*Custer-Keogh-Yates Battalions*—**.52 miles at 5 MPH**—Finding the going down Cedar Coulee too difficult and apparently veering away from the direction he wishes to go, Custer sees a cut in the left bank slope and moves out of the coulee moving more in the direction of the river.

2:12 PM—*Scouts*—**4 MPH-6 MPH, stopping along the way**—The three Crow scouts—Goes Ahead, White Man Runs Him, and Hairy Moccasin—begin heading north along the bluff line.

2:12 PM—*Pack Train*—**7.5 miles from the divide; 3.95 MPH**—McDougall arrives at the morass as the pack mules continue to be driven on. Five or six of the mules are stuck, however, and McDougall orders his men to extricate them.

2:15 PM—*Reno Battalion*—**⁸/₁₀ of a mile; 12 MPH**—Last of Company M arrives at the "brow" of the timber.

2:15 PM—**1 mile ± from lone tepee; 12 MPH**—Boston Custer reaches Middle Knoll; turns to the right on Custer's shod trail.

2:16 PM—**335 yards; 12 MPH**—Boston Custer reaches North Fork; pauses only briefly to let his horse gulp some water.

2:16 PM—*Reno Battalion*—Varnum tells the Company A horseholders to mount up and follow him.

2:17 PM–2:20 PM—At sometime within these three minutes, Bloody Knife is killed in the glade, his brains and blood splattering all over Reno. The troops, in the process of dismounting were immediately told by Reno to re-mount.

2:19 PM—**Martini: ¾ mile; Boston Custer: ½ mile; Martini: 5 MPH; Boston Custer: 13 MPH**—Boston Custer meets Martini. They pause for only seconds, Boston pointing the way to Martini and Martini telling Boston George Custer's whereabouts. Boston points out Martini's wounded horse.

- Martini meets one or two Company C troopers, probably Brennan and Fitzgerald.

2:19 PM—*Reno Battalion*—Varnum reaches Moylan.

2:19 PM—*Custer-Keogh-Yates Battalions*—**.48 miles at 3½ MPH**—After going cross-country Custer runs into Middle Coulee and finding it easier going takes it north.

2:20 PM–2:30 PM—*Scouts*—**To the ravine: 250 yards from high point 3.375; Reno Hill: 900–1,250 yards**—After hiding some of the Sioux ponies in a ravine to the east of the ridgeline, several Rees head toward Reno Hill. This is where they will see the soldiers in full flight, many scaling the bluffs to reach the hilltop.

2:21 PM—*Reno Battalion*—Varnum spends a minute or two with Gerard and Reynolds. They have a quick drink.

2:23 PM—forty-eight minutes after dismounting—Reno begins retreat.

2:23 PM—*Warriors*—**⅔ of a mile (1,150 yards); 3 MPH, including swimming the Little Big Horn River and climbing the bluffs**—Gall and Iron Cedar reach the top of the bluffs. Iron Cedar points toward the troops near the mouth of Cedar Coulee.

2:24 PM—**1 mile from Martini meeting; 13 MPH**—Boston Custer is now passing over Reno Hill.

- Reno's fight was visible to him for the next five minutes, so he could have at least reported this much to his brothers.

2:25 PM—*Custer-Keogh-Yates Battalions*—**1½ miles; 3+–5 MPH average, increasing to 8, then 10 MPH**—After tough going down Cedar Coulee, then up its slopes, cross-country, and into and down Middle Coulee, Custer reaches Medicine Tail Coulee and heads toward the Little Big Horn River and the village.

2:26 PM—*Warriors*—Gall and Iron Cedar watch as Custer turns into Medicine Tail Coulee.

2:26 PM—**⁴⁄₁₀ of a mile from mid-point of Reno Hill; 13 MPH**—Boston Custer is passing over 3,411; he looks into the valley briefly and sees Reno's command galloping from the timber, Indians in pursuit.

2:27 PM—*Pack Train*—**6 to 8 MPH**—McDougall's troops get the last of the stuck mules out of the morass and push them on.

2:28 PM—**1 to 1⅓ miles from the morass; 3.5 MPH**—Lead elements of the pack train begin reaching the opening to the "flats."

2:28 PM—*Scouts*—**2.1 miles from leaving the column; 5 MPH**—Curley and Black Fox reach Reno Creek. They stop and water their horses.

2:29 PM—*Warriors*—Gall and Iron Cedar turn to head back to the village.

2:30 PM—PVT Watson of Company C is picked up by the packs; he is told to ride with McDougall's Company B when it catches up.

2:30 PM—*Scouts*—**900–1,250 yards from sequestered horses**—Boy Chief and several other Rees—Little Sioux, Soldier, Stabbed, Strikes The Lodge, and Strikes Two—arrive at Reno Hill where they see Reno's men in full flight, many of the troopers scaling the bluffs, some beginning to reach the hilltop.

2:30 PM ±—*Terry-Gibbon Column*—*Brisbin's cavalry reaches Mission Bottom. They unsaddle and make camp. At this point they are still twenty-one miles from the Little Big Horn River.*

2:32 PM—*Custer-Keogh-Yates Battalions*—**⁹⁄₁₀ mile (2+ miles, total, from top of Cedar Coulee); 10 MPH**—Riding hard down Medicine Tail Coulee, Custer begins to move up the slopes to Luce Ridge.

2:32 PM—*Scouts*—**1⅓ miles from Weir Peaks; 4 MPH average, stopping and starting**—The three Crow—Goes Ahead, Hairy Moccasin, and White Man Runs Him—reach the far end of the bluffs overlooking Ford B.

2:32 PM–3:10 PM—**Halted on the bluffs**—The three Crow watch as Custer's command mounts the ridges to the north and east, then the Crow fire into the Indian village, their shots falling in the Sans Arc and Minneconjou camps.

2:35 PM—**1¾ miles from Reno Hill; 10 MPH, average**—Boston Custer turns into Medicine Tail Coulee. He increases his speed.

2:35 PM—*Benteen Battalion*—**3.4 miles from the morass; 7½ MPH**—Benteen reaches the lone tepee. Slows down a bit and rides around the burning structure. He stops momentarily and peers in, then continues on, increasing his speed.

- Benteen: "*I went at a slow trot [after he watered at the morass] until I came to a burning lodge with a dead body of an Indian in it on a scaffold. We did not halt.*" "*I... went on, I suppose about seven miles, when I came to a burning tepee. I rode around it, I am not sure whether I dismounted or not. I know it contained the dead body of a warrior. A mile or so from that tepee I met a sergeant coming back with instructions to the commanding officer of the pack train to 'hurry up the packs.'*"

2:36 PM–2:46 PM—*Reno Battalion*—De Rudio—still in the timber—watches as masses of Indians follow Reno's command to the crossing, fighting all along the way.

2:38 PM—**Variously, 1.14–1.38 miles; varying speeds, from 13+ MPH down to a crawl**—The first of Reno's troops begin reaching the hilltop.

- W. A. Graham: "A force large enough to prevent Reno from assuming the offensive was left and the surplus available force flew to the other end of the camp, where, finding the Indians there successfully driving Custer before them, instead of uniting with them, they separated into two parties and moved around the flanks of his cavalry."

2:38 PM—*Scouts*—**6 MPH**—Billy Cross, Bull, Red Bear, Soldier, Stab, Strikes Two, White Eagle, Red Star, Red Wolf, and Strikes The Lodge start back to the ravine where the stolen ponies are hidden with the intention of driving them back along Reno Creek.

2:39 PM—**2.6 miles; 3 MPH**—SGT Kanipe reaches Benteen.

2:39 PM—*Benteen Battalion*—**(½ mile west of the lone tepee); Benteen: 5 MPH, up to 8 MPH**—Kanipe reins up next to Benteen, but again, Benteen does not halt and directs Kanipe to the rear in the direction of the pack train.

- According to Kanipe, the packs would now be about two miles east of Benteen's command. This would put them some 3.2 miles east of the river. Not a bad guess by Kanipe.
- Some of Benteen's men heard Kanipe yell, "We've got them, boys," as he rode for the pack train.
- Godfrey: "*The sergeant was sent back to the train with [his] message; as he passed the column he said to the men, 'We've got 'em, boys.' From this and other remarks we inferred that Custer had attacked and captured the village.*"
- LT Godfrey: "*...recalled that it was shortly after they passed the old camp (Lone Teepee site) that they again stopped to water their horses.*"
- LT Godfrey: the gunfire from beyond the hills and ridges... "*became more distinct*" and the column "*increased gait.*" From the sound of the firing—sporadic, sometimes sharp, but no longer heavy and furious—the engagement rendered impression of ending rather than of beginning or continuing. LT Godfrey: "*I thought all was over and that it could only have been a small village to be over so soon.*"

- Kanipe remembered he was not in sight of the pack train when he met Benteen.
- Benteen told Kanipe he made a mistake delivering Custer's orders to him and that he should head for the packs and CPT McDougall.
- Kanipe rode down the column shouting, *"We've got 'em boys!"* and *"the Indians [are] on the run!"*
- Godfrey also heard Kanipe shouting these words.
- The command justly *"inferred Custer had attacked and captured the village."*

2:39 PM—*Warriors*—⅔ of a mile (1,150 yards); 4 MPH including swimming the **Little Big Horn River**—Gall and Iron Cedar have returned to the village and Gall seeks to rally any warriors he can find to head downstream and confront the new threat.

2:39 PM—*Custer-Keogh-Yates Battalions*—½ mile; 6 MPH—Custer reaches the top of Luce Ridge.

2:39 PM–2:54 PM—*Warriors*—Various; (8 MPH)—Gall rallies some warriors and begins to move toward Ford B. They are all mounted.

2:40 PM—*Benteen Battalion*—6 MPH, moving up to 7 and then 8 MPH—Hearing occasional firing only, LT Godfrey concluded the fight was over and they would have little to do but congratulate the others and help destroy the plunder. As the firing became more distinct, however, the command began to increase its speed.

2:41 PM—2.7 miles from just below the head of Cedar Coulee; down to a 4.2 MPH, average—Martini reaches Benteen in the "flats," less than one mile from the Little Big Horn.

2:41 PM—.83 miles west of the lone tepee (⅓ mile from meeting Kanipe); 8 MPH—Benteen halts momentarily to read the message from Cooke. He shows it to Tom Weir and Win Edgerly who have caught up. Benteen now continues toward the river.

2:42 PM—*Warriors*—6 to 8 MPH—Other Indians—primarily Cheyenne like American Horse and Brave Wolf—leave the valley fight and head back to their village.

2:42 PM—*Custer-Keogh-Yates Battalions*—1.4 miles; 12 MPH—Boston Custer reaches the top of Luce Ridge. He informs his brothers of all he has seen, including that Benteen is on the main trail.

2:42 PM—2:49 PM—Custer, Keogh, and Yates assess Boston Custer's information about Benteen. Custer decides he has between 1½–1¾ hours before Benteen arrives, so he needs to hurry his reconnaissance and position himself where he can meet Benteen.

2:44 PM—*Scouts*—1,100–1,300 yards from Reno Hill area—Several Ree scouts arrive back at the ravine where the stolen horses are sequestered. They begin culling out about fifteen.

2:45 PM—*Pack Train*—2+ miles from the morass; 3.5 MPH—Mathey continues to drive the pack train and is now less than 1½ miles east of the lone/burning tepee, fairly well confirming Kanipe's observation, above.

- According to Walter Mason Camp, it took Kanipe another twenty minutes after leaving Benteen to report to McDougall.
- Kanipe claimed to have seen the head of the pack train about two miles from where he had met Benteen as Benteen's battalion approached the lone tepee.
- Like Benteen said, Kanipe's orders specified reporting to McDougall.
- Both McDougall and Mathey said no one reported to them with a message from Custer. Mathey claimed he only met one person and that was a half-breed.
- Bruce Liddic considers McDougall's and Mathey's claim to be a lie, sworn to at the Reno Court of Inquiry. He also quotes a testimonial McDougall wrote for Kanipe when the latter was seeking a job with the U.S. Revenue Service (McDougall was living in Wellsville, NY; January 9, 1897): "*On the afternoon of June 25th, 1876 when the entire country was full of Indians, Sg't Knipe brought to me an order from General Custer 'to bring the pack train across the way' where I found Major Reno…. I take great pleasure in giving him this small certificate of merit.*" There is no substance to Liddic's accusation.
- There are, however, authors who agree with McDougall and Mathey and claim Kanipe, worried about meeting hostiles while riding between the two commands, simply lagged Benteen's battalion and never did deliver the message to McDougall. Kanipe: "*McDougall and his outfit rode on to the top of the hill and reinforced Major Reno as he retired from the bottom of the bluffs. The Indians were following close at their heels, shooting and yelling, and the men were dropping here and there. They, the Indians, would hop on them and scalp them before we could rescue them.*"
- Kanipe claimed that after he delivered the message to McDougall, he went on to Benteen to tell him as well. Yet he had already passed Benteen and told him.
- At the Reno Inquiry, the two civilian packers, Churchill and Frett, testified that a sergeant rode up to them and told them the column needed to hurry, that Custer was attacking. Two packers, however, do not equal McDougall and Mathey … who would have no reason to lie.

2:45 PM—under 2 miles from the morass; 6 to 8 MPH—McDougall with the recalcitrant mules catches up to the rear of the main body of the train, which is continuing to string out further.

2:46 PM—*Reno Battalion*—De Rudio watches as Indians continuing harassing Reno's command at the crossing. Some of the warriors stop and begin pointing upriver. De Rudio looks and sees troops approaching the ford where Reno crossed. He assumes it is Benteen. As the troops get closer to the ford they turn and disappear over a bluff.

2:48 PM—*Benteen Battalion*—1,525 yards from meeting Martini; 7 MPH—Benteen reaches the Little Big Horn River and has now seen friendly Indians on the bluffs just north of Reno Creek. These scouts direct him toward Reno Hill. It appears they were the young Crow, Curley, and the Ree, Black Fox, and may also have been joined by a couple more Rees with stolen ponies.

2:49 PM—*Custer-Keogh-Yates Battalions*—**At 6 MPH moving to 8 MPH**—After viewing the Little Big Horn valley and the hills to the north, Custer drops off Keogh with instructions to deploy his battalion and protect Custer's rear, then heads toward the river along the ridgeline with HQ and Yates' battalion.

2:49 PM—*Scouts*—(**At 3–5 MPH**)—Several Rees take about fifteen horses from the ravine and head down the hills toward Reno Creek. In all likelihood these are, Billy Cross, Bull, Red Bear, Soldier, Stab, Strikes Two, White Eagle, Red Star, Red Wolf, and Strikes The Lodge. They run into both Benteen's command and the pack train. After the packs turned toward the hills, trailing Sioux retrieved their horses and the Rees returned to the hilltop.

2:50 PM—*Reno Battalion*—**Variously, 1.14–1.38 miles**—SGT Culbertson reaches the hilltop.

2:50 PM—*Custer-Yates*—**8 MPH**—LT Algernon Smith and Company E break off from the Yates battalion and head into Medicine Tail Coulee.

2:50 PM—*Warriors*—Crazy Horse, now alerted to more troops mounting the bluffs and hearing that there are additional troops farther downstream, begins to gather his warriors to head off Custer's command.

2:52 PM—The Oglala warrior, Shave Elk, and several others begin to move up MTC. They see Smith's command and immediately turn around to head back to Ford B.

2:52 PM—*Benteen Battalion*—As Benteen's command begins to mount the bluffs and follow their commander, they are passed by several Indian scouts—not sure if they were Crow or Ree—driving some Sioux ponies, and the scouts yelled, "Soldiers," pointing to the hilltop to the right.

2:53 PM—*Warriors*—**1½ miles; 8–10 MPH**—Cheyenne warriors American Horse and Brave Wolf, having left the Reno fighting, reach the Ford B area of the Cheyenne village.

2:55 PM—(**8 MPH**)—Crazy Horse, with a number of his warriors, turns and heads toward the village.

2:55 PM—*Custer-Yates*—**⁶⁄₁₀ mile; 8 MPH**—Custer and Yates arrive at the bluff overlooking Ford B.

2:55 PM—As Yates' Company F pulls up, PVT William Brown's horse bolts and runs down the bluff, across the flats and into the river. Brown is dragged off by Indians and killed. (There is the possibility Brown may have been one of the Company F outriders.)

2:57 PM—*Benteen Battalion*—**6.3 miles from the morass; 8 MPH from meeting the scouts; 7.7 MPH, from the morass**—eighty-two minutes from the time Reno dismounted/112 minutes from the Custer-Reno separation—Benteen arrives on Reno Hill.

2:58 PM—*Custer-Yates*—**1 mile; 8 MPH**—LT Algernon Smith arrives at Ford B and proceeds to the river's edge, deploying his troops and dismounting some of his men. He sets up a screening force covering the troops on the ridge above him. There is also some evidence from Indian interviews that a soldier wearing buckskin was wounded at this time. That could have been Smith.

3 PM—*Reno Battalion*—After the command left the timber, LT De Rudio linked up with Gerard, PVT O'Neill, and Billy Jackson—he had run into them a few moments earlier—all of them fearing the progress of the fire. He then said the wind died down and a few drops of rain fell, impeding the fire's progress.

3 PM—*Benteen Battalion*—Benteen's troops begin arriving on Reno Hill.

3 PM—*Terry-Gibbon Column*—*Terry's infantry and battery arrive at Big Horn River.*

3:02 PM—*Warriors*—Indians still in full force in valley. Estimates ranged from 600 to 1,000 or more.

3:02 PM—*Benteen Battalion*—Weir tells Benteen and Reno they should move forward to find Custer. Reno refuses permission. LT Gibson, PVT Fox (D), and TMP Martini (H) overhear Reno's refusal.

3:05 PM—Last of Benteen's command reaches Reno Hill. Benteen directs his companies to form a dismounted skirmish line along the bluffs. Godfrey estimates 600 to 700 Indians in the valley with more arriving. In addition, he spots quite a number in the ravines on the east side of the river. He also sees dust from the packs and estimates they are some three to four miles away. In reality, the packs are within one-half mile of the lone tepee. Edgerly estimated 800–1,000. Benteen used a figure of 900.

3:05 PM—*Custer-Yates*—6 MPH—His rear protected by Smith's Gray Horse Troop at the ford, Custer moves across Custer's Bluff/Butler Ridge and into Deep Coulee, then the flats beyond, heading for the northern ridgeline and hilltop later named Finley-Finckle Ridge and Calhoun Hill.

3:06 PM—8 MPH—Trailed by sharp, sniping fire, Smith—his company fully remounted—begins moving away from Ford B. He heads for the Finley-Finckle Ridge area and Calhoun Hill. Yates protects his rear.

3:07 PM—*Keogh Battalion*—Keogh spots Indians coming down North MTC—in all likelihood Wolf Tooth and Big Foot—plus Indians along West Coulee's ridges, and orders his troops to open fire.

3:07 PM—*Custer-Yates*—Between 150 and 500 yards from Ford B; increasing to 8 MPH—As Custer enters Deep Coulee, TMP Dose is killed.

3:07 PM—*Reno-Benteen*—On Reno Hill, heavy or volley firing is heard from downstream. Loud firing continues for several minutes.

3:07 PM—Herendeen, still in Reno's timber, hears heavy firing from downstream. It lasted about an hour.

3:07 PM—*Warriors*—1½ miles—to this point—from the Reno retreat crossing; 8 MPH—Crazy Horse and his warriors—cantering back toward the village—hear the volley firing as they near the Hunkpapa circle of Sitting Bull.

3:09 PM—*Pack Train*—1.4 miles from last report; 3.4 miles from morass; 3.5 MPH down to 2 to 3 MPH—Lead mules of the pack train begin arriving in the vicinity of the lone tepee and Gerard's Knoll. Mathey slows down so the train can close up.

McDougall rides up to meet him. The tepee was smoldering and McDougall stops to peer inside where he sees three dead Indians.

- When Mathey reached the lone tepee, he halted the pack train to allow McDougall to try to catch up after corralling the mired mules and closing up the column.
- McDougall estimated "*it was about four miles from the morass to the tepee.*"
- Another point to be factored in: it was Kanipe who claimed—many years after the battle—that Tom Custer told him to tell McDougall to bring "*the pack train straight across the country.*"
- Mathey spots a good deal of smoke up ahead.
- A half-breed scout (possibly William Cross who was originally with Custer's column) passes Mathey and tells him there are too many Indians up ahead for Custer to handle.

3:09 PM—*Warriors*—**1½ miles; 6 MPH**—Gall arrives in the vicinity of Ford B; sees Smith's command (E Company) pulling back toward Finley-Finckle Ridge.

3:09 PM—*Keogh Battalion*—Keogh, seeing Custer and Smith pulling out, orders his troops to head for Nye-Cartwright Ridge. His troops continue to fire at the harassing Wolf Tooth band.

3:10 PM—*Warriors*—**8 MPH down to 6 MPH**—Crazy Horse and some followers pick their way through the Hunkpapa circle—still in great turmoil—and head toward their own camp.

3:10 PM—*Reno-Benteen*—As Benteen orders his men to consolidate the hilltop and set up a skirmish line, LT Edgerly sees they are still coming under some fire from Indians hidden on the hilltops and behind rocks and bushes. He also sees a number of Reno's wounded. Benteen orders the Indians to be driven away.

3:10 PM—*Scouts*—**6 MPH**—Goes Ahead, Hairy Moccasin, and White Man Runs Him leave the bluffs above Ford B and head back along the way they came. They now begin to move faster.

3:12 PM—*Custer-Yates*—**Dismount; 6–8 MPH for the horsemen**—Some of Smith's troops begin to dismount on the Deep Coulee flats to provide stable covering fire for the withdrawing horsemen.

3:12 PM—*Keogh Battalion*—**¼ mile; 8 MPH**—Keogh arrives on Nye-Cartwright Ridge where he continues to fire on marauding warriors.

3:12 PM–3:17 PM—Keogh, on Nye-Cartwright, sets up a mounted skirmish line and continues to fire at encroaching Indians.

3:12 PM—*Reno-Benteen*—A number of troops from Benteen's battalion head for the marauding Indians atop the hills to drive them away.

3:12 PM—*Scouts*—Black Fox—identifiable by a white bandana tied around his head—leaves Curley and joins fellow Rees driving stolen Sioux ponies.

3:13 PM–3:15 PM—*Warriors*—Some Indians—initially three Cheyenne and four Sioux warriors—cross the Little Big Horn and continue to harass Smith's men; this is the beginning of the Indian movement across Medicine Tail Ford. Wolf Tooth and Big Foot continue to engage Keogh's troops, albeit from a distance.

3:14 PM—*Pack Train*—**3 to 4 MPH**—Mathey starts the train moving again.

3:14 PM–3:17 PM—*Custer-Yates*—**8 MPH**—Custer and Yates, with Smith's Company E following to cover the move, begin arriving on Calhoun Hill to re-unite with Keogh.

Starting at 3:15 PM and continuing—*Warriors*—**650 yards to 1 mile; 10–12 MPH**—More Indians arrive at Medicine Tail Ford and begin crossing. Some on horseback ride up Deep Coulee for as far as one mile; others dismount and begin making their way on foot toward the Calhoun Coulee area.

3:15 PM—*Reno-Benteen*—CPT Weir discusses the situation and the firing heard downstream with his lieutenant, Win Edgerly. Edgerly assures him he would follow if Weir were to head north.

3:16 PM–(3:31 PM)—*Warriors*—**1 mile from where he heard the volley firing; 6 MPH**—Crazy Horse reaches his camp circle and pauses to prepare for more fighting.

3:17 PM—*Reno-Benteen*—Edgerly discusses the situation with the Company D first sergeant, 1SG Michael Martin. They agree that the command should go toward the sound of the firing.

3:17 PM—*Warriors*—More Indians begin leaving the valley and heading downstream.

3:17 PM—*Reno-Benteen*—CPT Weir decides to discuss the situation with MAJ Reno.

3:17 PM–3:25 PM—*Custer-Yates*—**1 to 1.1 miles from Ford B; 6 to 8 MPH**—Smith begins arriving on Calhoun Hill.

3:18 PM—*Warriors*—**.38 of a mile (670 yards) to 1 mile; 12 MPH (mounted); 5–6 MPH on foot**—Lead Indians on horseback—crossing at Ford B—dismount in Deep Coulee and begin infiltrating up the cut-bank, into the flats, and across toward Calhoun Coulee. Others continue to ride up the coulee toward Henryville.

3:18 PM—*Pack Train*—**¼ of a mile west of the burning tepee**—McDougall and Mathey watch as eight to ten Ree drive about fifteen captured Sioux ponies past them. One of them—possibly the half-breed, Billy Cross—tells Mathey there are too many Sioux to fight.

3:18 PM—*Scouts*—**2 miles from picking up the horses in the ravine; 5 MPH**—Eight to ten Ree drive about fifteen stolen Sioux ponies along Reno Creek and meet the pack train west of the lone tepee. One of them was the half-breed, Billy Cross. It appears some of the others were the Ree stragglers, Bull, Red Bear, Soldier, Stab, Strikes Two, and White Eagle, along with Red Star, Red Wolf, and Strikes The Lodge. After the packs turned toward the hills, trailing Sioux retrieved their horses and the Ree returned to the hilltop. These are the same scouts who passed Benteen on his way to Reno Hill.

3:18 PM—*Black Fox*—seen with a white handkerchief tied around his head—leaves the Rees and joins the pack train.

3:18 PM—*Reno-Benteen*—10 MPH—LT Hare is sent to get ammo mules from the pack train. LT Godfrey lends Hare his horse.

3:19 PM and continuing…—*Warriors*—¾ mile (1,350 yards); 5–6 MPH—Indians, mostly on foot and out of range of the cavalry carbines, make their way toward Greasy Grass Ridge and Calhoun Coulee.

3:20 PM—10 MPH—Wolf Tooth sees Keogh's movements and begins mounting and crossing the ridges, heading toward Calhoun Hill.

3:20 PM—*Reno-Benteen*—Benteen's troops who had chased the Indians from the hilltop return and stand-to-horse.

3:22 PM—*Keogh Battalion*—.86 of a mile (1,500 yards) from Nye-Cartwright; 8 MPH—Keogh arrives on Calhoun Hill.

3:23 PM–3:26 PM—*Custer-Keogh-Yates Battalions*—Custer, Keogh, Yates, and Cooke discuss their dispositions and the situation they see in the valley. Custer asks Boyer if there is a ford farther downstream, a ford beyond where they see the refugees gathering. Boyer assures him he will be able to find one farther north.

3:23 PM—*Scouts*—1⅓ miles from bluffs above Ford B; 6 MPH—The three Crow reach a point near Weir Peaks and instead of re-mounting the Weir complex, head over toward Cedar Coulee.

3:23 PM—*Pack Train*—Company B, now in advance of the packs, meets a Crow scout—in all likelihood, Curley—who explains in sign-language that "much soldiers down."

3:23 PM–3:27 PM—*Reno-Benteen*—CPT Weir is with MAJ Reno and CPT Benteen. Whether or not Weir seeks permission to move downstream has never been satisfactorily established, but he leaves the meeting and goes to get his striker. Edgerly claimed, "*He told me later that he hadn't spoken to Reno or Benteen, but rode out on the bluff hoping to see something of Custer's command.*" PVT Fox claimed to have heard Weir speaking with Reno just before Weir moved out from Reno Hill. "*Weir remarked, 'Custer must be around here somewhere and we ought to go to him.' Reno said 'We are surrounded by Indians and we ought to remain here.' Weir said, 'Well if no one else goes to Custer, I will go.' Reno replied, 'No you cannot go. For if you try to do it you will get killed and your Company with you.'*" Fox also claimed Moylan and Benteen overheard this conversation "and talked as though to discourage him," but neither man ever supported Fox' contention. [See 3:02 PM.]

3:25 PM–3:43 PM—*Warriors*—3.42 miles from Reno's retreat crossing; 8–10 MPH—Many Indians who left the Reno battlefield are arriving at Ford B. Some continue on toward Ford D. Others—who did not get into the valley fight—are arriving, as well.

3:25 PM—*Custer-Keogh-Yates Battalions*—Varying speeds; some men re-mounted, others—on foot—still firing at encroaching Indians—The last of Smith's Company E troops arrive on Calhoun Hill. These were the men who had dismounted and formed a rear guard for the leading horsemen.

3:27 PM—*Warriors*—1.14 miles (2,000 yards); 10 MPH—Part of Wolf Tooth's band reach upper Deep Coulee and the Henryville area. They sequester their horses in the ravine and begin infiltrating toward Calhoun Hill.

3:27 PM—*Custer-Yates*—10 MPH—Custer takes HQ and the Yates battalion and heads north in search of a crossing point.

3:27 PM—*Keogh Battalion*—Company L men take up skirmish line positions.

3:27 PM—*Reno-Benteen*—As Weir turns and leaves, Reno takes SGT Culbertson and several men and heads down the bluffs to find LT Hodgson's body.

3:27 PM–3:34 PM—Weir turns and leaves, and seeking out his striker, mounts up to head downstream.

3:27 PM–3:44 PM—*Keogh Battalion*—Keogh deploys his battalion, moving his horses into the swale area behind Calhoun Hill.

3:29 PM—*Pack Train*—1 ± mile from area of Gerard's Knoll; 3.5 MPH—Mathey and the lead mules are in the Middle Knoll area when LT Hare approaches. Mathey halts the train.

3:29 PM—*Warriors*—¾ mile (1,350 yards) up Deep Coulee; 5–6 MPH—Lead Indians on foot from Deep Coulee, begin reaching Calhoun Coulee, still out of effective range of the cavalry carbines atop Calhoun Hill and Battle Ridge. They begin their slower infiltration toward Calhoun Hill-Battle Ridge. Others continue up Deep Coulee into what is now called "Henryville."

3:30 PM—*Pack Train*—2 miles from Reno Hill; 10 MPH—LT Hare reaches the packs and Mathey cuts out two ammo mules.

3:31 PM—*Warriors*—At 8-10 MPH—Crazy Horse and a large band of warriors leave the Oglala camp heading for the Ford B area.

3:31 PM—*Pack Train*—Mathey—listening to Hare—orders two ammo mules cut out of the train to follow Hare.

3:32 PM—(10 MPH)—Hare begins the trip back to Reno Hill.

3:32 PM—(7 MPH)—The ammo mules follow right behind Hare, but at a slower pace.

3:32 PM—3.5 to 4 MPH—Mathey starts the pack train forward, following Hare's lead up the bluffs.

3:32 PM—8 MPH—Pistols drawn, CPT McDougall places one platoon of Company B behind the pack train, and one platoon ahead, and moves forward toward the men on the hilltop.

3:33 PM—*Warriors*—1.2 miles from Ford B crossing; 3 MPH—Gall, with more warriors, reaches the Henryville area.

3:34 PM–3:37 PM—570 yards into Calhoun Coulee (now, 1.1 miles from Ford B); 2½ to 4½ MPH—Lead Indians, infiltrating on foot, begin reaching a point within 100 yards of Battle Ridge/Calhoun Hill. Their arching arrows begin to threaten the troops and held horses in the swale and along the ridge.

3:35 PM—*Reno-Benteen*—6 MPH—CPT Tom Weir takes his orderly and starts downstream.

3:37 PM—*Custer-Yates*—**Forward and backtracking, 1–1½ miles; variously, 10–12 MPH**—The Company F scouts, backtracking, meet Custer and Yates. The scouts inform Custer that there appears to be a crossable ford ahead, and that they can see the full extent of the Indians gathering in Squaw-Chasing Creek. A brief, but sharp exchange occurs with Indians in front on the troops, probably some warriors from the Wolf Tooth/Big Foot band.

3:37 PM—*Warriors*—**Various speeds**—More and more Indians involved in the valley fighting begin to leave, heading downstream to the sound of the volley firing.

3:38 PM—*Scouts*—**1½ miles after turning from Weir Peaks; 6 MPH**—The three Crow arrive amidst the confusion on Reno Hill.

3:38 PM—*Warriors*—**1 mile from the Oglala village circle; 8–10 MPH**—Crazy Horse and his band reach Ford B. They stop momentarily to see what they can from the edge of the ford.

3:40 PM—**At 12 MPH**—Deciding not to cross at the Medicine Tail ford, Crazy Horse spurs his horse on and heads downriver for Deep Ravine ford.

3:40 PM—*Reno-Benteen*—6 MPH—Edgerly begins moving Company D downstream.

3:42 PM—*Custer-Yates*—**2.33 miles; 10 MPH**—Custer arrives at Ford D.

3:42 PM—*Keogh Battalion*—Keogh, Calhoun, and Harrington discuss the threat to their horses from arching arrows falling amongst them from Indians moving up Calhoun Coulee. Keogh orders Harrington to ready his company for a charge into the coulee.

3:43 PM—*Reno-Benteen*—10 MPH—Hare is approaching Reno Hill after cutting out a couple of ammo mules. He sees Edgerly and Company D beginning to head downstream.

3:43 PM—*Scouts*—The three Crow scouts meet up with the Ree, Red Bear and White Cloud, on Reno Hill, all of them milling around the pack mules.

3:44 PM—*Keogh Battalion*—**(650 yards [.37 miles]); (12 MPH)**—Keogh sends Company C into Calhoun Coulee to relieve pressure from Indians infiltrating up the coulee. (This was the beginning of the general firing heard by Fred Gerard after the "scattering" shots many described as volleys.)

3:44 PM–3:46 PM—**Up to 650 yards; 12 MPH**—Harrington charges into Calhoun Coulee, scattering Indians all around the coulee. He moves approximately 450–650 yards and orders his troops to dismount and set up a skirmish line.

3:45 PM—*Reno-Benteen*—**2 miles**—Hare reaches Reno Hill. The ammo mules are a couple hundred yards behind him.

3:45 PM—*Warriors*—Most of the Indians are now out of the valley, only about 100–150 remaining on both sides of the river.

3:46 PM—*Custer-Yates*—12 MPH—Custer begins moving away from Ford D.

3:47 PM–3:49 PM—*Keogh Battalion*—**825–850-yard length, north ridge to south ridge**—Harrington deploys his troops, possibly spreading them too thinly for as much as 850 yards. (An alternative scenario would have been his ordering the men into squads to occupy small enclaves.)

3:48 PM—*Warriors*—**1.43 miles (2,500 yards) from Ford B; 12 MPH**—Crazy Horse and his lead warriors reach the Deep Ravine crossing.

3:48 PM—*Reno-Benteen*—2 miles; 5–7 MPH—The two ammo mules reach Reno Hill and one of them is stripped immediately, the boxes broken into and ammo distributed.

3:48 PM—*Pack Train*—2 miles; 8 MPH—CPT McDougall and one platoon of his Company B approach and begin arriving at Reno Hill.

3:48 PM—*Reno-Benteen*—More stragglers from Reno's command reach the hilltop.

3:49 PM—*Warriors*—**(1,200 yards from the crossing to Battle Ridge); 6–7 MPH**—Crazy Horse is across the Deep Ravine crossing and starts up the ravine. He was followed by Crow King and his Hunkpapa warriors.

3:49 PM—*Keogh Battalion*—**At 6 MPH (foot) to 12 MPH (mounted)**—Company C is suddenly attacked and routed by hordes of warriors. Troops begin running for Finley-Finckle Ridge. (It is possible this ridge is where Yellow Nose snatched the company guidon.)

3:49 PM—*Reno-Benteen*—**1¼ miles from Reno Hill; 6 MPH**—CPT Weir reaches Weir Peaks and heads up its slope.

3:50 PM—*Custer-Yates*—½ mile; 7 MPH—Marc Kellogg, probably near the rear of Custer's command, is cut down and killed by trailing Indians.

3:50 PM—*Reno-Benteen*—⁹⁄₁₀ mile; 6 MPH **slowing to 4 MPH**—Edgerly and Company D reach the head of Cedar Coulee and begin descending it.

- Reno returns from searching for Hodgson's body. He sees Company D moving north and orders Hare to tell Weir to try to make contact with Custer. At the same time, Reno orders Varnum to take the shovels from the ammo mules and some men and go down the bluffs to bury Hodgson.
- At this same time, someone mentions to Reno that Custer's trail had been found. Reno went to see for himself.

3:51 PM—CPT Weir reaches the top of the northernmost peak.

3:52 PM—6 MPH—LT Hare leaves for Weir Point to tell CPT Weir to try to contact Custer.

3:52 PM—*Pack Train*—4–6 MPH—Lead elements of the main pack train are less than one mile from Reno Hill.

3:53 PM—*Keogh Battalion*—**5 MPH (foot) to 12 MPH (mounted)**—Company C breaks and makes a run—both on foot and on horseback—for Finley-Finckle Ridge.

3:53 PM—*Warriors*—**675 yards from river crossing; 7 MPH**—Crazy Horse reaches the head-cut of Deep Ravine and aims for the huge gap in Battle Ridge.

3:53 PM—*Keogh Battalion*—Keogh, having realized the threat, feverishly seeks to deploy Company I to head off the Indian attack emanating from Deep Ravine.

(3:53 PM–4:25 PM)—It is during this timeframe that the fighting on Calhoun Hill and the Keogh Sector becomes intense with panicked Company C troops fleeing up Finley-Finckle Ridge to Calhoun Hill; emboldened Indians beginning to storm the southern end of Calhoun Hill; and Crazy Horse assaulting Company I through the gap in Battle Ridge and across.

3:54 PM—*Pack Train*—Packs seen several hundred yards off; Reno orders the command to begin moving north and they do so, following Custer's trail.

3:54 PM—*Keogh Battalion*—LT Calhoun, watching the rout of Company C, quickly orders a partial shift of his skirmish line from south to west, ordering his troops to cover the retreating soldiers.

3:54 PM—*Custer-Yates*—**1¼–1½ miles from Ford D; 12 MPH**—Custer reaches Cemetery Ridge.

3:54 PM–3:59 PM—Custer rapidly sets up his dispositions on Cemetery Ridge. He and Yates confer as they see masses of Indians mounting the head-cut of Deep Ravine and heading up to Battle Ridge, effectively splitting the two commands.

3:55 PM—*Warriors*—**3.4 miles to Ford B; 2.3 miles to Ford D; 8 MPH through the camp; 12 MPH thereafter**—The first Indians from the Reno fight are beginning to arrive in the vicinity of Ford D at this time.

3:55 PM—*Keogh Battalion*—LT Harrington, still mounted and trailing about eight of his retreating troopers up Finley-Finckle Ridge, kills a Cheyenne warrior, then a Sioux Indian, before he himself is cut down.

3:55 PM–3:57 PM—**¼ mile (450 yards); 6–12 MPH, on foot and horse**—Lead elements of routed Company C reach Finley-Finckle Ridge, pursued mostly by Indians on foot coming up from Calhoun Coulee and the lower end of Deep Coulee.

3:55 PM–3:59 PM—*Warriors*—**525 yards from the Deep Ravine head-cut to Battle Ridge crest; 600 yards from the crest of Battle Ridge to Crazy Horse Ridge; 10 MPH**—Crazy Horse and his warriors—unaware of Custer and Yates to their northwest—crest Battle Ridge through a huge gap that feeds and forms Deep Ravine and charge down through Keogh's men, splitting his command off from Custer and the Yates battalion. They charge through the troops and up to the ridge to the east.

3:55 PM–4:25 PM—*Keogh Battalion*—Fighting in the Keogh Sector begins to rage, ultimately with panicking troops from companies C and L intermingling with Company I men. Indians pressing from the Calhoun Hill area force troops north along Battle Ridge, some soldiers fleeing westward across the ridge.

3:55 PM–4:17 PM—*Pack Train*—**2 miles from meeting Hare; 12.7 miles from divide crossing; 2⅔ to 4 MPH (3.51 MPH from divide crossing)**—Pack train begins arriving on Reno Hill. Benteen's timing would have put the arrival of the first mules at about 4:15 PM.

3:56 PM—*Keogh Battalion*—A number of LT Calhoun's troops, having established a second skirmish line facing toward Finley-Finckle Ridge, attempt to cover the withdrawal of Company C, but are faced with increasing dust and smoke making visibility difficult.

3:57 PM—(670 yards to Calhoun Hill); 6–12 MPH, on foot and mounted—Additional elements of Company C reach Finley-Finckle Ridge as others begin running toward Calhoun Hill. Fighting is hand-to-hand and the troops are overwhelmed.

3:57 PM—*Reno-Benteen*—³/₁₀ additional miles; 3 MPH—LT Edgerly and Company D, using Cedar Coulee, reach the east side of Weir Point.

3:57 PM—Varnum, having secured spades from the packs, starts down the bluffs to bury Hodgson.

3:58 PM—*Warriors*—Indians from the Henryville area and from the ridge east of Calhoun Hill—watching as Company L troops re-deploy and hearing the action of Crazy Horse's charge through Keogh's Company I—begin to charge Calhoun's men from their close-in positions.

3:58 PM—**Various speeds**—Indians from the Reno fight—having been told that soldiers were spotted across Ford D—begin fording the river at "D" to chase after Custer.

3:59 PM—*Custer-Yates*—(½ mile); 8 MPH—Custer sends Yates (F) into the "basin" area as a reserve and to try to head off the infiltration of Indians out of Deep Ravine.

3:59 PM—*Warriors*—Crazy Horse reaches the ridge east of Battle Ridge. He moves down its east slope and turns to head back and resume his attack. He pauses a few minutes to gather his warriors and discuss the situation with Indians who had come up from Deep Coulee.

4 PM—*Reno-Benteen*—5–7 MPH—The general move toward Weir Peaks begins, Benteen's command leading out. Godfrey first claimed he was third in line, then told Camp the order of march was M, K, H; Wallace said H, then K led. Edgerly said H, K, and M.

4 PM—*Pack Train*—As he arrives on Reno Hill, Tom McDougall sees the tail-end of Edgerly's troops in Cedar Coulee.

4 PM—*Terry-Gibbon Column*—*Terry moves out toward his cavalry. He leaves orders for the cavalry to move at five PM and for the infantry to move by at least four AM the next morning.*

4:02 PM—*Reno-Benteen*—1.6 miles, total, from Reno Hill; 3 to 4 MPH—Company D reaches its farthest point in advance of Weir Peaks. Edgerly stops his troops and sees CPT Weir motioning for him to return and come to the high ground. He begins turning his troops toward Weir.

4:04 PM–4:15 PM—*Warriors*—Crazy Horse and the Minneconjou warrior, White Bull, lead a charge from east of Battle Ridge, into the middle of panicking and re-deploying troopers, breaking the back of Keogh's command and overrunning Calhoun's Company L.

NOTE ... 4:05 PM—Keogh Battalion—1.15 miles from lower Finley-Finckle Ridge to Last Stand Hill; 5 MPH, average—This is the earliest any Company C troopers on foot could have possibly reached Last Stand Hill.

4:06 PM—*Custer-Yates*—½ mile (875 yards); 8 MPH—Yates and Company F arrive in the "basin" area. He deploys his men in an attempt to stem the flow of Indians from Deep Ravine.

4:07 PM–4:08 PM—*Warriors*—1 to as much as 1¾ miles; 12–14 MPH—Indians from the Ford D area now arrive north and west of Cemetery Ridge, putting extreme pressure on Custer. The Indians were both dismounted and on horseback.

4:09 PM—*Custer-Yates*—(⁴⁄₁₀ of a mile; 700 yards); At 6 MPH (foot), 8 MPH (mounted)—Now under increasing pressure, Custer begins moving up Cemetery Ridge to Last Stand Hill. Company E—partially dismounted—is overrun. Casualties are fairly heavy—maybe as many as six troops killed—and the unmounted horses are run off.

4:09 PM—*Reno-Benteen*—A cautious crawl—An orderly from Reno reaches Varnum mid-way down the bluffs and tells him to return to the command. They are moving downstream.

4:09 PM—1¼+ miles; 5–6 MPH—Hare, climbing the steep peaks, reaches CPT Weir and tells him of Reno's request that he try to contact Custer.

4:12 PM—*Custer-Yates*—(³⁄₁₀ of a mile; 525 yards); at 8 MPH—Yates, under heavy pressure and seeing Custer moving, re-mounts his troops and heads for Last Stand Hill.

4:13 PM—⁴⁄₁₀ of a mile; 8 MPH (mounted)—In a semi-controlled move protected by the mounted troops, lead elements of HQ and Company E reach Last Stand Hill.

4:14 PM—*Reno-Benteen*—1 mile; 5 MPH—LT Edgerly and Company D have moved back up Cedar Coulee and climbed the slopes of the Weir loaf to get in position.

4:14 PM—1¼ miles; now, 4 MPH—Benteen, French, and Godfrey approach Weir Point, the command stretched out behind them.

4:15 PM—*Custer-Yates*—⁴⁄₁₀ of a mile; 6 MPH (on foot), **pulling their horses with them**—Final stragglers of Company E reach Last Stand Hill.

4:15 PM—³⁄₁₀ of a mile; 8 MPH—Yates and Company F begin arriving at Last Stand Hill.

4:15 PM—*Warriors*—Crazy Horse and White Bull now join in the fighting for Last Stand Hill.

4:15 PM–4:25 PM—*Custer-Yates*—The fighting intensifies around the Custer command on the ridge, up to the top of the knoll. Stragglers from the Keogh debacle—no more than about eleven men—continue arriving, Indians chasing them slowing down, keeping their distance.

4:15 PM–4:40 PM—Indian fire north of Custer Hill threatens troops there.

4:17 PM—*Pack Train*—The last of the pack train arrives on Reno Hill.

4:18 PM—*Reno-Benteen*—Edgerly orders Company D to commence firing at Indians within range. These are the remnants of the Indians left behind after the valley fighting. Both Weir and the company "had stopped back at the south end of this sugarloaf and Edgerly said he would go out to the end of the sugarloaf to look down and see if he could see Custer while they were out there."

4:18 PM–4:25 PM—*Keogh Battalion*—(1¼–1⅓ miles); 12 MPH–15 MPH—CPL John Foley (Company C) bolts from the Keogh Sector fighting and tries to get away, south, toward Reno's troops now on and approaching Weir Point. He is pursued by three Indians one of who is the Minneconjou warrior, Turtle Rib.

4:20 PM–4:25 PM—*Warriors*—A cry goes up amongst the Indians that the suicide boys are arriving.

4:20 PM—*Reno-Benteen*—Varnum returns to Reno Hill from his foray to try to find and bury Hodgson. Sees most of the command heading downstream.

4:20 PM—Benteen climbs highest point of Weir Peaks and is now with CPT Weir. His first sight of the village was from "that high point." It was the only point from which the village could be seen and he estimated about 1,800 tepees. When Benteen reached Weir Peaks and saw for the first time the extent of the Indian village he realized they had bitten off too much.

4:20 PM–4:35 PM—Companies H, K, and M are positioning themselves alongside Company D on the Weir Point complex of hills.

- LT Godfrey moves his own Company K along the edge of the bluffs, closest to the river. "*Weir's and French's troops were posted on the high bluffs and to the front of them; my own troop along the crest of the bluffs next to the river....*"
- CPT French moves Company M all the way to "Edgerly" Peaks, where he can look down in the direction of Battle Ridge. When PVT Pigford first looked over in that direction he saw Indians firing from a large circle. It gradually closed until it "*converged into a large black mass on the side hill toward the river and all along the ridge.*" Hare said M, K, and H "*were strung out along bluffs behind Company D parallel with the river but not quite up to Company D.*"
- Edgerly described the Company H position as occupying the two peaks—as Benteen said, in a file—and Company D deployed on the loaf at a right angle to H. Edgerly said M was a little to H's rear. Godfrey's K seemed to be adjacent to D, on a narrow spur along the bluffs adjacent to the river.

4:21 PM—*Custer-Yates*—With the pressure mounting and the realization that they are surrounded, Company E men release their horses. Their remaining mounts stampede down the ridge toward the river, giving the impression of a charge.

4:25 PM—Company E men under the command of LT Sturgis prepare to charge off Custer/Last Stand Hill down the South Skirmish Line.

4:25 PM–4:31 PM—(550–875 yards); (5 to 10 MPH)—Company E troops charge down the South Skirmish Line. Some troops are mounted, but most are on foot.

4:25 PM–4:32 PM—*Reno-Benteen*—(1¼–1⅓ miles); (12 MPH–15 MPH)—SGT Flanagan of Company D sees a lone rider cresting the ridges just to the west of Luce/Nye-Cartwright ridges. This was CPL John Foley of Company C. Flanagan sees Indians in pursuit and suddenly Foley shoots himself in the head.

4:27 PM–4:31 PM—*Custer-Yates*—550–875 yards; 5 to 10 MPH—Company E troopers on horseback begin arriving parallel to the top of Deep Ravine. Those on foot take a little longer and because of the distance and the heat, they begin slowing. Initially, Indians in their way separate and retreat.

4:32 PM–4:36 PM—*Warriors*—350–700 yards (²⁄₁₀–⁴⁄₁₀ of a mile); 6 to 12 MPH—Led by the suicide boys, Indians on Cemetery Ridge charge off the ridge—some on horseback, many on foot—and burst in amongst the exhausted troopers along the so-called South Skirmish Line (SSL). At the same time, other Indians—including the suicide boys on Cemetery Ridge—charge up to Custer/Last Stand Hill. The final fighting becomes furious, all the more so because of the extreme dust and gun smoke.

4:34 PM–4:36 PM—700 yards; 6 to 12 MPH—Indians on foot and horseback overrun Custer/Last Stand Hill.

4:40 PM—*Custer-Yates*—The Custer battle is ending. The last of the Company E men are forced into Deep Ravine where they are slaughtered.

4:40 PM—*Reno-Benteen*—According to De Rudio, the firing from downstream died off 1½ hours after he heard it first.

4:42 PM—1¼ miles; 8 MPH—Varnum reaches the sugarloaf of Weir Point and joins Edgerly and Company D. "*I went to the position of Captain Weir's company at the far point of the ridge down-stream. At that time his men were firing at pretty long range—I should say seven or eight hundred yards—at Indians here and there. At that time I could see all over the plain where ... the Custer battlefield had been, and it was just covered with Indians in all directions, coming back towards us.*"

4:43 PM—At some point, the heavy firing from downstream ceased and Herendeen began his move out of the timber. This is more than a two-hour stay in the woods, though Herendeen claimed some three hours.

4:45 PM—*Warriors*—Word begins to spread amongst the Indians in the Calhoun-Custer sectors that additional soldiers can be seen on the high bluffs upstream. Some of the Indians in the Calhoun Hill area begin moving toward Weir Peaks.

4:50 PM—(2+ miles); 8–10 MPH—More Indians begin moving toward Weir Peaks.

4:51 PM—*Reno-Benteen*—(1± mile); 8 MPH—Benteen, seeing the Indians begin to move toward the troops, hustles back to Reno to tell him this position is untenable.

4:53 PM—Company D firing eases as it becomes apparent Indians are beginning to move toward the troops at Weir Point.

4:57 PM—¾ of a mile; 8–10 MPH—Benteen reaches Reno and tells him about the approaching Indians. Reno agrees to the pullback and orders Trumpeter Penwell (K) to inform French, Godfrey, and Weir. Penwell leaves immediately.

5 PM—Herendeen and the men from the timber would be arriving at Weir Peaks at this time.

5:03 PM—¾ of a mile; 10 MPH—TMP Penwell signals to French to begin pulling back, then reaches Godfrey and tells him of Reno's orders to withdraw.

5:03 PM—10 MPH—French's Company M begins its withdrawal. French yells over to Edgerly ordering Company D to withdraw.

5:04 PM—LT Godfrey directs LT Hare to take ten men and occupy some high ground on the right facing the Indians. Hare had just cut the men out when orders came—through TMP Penwell—to fall back as quickly as possible. Penwell informed Hare, who then told Godfrey.

5:04 PM—8-10 MPH—Company D begins its withdrawal. Edgerly sees everyone off before attempting to leave.

5:06 PM—As Hare moves to occupy the high ground, Godfrey orders Company K to mount up and prepare to move back.

5:07 PM—8-10 MPH—Last of Company D leaves the Weir sugarloaf down a draw and into Cedar Coulee. Edgerly struggles with his horse as his orderly, SGT Harrison stands nearby. Edgerly had trouble mounting and claimed Indians got within fifteen feet of him and his orderly, an old veteran. The horse kept moving away from him, so Harrison moved in such a way to prevent the horse from going any farther. He smiled and told Edgerly the Indians were bad marksmen from so close.

5:09 PM—8-10 MPH—Godfrey's Company K—the last one to leave the Weir Point complex—begins its move toward Reno Hill.

5:10 PM—*Warriors*—(As much as 3½-4 miles); 12-14 MPH—The Indians are moving toward Weir Peaks with the lead elements approaching the struggling Edgerly and SGT Harrison—no more than 150 to 200 yards away—on the Weir "sugarloaf."

5:10 PM—*Reno-Benteen*—According to Hare, it was about 1½ hours from the time Weir left Reno Hill to when the general engagement on Reno Hill began.

5:11 PM—¼ of a mile off the "sugarloaf"; 10 MPH—As Company D moves up Cedar Coulee in front of the on-coming Indians, Farrier Vincent Charley is hit in the hips and falls from his horse.

5:11 PM—*Warriors*—10-12 MPH—Finally, as Indians begin to reach the top of the "loaf," Edgerly has managed to mount his horse and he and Harrison fight their way off and down a draw toward Cedar Coulee.

5:11 PM—3½—4 miles; 8-14 MPH—There are now as many as 200 Indians near Weir Point, with many more closely behind. They slow, first to gather numbers, second to assess what the soldiers are doing.

5:14 PM–5:15 PM—*Reno-Benteen*—¼ of a mile off the "sugarloaf"; 12 MPH to a halt—Entering the coulee and riding hard toward its head, Edgerly and Harrison come across the injured and un-horsed Vincent Charley. Edgerly instructs him to crawl into a ravine and they would come back for him as soon as he could get reinforcements. As Edgerly and Harrison rode on and looked back, they saw the Indians finishing off Charley.

5:14 PM—*Warriors*—10 MPH—Warriors follow after Edgerly and Harrison.

5:17 PM—*Reno-Benteen*—1 mile from its position on the Weir complex; 8–10 MPH—As he headed back, Godfrey realized he needed to protect the rear of the retreating troops, so he halted, dismounted his men, and formed a skirmish line, sending his "fours" and their led-horses back, leaving about twenty-five men on the line. The Indians firing "was very hot," but none of his troopers was hit. Several horses were hit. They were about 500 yards from Reno Hill.

5:25 PM—1–1¼ miles—Based on the 3:55 PM time as the beginning of the general move from Reno Hill to Weir Peaks, a 1½-hour time frame would place the command back on Reno Hill at this time. This would be in general agreement with packer B.F. Churchill, who said the round trip to Weir and back took about one hour for the packs.

5:30 PM—1–1¼ miles—Varnum agreed with Hare, citing a 5:30 PM return to Reno Hill from Weir Peaks. Varnum's estimate was three hours, from Reno first reaching the hilltop at 2:30 PM. SGT Culbertson thought 1½ hours from beginning of move to Weir to the return to Reno Hill. Herendeen and Edgerly claimed they were back on Reno Hill by five PM (in all likelihood, too early an estimate).

5:30 PM—*Terry Gibbon Column*—*Terry moves out of Mission Bottom camp with the artillery and cavalry. Begins raining heavily. Once in Mission Coulee the going becomes extremely difficult. CPT Ball and LT McClernand act as guides. LT Bradley joins up with the cavalry column in Mission Coulee.*

5:45 PM—*Reno-Benteen*—under 2 MPH–6 MPH; 500–650 yards—The last of Godfrey's Company K troopers reaches the Reno Hill perimeter.

8

The Siege

Monday, June 26, and Beyond

JUNE 26, 1876—MONDAY—*Military Correspondence & Intelligence Reports—*

From the Acting Assistant Adjutant General, Department of the Platte—*"Reports departure of five Co's Infantry for Fetterman Capt Powell Commanding."*[1]

From the Acting Assistant Adjutant General, Department of the Platte—*"Repeats dispatch from Fetterman as follows: Train with wounded will reach here tomorrow. Capt Nickerson is with it."*[2]

From Col. Merritt—*"Dispatch rec'd. Leave at once for Laramie."*[3]

Terry-Gibbon Column—Some scattered showers early, then plenty of sun and heat.

   2 AM—Will Logan—sent out by Terry to try to locate Custer—hears war drums and voices in the distance; he halts.[4]

   BETWEEN 2 AM–3 AM—*Daybreak.*

Reno-Benteen—2:45 AM—First firing begins on Reno Hill[5]:

- Reno: about 2:30 AM
- Edgerly: about 2:30 AM
- McDougall: about 2:30 AM
- Wallace: before 3 AM
- Godfrey: between 2:30–3 AM
- (Godfrey: about 3 AM or earlier)
- Moylan: about 3 AM
- Benteen: about 3 AM
- Varnum: about 3 AM
- Herendeen: peep of the day

Steamer "Far West"—3:30 AM—The "Far West" starts out.

Terry-Gibbon Column—DAYLIGHT—Brisbin rouses Bradley and orders him out on a scout.

   3:30 AM—Bradley sends six Crow out in the lead.

   4 AM—Bradley leaves camp on his scout.

7th Cavalry—EARLY MORNING, BEFORE DAWN—LT De Rudio, PVT O'Neill, Fred Gerard, and Billy Jackson try to cross the river to reach Reno's command. Gerard, superstitious, says a prayer to the Indians' Great Spirit and tosses his watch in the river as a token, all this hoping to find a suitable crossing point. Gerard later denied the incident, claiming he lost his watch and threw his rifle into the river, trying to get it out of his way.[6]

- They wind up coming across Indians and Gerard and Jackson—the only ones with horses—take off (this was pre-arranged), leaving De Rudio and O'Neill hidden in the brush.

Terry-Gibbon Column—5 AM—The infantry column breaks camp and begins its move to catch up to the cavalry.

Steamer "Far West"—5:30 AM—"Far West" reaches a creek flowing into the Big Horn on its right bank; they encounter rapids and meet with a long delay.

Terry-Gibbon Column—EARLY MORNING—About six miles below the mouth of the LBH horse tracks are seen in the grass and a little way further, three Indians are spotted on the other side of the Big Horn. A lone horse was also spotted on the same side of the river as the soldiers were on; this was the horse the Crow had let go when they tried to swim the river.

- The three Indians proved to be the Crow, White Man Runs Him, Goes Ahead, and Hairy Moccasin.
- They inform Prevo that Custer and all with him have been wiped out.
- After questioning them, Prevo concluded they were certainly exaggerating and had no definitive knowledge of what had happened.

7:50 AM—Gatling gun battery arrives at the bivouac.

Reno-Benteen—[JUST BEFORE 9 AM—Willert claims this was when Benteen ordered the charge of companies B, D, G, and K.[7] Liddic claimed it was about 3 PM, but I think it may have been somewhat earlier because the Indian firing had all but ceased by 3 PM.]

Terry-Gibbon Column—9 AM—Carroll's trains break camp.

- They went 2 miles and came across some of the Crow scouts who were assigned to Custer.
- Crow scouts report big fight on the Little Big Horn with Custer being whipped badly.

9:15 AM—LT Bradley sees Terry and the head of the cavalry command appear on a ridge a couple of miles back and decides it is his duty to inform the general of what the Crow said.

- His staff and COL Gibbon, who had re-joined the command earlier that morning, surrounded Terry.
- Terry's diary mentions these reports as being of Sioux trails. Taylor reports more.
- Terry wanted to wait for his infantry to arrive, but now directed the command to move as soon as they could finish their coffee.
- [*It is fairly clear now Matthew Carroll and his trains are with Terry.*]

9:30 AM—"Far West" passes Terry's camp of June 25.
10 AM—Terry begins to move toward the LBH valley.

- The infantry command is seen moving toward them.

10 AM—Curley is far down Tullock's Creek.

Warriors and ***Reno-Benteen***—Indians started grass and brush fires, probably to conceal their movements and to prevent soldiers from approaching river for water.

- Historian Edgar Stewart felt there might have been "thousands" of Indians in the vicinity this day. "Captain Benteen stated later that there were *'picnic parties'* of Indians as large as a regiment standing around the river bottom looking on, and that fully 2,000 hostiles were idling about, waiting for a place from which to shoot. He declared … there was not a foot of unoccupied land anywhere and that there were Indians everywhere … the command was surrounded by from eight to nine thousand hostiles."[8]
- Varnum felt there were as many as 4,000 Indians, many of whom were never engaged. The men on the hill could see large masses of them a good ways off.
- Herendeen felt there were 400–500 in the surrounding hills.
- Moylan put the number at 900–1,000 around the command.[9]

MID-MORNING—A sergeant reports to Benteen—with LT Gibson's compliments—that the Indians are giving Company H a devil of a time. Benteen reports to Reno and asks for reinforcements. The major refuses, but Benteen demands Company M and with French's troops organizes a charge chasing the gathering Indians down a ravine and across the river.

A LITTLE BEFORE NOON—The trek down to the Little Big Horn River for water began.

- One soldier killed, six wounded, getting water.
- Benteen positions four marksmen to protect the water carriers:
  - ◊ SGT Geiger (H)
  - ◊ BSM Mechlin (H)
  - ◊ SAD Voit (H)
  - ◊ PVT Windolph (H)
  - ◊ SGT Fehler (A) (possibly stood in for Voit when Voit was wounded).[10]

Terry-Gibbon Column—12:30 PM—Having proceeded about 9½ miles up the LBH valley (on the east side of the river), the combined Terry/Gibbon command begins crossing the Little Big Horn River to its west side.

- The river here was about twenty yards across, 2½ feet deep, and cold.
- Ash growing along the stream.

Reno Battalion—1 PM—Godfrey: "*Indians had nearly all left us, but they still guarded the river….*"[11]

SOME TIME IN THE AFTERNOON—Varnum goes to Reno and volunteers to try to get a message out. SGT McDermott (A) offered to go with him. Reno refused permission, saying he couldn't afford to lose two good shots and that they would probably be killed anyway. Varnum responded, "*we might as well get killed trying to get relief as to get killed where we were. [Reno] said, 'Varnum, you are a very uncomfortable companion.'*"[12]

2 PM–EARLY AFTERNOON—The troops again came under heavy fire, this time from the north and east. Verified by Godfrey.[13]

Terry-Gibbon Column—ABOUT 2:20 PM—With the entire command across the river, Terry orders a halt.

- An advance guard of Muggins Taylor and Henry Bostwick is sent out, each by a different route, to reconnoiter and try to link up with Custer.

Reno-Benteen—3 PM—Benteen ordered another charge, but this time Reno led it or went with it. Companies B, D, G, and K moved forward about seventy yards before falling back with no casualties. Indian firing was intense.[14]

3 PM—Indian firing ceased altogether.[15]

- Large numbers of warriors seen returning to the village.

Terry-Gibbon Column—5 PM TO 5:20 PM—Terry's advance up the Little Big Horn valley begins again.

- The infantry formed the left column (nearest the river); the cavalry was on the right. Terry and Gibbon marched up front, in between the two columns.
- The Gatling guns were in the rear.
- Trains are with them.

Warriors—LATE AFTERNOON—The Indians begin firing the prairie in the valley. Under the cover of this fire—set to conceal their movements (as before)—the Indians broke camp and began to move away.

Terry-Gibbon Column—6:20 PM—Terry's column halts.

6:30 PM–6:40 PM—The scout, Henry Bostwick, sent out earlier to try to get a message to Custer comes riding back at a furious gallop. "*You have been looking for Indians all summer? You'll find all you want there!*"[16]

- Bostwick gestured excitedly up the valley, to a section of bench land about six miles up.
- Terry sends LT Roe (F/2C) toward the western bench land as an advanced guard along the column's right flank.
- LT Bradley moves up the left side of the column, through the timber and brush that grew along the river.
  - ◊ He continually saw Indians in the valley and on the bluffs to the right (where Roe was advancing), sometimes singly, pairs, or more. He also saw a group of 75–100, and heard rifle shots from the bluffs.
  - ◊ At one point, Bradley saw a timbered area jutting far into the valley. Indians were riding from the bluffs into that woods, and he felt there were more than 100, plus whatever number had already been there.
  - ◊ The Indians facing Roe were estimated to be as many as 300, their advance elements appearing to be wearing uniform jackets and carrying guidons. This group was between Roe and a large mass of people seeming to be moving from the Little Big Horn toward the Big Horn.
  - ◊ Roe sent a sergeant and three men forward to see who these people were … and quickly found out!

◊ Bradley felt there were at least 1,000 warriors to the command's front, *"with plenty more to cooperate with them."*[17]

- The Gatling guns and three companies of cavalry moved on the right in column, four companies of infantry were on the left, and one company of infantry in front and behind the pack mules in between the other two columns.

Warriors—7 PM—The Indian column emerges from the smoke of the prairie fire. The possessions of those who were in mourning were left behind, as was custom. That included the standing tepees.

Reno-Benteen—Some troopers estimated the Indian column's length at five miles. Benteen thought it to be three miles long and ½ mile wide. Benteen said, *"They had an advance guard, and platoons formed, and were in as regular military order as a corps or division."*[18]

- "Benteen, who was qualified to judge, estimated the strength of the hostiles as being equal to that of a full cavalry division. *'It* [the Indian column] *started about sunset and was in sight till darkness came. It was in a straight line about three miles long, and I think half a mile wide, as densely packed as animals could be. They had an advance guard and platoons formed, and were in as regular military order as a corps or division.'*"[19]
- "It is beyond doubt that the hostile camp on the banks of the Little Big Horn River had been one of the greatest gatherings of Indians ever seen upon the plains."[20]
- LT Godfrey: *"'… the Indian village moving … was, or seemed to be, about three miles long by ¾ [mile] wide and very closely packed'"*[21]
- PVT Windolph: *"The heavy smoke seemed to lift for a few moments, and there in the valley below we caught glimpses of thousands of Indians on foot and horseback, with their pony herds and travois, dogs and pack animals, and all the trappings of a great camp, slowly moving southward. It was like some Biblical exodus; the Israelites moving into Egypt; a mighty tribe on the march."*[22]
- LT Edgerly: *"I thought before the ponies commenced to move that it was like a lot of brown underbrush; it was the largest number of quadrupeds I ever saw in my life…. It looked as though a heavy carpet was being moved over the ground."*[23]
- Most troopers thought the Indians had run low on ammo or that Custer, with reinforcements, was coming to their rescue.
- The troopers on Reno Hill gave the Indians three cheers as they moved away![24]
- LT Roe, moving up the bench lands, comes across a large body of warriors, maybe as many as several hundred in number. He sends an orderly back to Terry. He also sees the tail end of the moving village and objects on the eastern bluffs he takes to be dead buffalo. He waits, a good distance away.
- Terry's column approaches a heavily timbered area, LT Bradley in the lead, and Indians are spotted amongst the trees and brush.
- Terry, in his June 27, 1876, battle dispatch, said both Benteen and Reno

estimated not less than 2,500 warriors, but other officers thought the number of Indians engaged was much more.[25]

Terry-Gibbon Column—8 PM—LT Roe leaves the bench land to re-join the main column.

8:40 PM–9 PM—Terry decides to go into bivouac, as it is getting dark. He camped on the site of the present-day Crow Agency, the schoolhouse marking the approximate center of his camp.

- The infantry had marched some 29 to 30 miles.
- The camp was about 11 miles as the Crow flies, from the mouth of the LBH and about 8–9 miles from Reno's position in the hills.
- There were fully 1,000 Indians to Terry's front, yet this was only the rear guard, as the rest of the village headed south.[26]
- Good camp: wide bottom, plenty of grass.
- Ten head of horses found during the day; not clear whose they were.
- Night passes quietly.

Benteen Battalion—SUNDOWN—No Indians to be seen.

DARKNESS—Gerard and Jackson leave the timber above Ford A and head toward Reno's command.

Steamer "Far West"—

9:30 PM—"Far West" moors on the west side of a large island near the right bank of the Big Horn. Maximum temperature recorded by SGT Wilson was 70°; minimum was 60°.

Reno-Benteen—11 PM—Gerard and Jackson reach Reno's command.

~11 PM—De Rudio and O'Neill reach Reno's command.

JUNE 27, 1876—TUESDAY—*Military Correspondence & Intelligence Reports*—From Col. Merritt—*"Notes receipt of dispatch to Chug. Leaves for the front tomorrow or next day."*[27]

From the Commanding Officer, Fort Lincoln—*"Scouts left last night with dispatches for Gen. Terry."*[28]

Reno-Benteen—EARLY MORNING, JUST AFTER FIRST LIGHT—Reno writes a message for Terry, whom he supposes is with Gibbon's command somewhere down the Big Horn or Little Bighorn valleys.

Camp of the Little Big Horn
Twenty miles from its mouth, June 27

Gen. Terry:

I have had a most terrific engagement with the hostile Indians. They left their camp last evening at sunset, moving due south, in the direction of the Big Horn mountains. I am very much crippled and cannot possibly pursue. Lieutenant Mackintosh [sic] and Dr. DeWolf are among the killed. I have many wounded, and many horses and mules shot. I have lost both my own horses. I have not seen or heard from Gen. Custer since he ordered me to charge with my battalion (3 companies), promising to support me. I charged about 2 PM, but meeting no support was forced back to the hills. At this point I was joined by Capt Benteen with 3 companies and the pack train (rear guard, 1 company). I have fought thousands and can still hold my own, but I cannot leave here on account of the wounded. Send me medical aid at once and rations.

M. A. Reno, Major 7th Cav[29]

- The message was given to scouts and they headed downstream. They returned shortly, however, with word that a number of "warriors" occupied the lower regions and they could not get through.

Steamer "Far West"—3:30 AM—The "Far West" starts again.

Terry-Gibbon Column—EARLY MORNING—Terry's command has a light breakfast and starts its move upriver.

- The Indians have disappeared.
- LT Bradley fords the LBH and begins his scout on the east side of the river.

7:30 AM—Terry's column begins its advance.

- Moved between 1½ to two miles and stopped for ten minutes.

7:40 AM—Terry moves onto a hill.

8:20 AM—Spots a few tepees about two miles in front.

Reno-Benteen—9 AM—Troops from Reno Hill see a body of people moving up the valley. It turns out to be Terry's force.[30]

9:30 AM—Godfrey uses this time when a cloud of dust was seen downriver.[31]

- Two officers ride out to meet Terry: LTs Wallace and Hare.

Steamer "Far West"—10 AM—The "Far West" reaches the confluence of the Little Big Horn and Big Horn rivers, approximately forty miles south of the Big Horn's mouth. CPT Baker offloads his troops to reconnoiter the south side of the Little Big Horn valley.

Terry-Gibbon Column—LATER MORNING—Terry's column advances into the abandoned Indian camp. Holmes Paulding finds Yates' gauntlets, Porter's buckskin shirt, and Sturgis' underclothing and spurs.

- Gibbon viewed the dead soldiers along Reno's retreat route and was then alerted to small dark figures atop the bluffs. Even with his binoculars he could not tell if they were soldiers or Indians. He was about 1½ miles away.
- Lodge poles and camp utensils found.

11 AM—Terry reaches Reno's position.

- Terry writes telegram to the Adjutant General of the Military District of the Missouri, Chicago, via Fort Ellis.

Reno-Benteen—SOME TIME DURING THE DAY—probably late morning—CPT McDougall and privates Ryan and Moore (Company B men) buried Hodgson on "*a little knoll between my position and the works on the hill and these two men and myself dug his grave and buried him.*"[32]

- Reno's wounded brought over to Terry's camp.
- Wagon master Matthew Carroll wrote he believed they would find many more dead Indians: had found twenty-five so far.
- Soldiers horribly mutilated.

Steamer "Far West"—

12:35 PM—The "Far West" starts again, continuing its move up the Big Horn River.

5:30 PM—The "Far West" reaches "Sitting Bull Rapids," taking one hour to ascend them.

8:30 PM—"Far West" ties up, unable to ascend further rapids. Total distance traveled from the mouth of the Big Horn was approximately 66 miles. The day's temperatures varied from a high to 76° to a low of 63°.

June 28, 1876—Wednesday—*Military Correspondence & Intelligence Reports*—

From the Acting Assistant Adjutant General, Department of the Platte—*"Major Arthur, Paymaster leaves tomorrow for Fetterman."*[33]

From the Acting Assistant Adjutant General, Department of the Platte—*"Forwards telegram from Gen. Crook rel. to paying troops of Big-horn Expedition."*[34]

From Capt Nickerson, ADC [or Crook's Adjutant]—*"Left Gen. Crook 21st inst. Met Schuyler at Crazy Woman's Creek night of 22nd and he probably reached Crook with dispatch the following day."*[35]

From Capt Nickerson, ADC—*"Reports having sent Courier with Gen. Sheridan's dispatch to Gen. Crook. Will start Infantry and Supply Train Monday morning."*[36]

From Col. W. Merritt—*"Reports forage and rations to include July 27th. Leaves for the command today."*[37]

Telegram dated June 28, 1876, Fort Fetterman, Wy, to Lieut. Gen. Sheridan, Chicago—*"Left Gen Crook morning twenty-first Camp on Goose Creek base Big Horn Mountain Schuyler met us at Crazy Woman's Creek. Night twenty-second & probably reached General's camp by ten next day with your dispatch. Your dispatch about Terry's movements probably reached him the following day or by twenty-four. Nickerson, ADC."*

Reno-Benteen—Reno abandons hill position. Combined command moved down the ridges and buried Custer's command.

- Establish bivouac next to Gibbon's men, on their right.
- Day was spent making litters to carry the wounded and burying the dead.

Steamer "Far West"—Morning—The "Far West," unable to proceed up the Big Horn any farther, turns and rapidly descends the river, mooring at the mouth of the LBH where it remained all day.

Terry-Gibbon Column—Morning—CPT Ball (H/2C) sent out to follow the Indian trail, south. He followed it for ten or twelve miles and it headed toward the Big Horn Mountains. On his way back he discovered a large fresh trail that led directly toward the village.

Steamer "Far West"—Noon—Engineer sergeant Wilson reports the arrival of the Crow scout, Curley.[38] James M. Sipes, who was a sometimes-barber aboard the "Far West"—but mostly just a sightseer along for the ride—was fishing on the left bank of the Little Big Horn with Grant Marsh; the ship's steward, Reuben Riley; and either James Boles or Walter "Bob" Burleigh, the ship's owner and Clerk, when he said

Curley rode into the water from the right bank. He had three ponies and a red Sioux blanket he had taken from a dead Sioux.[39]

Terry-Gibbon Column—8 PM—Terry moves camp 4½ miles down the valley. They had great trouble moving the wounded on their hand litters.

- After they made the litters for the wounded, *"two men were assigned to each hand-litter, but it was soon found that this was not sufficient, and the number had to be doubled, and, besides, two men had to be assigned to each horse-litter to steady it. Infantrymen and dismounted cavalrymen relieved each other every few minutes...."*[40]

JUNE 29, 1876—THURSDAY—*Combined Command*—Command remains in camp. Terry orders LT Maguire to make a survey of the battlefield. Also ordered horse litters made.

Steamer "Far West"—DURING THE DAY—Three scouts arrive at the "Far West" with news of the battle. The boat was immediately barricaded and preparations were made to receive the wounded.

Combined Command—Continued to make litters for the wounded.
6:30 PM—March commences again.
10 PM—The van of Terry's command reaches the "Far West."

JUNE 30, 1876—FRIDAY—*Military Correspondence & Intelligence Reports*—From the Acting Assistant Adjutant General, Department of the Platte— *"Repeats dispatch from C.O. Fort Laramie rel. to another fight with Indians the troops engaged not being Crook's."*[41]

Telegram dated June 30, 1876, Omaha, Neb., to Asst Adjt Genl, Mil. Div. Mo., Chicago, Ill.— *"The following dispatch from Commanding officer Fort Laramie just received. There is a report from Red Cloud that Indians coming in bring news of another fight with northern Indians. The troops not being Crook's. A village was entirely destroyed. Hawkins, Act. Ass't Adjt. Gen."*

Combined Command—1 AM TO 2 AM—Command reaches the "Far West."
4 PM—Troops remained in camp until now and then moved across the creek some ½ mile.

Steamer "Far West"—"Far West" leaves for Fort Pease (53 miles away).

- Showered on and off all day; grass in the area was good for the horses and mules.

JULY 1, 1876—SATURDAY—*Military Correspondence & Intelligence Reports*—From the Acting Assistant Adjutant General, Department of the Platte— *"Dispatch from Fetterman that 5 Companies from Medicine Bow arrived yesterday."*[42]

From the Acting Assistant Adjutant General, Department of the Platte— *"Relative to return of 40 Indians from Gen. Crook's Command who say that he is six days march ahead."*[43]

Combined Command—Trains—and troops—move back up their trail, camping on the Big Horn where they "nooned" previously, making 17 miles.

- A great deal of smoke was seen at the foot of the Big Horn Mountains.
- The opinion was that General Crook had struck the Sioux camp.

July 2, 1876—Sunday—*Military Correspondence & Intelligence Reports*—From Department of Dakota—*"Relative to movement of wounded to Steamer. New supplies required especially for horses for Cavalry."*[44]

Combined Command—Command continued to march, following the Tullock's Creek/Big Horn divide. Good cavalry road, but impracticable for wagons.

July 3, 1876—Monday—*Military Correspondence & Intelligence Reports*—From Brig. Gen. A.H. Terry—*"Telegraphs a copy of written instructions given to Gen. Custer."*[45]

Letter written by Major Marcus Reno, HQ 7th Reg. Cav'y, In the field, July 3, 1876, addressed to Adj't Gen USA—

> In consideration of the great loss of officers in the engagement of June 25 & 26 I have the [illegible] to request the immediate return of Cap't Bell, Jackson & Lt Larned, otherwise there is not an officer to accompany the companies. When there is an officer will be commanded by inexperienced & young men. I am [illegible] Very Respectfully. M.A. Reno, Maj 7th Ca'y.

Combined Command—It was on this day they found Curley—again.

July 4, 1876—Tuesday—*Military Correspondence & Intelligence Reports*—From the Assistant Adjutant General, Department of Dakota—*"Repeats telegram from Gen. Terry reporting his arrival at mouth of Rosebud river and giving disposition of troops."*[46]

From Col. W. Merritt—*"Relative to movements of his command."*[47]

Telegram dated July 4, 1876, from St. Paul, Minn., to Adj't General Division Missouri, Chicago—*"The following just received, mouth of Rosebud River June twenty-first via Bismarck July third arrived here this morning. No Indians met with as yet but traces of a large and recent camp discovered some twenty to thirty miles up the Rosebud, Gibbon's column moves this morning on the north side of the Yellowstone for the mouth of the big horn where it will be ferried across by the supply steamer and whence it will proceed to the mouth of the Little Horn and so on. Custer will go up the Rosebud tomorrow with his whole regiment and thence to the head waters of the Little Horn and thence down the Little Horn. I hope that one of the two columns will find the Indians. I go personally with Gibbons. Signed Alfred H. Terry. Ruggles, Asst Adjt Genl."*

Combined Command—Everything quiet; no news.

July 5, 1876—Wednesday—*Military Correspondence & Intelligence Reports*—From Department of the Platte—*"Report 150 Snake Indians leave Camp Stambaugh [?] today for Crook [?]."*[48]

Combined Command—In the evening, General Terry invited the officers over "for a sing." After that, the officers visited the officers of the 2nd Cavalry, then went to sleep around midnight.

Word of the Custer defeat was received at Fort Laramie on July 5. "At Fort Laramie the discussions centered as much on Custer's motives as on the obvious nature of the tragedy where so many soldiers were killed. *'Everyone seems to think that Custer made the attack prematurely to get glory for himself and his regiment,'* wrote Cynthia Capron to her husband."[49] (Cynthia Capron was the wife of 1LT Thaddeus Hurlbut Capron, Company C, 9th U.S. Infantry with Crook's Wyoming column.)

JULY 6, 1876—THURSDAY—*Military Correspondence & Intelligence Reports*— From C. McKeever, Assistant Adjutant General—*"Asks for particulars of Custer fight on Little Horn and with reference to the safety of Capt Keogh."*[50] LTC Chauncey McKeever had been the Army's Assistant Adjutant General since March 3, 1875.

From Lieut. Gen. P.H. Sheridan—*"Sends for news of Gen. Terry's Command. Newspapers report Custer and 300 men killed."*[51]

From E.D. Townsend, Adjutant General—*"Papers report disaster to Gen. Custer— Telegraph any information received."*[52] BG Edward Davis Townsend was the Army's Adjutant General. Appointed on February 22, 1869.

From the Commanding Officer, Fort Fetterman—*"Received dispatch to Gen. Crook. Expects Richard [half-breed scout, Louis Richaud] in with Scouts and will send him out at once."*[53]

From J.E. Kingsley—*"Brown received message will see that all dispatches for Gen. Sheridan reach him at once."*[54]

Partial letter from Fort Laramie, Wyo. Dated July 6, 1876, to A.A.G., Omaha, Nebraska—

> **Captain Jordan, Camp Robinson sends the following: About twenty Indians from hostile camp returned since second. They say that Sitting Bull had two thousand Indians in Rosebud fight and lost five killed and thirty wounded. Son of Dull Knife Cheyenne Chief killed. Son and son in law of Red Cloud in the fight. One Indian said he saw a great many soldiers charge on Sioux village when eight miles off: supposed to be Gibbon or Terry, or both. Agency Indians mourning a great deal and appear uneasy and frightened.**

Telegram dated July 6, 1876, at 8:20 AM [or possibly 8: 20 PM], Headquarters Dep't of Dakota upon Little Big Horn River, June 27, to Adjutant Gen. of Military Division of the Missouri at Chicago, Ill—*"It is my painful duty to report that 2 days before yesterday the twenty-fifth inst. a great disaster overtook Gen. Custer & the troops under his command. At twelve o'clock of the twenty-second he started with his whole regiment & a strong detachment of scouts & guards from the mouth of the Rosebud proceeding up that river about twenty miles. He struck a very heavy Indian trail which had previously been discovered & pursuing it found that it led as it was supposed that it would lead to the Little big horn river. Here he found a village of almost unexpected extent & at once attacked it with that portion of his force which was immediately at hand. Major Reno with three Companies A G & M of the regiment was sent into the valley of the stream at the point where the trail struct at. General Custer with five Companies C E F I & L attempted [illegible] to enter it about three miles lower down. Reno forded the river. Charged down its left bank dismounted & fought on foot until finally completely overwhelmed by numbers he was compelled to mount recross the river & seek a refuge on the high bluffs which overlooked its right bank. Just as he recrossed Capt Benteen who with three Companies D H & K was some two miles to the left of Reno when the action*

commenced but who had been ordered by Gen'l Custer to return came to the river &
rightly concluding that it was useless for his force to attempt to renew the fight in the
valley he joined Reno on the bluffs. Cap't McDougall with his Company B was at first at
some distance in the rear with a train of pack mules. He also came up to Reno. Soon this
united force was nearly surrounded by Indians many of whom armed with rifles occu-
pied positions which commanded the ground held by the cavalry ground from which
there was no escape rifle pits were dug & the fight was maintained though with heavy
loss from about half past two o'clock of the twenty-fifth till six o'clock of the twenty-sixth
when the Indians withdrew from the valley taking with them their village. Of the move-
ments of Gen. Custer & the five companies under his immediate command scarcely
anything is known from those who witnessed them for no officer or soldier who accom-
panied him has yet been found alive. His trail from the point where Reno crossed the
stream passes along & in the rear of the crest of the bluffs on the right bank for nearly or
quite three miles. Then it comes down to the bank of the river but at once diverges from
it as if he had unsuccessfully attempted to cross then turns upon itself almost completes
a circle & closes. It is marked by the remains of his officers & men. The bodies of his
horses some of them dropped/bobbed along the path others heaped where halts appear
to have been made there is abundant evidence that a gallant resistance was offered by
the troops but they were beset on all sides by overpowering numbers. The officers known
to be killed are Gen Custer Captains Keogh Yates & Custer Lieuts Cooke Smith McIn-
tosh Calhoun Porter Hodgson Sturgis & Reilly of the Cavalry Lieut Crittenden of the
twentieth infantry & acting ass't surgeon Dewolf Lieut Harrington of the Cavalry &
asst Surgeon Lord are missing. Capt Benteen & Lieut Varnum of the Cavalry are slightly
wounded. Mr Boston Custer a brother & Mr Reed a nephew of Gen'l Custer were with
him & were killed. No other officers than those whom I have named are among the
killed wounded & missing. It is impossible as yet to obtain a nominal/reliable list of the
enlisted men who were killed & wounded but the number of killed including officers
must reach two hundred & fifty the number of wounded is fifty-one. At the mouth of the
Rosebud I informed Gen'l Custer that I should take the steamer Far West up the Yellow-
stone to the ferry Gen'l Gibbon's column over the river that I should personally accom-
pany that column & that it would in all probability reach the mouth of the little big
horn on the twenty-sixth inst. The steamer reach Gen'l Gibbon's troops near the mouth
of the Big Horn early in the morning of the twenty-fourth [illegible] four o'clock in the
afternoon all his men & animals were across the Yellowstone at five o'clock the column
consisting of five companies of the seventh infantry four companies of the second cavalry
& a battery of three [?] Gatling guns marched out to & across Tullock's Creek. Start-
ing soon after five o'clock in the morning of the twenty-fifth the infantry made a march
of twenty-two miles over the most difficult country which I have ever seen in order that
scouts might be sent into the valley of the Little Big Horn the cavalry with the battery
was there pushed on thirteen or fourteen miles further reaching camp at midnight. The
scouts were set out at half past four on the morning of the twenty-sixth. The scout dis-
covered the Indians who were at first supposed to be Sioux but when over taken they
proved to be Crows who had been with Gen. Custer. They brought the first intelligence of
the battle their story was not credited it was supposed that some fighting perhaps severe
fighting had taken place but it was not believed that disaster could have overtaken so

large a force as twelve Companies of Cavalry. The infantry which had broken camp very early soon came up & the whole column entered & moved up the valley of the Little Big Horn during the afternoon. Efforts were made to send scouts through to what was supposed to be Gen. Custer's position & to obtain information of the condition of affairs but those who were sent out were driven back by parties of Indians who in increasing numbers were seen hovering in Gen. Gibbon's front at twenty minutes before nine o'clock in the evening the infantry had marched between twenty-nine & thirty miles. The men were very weary & daylight was failing. The column was therefore halted for the night at a point about eleven miles in a straight line above the mouth of the stream. This morning the movement was resumed & after a march of nine miles Major Reno's entrenched position was reached the withdrawal of the Indians from around Reno's command & from the valley was undoubtedly caused by the appearance of Gen. Gibbon's troops. Major Reno & Cap't Benton [sic; Benteen] both of whom are officers of great experience accustomed to see large masses of mounted men estimated the number of Indians engaged at not less than twenty-five hundred. Other officers think that the number was greater than this. The village in the valley was about three miles in length & about a mile in width besides the lodges proper a great number of temporary brush wood shelter was found in it indicating that many men besides its proper inhabitants had gathered together there. Major Reno is very confident that there were a number of white men fighting with the Indians. It is believed that the loss of the Indians was large. I have as yet received no official reports in regard to the battle but what is stated in as gathered from the officers who were on the ground then & from those who have been over it since. Alfred H. Terry, Brig. Gen'l."

Telegram dated July 6, 1876, 9 AM, from Camp on Yellowstone to the Adjt General, Military Division of the Missouri, Chicago, Ill.— *"In the evening of the twenty-eighth 28 we commenced moving down with the wounded but were able to get on but four 4 miles as our hand litters did not answer the purpose the mule litters did excellently well but they were insufficient in number. The twenty-ninth 29 therefore was spent making a full supply of them in the evening of the twenty-ninth 29th we started again & at two AM the wounded were placed on the steamer at the mouth of the Little Big Horn the afternoon of the thirtieth 30th they were brought down to the depot on the Yellowstone. I send them tomorrow by steamer to Ft Lincoln & with them one of my aides Capt E.W. Smith who will be able to answer any questions which you may desire to ask. I have brought down the troops to the same point they arrived tonight they need refitting particularly in the matter of transportation before starting again & although I had on the steamer a good supply of subsistence & forage there are other things we need and I should hesitate to trust the boat again the Big Horn. Col. Sheridan's dispatch informing me of the reported gathering of Indians on the Rosebud reached me after I came down here. I hear nothing of Gen Crook's movements at least a hundred horses are needed to remount the cavalry men now here. Alfred H. Terry, Brig. General."*

Telegram dated July 6, 1876, 11:30 AM, Louisville, Ky, to the Assistant Adjutant General, Division of Missouri, Chicago, Illinois— *"Have you any particulars of Custer fight on Little Horn friends of Captain Keogh are anxious to hear concerning him. Signed McKeever, Assistant Adjutant General."*

Telegram dated July 6, 1876, 11:26 AM, Philadelphia, Pa., to R.C. Drum, Adjt Gen'l, Chicago, Ills— "*Send any news that you receive from Terry's Command without delay newspaper report from Helena information second July that Custer & some three hundred men were killed in fight on the Little Horn. P.H. Sheridan, Lieut. Gen'l, Comd'g.*"

Telegram dated July 6, 1876, 5 PM, from Camp on Yellowstone near mouth Big Horn River, July 3 via Bismarck, DT, July 6, to the AA General, Headquarters, Military Div., Chicago, Ills— "*The following is a copy of the written orders given to Gen. Custer, Camp at mouth of Rosebud River, June twenty-third 23 Eighteen seventy-six 1876. Lieut. Col. Custer Seventh 7th Cavalry. Colonel, The brigadier general commanding directs that as soon as your regiment can be made ready for the march you proceed up the Rosebud in pursuit of the Indians whose trail was discovered by Major Reno a few days since it is of course impossible to give you any definite instructions in regard to this movement & were it not impossible to do so the dep't Commander places too much confidence in your zeal energy & ability to wish to impose upon you precise orders which might hamper your action when nearly in contact with the enemy [an illegible insert] however indicate to you his own views of what your action should be & he desires that you should conform to them unless you shall see sufficient reason for departing from them he thinks that you should proceed up the rosebud until you ascertain definitely the direction in which the trail above spoken of leads. Should it be found as it appears almost certain that it will be found to turn toward the Little (big) Horn he thinks that you should still proceed southward perhaps as far as the head waters of the Tongue & then turn towards the little horn feeling constantly however to your left so as to preclude the possibility of the escape of the Indians to the south or south east by passing around your left flank. The column of Col. Gibbon is now in motion for the mouth of the big horn as soon as it reaches that point it will cross the yellow stone & move up at least as far as the forks of the Big and Little horns. Of course its future movements must be controlled by circumstances as they arise, but it is hoped that the Indians if upon the Little Horn may be as nearly enclosed by the two 2 columns that their escape will be impossible. The department Commander desires that your move up the Rosebud you should thoroughly examine the upper part of Tullock's Creek & that you should endeavor to send a scout through to Col. Gibbon's column with information of the result of your examination the lower part of this creek will be examined by a detachment from Col. Gibbon's Command the supply steamer will be pushed up the Big Horn as far as the forks of the river is found to be navigable for that distance & the department Commander who will accompany the Column of Col. Gibbon desires you to report which then not later than the expiration of the time for which your troops are rationed unless in the meantime you receive further orders. Respectfully etc. Signed E.W. Smith, Cap't, Eighteenth Infantry, Acting Ass't Adj't Gen'l, Alfred H. Terry, Brig. Gen'l.*"

Telegram dated July 6, 1876, 6:20, 6:30, and 6:40 PM, from St. Paul, Minn., to the Adjutant General, Division Missouri, Chicago— "*Your dispatch received. Colonel Smith General Terry's aide de camp is at Bismarck & has telegraphed me from there today as follows: General Terry desires you to telegraph to Generals Sturgis & Crittenden the death of their sons in battle of June twenty-fifth 25th. Have you received dispatch via Ellis reporting the action. I am at Bismarck to correspond with division headquarters not having received the dispatch reporting the action. I so telegraphed to Colonel Smith & asked him for particulars. He replies as follows: on twenty-fifth ~~25th~~ of June Custer with his whole regiment attacked Indian village on Little Big Horn. Repulsed with loss of fifteen ~~15~~ officers & over three hundred ~~300~~ men. General Custer Colonels Custer Keogh Yates Cooke Lieutenants Smith McIntosh Calhoun Hodgson Reilly Porter Sturgis & Crittenden killed. Lieutenants Harrington & assistant surgeon Lord missing all other officers with expedition are well. Two hundred sixty-one ~~261~~ dead have been buried fifty-two ~~52~~ wounded brought away. Command is at mouth of Big Horn waiting to refit. Signed, Smith, aide de camp. I telegraphed this morning to Manager Western Union telegraph Company Omaha to hunt up & hurry up the missing dispatch from Fort Ellis. I also telegraphed Sturgis Crittenden & Mrs Crittenden. The following is from this evening's paper 'Special telegram to the Dispatch. Bismarck, D.T. July sixth ~~6th~~. The far west which left the Big Horn fifty miles above its mouth Monday traveling a distance of nine hundred miles since then arrived last night at eleven ~~11~~ o'clock bringing Col. Smith of Gen. Terry's staff & the wounded from Major M.A. Reno's three-day battle with the Indians. Custer's annihilation Gen. Custer with Companies C, I, L, F and E of the seventh ~~7th~~ Cavalry was entirely wiped out not a man being left to tell the tale. Among the killed are Gen. Custer Col. Custer Boston Custer Col. Calhoun a brother in law and Reed a nephew of Gen. Custer Col. Yates Col. Keogh Cap't McIntosh Cap't Smith Col. Cook Lieut. Crittenden a son of Gen. Crittenden Lieut. Sturgis son of Gen. Sturgis Lieut. Hodgson Lieut. Harrington Lieut. Porter Dr. Lord Dr. DeWolf Charles Reynolds Mark Kellogg the Bismarck Tribune special Correspondent & soldiers swelling the aggregate of killed to two hundred & sixty-nine ~~269~~ wounded fifty-two ~~52~~ thirty-eight ~~38~~ of whom arrived on the Far West. The battle occurred the twenty-fifth ~~25th~~ twenty-sixth ~~26th~~ & twenty-seventh ~~27th~~ June twenty ~~20~~ miles above the mouth of the Little Horn a branch of the Big Horn. Gen. Custer attacked a village of about four thousand ~~4,000~~ warriors on the right with five ~~5~~ companies & Reno on the left with seven ~~7~~ companies. Custer fought about one ~~1~~ hour when the entire command having been surrounded by twenty ~~20~~ times their number better armed than the Cavalry were killed. Reno's battle: Reno cut his way through the Indians surrounding him with a loss of forty-one ~~41~~ killed & many wounded & reached a bluff where he entrenched and repulsed repeatedly the assault of the Indians without further serious loss. Reno's battle raged for three days when Gen. Terry made his appearance and the Indians retreated in great confusion leaving their camp strewn with Buffalo robes fine dressed hides gorgeous & valuable costumes & trinkets one tepee containing the bodies on nine ~~9~~ chiefs painted gorgeously arranged etc and scores of their dead were found on or near the battlefield. Many of their dead with their wounded were carried away & it is believed their loss will exceed the loss of the whites. One ~~1~~ Crow scout of all those who went in with Gen. Custer lives &for three ~~3~~ days after the battle he could not give an intelligent account of it. He was so frightened he lay in a ravine near where Custer went. The wires are too much in use to give further details. Will telegraph when I get further particulars. Supposed Gen. Terry has telegraphed you direct. Bismarck line is reported crowded with business will have manager here hunt up and hurry up all dispatches for you. I know important dispatches have been sent you from what Smith has telegraphed. Ruggles, AA Gen'l.'"*

Telegram dated July 6, 1876, 10:12 PM, from St. Paul, Minn. to the Adjutant General, Division Missouri, Chicago—*"Manager Western Union Omaha telegraphs me he thinks cause of delay in receipt of report Custer's fight sent via Ellis is that lines have been down some days north of Ross Fork Idaho. Ruggles, AA Gen'l."*

Combined Command—Some Crow scouts came into camp and told of the Crook/Rosebud fight on the 17th of June. A courier was dispatched to Crook.

July 7, 1876—Friday—*Military Correspondence & Intelligence Reports*—Telegram dated July 7, 1876, 10:45 AM, from St. Paul, Minn., to the Adjutant General, Division Missouri, Chicago—*"If it has not already appeared in Chicago papers I can telegraph you graphic account from Eye Witness of what was found on field after Custer's fight as appears in this morning's St. Paul Pioneer Press. Ruggles, Ass't Adj't General."*

Telegram dated July 7, 1876, 11:51 AM, from Ft. Leavenworth, Ka, to Col. R.C. Drum, AAG, Chgo, Ill.—*"This department has now been stripped of so many officers and men for service north that I consider it dangerous to have so many officers absent from the posts of Sill Reno & Elliott in the midst of the large bodies of Indians in that region and I respectfully but urgently ask that all the officers from this Command now absent as witnesses in the trial of Gen. Belknap be at once returned to their posts. The departure of six Companies of the Fifth Infantry in addition to the eight Companies Fifth Cavalry heretofore sent makes it out of the question to send any officers to replace those now absent in Washington & I repeat that it is not safe to leave the posts in question stripped of so many officers. Jno. Pope, Bvt Maj. Gen., Cmd'g."*

Telegram dated July 7, 1876, 10:40 PM, from Camp on Little Horn, June 28, to Ass't Adj't Gen'l, Military Division of Missouri, Chicago, Ills—*"The wounded were brought down from the bluffs last night & made as comfortable as our means would permit. Today horse & hand litters have been constructed & this evening we shall commence moving them toward the north [the word 'mouth' was inserted over 'north'] of the Little Big Horn to which point I hope that the steamer has been able to come. The removal will occupy three or four days as the march must be short. A reconnaissance was made today by Cap't Ball of the Second Cavalry among [along] the trail made by the Indians when they left the valley he reports that they divided into two parties one of which kept along the valley of Long Fork making he thinks for the Big Horn Mountains. The other turned more to the Eastward. He also discovered a very heavy trail leading into the valley that is not more than five days old this trail is entirely distinct from one which Gen. Custer followed & would sum to show that at least two large bands united just before the battle. The dead were all interred today. Alfred H. Terry, Brig, Gen'l."*

Combined Command—The courier's horse came into camp.

July 8, 1876—Saturday—*Military Correspondence & Intelligence Reports*—Telegram dated July 8, 1876, St. Paul, Minn., to Lieutenant General P.H. Sheridan, Chicago, Ills—*"Your dispatch about remains of officers killed in Custer's battle received. These bodies were buried on the field. The graves are marked. With the means at hand it was simply impossible to bring in these bodies subsistence had to be thrown away to get transportation to bring in the wounded. Ruggles, Ass't Adj't Gen'l."*

Telegram dated July 8, 1876, from Bismarck, DT, to Adjutant General, Military Division of the Missouri, Chicago—*"Have just informed Major Ruggles that Fort Lincoln garrison has not one hundred rounds per man of rifle ammunition caliber forty-five command in the field has a reserve of only ten thousand rounds of same carbine and pistol ammunition sufficient. Smith ADC."*

Telegram dated July 8, 1876, Department of Dakota, A.A.G.—*"Our ord. returns show no reserved supply of musket, carbine or pistol ammunition on hand at Lincoln. We have none here. I recommend that such supply as your Ord. Officer may deem necessary be forwarded at once."* Added as an addendum: *"See tel. to Col. Ruggles, July 10, 1876."*

First Endorsement—"Headqrs Mil. Div. Mo., Chicago, July 8, 1876—Respectfully referred to the Chief Ordnance Officer of the Division for his information and such action as he may deem necessary. By Command of Lieut. Gen'l Sheridan, [signature illegible] Ass't Adj't General."

Telegram dated July 8, 1876, St. Paul, Minn., to Adj't Gen'l Division Missouri, Chicago—*"The following just received—Camp on Little Big Horn June twenty-seventh—Custer with his whole regiment & forty scouts and guides attacked an immense Indian village on the twenty-fifth & was defeated. I have telegraphed particulars to Division headquarters. The officers known to be killed are Gen'l Custer Captains Keogh Yates and Custer. Lieutenants Cook Smith McIntosh Calhoun Porter Hodgson Sturgis and Reilly of the Cavalry Lieut of the twentieth Infantry & acting asst surgeon Dewolf Lieut Harrington & asst Surgeon Lord are missing. Captain Benteen and Lieutenant Varnum are wounded but so slightly that they remain on duty. Mr Boston Custer the brother & Mr Reed the Nephew of General Custer were killed. Please telegraph to the Commanding officer at Forts Lincoln & Rice to break the news to the families of the deceased officers & inform the Commanding officer at Fort Totten of the death of Dewolf. Please telegraph also to General Crittenden at Fort Abercrombie & to General Sturgis at St Louis of the death of their sons. Inform Lieutenant Lord of the death at Fort Snelling that his brother is missing. It is impossible as yet to determine the number of killed but it must reach two hundred & fifty officers & men. There are fifty-one 5̶1̶ wounded. No other officers than those whom I have named were injured. It has been impossible as yet to obtain a nominal list of the killed & wounded among the enlisted men. Ask Division Headquarters for a copy of my dispatch. Signed Alfred H. Terry, Brig. Gen'l."*

Combined Command—The courier returned, having lost everything swimming the Big Horn. He saw about forty hostiles.

JULY 9, 1876—SUNDAY—LT Godfrey was Officer of the Day. Godfrey received a letter from his wife informing him Indians had attacked Fort Lincoln and drove off cattle from Fort Rice. Godfrey's good friend LT Bradley left camp in the morning for Fort Ellis.

JULY 10, 1876—MONDAY—*Military Correspondence & Intelligence Reports*— *Second Endorsement* to telegram of July 8, 1876: Headqrs. Mil. Div. Mo., Office of Chf. Ord. Officer, Chicago, July 10, 1876—*"Respectfully—to the Ass't Adj't General of the Division. There were shipped by Express from Rock Island Arsenal, invoiced to the Commanding Officer Fort Lincoln Da. on Saturday 9th ... 150,000 rounds Rifle* *ammunition; 100,000 rounds Carbine ammunition; 50,000 rounds Revolver ammunition. This reaches St. Paul at 5 PM this evening. I request that Gen'l Ruggles be notified of it, that he may expedite its shipment from there to its destination. J.M. Reilly [?], Captain of Ordnance, Chf Ord. Officer."*

Combined Command—Godfrey spent some time visiting his pickets.

- CPT Ball came in from a scout to Pompey's Pillar. He saw no signs of Indians.
- Godfrey saw the account of the Crook/Rosebud fight in the *New York Herald*. He believed Crook *"was somewhat worsted."* He noted that the 7th's men considered themselves *"very lucky in not being gobbled up whilst intrenched [sic]."*[55]

JULY 11, 1876—TUESDAY—Command ordered to have 100 rounds of ammunition issued to each man and 100 rounds per man on the mules.

JULY 12, 1876—WEDNESDAY—Command moved ½ mile downriver for better grass, but wound up on a dust-heap. No rain *"for several weeks & the ground is very dry."*[56] Spent a very pleasant evening singing with several officers from the 7th and Dr. Paulding, CPT Ball, and LTs Hamilton and Roe. Racked out around 11:30 PM.

JULY 13, 1876—THURSDAY—For Godfrey, nothing new: fished, swam; rained about ½ inch to ⅔ of an inch. Took a ride.[57]

JULY 14, 1876—FRIDAY—Huge thunderstorm after dark.

JULY 15, 1876—SATURDAY—Scouts were in the camp early. CPT Michaelis brought in a dispatch from General Sheridan. Six companies of the 5th Infantry were ordered from Department of the Missouri; six more—22nd Infantry—were applied for.

Steamer "Far West"—The boat was ordered downriver for Bismarck the following day.

JULY 16, 1876—SUNDAY—Combined Command—Godfrey wrote a long letter to his wife, enclosing a check drawn on the 1st National Bank of Yankton, D. T., *"for $25,385."* [*!!!*]

Steamer "Far West"—The steamer left at 11:30 AM. Terry and someone Godfrey called "Col. Burton" went down to meet the "Far West."[58] It seems CPT Moylan and CPT Louis H. Sanger (G/17I) were either there or were going with them to bring the wagon train up from the Powder River Depot. Godfrey went to Gibbon's tent, read *The Army and Navy Journal*, and had a *"jolly"* sing with officers of the 2nd Cavalry.[59]

Side Notes—There was no "COL Burton" on the expedition and a check of the Heitman Register showed no one of that description in the service at that time. The closest possibility could have been CPT George Hall Burton of the 21st Infantry Regiment, but Burton did not make lieutenant colonel until August 31, 1888, and had received no brevet to that rank previously. Also, there is no mention of the 21st Infantry being attached to either Terry or Gibbon by that time.

JULY 17, 1876—MONDAY—Combined Command—Godfrey received a letter from his wife (dated July 4) and another from his sisters (dated June 25). Apparently, no one had even heard of the battle when those letters were written.[60] Godfrey visited

HQ and saw Dr. Williams, LT Thompson (Terry's Acting Commissary of Subsistence [ACS]), and COL Gibbon.

A dispatch for Terry was received from CPT E.W. Smith and opened by Gibbon: *"the distress at Lincoln was indescribable and heartrending. That the country was ablaze with indignation that such a disaster should occur...."*[61]

JULY 18, 1876—TUESDAY—Godfrey is Officer of the Day. Montana newspapers arrived; great indignation and excitement at the 7th Cavalry's defeat.

JULY 19, 1876—WEDNESDAY—7 AM—Godfrey went over to some island with horses. He found the herders had gone and he *"made them return & report in compliance with orders. This was done as a lesson, but was disapproved by Col. Reno."*[62]

1 PM—Godfrey arrives for lunch and hears CPT Thompson (L/2C) committed suicide at 5:30 AM.

6:30 PM—CPT Thompson is buried. *"He had been suffering from disease, consumption, the germs of which were laid in 'Libby' Prison, Va. [,] during the war. He had been sick two days."*[63] Godfrey walked back to his tent with LT Edgerly who asked Godfrey to write to Mrs. Godfrey asking her to stop and see Mrs. Edgerly.[64]

JULY 20, 1876—THURSDAY—1 AM—Shots fired. Indians had passed by, probably trying to steal horses. Scouts saw tracks of about thirty horses.

JULY 21, 1876—FRIDAY—Despite a bad headache, Godfrey ate breakfast and then loafed at Tom McDougall's tent. Felt better in the evening.

JULY 22, 1876—SATURDAY—Ordered to move camp to about one mile below Fort Pease.

3:30 PM—Command begins move to a much better camp. Hostiles seen on the high bluffs, but soon disappeared. Had a sing at regimental HQ until about 11:30 PM.

JULY 23, 1876—SUNDAY—CPT Wheelan (G/2C), lieutenants Hamilton, Doane, and Low, with two companies of the 2nd Cavalry, a battery of artillery, and twenty-five Crow scouts head out to meet up with CPT Moylan, returning from the PRD.

JULY 24, 1876—MONDAY—4:30 PM UNTIL DARK—Rained. A scout came in with word from Terry, who was aboard the "Far West." No word from Crook. Gibbon placed Reno and CPT James Sanno (K/7I) under arrest.[65]

JULY 25, 1876—TUESDAY—One of the pickets drowned this morning trying to ford a ravine that had swollen. It seems he was thrown from his horse and could not swim the rapidly moving water. [*This was PVT Richard A. Wallace from Boston, MA, a Company B trooper.*]

- Reno received his arrest charges from Gibbon.
- LT Godfrey: *"It all comes from Col. R sending out some scouts as vedettes Saturday eve after we got into camp. I presume however Col Reno's manner has as much to do with the results, as his manner is rather aggressive & he protested against the scouts being taken from the Reg't."*[66]

AUGUST 2, 1876—Godfrey made a comment about General Terry telling of LT Larned's appointment as *"Prof. of D'g. He was mad & thot [sic] it was an outrage as we* *all think him a systematic shirk.*"[67] *["D'g," was "Drawing," in all likelihood, an engineering or map-making subject.]*

AUGUST 3, 1876—Troops of the 7th Infantry discover a dead cavalry horse, identified as belonging to the 7th Cavalry near the confluence of Rosebud Creek and the Yellowstone River. The horse was found a short distance south of the river, on the east side of the Rosebud. CPT Walter Clifford (E/7I) was among the first of the troops to examine the carcass.

Over the years, the following men remarked on this horse and a body found in 1886 along the Rosebud:

- CPT Walter Clifford (E/7I)
- 2LT Charles Booth (B/7I)
- 2LT George Young (E/7I)
- 1LT Edward Settle Godfrey (K/7C)
- 2LT Richard Thompson (K/6I; Acting Commissary of Subsistence, Dakota column)
- SGT Richard Hanley (C/7C)
- SGT Daniel Kanipe (C/7C)
- George Herendeen (Scout)
- PVT Frank Sniffen (M/7C)
- PVT George Glenn (H/7C)
- CPT Henry Freeman (H/7I)
- 1LT Charles King (K/5C; regimental adjutant)
- John Finnerty (Newsman)
- 1LT John Bourke (D/3C; Crook's aide and adjutant)
- PVT Ferdinand Widmayer (M/7C)
- PVT Jacob Adams (H/7C)
- PVT Anthony Gavin (G/22I)

AUGUST 5, 1876—LT Godfrey had four of his men—Charles Burckhardt (his cook); someone he misnamed Lahy, but whose name was actually John Foley; George Blunt; and Thomas Murphy—discharged. He regretted losing them, "*as they have been excellent soldiers.*"

AUGUST 7, 1876—8 AM—Mounted inspection held. LT Godfrey gave the following counts for his Company K: 44 men in the ranks; 1 teamster; 2 troops at Regimental HQ; 5 troops at Department HQ, Artillery and Ordnance Detachments; 8 absent; 47 serviceable horses; 3 unserviceable horses; 3 on details (horses?) After the inspection, Godfrey went back—probably to his tent—and wrote a letter "*to the Army and Navy Journal correcting the prevailing mistake that Col. Benteen's column at the Battle of the Little Big Horn was a 'Reserve' by design.*"[68]

AUGUST 8, 1876—The Nathan Short tale now enters the picture, though no name was used: "*A rumor spread that a man of C co. & his horse had been found both dead but it seems some 'Dough-boy' got it off as a joke.*"[69]

AUGUST 27, 1876—Godfrey and Benteen went fishing. Benteen told him he had been assigned to recruiting duty, apparently a coveted assignment. Godfrey wrote he was happy for Benteen, who "*certainly is entitled to it over everybody else.*"[70]

SEPTEMBER **6, 1876**—Godfrey put in an order to *Brooks Brothers* for a blouse and pants!

SEPTEMBER **14, 1876**—Godfrey is OD, but is troubled by constant diarrhea. The command breaks camp, but as it departs discovers the area is on fire. Godfrey heads back to determine its origin. It started in the Company A area, and Moylan, blaming SGT Culbertson, reduces him in rank.[71]

SEPTEMBER **23, 1876**—This was the first mention of 2LT Edwin P. Eckerson who had been appointed to Company L, vice, Braden, on May 2, 1876, but had only joined on August 2, 1876; and 2LT Ernest A. Garlington, who had just graduated from the USMA on June 15, 1876, and had been appointed to Company H, vice, De Rudio.

Chapter Notes

Prologue

1. MacLean, Colonel French L., *Custer's Best* (Atglen, PA: Schiffer Military History, 2011), 30, and footnote 96; citing Alexander Rose, *American Rifle: A Biography* (New York: Delacourt Press, 2008), 155–156.

2. *Ibid.*, 22, footnote vii; citing Rose, *American Rifle: A Biography*, 211.

3. *Ibid.*, 23.

4. Foley, James R., "Walter Camp & Ben Clark," John P. Hart, ed., *Custer and His Times* (Cordova, TN: The Little Big Horn Associates, Inc., 2008, Book Five), 117.

5. *Ibid.*, 118.

6. *Ibid.*, 124.

7. Stewart, Edgar I., *Custer's Luck* (Norman: University of Oklahoma Press, 1955 [1985]), 65, quoting George Bird Grinnell, *Two Great Scouts and Their Pawnee Battalion: The Experiences of Frank J. North and Luther H. North* (Cleveland, Ohio: The Arthur H. Clark Company, 1928), 242.

8. Michno, Gregory F., *The Mystery of E Troop* (Missoula, MT: Mountain Press Publishing Company, 1994), 173.

Chapter 1

1. *Briefs of Papers in Relation to the Sioux War of 1875, 1876, and 1877.*

2. *Ibid.*

3. *Ibid.*

4. *Ibid.*

5. Wright, Charles E., *Law at Little Big Horn* (Lubbock: Texas Tech University Press, 2016), 86.

6. *Ibid.*, footnote 39, 261; referencing House Executive

Document No. 184, report of E. C. Watkins dated November 9, 1875, entitled "Military Expedition against the Sioux Indians," 8–9.

7. Wright, *Law at Little Big Horn*, 87.

8. *Briefs of Papers in Relation to the Sioux War of 1875, 1876, and 1877.*

9. Willert, James, *To the Edge of Darkness* (El Segundo, CA: Upton and Sons, Publishers, 1998), 115.

10. *Briefs of Papers in Relation to the Sioux War of 1875, 1876, and 1877.*

11. *Ibid.*

12. *Ibid.*

13. All duty assignments from, Hedren, Paul L., *Fort Laramie and the Great Sioux War* (Lincoln: University of Nebraska Press, 1988), 53.

14. *Briefs of Papers in Relation to the Sioux War of 1875, 1876, and 1877.*

15. Carroll, John M., ed., *General Custer and the Battle of the Little Big Horn: The Federal View* (Bryan, TX, and Mattituck, NY: 1986), 9; hereafter referred to as *The Federal View.*

16. *Briefs of Papers in Relation to the Sioux War of 1875, 1876, and 1877.*

17. Facebook post by Ephriam D. Dickson III.

18. Darling, Roger, *A Sad and Terrible Blunder* (Vienna, VA: Potomac-Western Press, 1990), 41.

19. *Ibid.*, quoting Colonel Robert Patterson Hughes, "The Campaign Against the Sioux in 1876," *Journal of the Military Service Institution of the United States*, Vol. XVIII, January 1896,

5. At the time, Hughes was a captain in Company E, 3rd Infantry, and was General Terry's brother-in-law, the two men being extremely close.

20. Upton, Richard, ed., *Custer Catastrophe at the Little Big Horn* (El Segundo, CA: Upton and Sons, Publishers, 2012), 71; referencing Captain Charles King, "Custer's Last Battle," *Harper's Magazine*, August 1890.

21. *Briefs of Papers in Relation to the Sioux War of 1875, 1876, and 1877.*

22. *Ibid.*

23. *Ibid.*

24. Stewart, *Custer's Luck*, 81.

25. *Ibid.*, footnote 21.

26. *Ibid.*, 82.

27. *Ibid.*

28. *Ibid.*, 83.

29. *Briefs of Papers in Relation to the Sioux War of 1875, 1876, and 1877.*

30. Letters sent (entry 2538) from the Military Division of the Missouri, where Sheridan was commander in 1876, in the Records of United States Army Continental Commands (Record Group 393).

31. Gibbon, "Last Summer's Expedition…" *American Catholic Quarterly*, April 1877, in Upton, *Custer Catastrophe at the Little Big Horn*, 157].

32. Darling, *A Sad and Terrible Blunder*, 106.

33. Stewart, *Custer's Luck*, 84.

34. *Ibid.*, 85.

35. Gibbon, "Last Summer's Expedition…" *American Catholic Quarterly Review*, Upton, *Custer Catastrophe at the Little Big Horn*, 151; see March 17th entry.

36. See Neil C. Mangum,

Battle of the Rosebud: Prelude to the Little Bighorn (El Segundo, CA: Upton & Sons, 2012), 20. Hereafter referred to as *Battle of the Rosebud.*

37. *Briefs of Papers in Relation to the Sioux War of 1875, 1876, and 1877.*

38. *Ibid.*

39. Hutchins, James S., *The Army and Navy Journal on the Battle of the Little Bighorn and Related Matters 1876–1881* (El Segundo, CA: Upton and Sons, Publishers, 2003), 15, hereafter referred to as *The Army and Navy Journal.*

40. *Briefs of Papers in Relation to the Sioux War of 1875, 1876, and 1877.*

41. *Ibid.*

42. *Ibid.*

43. *Ibid.*

44. See John S. Gray, *Centennial Campaign: The Sioux War of 1876* (Norman: University of Oklahoma Press, 1988), 40; hereafter referred to as *Centennial Campaign.*

45. Willert, *To the Edge of Darkness,* 18.

46. Hutchins, *The Army and Navy Journal,* 16.

47. *Briefs of Papers in Relation to the Sioux War of 1875, 1876, and 1877.*

48. MacLean, *Custer's Best,* 31; citing, Records Group 393, Records of U.S. Army Continental Commands, 1821–1920, Part V, Military Installations, Fort Rice, SD, Entry 1.

49. Haines, Aubrey L. *An Elusive Victory* (Helena, MT: Falcon Publishing, Inc., 1999), 43–44, footnote 25, citing Robert M. Utley, *Frontier Regulars* (Lincoln: University of Nebraska Press, 1973), 17.

50. *Briefs of Papers in Relation to the Sioux War of 1875, 1876, and 1877.*

51. *Ibid.*

52. Carroll, *The Federal View,* 18; citing the Annual Report of Major G. L. Gillespie, Corps of Engineers, July 11, 1876.

53. Hutton, Paul Andrew, *The Apache Wars* (New York: Crown, 2016), 165.

54. *Ibid.,* 165 and 321.

55. Wright, *Law at Little Big Horn,* 255, footnote 22.

56. *Briefs of Papers in Relation to the Sioux War of 1875, 1876, and 1877.*

57. Willert, *To the Edge of Darkness,* 18, quoting Lieutenant Charles Francis Roe.

58. *Ibid.,* 18.

59. MacLean, *Custer's Best,* 31.

60. *Briefs of Papers in Relation to the Sioux War of 1875, 1876, and 1877.*

61. Willert, *To the Edge of Darkness,* 21.

62. *Briefs of Papers in Relation to the Sioux War of 1875, 1876, and 1877.*

63. Willert, *To the Edge of Darkness,* 21.

64. *Ibid.*

65. Mangum, *Battle of the Rosebud,* 4.

66. *Briefs of Papers in Relation to the Sioux War of 1875, 1876, and 1877.*

67. *Ibid.*

68. *Ibid.*

69. Carroll, *The Federal View,* 19.

70. Bradley, Lieutenant James H.; Edgar I. Stewart, ed., *The March of the Montana Column* (Norman: University of Oklahoma Press, 1961 [2001]), 8.

71. Willert, *To the Edge of Darkness,* 21, citing footnote 1, 29, *American Catholic Quarterly Review,* April and October 1877, Old Army Press, Bellevue, NE, 1969; also, Upton, *Custer Catastrophe at the Little Big Horn,* 151.

72. Mangum, *Battle of the Rosebud,* 5.

73. Marquis, Thomas B., *Which Indian Killed Custer?* (Privately published; limited edition, 1933), 3.

74. Mangum, *Battle of the Rosebud,* 6.

75. Neihardt, John G., *Black Elk Speaks* (Lincoln: University of Nebraska Press, 1932 [1988]), 91.

76. Carroll, *The Federal View,* 13.

77. Mangum, *Battle of the Rosebud,* 6.

78. *Ibid.,* 7.

79. *Ibid.,* 8.

80. Philbrick, Nathaniel, *The Last Stand* (New York, Viking, 2010), 67.

81. *Briefs of Papers in Relation to the Sioux War of 1875, 1876, and 1877.*

82. *Ibid.*

83. *Ibid.*

84. *Ibid.*

85. *Ibid.*

86. Stewart, *Custer's Luck,* 187–188; see as well, Marquis, *Which Indian Killed Custer?,* 3.

87. Marquis, Thomas B., *Wooden Leg* (Lincoln: University of Nebraska Press, 1931 [1963], 179.

88. *Briefs of Papers in Relation to the Sioux War of 1875, 1876, and 1877.*

89. *Ibid.*

90. *Ibid.*

91. *Ibid.*

92. Connell, Evan, *Son of the Morning Star* (San Francisco, CA: North Point Press, 1984), 264; and Stewart, *Custer's Luck,* 84.

93. Stewart, *Custer's Luck,* 84.

94. *Briefs of Papers in Relation to the Sioux War of 1875, 1876, and 1877.*

95. Mangum, *Battle of the Rosebud,* 9–10.

96. *Ibid.,* 24.

97. *Briefs of Papers in Relation to the Sioux War of 1875, 1876, and 1877.*

98. *Ibid.*

99. Willert, *To the Edge of Darkness,* 31, citing Gray, *Centennial Campaign,* 73; Terry to Gibbon, March 31, 1876, Military Division of the Missouri, Letters Received, RG393; NARS.

100. Stewart, *Custer's Luck,* 104.

Chapter 2

1. Willert, James, *Little Big Horn Diary* (El Segundo, CA: Upton and Sons, Publishers, 1997), 219.

2. Bradley, *The March of the Montana Column,* 30.

3. Philbrick, *The Last Stand,* 67.

4. *Briefs of Papers in Relation to the Sioux War of 1875, 1876, and 1877.*

5. *Ibid.*

6. Willert, *To the Edge of Darkness,* 38.

7. *Ibid.,* 39.

8. Bradley, *March of the Montana Column,* 48.

9. Willert, *To the Edge of Darkness*, 52–54.

10. Upton, *Custer Catastrophe at the Little Big Horn 1876*, 33. Godfrey's original article was "revised" in 1908, but was not re-published until 1921.

11. Stewart, *Custer's Luck*, 189.

12. Marquis, *Wooden Leg*, 180–181.

13. *Ibid.*, 184.

14. *Ibid.*, 185.

15. Willert, *To the Edge of Darkness*, 56; also see Gibbon, *American Catholic Quarterly* article, "Last Summer's Expedition Against the Sioux and its Great Catastrophe and Hunting Sitting Bull," in Upton, *Custer Catastrophe at the Little Big Horn 1876*, 154.

16. Gibbon, *American Catholic Quarterly* article, "Last Summer's Expedition Against the Sioux and its Great Catastrophe and Hunting Sitting Bull," in Upton, *Custer Catastrophe at the Little Big Horn 1876*, 154 and 156.

17. *Briefs of Papers in Relation to the Sioux War of 1875, 1876, and 1877.*

18. Bradley, *The March of the Montana Column*, 68; and Gibbon, *American Catholic Quarterly* article, "Last Summer's Expedition Against the Sioux and its Great Catastrophe and Hunting Sitting Bull," in Upton, *Custer Catastrophe at the Little Big Horn 1876*, 156.

19. Willert, *To the Edge of Darkness*, 65, quoting Gibbon's letter to Terry.

20. *Briefs of Papers in Relation to the Sioux War of 1875, 1876, and 1877.*

21. James Willert claimed twenty-two wagons: *To the Edge of Darkness*, 67.

22. Stewart, *Custer's Luck*, 115.

23. Philbrick, *The Last Stand*, 67.

24. Willert, *To the Edge of Darkness*, 71; Freeman's Journal.

25. *Briefs of Papers in Relation to the Sioux War of 1875, 1876, and 1877.*

26. *Ibid.*

27. Stewart, *Custer's Luck*, 117.

28. Upton, *Custer Catastrophe at the Little Big Horn 1876*, 157.

29. Philbrick, *The Last Stand*, 67.

Chapter 3

1. Gray, John S., *Custer's Last Campaign* (Lincoln: University of Nebraska Press, 1991, 146.

2. Willert, *To the Edge of Darkness*, 80, citing Gibbon, *American Catholic Quarterly Review*, 13. See also, Carroll, ed., *The Federal View*, 98. Gibbon's official report dated October 17, 1876, from Fort Shaw, M. T.

3. Darling, *A Sad and Terrible Blunder*, 44.

4. *Briefs of Papers in Relation to the Sioux War of 1875, 1876, and 1877.*

5. Stewart, *Custer's Luck*, 140.

6. *Briefs of Papers in Relation to the Sioux War of 1875, 1876, and 1877.*

7. Willert, *To the Edge of Darkness*, 84.

8. Stewart, *Custer's Luck*, 190.

9. *Briefs of Papers in Relation to the Sioux War of 1875, 1876, and 1877.*

10. Mangum, *Battle of the Rosebud*, 24–25.

11. Roe, Charles Francis, General, "Custer's Last Battle," published by Robert Bruce at the office of the National Highways Association, Old Slip, New York City, 1927, 3. Probably written some time during or after 1898; published in 1927, in cooperation with Josephine Roe Slade, 630 Park Avenue, New York, New York.

12. Philbrick, *The Last Stand*, 67.

13. Hutchins, *The Army and Navy Journal*, 22, from a May 20, 1876, article, 655–656.

14. Connell, *Son of the Morning Star*, 264. Edgar Stewart wrote, "From this message it is obvious that Terry appreciated the strength of the enemy and should, from an estimate based on the number of lodges, have expected to encounter a force of between 4,500 and 6,000 warriors" [*Custer's Luck*, 139].

15. O'Neil, Tom, compiled by. *The Field Diary and Official Report of General Alfred H. Terry* (Brooklyn, NY: Arrow and Trooper), 11. Hereafter referred to as *The Field Diary of General Terry*. Roger Darling, in *A Sad and Terrible Blunder*, 42, claimed this telegram was dispatched on the 15th.

16. Heski, Tom, Facebook quote, "Little Big Horn Discussion Group" site, May 27, 2017.

17. According to the diary of the wagon master, Matthew Carroll, this convoy left the following day. *Diary of Matthew Carroll: Master in Charge of Transportation for Colonel John Gibbon's Expedition Against the Sioux Indians, 1876*, Contributions to the Historical Society of Montana (Kindle Locations 5953–6128), Vol. 2. Helena, Montana: Rocky Mountain Publishing Company. Hereafter referred to as *Diary of Matthew Carroll*. The diary was printed without page numbers, referring only to dates.

18. *Briefs of Papers in Relation to the Sioux War of 1875, 1876, and 1877.*

19. *Ibid.*

20. *Ibid.*

21. In his diary, Carroll wrote "Diamond-E" train.

22. Stewart, *Custer's Luck*, 145.

23. Gray, *Custer's Last Campaign*, 153.

24. *Briefs of Papers in Relation to the Sioux War of 1875, 1876, and 1877.*

25. *Ibid.*

26. Liddic, Bruce R., *Vanishing Victory* (El Segundo, CA: Upton & Sons, Publishers, 2004), 32. Liddic claimed the breakdown under Benteen was Weir: D, H, and K; and French: A, G, and M.

27. See Wagner III, Frederic C., *Participants in the Battle of the Little Big Horn*, 2nd edition (Jefferson, NC: McFarland & Company, Inc., Publishers, 2016), 233–235.

28. Willert, *Little Big Horn Diary*, 16.

29. Connell, *Son of the Morning Star*, 264.

30. Wagner, *Participants in the Battle of the Little Big Horn*, 233–235.

31. Carroll, *The Federal View*, 77; Sheridan's Annual Report.

32. Willert, *Little Big Horn Diary*, 2.

33. Stewart, *Custer's Luck*, 244; also, footnote 34, citing Byrne and Marquis.

34. Willert, *Little Big Horn Diary*, 44.

35. *Ibid.*

36. *Ibid.*, 97.

37. Godfrey, Captain Edward S., "Custer's Last Battle 1876," *Century Magazine,* January 1892. OUTBOOKS, Olympic, CA, 1976, 14.

38. Hammer, Kenneth, ed., *Custer in '76* (Norman: University of Oklahoma Press, 1976 [1990]), 212, footnote 2.

39. Willert, *Little Big Horn Diary*, xxii.

40. *Ibid.*, 9.

41. Carroll, *The Federal View*, 19.

42. *Ibid.*, 26.

43. Hutchins, *The Army and Navy Journal*, 36.

44. Connell, *Son of the Morning Star*, 102.

45. MacLean, *Custer's Best*, 56–57.

46. *Ibid.*, 56.

47. *Ibid.*

48. *Ibid.*

49. Hutchins, *The Army and Navy Journal*, 35–36.

50. Connell, *Son of the Morning Star*, 400.

51. Godfrey, "Custer's Last Battle 1876," 5. Godfrey's time is listed there.

52. *Ibid.*

53. Willert, *Little Big Horn Diary*, 4.

54. General Terry noted in his diary that he and the main body arrived at the Heart River Camp 1 at 2 pm; total distance 13½ miles.

55. Carroll, *The Federal View*, 35; Lieutenant Edward Maguire's Annual Report.

56. Godfrey, "Custer's Last Battle 1876," 9.

57. Brigadier General Alfred H. Terry, in a letter to his sister Harriet. Also found in Willert, *Little Big Horn Diary*, 7.

58. Godfrey, "Custer's Last Battle 1876," 9.

59. Willert, *Little Big Horn Diary*, 12.

60. Overfield II, Loyd J., *The Little Big Horn* (Lincoln: University of Nebraska Press/Arthur H. Clark Company/Bison Books, 1971 [1990]), *1876*, 132.

61. Carroll, *Diary of Matthew Carroll*.

62. Philbrick, *The Last Stand*, 67.

63. *Briefs of Papers in Relation to the Sioux War of 1875, 1876, and 1877.*

64. Willert, *Little Big Horn Diary*, 21.

65. Carroll, *Diary of Matthew Carroll*.

66. *Ibid.*

67. *Briefs of Papers in Relation to the Sioux War of 1875, 1876, and 1877.*

68. Willert, *To the Edge of Darkness*, 105.

69. Marquis, *Wooden Leg*, 186.

70. *Ibid.*, 187.

71. *Ibid.*, 188.

72. Willert, *Little Big Horn Diary*, 26; also, Marquis, *Wooden Leg*, 185.

73. *Briefs of Papers in Relation to the Sioux War of 1875, 1876, and 1877.*

74. *Ibid.*

75. Chorne, Laudie J., *Following the Custer Trail of 1876* (Bismarck, ND: Printing Plus, 1997), 43.

76. Willert, *Little Big Horn Diary*, 28.

77. See the Roe journal, Willert, *To the Edge of Darkness*, 105.

78. *Briefs of Papers in Relation to the Sioux War of 1875, 1876, and 1877.*

79. Willert, *Little Big Horn Diary*, 32.

80. Carroll, *Diary of Matthew Carroll*.

81. Heski, Tom, Facebook quote, "Little Big Horn Discussion Group" site, May 22, 2017.

82. Carroll, *Diary of Matthew Carroll*.

83. Marquis, *Wooden Leg*, 186, and Willert, *Little Big Horn Diary*, 39.

84. Willert, *Little Big Horn Diary*, 40.

85. *Ibid.*

86. *Ibid.*

87. Heski, Tom, Facebook quote, "Little Big Horn Discussion Group" site, May 23, 2017.

88. Carroll, *Diary of Matthew Carroll*.

89. *Briefs of Papers in Relation to the Sioux War of 1875, 1876, and 1877.*

90. Willert, *Little Big Horn Diary*, 44.

91. Heski, Tom, Facebook quote, "Little Big Horn Discussion Group" site, May 24, 2017.

92. *Briefs of Papers in Relation to the Sioux War of 1875, 1876, and 1877.*

93. *Ibid.*

94. Willert, *Little Big Horn Diary*, 48.

95. Marquis, *Wooden Leg*, 189.

96. *Briefs of Papers in Relation to the Sioux War of 1875, 1876, and 1877.*

97. Willert, *Little Big Horn Diary*, 51.

98. Willert, in *Little Big Horn Diary*, 51, gives a good description of the steamboat, "Far West," and names several of her crew.

99. Carroll, *Diary of Matthew Carroll*.

100. *Briefs of Papers in Relation to the Sioux War of 1875, 1876, and 1877.*

101. See Willert, *Little Big Horn Diary*, 55.

102. Heski, Tom, Facebook quote, "Little Big Horn Discussion Group" site, May 27, 2017.

103. Hutchins, *The Army and Navy Journal*, 23 [673–674].

104. Gray, *Custer's Last Campaign*, 157.

105. Willert, *To the Edge of Darkness*, 119.

106. Gray, *Custer's Last Campaign*, 157.

107. Stewart, *Custer's Luck*, 154.

108. Gray, *Custer's Last Campaign*, 157.

109. Willert, *Little Big Horn Diary*, 57, and *To the Edge of Darkness*, 120.

110. Heski, Tom, Facebook quote, "Little Big Horn Discussion Group" site, May 27, 2017.

111. Gray, *Custer's Last Campaign*, 157–158.

112. Bradley, *The March of the Montana Column*, 126; and Stewart, *Custer's Luck*, 154, footnote 33, referencing Roe, *Custer's Last Battle*, 2.

113. Bradley, *The March of the Montana Column*, 126.

114. *Ibid.*
115. Gibbon, "Last Summer's Expedition…" *American Catholic Quarterly Review,* Upton, *Custer Catastrophe at the Little Big Horn,* 160.
116. Upton, *Custer Catastrophe at the Little Big Horn,* 177–178.
117. *Briefs of Papers in Relation to the Sioux War of 1875, 1876, and 1877.*
118. Heski, Tom, Facebook quote, "Little Big Horn Discussion Group" site, May 28, 2017.
119. Willert, *Little Big Horn Diary,* 62.
120. Bradley, *The March of the Montana Column,* 127.
121. Carroll, *Diary of Matthew Carroll.*
122. John Gray, in his book, *Custer's Last Campaign,* used an "R"-system to denote mileages up the Rosebud Creek, as shown in the test. I shall continue to use this system throughout.
123. Marquis, *Wooden Leg,* 190.
124. *Briefs of Papers in Relation to the Sioux War of 1875, 1876, and 1877.*
125. *Ibid.*
126. Stewart, *Custer's Luck,* 217.
127. Heski, Tom, Facebook quote, "Little Big Horn Discussion Group" site, May 29, 2017.
128. Gray, *Custer's Last Campaign,* 160.
129. Mangum, *Battle of the Rosebud,* 28.
130. Carroll, *The Federal View,* 19.
131. *Briefs of Papers in Relation to the Sioux War of 1875, 1876, and 1877.*
132. Willert, *Little Big Horn Diary,* 70; spelling corrected.
133. Carroll, *Diary of Matthew Carroll.*
134. Mangum, *Battle of the Rosebud,* 30.
135. *Ibid.,* citing Bourke's *Diary.*
136. Heski, Tom, Facebook quote, "Little Big Horn Discussion Group" site, May 31, 2017.

Chapter 4

1. Heski, Tom, Facebook quote, "Little Big Horn Discussion Group" site, June 1, 2017.
2. Carroll, *Diary of Matthew Carroll.*
3. Mangum, *Battle of the Rosebud,* 31.
4. *Briefs of Papers in Relation to the Sioux War of 1875, 1876, and 1877.*
5. *Ibid.*
6. Lore, Aaron, Facebook quote, "Little Big Horn Discussion Group" site, June 1, 2017.
7. Carroll, *Diary of Matthew Carroll.*
8. Marquis, *Wooden Leg,* 191.
9. Mangum, *Battle of the Rosebud,* 31.
10. *Ibid.,* 31–32.
11. *Briefs of Papers in Relation to the Sioux War of 1875, 1876, and 1877.*
12. Terry/Willert, *Little Big Horn Diary,* footnote, 85.
13. *Ibid.,* 86.
14. Gray, *Custer's Last Campaign,* 169.
15. Heski, Tom, Facebook quote, "Little Big Horn Discussion Group" site, June 3, 2017.
16. *Ibid.*
17. *Briefs of Papers in Relation to the Sioux War of 1875, 1876, and 1877.*
18. Monnett, John H., *Where a Hundred Soldiers Were Killed* (Albuquerque: University of New Mexico Press, 2008 [2010], 18.
19. Heski, Tom, Facebook quote, "Little Big Horn Discussion Group" site, June 4, 2017.
20. Willert, *Little Big Horn Diary,* 90.
21. *Briefs of Papers in Relation to the Sioux War of 1875, 1876, and 1877.*
22. *Ibid.*
23. *Ibid.*
24. *Ibid.*
25. Heski, Tom, Facebook quote, "Little Big Horn Discussion Group" site, June 5, 2017.
26. Carroll, *Diary of Matthew Carroll.*
27. *Briefs of Papers in Relation to the Sioux War of 1875, 1876, and 1877.*
28. *Ibid.*
29. Mangum, *Battle of the Rosebud,* 35–36.
30. *Ibid.,* 36.
31. *Briefs of Papers in Relation*

to the Sioux War of 1875, 1876, and 1877.*
32. Willert, James, and Tom Heski, "Another Look at the Reno Scout," *Research Review,* Vol. 14, No. 2, Summer 2000, 17.
33. Willert, *Little Big Horn Diary,* 98.
34. *Ibid.,* 99.
35. Stewart, *Custer's Luck,* 222.
36. *Ibid.,* 223.
37. Willert/Heski, "Another Look at the Reno Scout," 17.
38. Heski, Tom, Facebook quote, "Little Big Horn Discussion Group" site, June 7, 2017.
39. Carroll, *Diary of Matthew Carroll.*
40. Willert, *Little Big Horn Diary,* 99.
41. Mangum, *Battle of the Rosebud,* 17.
42. *Briefs of Papers in Relation to the Sioux War of 1875, 1876, and 1877.*
43. *Ibid.*
44. Gray, *Custer's Last Campaign,* 173.
45. *Ibid.,* 174.
46. See Willert, *Little Big Horn Diary,* 105.
47. Heski, Tom, Facebook quote, "Little Big Horn Discussion Group" site, June 8, 2017.
48. *Briefs of Papers in Relation to the Sioux War of 1875, 1876, and 1877.*
49. *Ibid.*
50. Stewart, *Custer's Luck,* 190.
51. Willert, *To the Edge of Darkness,* 141.
52. Gray, *Custer's Last Campaign,* 176.
53. Marquis, *Wooden Leg,* 197.
54. *Briefs of Papers in Relation to the Sioux War of 1875, 1876, and 1877.*
55. *Ibid.*
56. See Darling, *A Sad and Terrible Blunder,* 1.
57. Barnard, Sandy, *I Go With Custer* (Bismarck, ND: The Bismarck Tribune, 1996), 115.
58. Gray, *Custer's Last Campaign,* 183. From a June 22 dispatch by Custer. This is *not* borne out by the official orders as shown.
59. It is extremely interesting to note there is *no* mention

of Reno *not* going to the Rose-bud in these orders. James Willert brings out the same point. See *Little Big Horn Diary*, 124.

60. O'Neil, *The Field Diary of General Terry*, 5.

61. Willert, *Little Big Horn Diary*, 119.

62. Libby, Orin G., ed., *The Arikara Narrative of Custer's Campaign and the Battle of the Little Bighorn* (Norman: University of Oklahoma Press, 1920 [1998]), 69; hereafter referred to as *The Arikara Narrative*.

63. John Gray claimed Reno took 100 mules, but sixty-six makes more sense. James Willert says sixty-six mules were taken, eleven for each company. See *Little Big Horn Diary*, 118.

64. Godfrey, "Custer's Last Battle," 10.

65. Willert, *Little Big Horn Diary*, 119; quoting from Terry's diary, 5.

66. Willert/Heski, "Another Look at the Reno Scout," 20.

67. Also see June 14. If the Indians stayed at the Busby camp for only one night, then they moved about this date, camping in Davis Creek on the east side of the divide. See as well, Marquis, *Wooden Leg*, 197.

68. Graham, *The Custer Myth*, 147.

69. Marquis, *Wooden Leg*, 198.

70. *Ibid.*

71. Mangum, *Battle of the Rosebud*, 41.

72. *Briefs of Papers in Relation to the Sioux War of 1875, 1876, and 1877.*

73. *Ibid.*

74. Willert, *Little Big Horn Diary*, 127.

75. Willert, *To the Edge of Darkness*, 153–154.

76. Willert, *Little Big Horn Diary*, 128.

77. Carroll, *Diary of Matthew Carroll.*

78. Hedren, *Fort Laramie and the Great Sioux War*, 111. Hedren, however, has Sheridan arriving in Cheyenne on the following day, the 13th. Our entry is based on the telegram shown above.

79. *Ibid.*, 111–112.

80. *Briefs of Papers in Relation to the Sioux War of 1875, 1876, and 1877.*

81. Graham, *The Custer Myth*, 29.

82. In his book, *Lakota Noon* (Missoula, Montana: Mountain Press Publishing Company, 1998), 288, Gregory F. Michno quotes an Indian named White Shield: "They had sabers with them." And the body White Shield thought might have been Custer's was found with a six-shooter and a saber next to it. Sheer fantasy! Archaeology and participant accounts support the fact that with the exception of only Lieutenant Charles De Rudio, no sabers were carried at the Little Big Horn.

83. Willert, *Little Big Horn Diary*, 130.

84. Willert/Heski, "Another Look at the Reno Scout," 22.

85. *Ibid.*, 23.

86. *Briefs of Papers in Relation to the Sioux War of 1875, 1876, and 1877.*

87. Willert, *To the Edge of Darkness*, 158; see also Willert/Heski, "Another Look at the Reno Scout," 23.

88. Willert/Heski, "Another Look at the Reno Scout," 23.

89. Mangum, *Battle of the Rosebud*, 43.

90. Willert, *Little Big Horn Diary*, 139.

91. *Briefs of Papers in Relation to the Sioux War of 1875, 1876, and 1877.*

92. *Ibid.*

93. *Ibid.*

94. *Ibid.*

95. Carroll, *The Federal View*, 42; Lieutenant Edward Maguire, Annual Report, 1877.

96. Graham, *The Custer Myth*, 233.

97. *Ibid.*

98. *Ibid.*

99. Willert/Heski, "Another Look at the Reno Scout," 23.

100. *Ibid.*, 25.

101. Willert, *Little Big Horn Diary*, 146, quoting Hammer, *Custer in '76.*

102. *Briefs of Papers in Relation to the Sioux War of 1875, 1876, and 1877.*

103. Willert, *Little Big Horn Diary*, 147 and 437.

104. Willert/Heski, "Another Look at the Reno Scout," 25.

105. Gray, *Custer's Last Campaign*, 189.

106. Willert, *To the Edge of Darkness*, 163.

107. Willert/Heski, "Another Look at the Reno Scout," 26–27.

108. *Ibid.*, 27.

109. See and refer to, *Ibid.*, 27.

110. Willert, *To the Edge of Darkness*, 164.

111. Stewart, *Custer's Luck*, 236.

112. Willert, *To the Edge of Darkness*, 164.

113. Bradley, *The March of the Montana Column*, 141.

114. Darling, *A Sad and Terrible Blunder*, 69.

115. *Ibid.*

116. Neil Mangum claimed estimates of warrior strength ran "from a low of 750 upwards to 2,000 or more." See Mangum, *Battle of the Rosebud*, 48.

117. Stewart, *Custer's Luck*, 234.

118. Connell, *Son of the Morning Star*, 267.

119. Donovan, James, *A Terrible Glory* (New York: Little, Brown and Company, 2008), 165.

120. Gray, *Custer's Last Campaign*, 192.

121. *Ibid.*

122. Mangum, *Battle of the Rosebud*, 51.

123. *Ibid.*, 52.

124. *Ibid.*, 52–53.

125. *Ibid.*, 53.

126. *Ibid.*

127. *Ibid.*, 54.

128. Hammer, *Custer in '76*, 212.

129. Stewart, *Custer's Luck*, 192.

130. *Ibid.*

131. *Ibid.*, 199, citing in footnote 66, *Billings Gazette*, July 17, 1932.

132. Mangum, *Battle of the Rosebud*, 55.

133. *Ibid.*, 56.

134. Willert, *Little Big Horn Diary*, 162.

135. Donovan, *A Terrible Glory*, 151; quoting Bourke's *On the Border with Crook*, 312.

136. Mangum, *Battle of the Rosebud*, 57.

137. *Ibid.*, 60; citing, Captain

Henry Rowan Lemly, "The Fight on the Rosebud," *Valor in Arms,* Summer 1975, 9–10.

138. Mangum, *Battle of the Rosebud,* 68.

139. *Ibid.,* 69; citing Lemly, "The Fight on the Rosebud," 8.

140. Mangum, *Battle of the Rosebud,* 79.

141. See *Ibid.,* 81.

142. Willert, *Little Big Horn Diary,* footnote, 438.

143. *Ibid.,* 169.

144. Carroll, *The Federal View,* 74.

145. Willert, *Little Big Horn Diary,* 170–171.

146. Graham, *The Custer Myth,* 52.

147. Willert, *Little Big Horn Diary,* 174.

148. Stewart, *Custer's Luck,* 200.

149. Donovan, *A Terrible Glory,* 147; quoting Charles Eastman.

150. *Ibid.,* 154.

151. *Briefs of Papers in Relation to the Sioux War of 1875, 1876, and 1877.*

152. *Ibid.*

153. Willert, *Little Big Horn Diary,* 181–182.

154. Bradley, *The March of the Montana Column,* 142.

155. Marquis, *Wooden Leg,* 203.

156. *Ibid.*

157. *Ibid.*

158. Willert, *Little Big Horn Diary,* 179.

159. Hedren, *Fort Laramie and the Great Sioux War,* 117–118.

160. *Ibid.,* 119.

161. *Briefs of Papers in Relation to the Sioux War of 1875, 1876, and 1877.*

162. *Ibid.*

163. *Ibid.*

164. *Ibid.*

165. Willert, *Little Big Horn Diary,* 185.

166. Gray, *Custer's Last Campaign,* 196.

167. Willert, *Little Big Horn Diary,* 131.

168. *Ibid.,* 189.

169. Darling, *A Sad and Terrible Blunder,* 32.

170. *Ibid.,* 34.

171. Willert, *Little Big Horn Diary,* footnote from Gibbon,

186; also, *To the Edge of Darkness,* 173.

172. Bradley, *The March of the Montana Column,* 142.

173. Willert, *Little Big Horn Diary,* 187.

174. *Briefs of Papers in Relation to the Sioux War of 1875, 1876, and 1877.*

175. *Ibid.*

176. *Ibid.*

177. *Ibid.*

178. *Ibid.*

179. *Ibid.*

180. *Ibid.*

181. Gibbon, "Last Summer's Expedition Against the Sioux…" *American Catholic Quarterly,* April 1877; Upton, *Custer Catastrophe at the Little Big Horn,* 162.

182. Stewart, *Custer's Luck,* 239.

183. Darling, *A Sad and Terrible Blunder,* 1.

184. O'Neil, *The Field Diary of General Terry,* 6.

185. Donovan, *A Terrible Glory,* 428, footnote (9) 3.

186. Willert, *Little Big Horn Diary,* 197.

187. *Ibid.,* footnote quoting Captain Robert Hughes, 199.

188. Bradley, *The March of the Montana Column,* 143.

189. Gibbon, "Last Summer's Expedition Against the Sioux…" *American Catholic Quarterly,* April 1877; Upton, *Custer Catastrophe at the Little Big Horn,* 163.

190. Willert, *Little Big Horn Diary,* 200.

191. Upton, *Custer Catastrophe at the Little Big Horn,* 162.

192. Willert, *Little Big Horn Diary,* 189.

193. Bartsch, Bob, Facebook post on the "Little Big Horn Discussion Group" site, February 2017. It has been edited.

194. Graham, *The Custer Myth,* 147.

195. *Ibid.*

196. O'Neil, *The Field Diary of General Terry,* 12, and Graham, *The Custer Myth,* 147.

197. See Darling, *A Sad and Terrible Blunder,* 4.

198. Stewart, *Custer's Luck,* 242–243.

199. Mangum, Neil, "The

Little Big Horn Campaign," *Blue & Gray,* 2006, 19–20.

200. Liddic, *Vanishing Victory,* 40.

201. Willert, *Little Big Horn Diary,* 215.

202. Hutchins, *The Army and Navy Journal,* 37.

203. Libby, *The Arikara Narrative,* 77.

204. Willert, *Little Big Horn Diary,* 204.

205. Hammer, *Custer in '76,* 247; interview with Lieutenant Richard E. Thompson, Terry's Acting Commissary of Subsistence.

Chapter 5

1. Provided through the courtesy of Bruce R. Liddic.

2. As described by French MacLean, *Custer's Best,* 70.

3. Graham, *The Custer Myth,* 236.

4. O'Neil, *The Field Diary of General Terry,* 12.

5. *Ibid.*

6. Willert, *Little Big Horn Diary,* 234.

7. Graham, *The Custer Myth,* 155–156.

8. Kuhlman, Charles, *Legend into History* (Harrisburg, Pennsylvania: The Stackpole Company, 1952), 30.

9. Graham, *The Custer Myth,* 177.

10. Gibbon, "Last Summer's Expedition Against the Sioux and its Great Catastrophe," *American Catholic Quarterly,* April 1877.

11. Godfrey, "Custer's Last Battle 1876," 15.

12. Graham, *The Custer Myth,* 187; from the July 2, 1876 letter, from Benteen to his wife, the July 23rd segment.

13. Nichols, Ronald H., ed., *Reno Court of Inquiry* (Hardin, Montana: Custer Battlefield & Museum Association, Inc., 1996), 559–560.

14. Hammer, *Custer in '76,* 74; Walter Mason Camp correspondence, early 1900s.

15. Carroll, *The Federal View,* 64–66; "Report of the Chief of Engineers, Appendix PP, Report of Lieutenant George D. Wallace,

7th Cavalry, St. Paul, MN, January 27, 1877."

16. *Ibid.*, 65.

17. Smalley, Vern, *Little Bighorn Mysteries* (Bozeman, Montana: Little Buffalo Press, 2005), 2–2; verified by Lieutenant Godfrey.

18. Godfrey, "Custer's Last Battle 1876," 16.

19. Gray, *Custer's Last Campaign,* 208; this also ties in perfectly with what Evan Connell wrote about the agencies.

20. Godfrey, "Custer's Last Battle 1876," 17.

21. Smalley, *Little Bighorn Mysteries,* 2–9.

22. Nichols, *Reno Court of Inquiry,* 491.

23. Mills, Charles K., *Harvest of Barren Regrets* (Glendale, CA: The Arthur H. Clark Company, 1985), 240.

24. Godfrey, "Custer's Last Battle 1876," 16.

25. *Ibid.*, 17.

26. *Ibid.*

27. *Ibid.*

28. *Briefs of Papers in Relation to the Sioux War of 1875, 1876, and 1877.*

29. *Ibid.*

30. *Ibid.*

31. *Ibid.*

32. *Ibid.*

33. *Ibid.*

34. *Ibid.*

35. *Ibid.*

36. *Ibid.*

37. Willert, *Little Big Horn Diary,* 226.

38. Smalley, *Little Bighorn Mysteries,* 2–3.

39. MacLean, *Custer's Best,* 71.

40. Carroll, *The Federal View,* 64–66; "Report of the Chief of Engineers, Appendix PP, Report of Lieutenant George D. Wallace, 7th Cavalry, St. Paul, MN, January 27, 1877."

41. Smalley, Vern, *More Little Bighorn Mysteries* (Bozeman, Montana: Little Buffalo Press, 2005), 1–4.

42. Willert, *Little Big Horn Diary,* 227.

43. *Ibid.*, quoting Charles Varnum.

44. *Ibid.*, 228; quoting Godfrey, "Custer's Last Battle 1876," 17.

45. Connell, *Son of the Morning Star,* 264.

46. *Ibid.*, 265.

47. Other than this quote is from Reno's autobiography, the source is unknown.

48. Varnum, Charles A., John M. Carroll, ed., *I, Varnum* (Mattituck, New York: J. M. Carroll & Company, 1982), 85.

49. Stewart, *Custer's Luck,* 259.

50. Willert, *Little Big Horn Diary,* 229.

51. Godfrey, "Custer's Last Battle 1876," 18.

52. Smalley, *Little Bighorn Mysteries,* 2–3.

53. Godfrey, "Custer's Last Battle 1876," 17–18.

54. Stewart, *Custer's Luck,* 261.

55. Willert, *Little Big Horn Diary,* 238.

56. Marquis, *Wooden Leg,* 207.

57. *Briefs of Papers in Relation to the Sioux War of 1875, 1876, and 1877.*

58. *Ibid.*

59. *Ibid.*

60. *Ibid.*

61. Carroll, *The Federal View,* 64–66; "Report of the Chief of Engineers, Appendix PP, Report of Lieutenant George D. Wallace, 7th Cavalry, St. Paul, MN, January 27, 1877."

62. Mills, *Harvest of Barren Regrets,* 243.

63. MacLean, *Custer's Best,* 71.

64. Willert, *Little Big Horn Diary,* 236.

65. Carroll, *The Federal View,* 67; from engineer sergeant, James Wilson's report, January 3, 1877.

66. Godfrey, "Custer's Last Battle 1876," 18.

67. Willert, *Little Big Horn Diary,* 237.

68. *Ibid.*

69. Godfrey, "Custer's Last Battle 1876," 18.

70. *Ibid.*

71. Hedren, Paul, "More on the Personal and Designating Flags of the Great Sioux War," *Custer and His Times, Book Five* (Cordova, TN: The Little Big Horn Associates, Inc., 2008), 141–142.

72. Connell, *Sun of the Morning Star,* 267.

73. Heski, Tom, "Don't Let Anything Get Away," *Research Review,* Summer 2007, 9.

74. See Darling, *A Sad and Terrible Blunder,* footnote 48, 186.

75. Herendeen/Willert, *Little Big Horn Diary,* 237.

76. Godfrey, "Custer's Last Battle 1876," 18.

77. Kuhlman, *Legend into History,* 34.

78. Godfrey, "Custer's Last Battle 1876," 18.

79. Darling, *A Sad and Terrible Blunder,* 159–160.

80. *Ibid.*, 169.

81. Bradley, *The March of the Montana Column,* 147.

82. Varnum/Carroll, *I, Varnum,* 60 and 85; also, Hammer, *Custer in '76,* 59, Walter Mason Camp's notes.

83. Connell, *Son of the Morning Star,* 267; see June 17th.

84. Kuhlman, *Legend into History,* 34.

85. Stewart, *Custer's Luck,* 192.

86. Gray, *Custer's Last Campaign,* 215.

87. *Ibid.*

88. Heski, "'Don't Let Anything Get Away,'" 10.

89. *Ibid.*, 11, citing the Walter Mason Camp Field Notes, folders 40–41, BYU Library.

90. *Ibid.*, 11.

91. Kuhlman, *Legend into History,* 34.

92. Willert, *Little Big Horn Diary,* 240.

93. Gray, *Custer's Last Campaign,* 217; from Lieutenant Wallace.

94. *Ibid.*; from George Herendeen.

95. Donovan, *A Terrible Glory,* 198.

96. Darling, *A Sad and Terrible Blunder,* 166.

97. Willert, *Little Big Horn Diary,* 241.

98. Godfrey, "Custer's Last Battle 1876," 18.

99. Heski, "'Don't Let Anything Get Away,'" 12; citing Frazier and Robert Hunt, *I Fought With Custer* (Lincoln: University of Nebraska Press, 1947 [1987]), 73.

100. Hutchins, *The Army and Navy Journal*, 40; Herendeen, "Narrative of A Scout, July 7, 1876."

101. Marquis, *Wooden Leg*, 206.

102. *Ibid.*, 208–209.

103. *Ibid.*, 210.

104. See Wagner, *Participants in the Battle of the Little Big Horn*, 2nd edition, 234.

105. Marquis, *Wooden Leg*, 209.

106. Scott, Douglas D., *Uncovering History* (Norman: University of Oklahoma Press, 2013), 26.

107. Darling, *A Sad and Terrible Blunder*, 160.

108. Willert, *Little Big Horn Diary*, 243.

109. Gray, *Custer's Last Campaign*, 219.

110. *Ibid.*, 220–221.

111. Varnum/Carroll, ed., *I, Varnum*, 87. Author Vern Smalley says Red Foolish Bear, not Red Bear, *More Little Bighorn Mysteries*, 1–8; and Heski calls him Bear, "Don't Let Anything Get Away," 14.

112. Hammer, *Custer in '76*, 60; footnote 2.

113. Godfrey, "Custer's Last Battle 1876," 19.

114. *Ibid.*

115. Liddic, *Vanishing Victory*, 23.

116. *Ibid.*

117. *Ibid.*

118. *Ibid.*

119. Hammer, *Custer in '76*, 229.

120. Heski, "Don't Let Anything Get Away," 14.

121. *Ibid.*, 31, footnote 119.

122. Smalley, *Little Bighorn Mysteries*, 2–4.

123. Heski, "Don't Let Anything Get Away," 15, footnote 72; citing John M. Carroll, ed., *The Benteen-Goldin Letters on Custer and His Last Battle* (Lincoln: University of Nebraska Press, 1974 [1991]), 179–180, hereafter referred to as *The Benteen-Goldin Letters*.

124. Heski, "Don't Let Anything Get Away," 15.

125. *Ibid.*, citing Carroll, *The Federal View*, 65.

Chapter 6

1. *Briefs of Papers in Relation to the Sioux War of 1875, 1876, and 1877*.

2. Stewart, *Custer's Luck*, 269–270.

3. USGS series 7.5' series quadrangle map NW quarter of Section 34, T4S, R37E.

4. Willert, *Little Big Horn Diary*, footnote, quoting Fred Dustin, 444.

5. *Ibid.*, footnote, quoting Edgar Stewart.

6. *Ibid.*, 252.

7. Carroll, *Diary of Matthew Carroll*.

8. Varnum/Carroll, *I, Varnum*, 87.

9. Graham, *The Custer Myth*, 32; excerpted from *The Arikara Narrative*.

10. Hammer, *Custer in '76*, 60–61.

11. O'Neil, *The Field Diary of General Terry*, 7.

12. Godfrey, "Custer's Last Battle 1876," 19.

13. Graham, *The Custer Myth*, 262. From a statement made by Herendeen in Bozeman, Montana Territory, on January 4, 1878, and published in the *New York Herald*, January 22, 1878.

14. This is a wildly inflated number. As we have seen, the distance from the first halt area to the vicinity of the Crow's Nest—therefore, Halt Two—is only between 3½ and 4½ miles, depending on where one prefers to mark the spot. Tom Heski puts the distance between halts one and two at four miles, point-to-point. See, "Don't Let Anything Get Away," 25.

15. Heski, "Don't Let Anything Get Away," 24, citing Carroll, *Three Hits and a Miss*, 71.

16. Nichols, *Reno Court of Inquiry*, 214.

17. *Ibid.*

18. *Ibid.*

19. Hammer, *Custer in '76*, 59–60; from a series of letters between Camp and Varnum.

20. Willert, *Little Big Horn Diary*, 257; also, footnote, 444.

21. See Gray, *Custer's Last Campaign*, 238. Varnum claimed it was Boyer who made this remark, Varnum/Carroll, *I, Varnum*, 64 and 88.

22. Varnum/Carroll, *I, Varnum*, 63.

23. Willert, *Little Big Horn Diary*, 13.

24. Liddic, *Vanishing Victory*, 26.

25. *Ibid.*

26. Willert, *Little Big Horn Diary*, 259.

27. Smalley, *Little Bighorn Mysteries*, 2–5.

28. Liddic, *Vanishing Victory*, 27.

29. Gray, *Custer's Last Campaign*, 241.

30. Liddic, *Vanishing Victory*, 25.

31. See Gray, *Custer's Last Campaign*, 243.

32. Liddic, *Vanishing Victory*, 28. See Godfrey, "Custer's Last Battle 1876."

33. Godfrey, "Custer's Last Battle 1876," 21.

34. Heski, "Don't Let Anything Get Away," 29, citing Hammer, Maguire interview, Camp Field Notes, folder 79, FN 3, BYU Library, 124.

35. Liddic, *Vanishing Victory*, 29. Also see MacLean, *Custer's Best*, 72, citing Charles M. Robinson, *A Good Year to Die: The Story of the Great Sioux War* (New York: Random House, 1995), xxvii.

36. See Stewart, *Custer's Luck*, 276 and 323.

37. Hammer, *Custer in '76*, 64.

38. A second trip to view the valley makes sense. First of all, we have Hare's recollection of such, and based on the accounts of others, Custer would have been foolish to ignore Boyer's admonitions.

Chapter 7

1. Kuhlman, *Legend into History*, 180.

2. Sklenar, Larry, "Private Theodore W. Goldin: Too Soon Discredited?" *Research Review*, Vol. 9, No. 1, January 1995, 9–17.

3. Stewart, *Custer's Luck*, 345–346.

4. See Michno, *Lakota Noon*, 93. The picture clearly shows Cedar Coulee's junction with

Medicine Tail Coulee, so Gall's account could be accurate.

Chapter 8

1. "Briefs of Papers in Relation to the Sioux War of 1875, 1876, and 1877."
2. *Ibid.*
3. *Ibid.*
4. Coburn, Wallace David, *The Battle of the Little Big Horn* (Hollywood, CA: January 1, 1936), no page number cited.
5. Smalley, *Little Bighorn Mysteries*, 2–7.
6. Willert, *Little Big Horn Diary*, 392–393.
7. *Ibid.*, 403.
8. Stewart, *Custer's Luck*, 422.
9. *Ibid.*, 422–423.
10. Smalley, *Little Bighorn Mysteries*, 15–12.
11. Godfrey, "Custer's Last Battle 1876," 31.
12. Varnum/Carroll, ed., *I, Varnum*, 94.
13. Godfrey, "Custer's Last Battle 1876," 31.
14. Liddic, *Vanishing Victory*, 179.
15. Godfrey, "Custer's Last Battle 1876," 31.
16. Willert, *Little Big Horn Diary*, 410; quoting General Charles F. Roe, *Custer's Last Battle*, 7.
17. Bradley, *The March of the Montana Column*, 161.
18. Connell, *Son of the Morning Star*, 76.
19. Stewart, *Custer's Luck*, 428.

20. *Ibid.*
21. Willert, *Little Big Horn Diary*, 411; quoting Godfrey's *Diary of the Little Big Horn*, 17.
22. Connell, *Son of the Morning Star*, 76–77.
23. *Ibid.*, 77.
24. Kuhlman, *Legend into History*, 138.
25. O'Neil, *The Field Diary of General Terry*, 15.
26. Stewart, *Custer's Luck*, 304.
27. "Briefs of Papers in Relation to the Sioux War of 1875, 1876, and 1877."
28. *Ibid.*
29. Willert, *Little Big Horn Diary*, 418; from the *Chicago Times*, February 9, 1879, 10.
30. Varnum/Carroll, ed., Varnum, *I, Varnum*, 74.
31. Godfrey, "Custer's Last Battle 1876," 35.
32. Kuhlman, *Legend into History*, 139.
33. "Briefs of Papers in Relation to the Sioux War of 1875, 1876, and 1877."
34. *Ibid.*
35. *Ibid.*
36. *Ibid.*
37. *Ibid.*
38. Carroll, *The Federal View*, 67–68. In Hammer, *Custer in '76*, 241, a civilian named James M. Sipes said this was on "Tuesday" morning.
39. A slight variation of this story appears in Stewart, *Custer's Luck*, 479–480.
40. Gibbon, "Hunting Sitting Bull," *American Catholic*

Quarterly Review, Upton, *Custer Catastrophe at the Little Big Horn*, 171–172.
41. "Briefs of Papers in Relation to the Sioux War of 1875, 1876, and 1877."
42. *Ibid.*
43. *Ibid.*
44. *Ibid.*
45. *Ibid.*
46. *Ibid.*
47. *Ibid.*
48. *Ibid.*
49. Hedren, *Fort Laramie and the Great Sioux War*, 131, footnote 55, 264, citing Capron Journal no. 12, 102–103.
50. "Briefs of Papers in Relation to the Sioux War of 1875, 1876, and 1877."
51. *Ibid.*
52. *Ibid.*
53. *Ibid.*
54. *Ibid.*
55. Godfrey, *Field Diary*, 22.
56. *Ibid.*
57. *Ibid.*
58. *Ibid.*
59. *Ibid.*, 24.
60. *Ibid.*, 25.
61. *Ibid.*
62. *Ibid.*
63. *Ibid.*
64. *Ibid.*, 25–26.
65. *Ibid.*, 27.
66. *Ibid.*
67. *Ibid.*, 30.
68. *Ibid.*, 32.
69. *Ibid.*, 33.
70. *Ibid.*, 42.
71. *Ibid.*, 51–52.

Bibliography

Books

Barnard, Sandy, ed. *Ten Years with Custer*. Terre Haute, IN: AST Press, 2001.

Bourke, John G. *On the Border with Crook*. New York: Charles Scribner's Sons, 1981.

Bradley, Lieutenant James H.; Edgar I. Stewart, ed. *The March of the Montana Column*. Norman: University of Oklahoma Press, 2001.

Brady, Charles T. *Indian Fights and Fighters*. New York: Doubleday, 1904.

Bray, Kingsley M. *Crazy Horse*. Norman: University of Oklahoma Press, 2006.

Brininstool, E. A. *A Trooper with Custer and Other Historic Incidents of the Battle of the Little Big Horn*. Columbus, OH: The Hunter-Trader-Trapper Co., 1925.

Brust, James S.; Brian C. Pohanka; and Sandy Barnard. *Where Custer Fell*. Norman: University of Oklahoma Press, 2005.

Byrne, Patrick E. *Soldiers of the Plains*. New York: Minton, Balch and Co., 1926.

Carroll, John. *The Gibson and Edgerly Narratives*. Bryan, TX: privately printed, undated.

Carroll, John M., ed. *The Benteen-Goldin Letters on Custer and His Last Battle*. New York: Liveright, 1974.

Carroll, John M., ed. *General Custer and the Battle of the Little Big Horn: The Federal View*. Bryan, TX, and Mattituck, NY: J. M. Carroll & Company, 1986.

Chorne, Laudie J. *Following the Custer Trail of 1876*. Bismarck, ND: Printing Plus, 1997.

Clark, George M. *Scalp Dance*. Oswego, NY: Heritage Press, 1985.

Coburn, Wallace David. *The Battle of the Little Big Horn*. Hollywood, CA: January 1, 1936.

Coffeen, Herbert. *The Custer Battle Book*. New York: A Reflection Book, Carlton Press, Inc., 1964.

Connell, Evan. *Son of the Morning Star*. New York: HarperCollins Publishers, 1984.

Cooke, Philip St. George. *The 1862 U. S. Cavalry Tactics*. Mechanicsburg, PA: Stackpole Books, 2004.

Cross, Walt. *Custer's Lost Officer*. Stillwater, OK: Cross Publications, 2006.

Curtis, Edward Sheriff. *Visions of a Vanishing Race*. Edison, NJ: Promontory Press, 1974–1976 (1994).

Custer, Elizabeth Bacon, *"Boots and Saddles," or Life in Dakota with General Custer*. New York: Harper and Brothers, 1885.

Darling, Roger. *Benteen's Scout*. El Segundo, CA: Upton & Sons Publishers, 2000.

Darling, Roger. *A Sad and Terrible Blunder*. Vienna, VA: Potomac-Western Press, 1990.

DeMallie, Raymond J., ed. *The Sixth Grandfather*. Lincoln: University of Nebraska Press/Bison Books, 1985.

Dickson, Ephriam D., III. *The Sitting Bull Surrender Census: The Lakotas at Standing Rock Agency, 1881*. Pierre, SD: South Dakota State Historical Society Press, 2010.

Dixon, Joseph Kossuth. *The Vanishing Race*. Garden City, NY: Doubleday, Page, and Company, 1913.

Donahue, Michael N. *Drawing Battle Lines*. El Segundo, CA: Upton and Sons, Publishers, 2008.

Donahue, Michael N. *Where the Rivers Ran Red*. Montrose, CO: San Juan Publishing Group, Inc., 2018.

Donovan, James. *Custer and the Little Bighorn*. Stillwater, MN: Voyageur Press, 2001.

Donovan, James. *A Terrible Glory*. New York: Little, Brown and Company, 2008.

Doran, Robert E. *Horsemanship at Little Big Horn*. West Conshohocken, PA: Infinity Publishing, 2007.

Du Bois, Charles G. *The Custer Mystery*. El Segundo, CA: Upton and Sons, 1986.

Dustin, Fred. *The Custer Tragedy*. El Segundo, CA: Upton & Sons, 2011 (Ann Arbor, MI: Edwards Brothers, Inc., 1939 [1965]).

Eastman, Charles. *Indian Heroes and Great Chieftans*. Boston: Little, Brown, 1918.

Finerty, John F. *War-path and Bivouac: The Bighorn and Yellowstone Expedition*. Chicago, IL: Lakeside Press, 1955.

Foote, Shelby. *The Civil War: A Narrative*. Volumes 1–3. New York: Random House, 1958, 1963, 1974.

Fox, Richard Allan, Jr. *Archaeology, History, and Custer's Last Battle*. Norman: University of Oklahoma Press, 1993.

Godfrey, Edward S.; Edgar I. Stewart, ed. *The Field Diary of Lieutenant Edward Settle Godfrey (1876)*. Portland, OR: The Champoeg Press, 1957.

Graham, Colonel William A. *The Custer Myth*. Mechanicsburg, PA: Stackpole Books, 2000.

Gray, John S. *Centennial Campaign*. Fort Collins, CO: Old Army Press, 1976.

261

Gray, John S. *Custer's Last Campaign*. Lincoln: University of Nebraska Press, 1993.

Greene, Jerome A. *Evidence and the Custer Enigma*. Silverthorne, CO: Vistabooks, 1995.

Grinnell, George Bird. *Two Great Scouts and Their Pawnee Battalion: The Experiences of Frank J. North and Luther H. North*. Cleveland, Ohio: The Arthur H. Clark Company, 1928.

Haines, Aubrey L. *An Elusive Victory*. Helena, MT: Falcon Publishing, Inc., 1999.

Hammer, Kenneth, ed. *Custer in '76*. Norman: University of Oklahoma Press, 1990.

Hammer, Kenneth; Ronald H. Nichols, ed. *Men with Custer: Biographies of the 7th Cavalry*. Hardin, MT: Custer Battlefield Historical & Museum Association, Inc., 1995.

Hardorff, Richard G. *The Custer Battle Casualties*. El Segundo, CA: Upton and Sons, Publishers, 2002.

Hardorff, Richard G. *Hokahey! A Good Day to Die!* Lincoln: Bison/University of Nebraska Press, 1999.

Hardorff, Richard G., ed. *Camp, Custer and the Little Bighorn*. El Segundo, CA: Upton and Sons, Publishers, 1997.

Hardorff, Richard G., ed. *Cheyenne Memories of the Custer Fight*. Lincoln: University of Nebraska Press, 1998.

Hardorff, Richard G., ed. *The Custer Battle Casualties, II*. El Segundo, CA: Upton and Sons, Publishers, 1999.

Hardorff, Richard G., ed. *Indian Views of the Custer Fight*. Norman: University of Oklahoma Press, 2005.

Hardorff, Richard G., ed. *Lakota Recollections of the Custer Fight*. Lincoln: University of Nebraska Press/Bison Books, 1997.

Hardorff, Richard G., ed. *On the Little Bighorn with Walter Camp*. El Segundo, CA: Upton & Sons Publishers, 2002.

Hart, John P., ed. *Custer and His Times*. Cordova, TN: The Little Big Horn Associates, Inc., 2008. Book Five.

Hedren, Paul L. *Fort Laramie and the Great Sioux War*. Lincoln: University of Nebraska Press, 1988.

Heitman, Francis B. *Historical Register and Dictionary of the United States Army*. Washington, D.C.: U. S. Government Printing Office, 1903 (Urbana, IL: University of Illinois Press, 1965), Vol. 2.

Horn, W. Donald. *Fifty Years on Custer's Trail*. Privately published, West Orange, NJ: David McMillin, 2010.

Hutchins, James S., ed. *The Army and Navy Journal on the Battle of The Little Bighorn and Related Matters, 1876-1881*. El Segundo, CA: Upton and Sons, Publishers, 2003.

Hutton, Paul Andrew. *The Apache Wars*. New York: Crown/Penguin Random House LLC, 2016.

Johnson, Barry C. *A Captain of "Chivalric Courage."* London: The English Westerners' Society, 1989.

Johnson, Barry C. *Case of Marcus A. Reno*. London: The English Westerners' Society, 1969.

Kershaw, Robert J. *Red Sabbath*. Hersham, Surrey, England: Ian Allan Publishing, 2005.

King, W. Kent. *Massacre: The Custer Cover-Up*. El Segundo, CA: Upton & Sons, 1989.

Klokner, James B. *The Officer Corps of Custer's Seventh Cavalry: 1866-1876*. Atglen, PA: Schiffer Military History, 2007.

Kuhlman, Charles. *Legend into History*. Harrisburg, PA: The Stackpole Company, 1952.

Libby, Orin G., ed. *The Arikara Narrative of Custer's Campaign and the Battle of the Little Bighorn*. Norman: University of Oklahoma Press, 1920 (1998).

Liberty, Margot; and John Stands In Timber. *Cheyenne Memories*. New Haven, CT: Yale University Press, 1967 (1998).

Liddic, Bruce R. *Vanishing Victory*. El Segundo, CA: Upton & Sons Publishers, 2004.

Liddic, Bruce R.; and Paul Harbaugh. *Camp on Custer*. Spokane, WA: The Arthur H. Clark Company, 1995.

Mackintosh, John D. *Custer's Southern Officer*. Lexington, SC: Cloud Creek Press, 2002.

MacLean, French L., Colonel. *Custer's Best*. Atglen, PA: Schiffer Military History, 2011.

Mangum, Neil. *Battle of the Rosebud: Prelude to the Little Bighorn*. El Segundo, CA: Upton & Sons Publishers, 2012.

Marquis, Thomas B. *Keep the Last Bullet for Yourself: The True Story of Custer's Last Stand*. Algonac, MI: Reference Publications, 1976.

Marquis, Thomas B., int. *Wooden Leg*. Lincoln: University of Nebraska Press, 1931 [1965].

Martinez, David. *The Legends & Lands of Native North Americans*. New York: Sterling Publishing Co., Inc., 2003.

McChristian, Douglas C. *The U. S. Army in the West, 1870-1880*. Norman: University of Oklahoma Press, 1995.

McCreight, M. I. *Firewater and Forked Tongues*. Trail's End Publishing Co.: Pasadena, CA, 1947.

Michno, Gregory F. *Lakota Noon*. Missoula, MT: Mountain Press Publishing Company, 1997.

Michno, Gregory F. *The Mystery of E Troop*. Missoula, MT: Mountain Press Publishing Company, 1994.

Miller, David Humphreys. *Echoes of the Little Bighorn*. Rockville, MD: American Heritage Publishing Company, Inc., 1971.

Mills, Charles K. *Harvest of Barren Regrets*. Glendale, CA: The Arthur H. Clark Company, 1985.

Monnett, John H. *Where a Hundred Soldiers Were Killed*. Albuquerque: University of New Mexico Press, 2008 [2010].

Moore, Donald W. *Where the Custer Fight Began*. El Segundo, CA: Upton and Sons, Publishers, 2011.

Neihardt, John G. *Black Elk Speaks*. Lincoln: University of Nebraska Press, 1932 (1988).

Nichols, Ronald H., ed. *Men with Custer*. Hardin, MT: Custer Battlefield Historical & Museum Association, Inc., 2000.

Nichols, Ronald H., ed. *Reno Court of Inquiry*. Hardin, MT: Custer Battlefield Historical & Museum Association, Inc., 1996.

O'Neil, Tom, compiled by. *The Field Diary and*

Official report of General Alfred H. Terry. Brooklyn, NY: Arrow and Trooper, date unknown.

Overfield, Loyd J., II. *The Little Big Horn, 1876: The Official Communications, Documents and Reports.* Lincoln: University of Nebraska Press, 1990.

Panzeri, Peter. *Little Big Horn 1876.* Oxford, UK: Osprey Publishing, 1995.

Pennington, Jack. *The Battle of the Little Bighorn.* El Segundo, CA: Upton & Sons Publishers, 2001.

Schultz, James Willard. *William Jackson, Indian Scout.* New York: Houghton Mifflin Company, 1926.

Scott, Douglas D. *Uncovering History.* Norman: University of Oklahoma Press, 2013.

Scott, Douglas D.; and Richard A. Fox, Jr. *Archaeological Insights into the Custer Battle.* Norman: University of Oklahoma Press, 1987.

Scott, Douglas D.; P. Willey; and Melissa A. Connor. *They Died with Custer.* Norman: University of Oklahoma Press, 1998.

Scott, Douglas D.; Richard A. Fox, Jr.; Melissa A. Connor; and Dick Harmon. *Archaeological Perspectives on the Battle of the Little Bighorn.* Norman: University of Oklahoma Press, 1989.

Scudder, Ralph E. *Custer Country.* Portland, OR: Binfords & Mort, 1963.

Smalley, Vern. *Little Bighorn Mysteries.* Bozeman, MT: Little Buffalo Press, 2005.

Smalley, Vern. *More Little Bighorn Mysteries.* Bozeman, MT: Little Buffalo Press, 2005.

Stewart, Edgar I. *Custer's Luck.* Norman: University of Oklahoma Press, 1955.

Swanson, Glenwood J. *G. A. Custer, His Life and Times.* Agua Dulce, CA: Swanson Productions, Inc, 2004.

Taylor, William O.; Greg Martin, ed. *with Custer on the Little Bighorn.* New York: Viking Penguin, 1996.

Tillett, Leslie. *Wind on the Buffalo Grass.* New York: Crowell, 1976.

Upton, Richard, compiled and introduced by. *Custer Catastrophe at the Little Big Horn, 1876.* El Segundo, CA: Upton and Sons, Publishers, 2012.

Utley, Robert M. *Frontier Regulars.* Lincoln: University of Nebraska Press, 1973.

Varnum, Charles A.; John Carroll, ed. *I, Varnum.* Mattituck, NY: J. M. Carroll & Co., 1982.

Viola, Herman J. *Little Bighorn Remembered.* New York: Times Books/Random House, Inc., 1999.

Wagner, Frederic C., III. *Participants in the Battle of the Little Big Horn,* 2nd edition. Jefferson, NC: McFarland, 2016.

Wagner, Frederic C., III. *Participants in the Battle of the Little Big Horn.* Jefferson, NC: McFarland, 2011.

Wagner, Frederic C., III. *The Strategy of Defeat at the Little Big Horn.* Jefferson, NC: McFarland, 2014. 2nd edition.

Wagner, Glendolin Damon. *Old Neitriment.* Lynden, WA: Sol Lewis, 1973

Willert, James. *Little Big Horn Diary.* El Segundo, CA: Upton and Sons Publishers, 1997.

Willert, James. *March of the Columns.* El Segundo, CA: Upton and Sons, Publishers, 1994.

Willert, James. *To the Edge of Darkness.* El Segundo, CA: Upton and Sons, Publishers, 1998.

Williams, Roger L. *Military Register of Custer's Last Command.* Norman: The Arthur H. Clark Company, 2009.

Windolph, Charles; Frazier Hunt and Robert Hunt, eds. *I Fought with Custer.* Lincoln: University of Nebraska Press, 1947.

Articles, At-Large Publications, Broadcast Media, Journals, Maps, Newspapers, Pamphlets, Periodicals, and Organizations

Abrams, Marc H., ed. *Newspaper Chronicle of the Indian Wars,* Vol. 5, January 1, 1876—July 12, 1876. Brooklyn, NY: Abrams Publishing, 2010.

Anderson, Harry H., "Cheyennes at the Little Big Horn." Russell Reid, ed., *North Dakota History,* Volume 27, No. 2, Spring, 1960. Bismarck, North Dakota: State Historical Society of North Dakota, 1961.

Army Quarterly, Vol. 36, April—July 1938.

Bates, Colonel Charles Francis. *Custer's Indian Battles.* Bronxville, NY, 1936.

Belle Fourche Bee, 1922 and 1923.

Bighorn-Yellowstone Journal, Summer 1992, Vol. 1, No. 3.

Billings Gazette, July 17, 1932.

Bonafede, Mike. *Little Bighorn Battlefield Map.* Loveland, CO: Atalissa, Inc., 1999.

Bray, Kingsley M. "Teton Sioux: Population History, 1655–1881," *Nebraska History,* Vol. 75, 1994.

Brininstool, E. A.; and others. "Chief Crazy Horse, His Career and Death," *Nebraska History Magazine,* January-March 1926, Vol. XII, No. 1. Lincoln: Nebraska State Historical Society.

Camp, Walter Mason. Field Notes, Folder 94, Brigham Young University Library.

Carroll, John M. *Battles of the Little Big Horn.* From a letter written by Morris to Robert Bruce, May 23, 1928. Listed on Amazon.com as *Battles of the Little Bighorn: General Fry [i.e., Roe] on the Custer battle, William E. Morris to Robert Bruce, Lieutenant Roe to his wife, General Roe article.* Out of print.

Carroll, John M., ed. *The Sunshine Magazine Articles.* John P. Everett, "Bullets, Boots, and Saddles," Sioux Falls, SD, 1930. Privately re-published, Bryan, TX, 1979.

Carroll, Matthew. "Diary of Matthew Carroll: Master in Charge of Transportation for Colonel John Gibbon's Expedition Against the Sioux Indians, 1876." Historical Society of Montana, *Contributions to the Historical Society of Montana,* Volume 2.

Cavalry Journal, Fort Riley, KS: July 1923.

Crow Agency Quadrangle, Montana, Big Horn County, 7.5' series; 1:24,000. Specifically: Crow Agency Montana, N4530-W10722.5/ 7.5, 1967, AMS 4575 III SW, series V894; Crow Agency SE

Montana, N4530-W10715/ 7.5, 1967, AMS 4575 III SE, series V894; Benteen Quadrangle, Benteen Montana, 45107-D4-TF-024, 1967, DMA 4574 IV NW, series V894; and, Lodge Grass NE Quadrangle, Lodge Grass NE, Montana, 45107-D3-TF-024, 1967, DMA 4574 IV NE, series V894.

Daily Record, Greensboro, NC, April 27, 1924.

Dickson, Ephriam D., III. "The Big Road Roster," 21st Annual Symposium, Custer Battlefield Historical & Museum Association, Inc., Hardin, MT: June 22, 2007.

Dickson, Ephriam D., III. "The Sitting Bull Surrender Census," 21st Annual Symposium, Custer Battlefield Historical & Museum Association, Inc., Hardin, MT: June 22, 2007.

Du Bois, Charles G. *Kick the Dead Lion.* Billings, MT: Reporter Printing & Supply Co., 1961.

Eastman, Charles A. "The Story of the Little Big Horn." *Chautauquan,* No. 31, July 1900.

Ellison, Douglas W. *Mystery of the Rosebud.* Medora, ND: Western Edge Book Distributing, 2002.

Fox, Richard A., Jr.; Charles E. Rankin, ed. "West River History," *Legacy,* Helena, MT: Montana Historical Society Press, 1996.

The *Frank L. Anders-R. G. Cartwright Correspondence,* Volume 1, 95–96; Anders letter to Cartwright, February 7, 1948.

Freeman, Captain Henry B. *The Original Manuscript Journal of General Henry Freeman During the Custer Campaign Against the Sioux Indians in 1876.* March 21-October 5, 1876.

Gibbon, Colonel John. "Gibbon on the Sioux Campaign of 1876," *American Catholic Quarterly,* April and October 1877, Old Army Press, Bellevue, NE, 1969.

Godfrey, E. S. "Custer's Last Battle." *Century Magazine,* January 1892. Reprint by Outbooks, Olympic Valley, CA, 1976.

Helena Herald, Helena, M. T., July 15, 1876.

Heski, Thomas M. "'Don't Let Anything Get Away,'" *Research Review,* Vol. 21, No. 2, Summer, 2007.

Hinman, Eleanor H. "Oglala Sources on the Life of Crazy Horse, Interviews Given to Eleanor H. Hinman," *Nebraska History* 57 (1976).

Horn, W. Donald. "Did Custer Plan to Follow Reno Into the Valley?" Unpublished article, 2012.

Horn, W. Donald. "Girard Knoll Considered," *Research Review,* Vol. 14, No. 2, Summer 2000.

Indian School Journal, Oklahoma, November 1905.

Kanipe, Daniel A., "A New Story of Custer's Last Battle Told by the Messenger Boy Who Survived," *Contributions to the Historical Society of Montana,* Vol. IV, 1903.

Knight, Oliver, "Mark Kellogg Telegraphed for Custer's Rescue." Russell Reid, ed., *North Dakota History,* Volume 27, No. 2, Spring, 1960. Bismarck, North Dakota: State Historical Society of North Dakota, 1961.

Leavenworth Times, Leavenworth, KS, August 18, 1881.

Little Big Horn Battlefield, Montana Territory, June 1876. Olean, NY: McElfresh Map Co., 1996.

Luce, Lieutenant Colonel Edward S. Letter to

Charles G. Du Bois, dated February 26, 1953. Charles G. Du Bois Historical Collection. Provided through the courtesy of Bruce R. Liddic.

Mangum, Neil C. "The Little Bighorn Campaign." *Blue & Gray,* 2006, Vol. XXIII, No. 2.

Marquis, Thomas B. *Custer Soldiers Not Buried.* Hardin, MT, Privately Published, 1933.

Marquis, Thomas B. *Sketch Story of the Custer Battle.* Hardin, MT, Privately Published, 1933.

Marquis, Thomas B. *Which Indian Killed Custer?* Hardin, MT, Privately Published, 1933.

Myers, Stephen W. "Roster of Known Hostile Indians at the Battle of the Little Big Horn," *Research Review,* Vol. 5, No. 2, June 1991.

National Archives and Record Service (NARS): Terry to Gibbon, March 31, 1876, Military Division of the Missouri, Letters Received, RG393.

New York Herald, August 8, 1876.

New York Herald, January 22, 1878.

New York Herald, January 4, 1878.

New York Herald, July 8, 1876.

New York Herald, September 24, 1876.

Oregon Sunday Journal, January 14, 1912.

Pioneer Press, St. Paul, MN, July 18, 1886.

Pioneer Press, St. Paul, MN, May 19, 1883.

Pitsch, Jason; Keith T. Werts, ed., "The Reno Valley Fight: Assessing river and land changes," *Greasy Grass,* Vol. 23, May 2007.

Public Broadcasting System, www.pbs.org/weta/thewest/resources/archives/six/bighorn.htm.

Rapid City Journal, Charles G. du Bois, "'Battle of Little Big Horn' Fought 91 Years Ago"; "The Edgerly Narrative," June 25–27, 1967.

Robbins, James S.; John P. Hart, ed. "Custer: The Goat at West Point and at War," *Custer and His Times, Book Five.* The Little Big Horn Associates, Inc.: Cordova, TN, 2008.

Roe, Charles Francis, Diary, Library of the U. S. Military Academy, West Point, New York.

Rumsey, David, Map Collection.

Scott, Douglas D. and Peter Bleed. *A Good Walk Around the Boundary.* Lincoln: A Special Publication of the Nebraska Association of Professional Archaeologists and the Nebraska State Historical Society, 1997 (2006).

Scott, Douglas D.; Charles E. Rankin, ed. "Archaeological Perspectives on the Battle of the Little Bighorn," *Legacy,* Helena: Montana Historical Society Press, 1996.

Sheridan, Lieutenant General P. H.; and Marc Abrams, ed. *Record of Engagements with Hostile Indians within the Military Division of the Missouri From 1868–1882.* Chicago: Headquarters Military Division of the Missouri, 1882.

Sklenar, Larry. "Too Soon Discredited?" *Research Review,* January 1995, Vol. 9, No. 1.

Sundstrom, Linea. *The Thin Elk/Steamboat Winter Count: A Study in Lakota Pictography.* Privately Published by Linea Sundstrom, 2003.

Taunton, Francis B. *Sufficient Reason?* London: The English Westerners' Society, 1977.

Tepee Book, June 1916.

Thompson, Peter. "The Experience of a Private

Soldier in the Custer Massacre," *Belle Fourche* (South Dakota) *Bee,* 1922 or 1923. State Historical Society of North Dakota.

Time-Life Books, The Editors of. *Echoes of Glory: Arms and Equipment of the Union.* Alexandria, VA: 1996.

Trinque, Bruce A. "Elusive Ridge," *Research Review,* January 1995, Vol. 9, No. 1.

United States Army Center of Military History: Style.

United States Geological Survey, Reston, Virginia. United States Naval Observatory, Washington, D.C.

Wagner, Frederic C., III. "Frederic Francis Gerard: A Questionable Cause and an Unforeseen Effect," *Research Review,* Winter 2007, Vol. 21, No. 1.

Wagner, Frederic C., III. "From A Different View to the Same Kill," *Research Review,* Vol. 22, No. 2, Summer 2008.

Willert, James, "Another Look at the Reno Scout," *Research Review,* Vol. 14, No. 2, Summer 2000, 17–30.

Yellow Nose; Guerriere, Edward, trans. *The Big Horn-Yellowstone Journal,* Summer, 1992, Vol. 1, No. 3, 15. Article in the *Chicago Record-Herald.* Originally appeared in *The Indian School Journal,* November 1905.

Index